PENGUIN BOOKS

KEY POETS

Jenny Green has been an English teacher and examiner for over twenty years, and loved books and poetry all her life. She currently teaches GCSE English part-time to adults, and works for half the week on Penguin's Schools Line, giving advice and information on Penguin books to schools. She also writes articles and short stories and has recently written a booklet for Penguin on *Stretching the Gifted Reader*. She is married with three children and lives in Watford.

Books are to be returned on or before the last date stamped below.

PENGUIN BOOKS

Published by the Penguin Group
Penguin Books Ltd, 27 Wrights Lane, London w8 5tz, England
Penguin Books USA Inc., 375 Hudson Street, New York, New York 10014, USA
Penguin Books Australia Ltd, Ringwood, Victoria, Australia
Penguin Books Canada Ltd, 10 Alcorn Avenue, Toronto, Ontario, Canada m4v 3b2
Penguin Books (NZ) Ltd, 182–190 Wairau Road, Auckland 10, New Zealand

Penguin Books Ltd, Registered Offices: Harmondsworth, Middlesex, England

Published in Penguin Books 1995
10 9 8 7 6 5 4 3 2

Excerpts from *The Canterbury Tales* by Geoffrey Chaucer, translated by Nevill Coghill (Penguin
Classics, 1951, Fourth revised edition, 1977) copyright © Nevill Coghill, 1951, 1958, 1960, 1975,
1977. Reproduced by permission of Penguin Books Ltd.

Typeset by Datix International Limited, Bungay, Suffolk
Printed in Great Britain by Clays Ltd, St Ives plc
Filmset in 10.25/12.5 pt Garamond Monophoto

Contents

Preface

The National Curriculum now requires secondary-school children to read works by at least four of the twenty-eight poets included in this anthology. This is as it should be; they are as much part of our children's heritage as our landscape. Imagine the Lake District without Wordsworth, the Yorkshire moors without Emily Brontë! The road to Canterbury is still peopled by Chaucer's pilgrims, and the spirit of Andrew Marvell still complains elegantly beside the Humber.

It is impossible to predict which poem will fire a particular child's imagination. At primary school, I learned Wordsworth's 'She dwelt among the untrodden ways' and responded to its sadness. At eleven I fell in love with Flecker's 'The Old Ships', my imagination seized by 'Famagusta and the hidden sun/That rings black Cyprus with a lake of fire', and the thought of the aeons of history and legend encompassed by the Mediterranean Sea. In my early teens I learned 'Kubla Khan' by heart, because I wanted always to have it in my head.

It is so easy to think that poetry must always be 'relevant', and that children must be able to understand it easily to gain anything from it. But the imagination creates its own relevance, and the work of creating understanding often allows a deeper response. Of course children must also read works that deal with the modern world and its concerns, but some themes are eternal.

Some poems have passed so deeply into our language and thought that they are given almost proverbial status. Others have left images etched on our collective consciousness. People who never read poetry may still think of autumn as a season of 'mists and mellow fruitfulness', or understand the idea of wandering 'lonely as a cloud'. In the same way that we know that traditional fairy tales set in medieval forests have something valuable to offer modern children, we can accept that the greatest poems of the last seven hundred years can still feed a child's imagination.

I should like to thank Frances Hendry and Barbara Lammas for their invaluable suggestions for the sections on Burns and Milton, and my husband and family for their unstinting support.

Geoffrey Chaucer

(?1342–1400)

Little is known of Chaucer's early life apart from a few official records. His family were wine-merchants who lived in London, and Chaucer was probably educated at St Paul's Almonry.

Chaucer next became a page to the Countess of Ulster, wife of King Edward III's third son Prince Lionel. In 1357 her household accounts record that she bought him a short cloak, a pair of shoes and some black and red breeches. Although a page's duties included running errands and making beds, the post enabled an ambitious boy to acquire the best possible lessons in good manners and courtly behaviour and meet many people who could influence his future career. For Chaucer, one of these was the King's fourth son, John of Gaunt, Duke of Lancaster, who became his patron. Indeed, Chaucer later married Philippa de Roet, the sister of Catherine Swynford, who was for many years Gaunt's mistress and eventually became his third wife.

In 1359 Chaucer went to France as a soldier in one of the many battles later known as the Hundred Years War. He was taken prisoner, and ransomed by King Edward III for £16. Chaucer was greatly impressed by the elegance of French poetry and its tales of courtly love, in which lovers yearned for an unattainable mistress and did dangerous deeds in her service. Later, the *Book of the Duchess*, an elegy for the death of John of Gaunt's first wife, used many of the ideas of courtly love.

Edward III valued Chaucer's services and employed him as a valet, later sending him on trade missions abroad, including two trips to Italy in 1372 and 1378. These sparked his interest in Italian literature. Chaucer had an excellent memory, and could read in Latin, French, Anglo-Norman and Italian. He read much of the literature and the scientific and historical works then available, including the classical Roman writers and the Italian writers Dante, Petrarch and Boccaccio. The style and content of many of these stories influenced his later works *The House of Fame*, *The Parliament of Fowls*, *The Legend of Good Women* and *Troilus and Criseyde*.

Meanwhile, Chaucer became wealthy through various posts given to him by the King. From 1374 to 86 he was controller of customs for London, a Justice of the Peace and a Knight of the Shire. When a military expedition took John of Gaunt to Spain, Chaucer's career suffered a setback until Gaunt's return. With more time for writing, it was probably then that he began to create *The Canterbury Tales*.

By this time, Chaucer was an experienced writer. As well as literary works, he had translated and adapted works of history and philosophy. Since 1066 French had been regarded as the language of the court and therefore the best language for literature. Latin was the language of the Church and the classics. However, Chaucer felt that the freshness and flexibility of the emerging English language made it suitable for poetry. He was the first English poet to use iambic pentameter and the heroic couplet.

The Canterbury Tales is a collection of stories told by a group of pilgrims journeying to the shrine of St Thomas à Becket at Canterbury. Chaucer tells us in the Prologue that he joins them at the Tabard Inn in Southwark. Although his short descriptions of each member of the party are detailed and individual, together they create a portrait of the men and women of medieval England in every walk of life. Their tales are as individual and contrasting as the people themselves, ranging from courtly romances to downright vulgarity and bringing to life the personalities, opinions and disagreements of the tellers.

The first two paragraphs of the Prologue are printed here in the original Middle English, but the rest is a translation by Professor Nevill Coghill. Many of the words Chaucer used have now been lost or changed their meanings or their spelling, although much is still recognizable today. We do not know exactly how they were pronounced, but many letters now silent, such as a final 'e', were sounded at that time. If the lines are read aloud with a feeling for their rhythmical flow, the possible pronunciation and meaning become clearer.

from THE CANTERBURY TALES

The Prologue

Whan that Aprille with his shoures soote
The droghte of March hath perced to the roote,
And bathed every veyne in swich licour
Of which vertu engendred is the flour;
Whan Zephirus eek with his sweete breeth
Inspired hath in every holt and heeth
The tendre croppes, and the yonge sonne
Hath in the Ram his halve cours yronne,
And smale fowles maken melodye,
10 That slepen al the nyght with open ye
(So priketh hem nature in her corages);
Thanne longen folk to goon on pilgrimages,
And palmeres for to seken straunge strondes,
To ferne halwes, kowthe in sondry londes;
And specially from every shires ende
Of Engelond to Caunterbury they wende,
The hooly blisful martir for to seke,
That hem hath holpen whan that they were seeke.
Bifil that in that seson on a day,
20 In Southwerk at the Tabard as I lay
Redy to wenden on my pilgrimage
To Caunterbury with ful devout corage,
At nyght was come into that hostelrye
Wel nyne and twenty in a compaignye,
Of sondry folk, by aventure yfalle
In felaweshipe, and pilgrims were they alle,
That toward Caunterbury wolden ryde.
The chambres and the stables weren wyde,
And wel we weren esed atte beste.
30 And shortly, whan the sonne was to reste,

So hadde I spoken with hem everichon
That I was of their felaweship anon,
And made forward erly for to ryse,
To take oure wey ther as I yow devyse.

from THE CANTERBURY TALES

The Prologue

When in April the sweet showers fall
And pierce the drought of March to the root, and all
The veins are bathed in liquor of such power
As brings about the engendering of the flower,
When also Zephyrus[1] with his sweet breath
Exhales an air in every grove and heath
Upon the tender shoots, and the young sun
His half-course in the sign of the *Ram*[2] has run,
And the small fowl are making melody
10   That sleep away the night with open eye
(So nature pricks them and their heart engages)
Then people long to go on pilgrimages
And palmers long to seek the stranger strands
Of far-off saints, hallowed in sundry lands,
And specially, from every shire's end
Of England, down to Canterbury they wend
To seek the holy blissful martyr,[3] quick
To give his help to them when they were sick.
      It happened in that season that one day
20   In Southwark, at *The Tabard*, as I lay
Ready to go on pilgrimage and start
For Canterbury, most devout at heart,
At night there came into that hostelry
Some nine and twenty in a company

1. The west wind.
2. The zodiac sign of Aries.
3. St Thomas à Becket.

Of sundry folk happening then to fall
In fellowship, and they were pilgrims all
That towards Canterbury meant to ride.
The rooms and stables of the inn were wide:
They made us easy, all was of the best.
30   And, briefly, when the sun had gone to rest,
I'd spoken to them all upon the trip
And was soon one with them in fellowship,
Pledged to rise early and to take the way
To Canterbury, as you heard me say.

*   *   *

THE PRIORESS

There also was a *Nun*, a Prioress,
Her way of smiling very simple and coy.[1]
Her greatest oath was only 'By St Loy!'
And she was known as Madam Eglantyne.
And well she sang a service, with a fine
40   Intoning through her nose, as was most seemly,
And she spoke daintily in French, extremely,
After the school of Stratford-atte-Bowe;[2]
French in the Paris style she did not know.
At meat her manners were well taught withal;
No morsel from her lips did she let fall,
Nor dipped her fingers in the sauce too deep;
But she could carry a morsel up and keep
The smallest drop from falling on her breast.
For courtliness she had a special zest,
50   And she would wipe her upper lip so clean
That not a trace of grease was to be seen
Upon the cup when she had drunk; to eat,
She reached a hand sedately for the meat.

1. Quiet.
2. With an English accent.

She certainly was very entertaining
Pleasant and friendly in her ways, and straining
To counterfeit a courtly kind of grace,
A stately bearing fitting to her place,
And to seem dignified in all her dealings.
As for her sympathies and tender feelings,
60 She was so charitably solicitous
She used to weep if she but saw a mouse
Caught in a trap, if it were dead or bleeding.
And she had little dogs she would be feeding
With roasted flesh, or milk, or fine white bread.
And bitterly she wept if one were dead
Or someone took a stick and made it smart;
She was all sentiment and tender heart.
Her veil was gathered in a seemly way,
Her nose was elegant, her eyes glass-grey;
70 Her mouth was very small, but soft and red,
Her forehead, certainly, was fair of spread,
Almost a span across the brows, I own;
She was indeed by no means undergrown.
Her cloak, I noticed, had a graceful charm.
She wore a coral trinket on her arm,
A set of beads, the gaudies tricked in green,[1]
Whence hung a golden brooch of brightest sheen
On which there first was graven a crowned A,
And lower, *Amor vincit omnia*.[2]
80 Another *Nun*, the secretary at her cell,
Was riding with her, and *three Priests* as well.

* * *

1. Her rosary beads had large green beads for the Paternosters.
2. 'Love conquers all' – at that time this was as appropriate for
religious love as for human love.

THE SHIPMAN

There was a *Skipper* hailing from far west;
He came from Dartmouth, so I understood.
He rode a farmer's horse as best he could,
In a woollen gown that reached his knee.
A dagger on a lanyard falling free
Hung from his neck under his arm and down.
The summer heat had tanned his colour brown,
And certainly he was an excellent fellow.
90 Many a draught of vintage, red and yellow,
He'd drawn at Bordeaux, while the trader snored.
The nicer rules of conscience he ignored.
If, when he fought, the enemy vessel sank,
He sent his prisoners home; they walked the plank.
As for his skill in reckoning his tides,
Currents and many another risk besides,
Moons, harbours, pilots, he had such dispatch
That none from Hull to Carthage was his match.
Hardy he was, prudent in undertaking;
100 His beard in many a tempest had its shaking,
And he knew all the havens as they were
From Gottland to the Cape of Finisterre,
And every creek in Brittany and Spain;
The barge he owned was called *The Maudelayne*.

*   *   *

THE WIFE OF BATH

A worthy *woman* from beside *Bath* city
Was with us, somewhat deaf, which was a pity.
In making cloth she showed so great a bent
She bettered those of Ypres and of Ghent.
In all the parish not a dame dared stir
110 Towards the altar steps in front of her,
And if indeed they did, so wrath was she

As to be quite put out of charity.[1]
Her kerchiefs[2] were of finely woven ground;
I dared have sworn they weighed a good ten pound,
The ones she wore on Sunday, on her head.
Her hose were of the finest scarlet red
And gartered tight; her shoes were soft and new.
Bold was her face, handsome, and red in hue.
A worthy woman all her life, what's more
120   She'd had five husbands, all at the church door,
Apart from other company in youth;
No need just now to speak of that, forsooth.
And she had thrice been to Jerusalem,
Seen many strange rivers and passed over them;
She'd been to Rome and also to Boulogne,
St James of Compostella and Cologne,[3]
And she was skilled in wandering by the way.
She had gap-teeth, set widely, truth to say.
Easily on an ambling horse she sat
130   Well wimpled up, and on her head a hat
As broad as is a buckler or a shield;
She had a flowing mantle that concealed
Large hips, her heels spurred sharply under that.
In company she liked to laugh and chat
And knew the remedies for love's mischances,
An art in which she knew the oldest dances.

*   *   *

THE MILLER

The *Miller* was a chap of sixteen stone,
A great stout fellow big in brawn and bone.

1. People went up to the altar in order of their importance.
2. A headdress of a style that had been out of fashion for many years.
3. All places of pilgrimage.

He did well out of them, for he could go
140   And win the ram at any wrestling show.
Broad, knotty and short-shouldered, he would boast
He could heave any door off hinge and post,
Or take a run and break it with his head.
His beard, like any sow or fox, was red
And broad as well, as though it were a spade;
And, at its very tip, his nose displayed
A wart on which there stood a tuft of hair
Red as the bristles in an old sow's ear.
His nostrils were as black as they were wide.
150   He had a sword and buckler at his side,
His mighty mouth was like a furnace door.
A wrangler and buffoon, he had a store
Of tavern stories, filthy in the main.
His was a master-hand at stealing grain.
He felt it with his thumb and thus he knew
Its quality and took three times his due –
A thumb of gold, by God, to gauge an oat!
He wore a hood of blue and a white coat.
He liked to play his bagpipes up and down
160   And that was how he brought us out of town.

*   *   *

THE SUMMONER

There was a *Summoner*[1] with us at that Inn,
His face on fire, like a cherubin,[2]
For he had carbuncles. His eyes were narrow,
He was as hot and lecherous as a sparrow.
Black scabby brows he had, and a thin beard.
Children were afraid when he appeared.
No quicksilver, lead ointment, tartar creams,
No brimstone, no boracic, so it seems,

1. A man paid to summon sinners to trial before an ecclesiastical court.
2. In medieval art, cherubs are usually shown with flame-coloured faces.

Could make a salve that had the power to bite,
170 Clean up or cure his whelks of knobby white
Or purge the pimples sitting on his cheeks.
Garlic he loved, and onions too, and leeks,
And drinking strong red wine till all was hazy.
Then he would shout and jabber as if crazy,
And wouldn't speak a word except in Latin
When he was drunk, such tags as he was pat in;
He only had a few, say two or three,
That he had mugged up out of some decree;
No wonder, for he heard them every day.
180 And, as you know, a man can teach a jay
To call out 'Walter' better than the Pope.[1]
But had you tried to test his wits and grope
For more, you'd have found nothing in the bag.
Then '*Questio quid juris*'[2] was his tag.
He was a noble varlet and a kind one,
You'd meet none better if you went to find one.
Why, he'd allow – just for a quart of wine –
Any good lad to keep a concubine
A twelvemonth and dispense him altogether!
190 And he had finches of his own to feather:[3]
And if he found some rascal with a maid
He would instruct him not to be afraid
In such a case of the Archdeacon's curse
(Unless the rascal's soul were in his purse)
For in his purse the punishment should be.
'Purse is the good Archdeacon's Hell,' said he.
But well I know he lied in what he said;
A curse should put a guilty man in dread,
For curses kill, as shriving brings, salvation.
200 We should beware of excommunication.

1. In the Middle Ages, jays were taught to call out 'Watte' in the same way that parrots are now taught to say 'Polly'.
2. 'The question is, what is the point in law.'
3. He indulged in the same sin for which he had just excused others.

Thus, as he pleased, the man could bring duress[1]
On any young fellow in the diocese.
He knew their secrets, they did what he said.
He wore a garland set upon his head
Large as the holly-bush upon a stake[2]
Outside an ale-house, and he had a cake,
A round one, which it was his joke to wield
As if it were intended for a shield.

1. Bring them to court.
2. A bush on a stake was a common sign for an ale-house.

from THE CANTERBURY TALES

The Nun's Priest's Tale

Once, long ago, there dwelt a poor old widow
In a small cottage, by a little meadow
Beside a grove and standing in a dale.
This widow-woman of whom I tell my tale
Since the sad day when last she was a wife
Had led a very patient, simple life.
Little she had in capital or rent,
But still, by making do with what God sent,
She kept herself and her two daughters going.
10 Three hefty sows – no more – were all her showing,
Three cows as well; there was a sheep called Molly.
  Sooty her hall, her kitchen melancholy,
And there she ate full many a slender meal;
There was no *sauce piquante* to spice her veal,
No dainty morsel ever passed her throat,
According to her cloth she cut her coat.
Repletion never left her in disquiet
And all her physic was a temperate diet,
Hard work for exercise and heart's content.
20 And rich man's gout did nothing to prevent

Her dancing, apoplexy struck her not;
She drank no wine, nor white, nor red had got.
Her board was mostly served with white and black,
Milk and brown bread, in which she found no lack;
Broiled bacon or an egg or two were common,
She was in fact a sort of dairy-woman.

    She had a yard that was enclosed about
By a stockade and a dry ditch without,
In which she kept a cock called Chanticleer.
30 In all the land for crowing he'd no peer;
His voice was jollier than the organ blowing
In church on Sundays, he was great at crowing.
Far, far more regular than any clock
Or abbey bell the crowing of this cock.
The equinoctial wheel and its position[1]
At each ascent he knew by intuition;
At every hour – fifteen degrees of movement –
He crowed so well there could be no improvement.
His comb was redder than fine coral, tall
40 And battlemented like a castle wall,
His bill was black and shone as bright as jet,
Like azure were his legs and they were set
On azure toes with nails of lily white,
Like burnished gold his feathers, flaming bright.

    This gentlecock was master in some measure
Of seven hens, all there to do his pleasure.
They were his sisters and his paramours,[2]
Coloured like him in all particulars;
She with the loveliest dyes upon her throat
50 Was known as gracious Lady Pertelote.
Courteous she was, discreet and debonair,
Companionable too, and took such care

1. The great circle of the heavens. Fifteen degrees ascend every hour.
In Chaucer's time people believed that cocks crew punctually on the hour.
2. Lovers.

In her deportment, since she was seven days old
She held the heart of Chanticleer controlled,
Locked up securely in her every limb;
O what a happiness his love to him!
And such a joy it was to hear them sing,
As when the glorious sun began to spring,
In sweet accord, *My Love is far from land*
60 – For in those far off days I understand
All birds and animals could speak and sing.

Now it befell, as dawn began to spring,
When Chanticleer and Pertelote and all
His wives were perched in this poor widow's hall
(Fair Pertelote was next him on the perch),
This Chanticleer began to groan and lurch
Like someone sorely troubled by a dream,
And Pertelote who heard him roar and scream
Was quite aghast and said, 'O dearest heart,
70 What's ailing you? Why do you groan and start?
Fie, what a sleeper! What a noise to make!'
'Madam,' he said, 'I beg you not to take
Offence, but by the Lord I had a dream
So terrible just now I had to scream;
I still can feel my heart racing from fear.
God turn my dream to good and guard all here,
And keep my body out of durance vile!
I dreamt that roaming up and down a while
Within our yard I saw a kind of beast,
80 A sort of hound that tried or seemed at least
To try and seize me . . . would have killed me dead!
His colour was a blend of yellow and red,
His ears and tail were tipped with sable fur
Unlike the rest; he was a russet cur.
Small was his snout, his eyes were glowing bright.
It was enough to make one die of fright.
That was no doubt what made me groan and swoon.'
'For shame,' she said, 'you timorous poltroon!¹

1. Coward.

Alas, what cowardice! By God above,
You've forfeited my heart and lost my love.
I cannot love a coward, come what may.
For certainly, whatever we may say,
All women long – and O that it might be! –
For husbands tough, dependable and free,
Secret, discreet, no niggard, not a fool
That boasts and then will find his courage cool
At every trifling thing. By God above,
How dare you say for shame, and to your love,
That there was anything at all you feared?
Have you no manly heart to match your beard?
And can a dream reduce you to such terror?
Dreams are a vanity, God knows, pure error.
Dreams are engendered in the too-replete
From vapours in the belly, which compete
With others, too abundant, swollen tight.
　'No doubt the redness in your dream to-night
Comes from the superfluity and force
Of the red choler[1] in your blood. Of course.
That is what puts a dreamer in the dread
Of crimsoned arrows, fires flaming red,
Of great red monsters making as to fight him,
And big red whelps and little ones to bite him;
Just so the black and melancholy vapours
Will set a sleeper shrieking, cutting capers
And swearing that black bears, black bulls as well,
Or blackest fiends are haling him to Hell.
And there are other vapours that I know
That on a sleeping man will work their woe,
But I'll pass on as lightly as I can.
　'Take Cato[2] now, that was so wise a man,

90

100

110

120

1. Medieval medicine taught that mankind was made up of four 'humours' – choler, bile, blood and phlegm. If they were in balance, the health was good. If one predominated, various illnesses resulted. Anger and the colour red were associated with an excess of choler.
2. A Roman politician, famed for his self-denying habits, strict sense of justice and blunt speech.

Did he not say, "Take no account of dreams"?
Now, sir,' she said, 'on flying from these beams,
For love of God do take some laxative;
Upon my soul that's the advice to give
For melancholy choler; let me urge
You free yourself from vapours with a purge.
And that you may have no excuse to tarry
By saying this town has no apothecary,
I shall myself instruct you and prescribe
130　Herbs that will cure all vapours of that tribe,
Herbs from our very farmyard! You will find
Their natural property is to unbind
And purge you well beneath and well above.
Now don't forget it, dear, for God's own love!
Your face is choleric and shows distension;
Be careful lest the sun in his ascension
Should catch you full of humours, hot and many.
And if he does, my dear, I'll lay a penny
It means a bout of fever or a breath
140　Of tertian ague. You may catch your death.
　　'Worms for a day or two I'll have to give
As a digestive, then your laxative.
Centaury, fumitory, caper-spurge
And hellebore will make a splendid purge;
And then there's laurel or the blackthorn berry,
Ground-ivy too that makes our yard so merry;
Peck them right up, my dear, and swallow whole.
Be happy, husband, by your father's soul!
Don't be afraid of dreams. I'll say no more.'
150　　'Madam,' he said, 'I thank you for your lore,
But with regard to Cato all the same,
His wisdom has, no doubt, a certain fame,
But though he said that we should take no heed
Of dreams, by God, in ancient books I read
Of many a man of more authority
Than ever Cato was, believe you me,
Who say the very opposite is true

And prove their theories by experience too.
Dreams have quite often been significations
160 As well of triumphs as of tribulations
That people undergo in this our life.
This needs no argument at all, dear wife,
The proof is all too manifest indeed.

*   *   *

So let me say in very brief conclusion
My dream undoubtedly foretells confusion,
It bodes me ill, I say. And, furthermore,
Upon your laxatives I set no store,
For they are venomous. I've suffered by them
Often enough before, and I defy them.
170   'And now, let's talk of fun and stop all this.
Dear Madam, as I hope for Heaven's bliss,
Of one thing God has sent me plenteous grace,
For when I see the beauty of your face,
That scarlet loveliness about your eyes,
All thought of terror and confusion dies.
For it's as certain as the Creed, I know,
Mulier est hominis confusio
(A Latin tag, dear Madam, meaning this:
"Woman is man's delight and all his bliss"),
180 For when at night I feel your feathery side,
Although perforce I cannot take a ride
Because, alas, our perch was made too narrow,
Delight and solace fill me to the marrow
And I defy all visions and all dreams!'
      And with that word he flew down from the beams,
For it was day, and down his hens flew all,
And with a chuck he gave the troupe a call
For he had found a seed upon the floor.
Royal he was, he was afraid no more.
190 He feathered Pertelote in wanton play
And trod her twenty times ere prime of day.
Grim as a lion's was his manly frown

As on his toes he sauntered up and down;
He scarcely deigned to set his foot to ground
And every time a seed of corn was found
He gave a chuck, and up his wives ran all.
Thus royal as a prince who strides his hall
Leave we this Chanticleer engaged on feeding
And pass to the adventure that was breeding.

200   Now when the month in which the world began,
March, the first month, when God created man,
Was over, and the thirty-second day
Thereafter ended, on the third of May
It happened that Chanticleer in all his pride,
His seven wives attendant at his side,
Cast his eyes upward to the blazing sun,
Which in the sign of *Taurus* then had run
His twenty-one degrees and somewhat more,
And knew by nature and no other lore
210 That it was nine o'clock. With blissful voice
He crew triumphantly and said, 'Rejoice,
Behold the sun! The sun is up, my seven.
Look, it has climbed forty degrees in heaven,
Forty degrees and one in fact, by this.
Dear Madam Pertelote, my earthly bliss,
Hark to those blissful birds and how they sing!
Look at those pretty flowers, how they spring!
Solace and revel fill my heart!' He laughed.
     But in that moment Fate let fly her shaft;
220 Ever the latter end of joy is woe,
God knows that worldly joy is swift to go.
A rhetorician with a flair for style
Could chronicle this maxim in his file
Of Notable Remarks with safe conviction.
Then let the wise give ear; this is no fiction.
My story is as true, I undertake,
As that of good Sir Lancelot du Lake
Who held all women in such high esteem.
Let me return full circle to my theme.

230   A coal-tipped fox of sly iniquity
        That had been lurking round the grove for three
        Long years, that very night burst through and passed
        Stockade and hedge, as Providence forecast,
        Into the yard where Chanticleer the Fair
        Was wont, with all his ladies, to repair.
        Still, in a bed of cabbages, he lay
        Until about the middle of the day
        Watching the cock and waiting for his cue,
        As all these homicides so gladly do
240   That lie about in wait to murder men.
        O false assassin, lurking in thy den!

                    *   *   *

        Merrily in her dust-bath in the sand
        Lay Pertelote. Her sisters were at hand
        Basking in sunlight. Chanticleer sang free,
        More merrily than a mermaid in the sea
        (For *Physiologus* reports the thing[1]
        And says how well and merrily they sing).
        And so it happened as he cast his eye
        Towards the cabbage at a butterfly
250   It fell upon the fox there, lying low.
        Gone was all inclination then to crow.
        'Cok cok,' he cried, giving a sudden start,
        As one who feels a terror at his heart,
        For natural instinct teaches beasts to flee
        The moment they perceive an enemy,
        Though they had never met with it before.
            This Chanticleer was shaken to the core
        And would have fled. The fox was quick to say
        However, 'Sir! Whither so fast away?
260   Are you afraid of me, that am your friend?
        A fiend, or worse, I should be, to intend

1. A book in Latin about nature and the animal world, which had a
chapter on mermaids.

You harm, or practise villainy upon you;
Dear sir, I was not even spying on you!
Truly I came to do no other thing
Than just to lie and listen to you sing.
You have as merry a voice as God has given
To any angel in the courts of Heaven;
To that you add a musical sense as strong
As had Boethius[1] who was skilled in song.
270 My Lord your Father (God receive his soul!),
Your mother too – how courtly, what control! –
Have honoured my poor house, to my great ease;
And you, sir, too, I should be glad to please.
For, when it comes to singing, I'll say this
(Else may these eyes of mine be barred from bliss),
There never was a singer I would rather
Have heard at dawn than your respected father.
All that he sang came welling from his soul
And how he put his voice under control!
280 The pains he took to keep his eyes tight shut
In concentration – then the tip-toe strut,
The slender neck stretched out, the delicate beak!
No singer could approach him in technique
Or rival him in song, still less surpass.
I've read the story in *Burnel the Ass*,[2]
Among some other verses, of a cock
Whose leg in youth was broken by a knock
A clergyman's son had given him, and for this
He made the father lose his benefice.
290 But certainly there's no comparison
Between the subtlety of such a one
And the discretion of your father's art
And wisdom. Oh, for charity of heart,
Can you not emulate your sire and sing?'
    This Chanticleer began to beat a wing

1. A Roman philosopher and writer. Chaucer had translated his work
Of the consolations of philosophy.
2. A twelfth-century poem.

As one incapable of smelling treason,
So wholly had this flattery ravished reason.
Alas, my lords! there's many a sycophant
And flatterer that fill your courts with cant
300 And give more pleasure with their zeal forsooth
Than he who speaks in soberness and truth.
Read what *Ecclesiasticus*[1] records
Of flatterers. 'Ware treachery, my lords!

This Chanticleer stood high upon his toes,
He stretched his neck, his eyes began to close,
His beak to open; with his eyes shut tight
He then began to sing with all his might.

Sir Russel Fox leapt in to the attack,
Grabbing his gorge he flung him o'er his back
310 And off he bore him to the woods, the brute,
And for the moment there was no pursuit.

O Destiny that may not be evaded!
Alas that Chanticleer had so paraded!
Alas that he had flown down from the beams!
O that his wife took no account of dreams!
And on a Friday too to risk their necks!
O Venus, goddess of the joys of sex,
Since Chanticleer thy mysteries professed
And in thy service always did his best,
320 And more for pleasure than to multiply
His kind, on thine own day, is he to die?

O Geoffrey, thou my dear and sovereign master[2]
Who, when they brought King Richard to disaster
And shot him dead, lamented so his death,
Would that I had thy skill, thy gracious breath,
To chide a Friday half so well as you!
(For he was killed upon a Friday too.)

1. Chapter 6: v. 5, 'It is better for a man to hear the rebuke of the wise than to hear the song of fools.'
2. Geoffrey de Vinsauf, an author on the art of Rhetoric, who greatly influenced Chaucer. He wrote about the death of Richard Coeur de Lion, making many plays on the word Friday, the day of Richard's death. Chaucer is gently poking fun at him here.

Then I could fashion you a rhapsody
For Chanticleer in dread and agony.
330   Sure never such a cry or lamentation
Was made by ladies of high Trojan station,
When Ilium fell and Pyrrhus with his sword
Grabbed Priam by the beard, their king and lord,
And slew him there as the *Aeneid* tells,
As what was uttered by those hens. Their yells
Surpassed them all in palpitating fear
When they beheld the rape of Chanticleer.
Dame Pertelote emitted sovereign shrieks
That echoed up in anguish to the peaks
340 Louder than those extorted from the wife
Of Hasdrubal, when he had lost his life
And Carthage all in flame and ashes lay.
She was so full of torment and dismay
That in the very flames she chose her part
And burnt to ashes with a steadfast heart.
O woeful hens, louder your shrieks and higher
Than those of Roman matrons when the fire
Consumed their husbands, senators of Rome,
When Nero burnt their city and their home;
350 Beyond a doubt that Nero was their bale!
    Now let me turn again to tell my tale;
This blessed widow and her daughters two
Heard all these hens in clamour and halloo
And, rushing to the door at all this shrieking,
They saw the fox towards the covert streaking
And, on his shoulder, Chanticleer stretched flat.
'Look, look!' they cried, 'O mercy, look at that!
Ha! Ha! the fox!' and after him they ran,
And stick in hand ran many a serving man,
360 Ran Coll our dog, ran Talbot, Bran and Shaggy,
And with a distaff in her hand ran Maggie,
Ran cow and calf and ran the very hogs
In terror at the barking of the dogs;
The men and women shouted, ran and cursed,

They ran so hard they thought their hearts would burst,
They yelled like fiends in Hell, ducks left the water
Quacking and flapping as on point of slaughter,
Up flew the geese in terror over the trees,
Out of the hive came forth the swarm of bees;
370 So hideous was the noise – God bless us all,
Jack Straw and all his followers in their brawl[1]
Were never half so shrill, for all their noise,
When they were murdering those Flemish boys,
As that day's hue and cry upon the fox.
They grabbed up trumpets made of brass and box,
Of horn and bone, on which they blew and pooped,
And therewithal they shouted and they whooped
So that it seemed the very heavens would fall.
     And now, good people, pay attention all.
380 See how Dame Fortune quickly changes side
And robs her enemy of hope and pride!
This cock that lay upon the fox's back
In all his dread contrived to give a quack
And said, 'Sir Fox, if I were you, as God's
My witness, I would round upon these clods
And shout, "Turn back, you saucy bumpkins all!
A very pestilence upon you fall!
Now that I have in safety reached the wood
Do what you like, the cock is mine for good;
390 I'll eat him there in spite of every one."'
     The fox replying, 'Faith, it shall be done!'
Opened his mouth and spoke. The nimble bird,
Breaking away upon the uttered word,
Flew high into the tree-tops on the spot.
And when the fox perceived where he had got,
'Alas,' he cried, 'alas, my Chanticleer,
I've done you grievous wrong, indeed I fear

1. Jack Straw was one of the leaders of the London riots during the Peasants' Revolt of 1381. He and his gang massacred some Flemish boys, after which he was captured and beheaded.

I must have frightened you; I grabbed too hard
When I caught hold and took you from the yard.
400 But, sir, I meant no harm, don't be offended,
Come down and I'll explain what I intended;
So help me God I'll tell the truth – on oath!'
'No,' said the cock, 'and curses on us both,
And first on me if I were such a dunce
As let you fool me oftener than once.
Never again, for all your flattering lies,
You'll coax a song to make me blink my eyes;
And as for those who blink when they should look,
God blot them from his everlasting Book!'
410 'Nay, rather,' said the fox, 'his plagues be flung
On all who chatter that should hold their tongue.'

    Lo, such it is not to be on your guard
Against the flatterers of the world, or yard,
And if you think my story is absurd,
A foolish trifle of a beast and bird,
A fable of a fox, a cock, a hen,
Take hold upon the moral, gentlemen.

    St Paul himself, a saint of great discerning,
Says that all things are written for our learning;
420 So take the grain and let the chaff be still.
And, gracious Father, if it be thy will
As saith my Saviour, make us all good men,
And bring us to his heavenly bliss.

                        Amen.

Sir Thomas Wyatt

(1503–1542)

Sir Thomas Wyatt was born at Allington Castle, near Maidstone in Kent. His father, Henry Wyatt, had been a Privy Councillor to Henry VII and remained a trusted adviser when Henry VIII came to the throne in 1509. Thomas followed his father to court after his education at St John's College, Cambridge.

Wyatt married Lord Cobham's daughter, Elizabeth Brooke, in 1520. They had a son the following year, but separated in 1525 after Wyatt charged his wife with adultery. He may have become friendly with Anne Boleyn at this time.

In 1526 Henry VIII sent Wyatt on diplomatic missions abroad. During his travels he met many French and Italian writers, learning to speak and read their languages. Although he came back for a short time, he was soon made High Marshal of Calais and sent there for a couple of years, perhaps to keep him away from court because Henry wanted to marry Anne Boleyn.

After Henry and Anne were married in 1533, Wyatt returned to England and was knighted in 1535. By this time, he had befriended the King's chief minister, Thomas Cromwell. Cromwell was high in the King's favour, having masterminded his divorce from Queen Katherine and enriched him with the profits of the dissolution of the monasteries after Henry declared himself head of the Church of England.

When Henry married Anne, he hoped that she would have a son to be his heir. His only living legitimate child at that time was his daughter Mary. However, by 1536 Anne had given birth to one daughter, Elizabeth, and had suffered a miscarriage. Henry transferred his affections to Jane Seymour, and looked for a way to make himself free to marry her.

In April and May of 1536, several gentlemen of the court, including Wyatt, were accused of adultery with the Queen and imprisoned in the Tower of London. There is no evidence about the reason for Wyatt's arrest, although people assumed he was one of the Queen's lovers or had information about her 'crimes'. Wyatt himself thought that the Duke of Suffolk had a grudge against him and had encouraged the King to have him arrested. Within a month, the other prisoners and Anne herself were executed on Tower Hill, probably within sight of Wyatt's cell.

Henry married Jane Seymour at the end of May, and Wyatt was released and sent home to his father at Allington 'to address himself better'. Sir Henry Wyatt entertained the King and his new Queen at Allington in July, and perhaps his long years of service to the crown softened the King's heart, because Thomas was made Steward of Conisborough Castle in September. After his father died in November he was also made Sheriff of Kent and granted possession of the lands he inherited from his father.

From 1537 to 1539 Wyatt was sent abroad again, as ambassador to the court of the Holy Roman Emperor, Charles V. Jane Seymour had died after giving birth to a son in October 1537, and Henry VIII needed to arrange a new marriage to cement his political alliances. Cromwell encouraged a marriage with Anne of Cleves, but when Henry met her, he found her too ugly to bear and had the marriage annulled immediately. Cromwell's other political moves were also out of tune with the King's thinking at that time, and he was arrested and executed in 1540. With his patron and protector removed, Wyatt was once more arrested and charged with treason. He was said to have secretly worked against the King's interests while abroad, and wasted the King's money on riotous living. Wyatt defended himself vigorously against these allegations and was eventually pardoned by the King. He died suddenly after contracting a fever while riding on the King's business.

Wyatt is credited with introducing the sonnet into English poetry. He translated several sonnets by the Italian poet Petrarch and wrote others of his own. He also experimented with other poetic forms such as the rondeau, and wrote songs and satires. His best known poems are those that deal with the trials of romantic love. Most of his poems were published after his death.

Sonnet

I find no peace and all my war is done.
I fear and hope, I burn and freeze like ice.
I fly above the wind yet can I not arise.
And naught I have and all the world I seize on.
That looseth nor locketh, holdeth me in prison
And holdeth me not, yet can I scape[1] no wise,[2]
Nor letteth me live nor die at my device
And yet of death it giveth me occasion.
Without eyen I see and without tongue I plain.[3]
10 I desire to perish and yet I ask health.
I love another and thus I hate myself.
I feed me in sorrow and laugh in all my pain.
Likewise displeaseth me both death and life,
And my delight is causer of this strife.

1. Escape.
2. Way.
3. Lament.

Sonnet

The pillar perished is whereto I leant,
The strongest stay[1] of mine unquiet mind;
The like of it no man again can find –
From east to west still seeking though he went –
To mine unhap, for hap away hath rent[2]
Of all my joy the very bark and rind,
And I, alas, by chance am thus assigned
Dearly to mourn till death do it relent.
But since that thus it is by destiny,

1. Support.
2. Torn.

10   What can I more but have a woeful heart,
     My pen in plaint, my voice in woeful cry,
     My mind in woe, my body full of smart,
     And I myself myself always to hate
     Till dreadful death do cease my doleful state?

Ballade

     They flee from me that sometime did me seek
     With naked foot stalking in my chamber.
     I have seen them gentle, tame, and meek
     That now are wild and do not remember
     That sometime they put themself in danger
     To take bread at my hand; and now they range
     Busily, seeking with a continual change.

     Thanked be fortune it hath been otherwise
     Twenty times better, but once in special,
10   In thin array after a pleasant guise,
     When her loose gown from her shoulders did fall
     And she me caught in her arms long and small,
     Therewithal sweetly did me kiss
     And softly said, 'Dear heart, how like you this?'

     It was no dream: I lay broad waking.
     But all is turned thorough my gentleness
     Into a strange fashion of forsaking.
     And I have leave to go of her goodness
     And she also to use newfangleness.
20   But since that I so kindly am served
     I would fain¹ know what she hath deserved.

     1. Wish to.

Song

And wilt thou leave me thus?
Say nay, say nay, for shame,
To save thee from the blame
Of all my grief and grame.
And wilt thou leave me thus?
   Say nay, say nay.

And wilt thou leave me thus
That hath loved thee so long
In wealth and woe among?
And is thy heart so strong
As for to leave me thus?
   Say nay, say nay.

And wilt thou leave me thus
That hath given thee my heart
Never for to depart,
Nother for pain nor smart?
And wilt thou leave me thus?
   Say nay, say nay.

And wilt thou leave me thus
And have no more pity
Of him that loveth thee?
Helas,[1] thy cruelty!
And wilt thou leave me thus?
   Say nay, say nay!

1. Alas.

Epistolary Satire

My mother's maids when they did sew and spin,
>   They sang sometime a song of the field mouse
>   That, for because her livelood[1] was but thin,
Would needs go seek her townish sister's house.
>   She thought herself endured too much pain.
>   The stormy blasts her cave so sore did souse[2]
That when the furrows swimmed with the rain
>   She must lie cold and wet in sorry plight.
>   And worse than that, bare meat there did remain
10 To comfort her when she her house had dight[3] –
>   Sometime a barley corn, sometime a bean
>   For which she laboured hard both day and night
In harvest time whilst she might go and glean;[4]
>   And when her store was 'stroyed[5] with the flood,
>   Then wellaway, for she undone[6] was clean.
Then was she fain[7] to take instead of food
>   Sleep, if she might, her hunger to beguile.[8]
>   'My sister,' quod[9] she, 'hath a living good
And hence from me she dwelleth not a mile.
20 In cold and storm she lieth warm and dry
>   In bed of down. The dirt doth not defile
Her tender foot. She laboureth not as I.
>   Richly she feedeth and at the rich man's cost,
>   And for her meat she needs not crave nor cry.

1. Livelihood.
2. Soak.
3. Cleaned.
4. Pick up stray ears of corn.
5. Destroyed.
6. Ruined.
7. Wishing.
8. Deceive.
9. Said.

By sea, by land, of the delicates the most
    Her cater seeks and spareth for no peril.
    She feedeth on boiled bacon meat and roast
And hath thereof neither charge nor travail.[1]
    And when she list,[2] the liquor of the grape
30   Doth glad her heart till that her belly swell.'
And at this journey she maketh but a jape.
    So forth she goeth, trusting of all this wealth
    With her sister her part so for to shape
That, if she might keep herself in health,
    To live a lady while her life doth last.
    And to the door now is she come by stealth
And with her foot anon she scrapeth full fast.
    Th'other for fear durst[3] not well scarce appear,
    Of every noise so was the wretch aghast.
40 At last she asked softly who was there.
    And in her language as well as she could
    'Peep,' quod the other, 'sister, I am here.'
'Peace,' quod the town mouse, 'why speakest thou so loud?'
    And by the hand she took her fair and well.
    'Welcome,' quod she, 'my sister, by the Rood.'[4]
She feasted her, that joy it was to tell
    The fare they had. They drank the wine so clear
    And, as to purpose now and then it fell,
She cheered her with 'How sister, what cheer!'
50   Amidst this joy befell a sorry chance
    That, wellaway, the stranger bought full dear
The fare she had. For as she looked askance,
    Under a stool she spied two steaming eyes
    In a round head with sharp ears. In France
Was never mouse so feared, for though th'unwise
    Had not yseen[5] such a beast before,

1. Work.
2. Likes.
3. Dared.
4. Cross.
5. Seen.

Yet had nature taught her after her guise
To know her foe and dread him evermore.
The towny mouse fled; she knew whither to go.
60   Th'other had no shift, but wondrous sore
Feared of her life. At home she wished her tho!
And to the door, alas, as she did skip,
Th'heaven it would, lo, and eke her chance was so,
At the threshold her silly foot did trip,
And ere she might recover it again
The traitor cat had caught her by the hip
And made her there against her will remain,
That had forgotten her poor surety and rest
For seeming wealth wherein she thought to reign.
70 Alas, my Poyntz,[1] how men do seek the best
And find the worst by error as they stray!
And no marvel, when sight is so oppressed,
And blind the guide, anon, out of the way
Goeth guide and all in seeking quiet life.
O wretched minds, there is no gold that may
Grant that ye seek, no war, no peace, no strife.
No, no, although thy head were hooped with gold,
Sergeant with mace, halberd,[2] sword, nor knife
Cannot repulse the care that follow should.
80   Each kind of life hath with him his disease.
Live in delight even as thy lust would
And thou shalt find, when lust doth most thee please,
It irketh[3] straight and by itself doth fade.
A small thing it is that may thy mind appease.
None of ye all there is that is so mad
To seek grapes upon brambles or briers,
Nor none, I trow,[4] that hath his wit so bad
To set his hay for conies[5] over rivers;

1. The name of a friend of Wyatt.
2. Weapons.
3. Annoys, irritates.
4. Think, believe.
5. Rabbits.

Ne ye[1] set not a drag-net for a hare.
90   And yet the thing that most is your desire
Ye do mis-seek with more travail and care.
        Make plain thine heart that it be not knotted
        With hope or dread, and see thy will be bare
From all affects whom vice hath ever spotted.
        Thyself content with that is thee assigned
        And use it well that is to thee allotted.
Then seek no more out of thyself to find
        The thing that thou hast sought so long before,
        For thou shalt feel it sitting in thy mind.

1. Nor you.

Ballade

Horrible of hue, hideous to behold,
Careful of countenance, his hair all clustered,
With dead droppy blood that down his face rolled,
Pale, painful, and piteously pierced,
His heart in sunder[1] sorrowfully shivered,
Methought a man, thus marvellously murdered,
This night to me came and carefully cried:

'O man misfortunate, more than any creature,
That painfully yet lives more pain to perceive,
10   What hardened hath thy heart this harm to suffer?
Thy doubtful hope, it do thee but deceive.
No good nor grace to glad thee shalt receive.
By pain from thy pain then pain to procure,
Moe[2] bitter it were than death to endure.

1. Broken.
2. More.

'Follow me,' saith he, 'hold here my hand.
Too long is death in tears to groan.
The sea shall sooner quench the brand
Of the desire that hath thee thus undone
Or sooner send thee to a deadly swoon.
Hold in thy hand the haft here of this knife
And with the blade boldly bereave thy life.

'Come off,' quod[1] he. 'I come,' quod I.
Then therewith as methought
My breast I pierced painfully.
My heart right soon I it raught.
But, lord, alas, it was for naught
For with that stroke I did awake.
My heart for sorrow yet feel I quake.

1. Said.

Song

Forget not yet the tried intent
Of such a truth as I have meant,
My great travail so gladly spent.
    Forget not yet.

Forget not yet when first began
The weary life ye know since when,
The suit, the service none tell can.
    Forget not yet.

Forget not yet the great assays,[1]
The cruel wrong, the scornful ways,
The painful patience in denays.[2]
    Forget not yet.

1. Attempts.
2. Denies.

Forget not yet, forget not this:
How long ago hath been and is
The mind that never meant amiss.[1]
  Forget not yet.

Forget not then thine own approved
The which so long hath thee so loved
Whose steadfast faith yet never moved.
20   Forget not this.

1. Wrong.

Edmund Spenser

(?1552–1599)

Records of births in Elizabethan England were not kept systematically, but Spenser is thought to have been born in London. He was the eldest son of John Spenser, a gentleman probably related to the Spencer family of Althorp from which the Princess of Wales descends. His father made a living in cloth-making, and Spenser was educated at Merchant Taylors' school for the sons of such traders.

Spenser then went to Pembroke Hall, Cambridge, where he took a degree in 1576. While still at Cambridge he published several short poems. Through the influence of a college friend, he obtained a place in the household of Robert Dudley, the Earl of Leicester and a favourite of Queen Elizabeth I. There, he mixed with many famous people, including the poet Sir Philip Sidney, to whom Spenser dedicated his first major poem, *The Shepheardes Calendar*. This was a series of twelve poems, one representing each month of the year, written in a variety of metres and using out-of-date words to give the impression of antiquity.

Sidney and Spenser, with several other literary men, formed a club called the Areopagus. Their purpose was to write English verse using a naturalized form of the metres of Greek and Latin poetry, which was then thought to be the most noble style of literary expression.

Spenser began writing his longest and most ambitious work, *The Faerie Queene*, while he was living in Leicester's household. However, in 1580 he became the secretary to Lord Grey de Wilton, the lord deputy of Ireland. Spenser moved to Ireland with Wilton and bought Kilcolman Castle in county Cork, where he mainly lived for the rest of his life. He was not happy in Ireland, regarding it as a form of exile, broken only by trips to London to prepare *The Faerie Queene* for publication.

The success of *The Shepheardes Calendar* and the first three volumes of *The Faerie Queene* led to the publication of Spenser's minor verse, including *Complaints, containing sundry small poems of the world's vanitie*, one example of which is printed here. He also wrote a poem dedicated to Sir Walter Raleigh, which tells of his experiences in the English court and ends by praising the simple country life. In 1594 Spenser married Elizabeth Boyle; his beautiful wedding song, *Epithalamion*, is thought to celebrate this event.

The second batch of three books of *The Faerie Queene* was published in 1596 while Spenser was staying with the Earl of Essex. He had hoped for a place at court, but had to return to Ireland, disappointed and in poor health. His home was looted and burned by Irish rebels in October 1598, and the lost books of *The Faerie Queene* were probably destroyed at that time. Spenser and his wife and four children fled to Cork, and then to London, where he died early the following year. He was buried near his favourite poet, Chaucer, in Westminster Abbey.

The Faerie Queene was a poem designed to glorify Queen Elizabeth I. She features in the poem under the names of Belphoebe, Mercilla and Gloriana. Twelve knights, representing twelve virtues, each undertake adventures designed to show their virtue triumphant. Book I describes the adventures of the Red-cross Knight of Holiness, representing the Anglican Church, who defends the virgin Una, representing the true religion, from a dragon representing Error. The remaining five completed books tell legends of Temperance, Chastity, Friendship, Justice and Courtesy. A fragment of the seventh book, which celebrates the virtue of Constance, includes a beautiful description of the seasons and months of the year incorporating the signs of the zodiac and references to classical mythology.

Spenser invented a stanza for *The Faerie Queene* which was later used by Keats in *The Eve of St Agnes* and also by Shelley and Byron. It has eight lines with ten syllables and five beats and a ninth with twelve syllables and six beats, rhyming *ababbcbcc*. Some of Spenser's vocabulary is now obsolete, but that was partly a deliberate ploy to give his work the appearance of age. I have modernized his spelling, except where to do so would interfere with the rhythmic flow of the lines or with the rhyme scheme.

from *Visions of the World's Vanity*

[*The Crocodile Bird*]

Beside the fruitful shore of muddy Nile,
Upon a sunny bank outstretched lay
In monstrous length, a mighty Crocodile,
That crammed with guiltless blood, and greedy prey
Of wretched people travailing that way,
Thought all things less than his disdainful pride.
I saw a little bird, called *Tedula*,[1]
The least of thousands which on earth abide,
That forced this hideous beast to open wide
10   The grisly gates of his devouring hell,
And let him feed, as Nature doth provide,
Upon his jaws, that with black venom swell.
Why then should greatest things the least disdain,
Since that so small so mighty can constrain?

1. The crocodile bird, which picks bits out of a crocodile's teeth.

from EPITHALAMION[1]

Bring with you all the Nymphs that you can hear
Both of the rivers and the forests green:
And of the sea that neighbours to her near,
All with gay garlands goodly well beseen.[2]
And let them also with them bring in hand,
Another gay garland
For my fair love of lilies and of roses,
Bound truelove-wise with a blue silken riband.[3]

1. A song written for a wedding – in this case, Spenser's own marriage.
2. Of good appearance.
3. A ribbon tied in true lovers' knots.

And let them make great store of bridal posies,
10 And let them eke[1] bring store of other flowers
To deck the bridal bowers.
And let the ground whereas her foot shall tread,
For fear the stones her tender foot should wrong
Be strewed with fragrant flowers all along
And diapered[2] like the discoloured mead.
Which done, do at her chamber door await,
For she will waken straight,
The whiles do ye this song unto her sing,
The woods shall to you answer and your Echo ring.

*   *   *

20 Lo where she comes along with portly[3] pace
Like Phoebe[4] from her chamber of the East,
Arising forth to run her mighty race,
Clad all in white, that seems[5] a virgin best.
So well it her beseems that ye would ween[6]
Some angel she had been.
Her long loose yellow locks like golden wire,
Sprinkled with pearl, and pearling flowers between,
Do like a golden mantle her attire,
And being crowned with a garland green,
30 Seem like some maiden Queen.
Her modest eyes abashed to behold
So many gazers, as on her do stare,
Upon the lowly ground affixed are.
Nor dare lift up her countenance too bold,
But blush to hear her praises sung so loud,

1. Also.
2. Covered.
3. Stately.
4. Phoebe, or the male version Phoebus, was the driver of the chariot
of the Sun.
5. Is most suitable for.
6. Think.

So far from being proud.
Nathless[1] do ye still loud her praises sing
That all the woods may answer and your echoes ring.

1. Nevertheless.

from THE FAERIE QUEENE

BOOK I, CANTO I

[*The Red-cross Knight Fights the Dragon of Error*]

1

A Gentle Knight was pricking[1] on the plain,
All clad in mighty arms and silver shield,
Wherein old dints of deep wounds did remain,
The cruel marks of many a bloody field;
Yet arms till that time did he never wield:
His angry steed did chide his foaming bit,
As much disdaining to the curb to yield:
Full jolly knight he seemed, and fair did sit,
As one for knightly jousts and fierce encounters fit.

2

10 But on his breast a bloody Cross he bore,
The dear remembrance of his dying Lord,
For whose sweet sake that glorious badge he wore,
And dead as living ever him adored:
Upon his shield the like was also scored,
For sovereign hope, which in his help he had:
Right faithful true he was in deed and word,
But of his cheer did seem too solemn-sad,
Yet nothing did he dread, but ever was ydrad.[2]

1. Riding fast.
2. Dreaded.

3

Upon a great adventure he was bond,[1]
20   That greatest *Gloriana*[2] to him gave,
That greatest Glorious Queen of *Faerie* lond,[3]
To win him worship, and her grace to have,
Which of all earthly things he most did crave;
And ever as he rode, his heart did yearn
To prove his puissance[4] in battle brave
Upon his foe, and his new force to learn;
Upon his foe, a Dragon horrible and stern.

*   *   *

14

But full of fire and greedy hardiment,[5]
The youthful knight could not for ought be stayed,
30   But forth unto the darksome hole he went,
And looked in: his glistering armour made
A little glooming light, much like a shade,
By which he saw the ugly monster plain,
Half like a serpent horribly displayed,
But th'other half did woman's shape retain,
Most loathsome, filthy, foul and full of vile disdain.

15

And as she lay upon the dirty ground,
Her huge long tail her den all overspread,
Yet was in knots and many boughts[6] upwound,

1. Bound.
2. Gloriana, queen of the fairies, represents Queen Elizabeth I.
3. Land
4. Power.
5. Boldness.
6. Coils.

40   Pointed with mortal sting. Of her there bred
     A thousand young ones, which she daily fed,
     Sucking upon her poisonous dugs,[1] each one
190 Of sundry shapes, yet all ill-favoured:
     Soon as that uncouth light upon them shone,
     Into her mouth they crept, and sudden all were gone.

     16

     Their dam upstart, out of her den afraid,
     And rushed forth, hurling her hideous tail
     About her cursed head, whose folds displayed
     Were stretched now forth at length without entrail.[2]
50   She looked about, and seeing one in mail
     Armed to point, sought back to turn again;
     For light she hated as the deadly bale,[3]
     Ay wont[4] in desert darkness to remain,
     Where plain none might see her, nor she see any plain.

     17

     Which when the valiant Elf[5] perceived, he leapt
     As Lion fierce upon the flying prey,
     And with his trenchant[6] blade her boldly kept
     From turning back, and forced her to stay:
     Therewith enraged she loudly 'gan[7] to bray,
60   And turning fierce, her speckled tail advanced,
     Threatening her angry sting, him to dismay:
     Who nought aghast, his mighty hand enhanced:
     The stroke down from her head unto her shoulder glanced.

     1. Nipples.
     2. Twisting.
     3. Injury, fatal influence.
     4. For ever used.
     5. Knight.
     6. Sharp and slicing.
     7. Began.

18

Much daunted with that dint, her sense was dazed,
Yet kindling rage, herself she gathered round,
And all at once her beastly body raised
With doubled forces high above the ground:
Though wrapping up her wreathed stern around,
Leapt fierce upon his shield, and her huge train
70 All suddenly about his body wound,
That hand or foot to stir he strove in vain:
God help the man so wrapped in *Error's* endless train.

19

His Lady sad to see his sore constraint,
Cried out, Now now Sir knight, show what ye be,
Add faith unto your force and be not faint:
Strangle her, else she sure will strangle thee.
That when he heard, in great perplexity,
His gall did grate[1] for grief and high disdain,
And knitting all his force got one hand free,
80 Wherewith he gripped her gorge[2] with so great pain,
That soon to loose her wicked bands did her constrain.

20

Therewith she spewed out of her filthy maw[3]
A flood of poison horrible and black,
Full of great lumps of flesh and gobbets raw,
Which stunk so vilely, that it forced him slack
His grasping hold, and from her turn him back:
Her vomit full of books and papers was,
With loathly frogs and toads which eyes did lack,
And creeping sought way in the weedy grass:
90 Her filthy parbreak[4] all the place defiled has.

*   *   *

1. Harass.
2. Throat.
3. Mouth.
4. Vomit.

24

Thus ill-bestead,[1] and fearful more of shame,
Than of the certain peril he stood in,
Half-furious unto his foe he came,
Resolved in mind all suddenly to win,
Or soon to lose, before he once would lin;
And struck at her with more than manly force,
That from her body full of filthy sin
He raft[2] her hateful head without remorse;
A stream of coal-black blood forth gushed from her corse.[3]

1. Beset.
2. Cut off.
3. Corpse.

from THE FAERIE QUEENE

BOOK II, CANTO VII

[*The Cave of Mammon*]

28

The house's form within was rude and strong,
Like an huge cave, hewn out of rocky clift,[1]
From whose rough vault the ragged breaches[2] hung,
Embossed with massy gold of glorious gift,
And with rich metal loaded every rift,
That heavy ruin they did seem to threat;
And over them *Arachne*[3] high did lift
Her cunning web, and spread her subtle net,
Enwrapped in foul smoke and clouds more black than jet.

1. Cliff.
2. Stalactites.
3. In Greek mythology Arachne was a girl famous for her ability to weave. She challenged Athene to a contest, and when she produced a tapestry more beautiful than Athene's, the angry goddess turned her into a spider. Spiders are still called arachnids because of this story.

29

10 Both roof, and floor, and walls were all of gold,
But overgrown with dust and old decay,
And hid in darkness, that none could behold
The hue thereof: for view of cheerful day
Did never in that house itself display,
But a faint shadow of uncertain light;
Such as a lamp, whose life does fade away:
Or as the Moon clothed with cloudy night,
Does show to him, that walks in fear and sad affright.

30

In all that room was nothing to be seen,
20 But huge great iron chests and coffers strong,
All barred with double bands, that none could ween[1]
Them to efforce[2] by violence or wrong;
On every side they placed were along.
But all the ground with skulls was scattered,
And dead men's bones, which round about were flung,
Whose lives, it seemed, whilom[3] there were shed,
And their vile carcases now left unburied.

1. Think.
2. Force off.
3. Formerly.

from THE FAERIE QUEENE

BOOK II, CANTO VIII

[*The Guardians of the Cave of Mammon*]

21

At length they came into a larger space,
That stretched itself into an ample plain,
Through which a beaten broad highway did trace,
That straight did lead to *Pluto's*[1] grisly reign:
By that way's side, there sat infernal Pain,
And fast beside him sat tumultuous Strife:
The one in hand an iron whip did strain,
The other brandished a bloody knife,
And both did gnash their teeth, and both did threaten life.

22

10 On th'other side in one consort[2] there sat,
Cruel Revenge, and rancorous Despite,[3]
Disloyal Treason, and heart-burning Hate,
But gnawing Jealousy out of their sight
Sitting alone, his bitter lips did bite,
And trembling Fear still to and fro did fly,
And found no place, where safe he shroud him might,
Lamenting Sorrow did in darkness lie,
And Shame his ugly face did hide from living eye.

1. King of the underworld in Greek mythology.
2. Group.
3. Malice or spite.

23

And over them sad Horror with grim hue,
20   Did always soar, beating his iron wings;
And after him Owls and Night-Ravens flew,
The hateful messengers of heavy things,
Of death and dolour[1] telling sad tidings;
Whiles sad *Celeno*,[2] sitting on a clift,
A song of bale and bitter sorrow sings,
That heart of flint asunder could have rift:
Which having ended, after him she flyeth swift.

1. Grief.
2. A harpy. Harpies were mythological monsters with the bodies of
women and the wings and claws of birds.

from THE FAERIE QUEENE

BOOK III, CANTO IV

[*Night*]

55

Night thou foul Mother of annoyance sad,
Sister of heavy death, and nurse of woe,
Which wast begot in heaven, but for thy bad
And brutish shape thrust down to hell below,
Where by the grim flood of *Cocytus*[1] slow
Thy dwelling is, in *Herebus*[2] black house,
(Black *Herebus* thy husband is the foe
Of all the Gods) where thou ungracious,
Half of thy days dost lead in horror hideous.

1. The river in Hell.
2. Erebus was the husband of Night and parent of many horrors.

56

10 What had th'eternal Maker need of thee,
The world in his continual course to keep,
That dost all things deface, nor lettest see
The beauty of his work? Indeed in sleep
The slothful body, that doth love to steep
His lustless limbs, and drown his baser mind,
Doth praise thee oft, and oft from *Stygian*[1] deep
Calls thee, his goddess in his error blind,
And great Dame Nature's handmaid, cheering every kind.

57

But well I wote,[2] that to an heavy heart
20 Thou art the root and nurse of bitter cares,
Breeder of new, renewer of old smarts:
Instead of rest thou lendest railing tears,
Instead of sleep thou sendest troublous fears,
And fearful visions, in the which alive
The dreary image of sad death appears:
So from the weary spirit thou dost drive
Desired rest, and men of happiness deprive.

58

Under thy mantle black there hidden lie,
Light-shunning theft and traitorous intent,
30 Abhorred bloodshed, and vile felony,
Shameful deceit, and danger imminent;
Foul horror, and eke[3] hellish dreariment:
All these I wote in thy protection be,
And light do shun, for fear of being shent:[4]
For light alike is loathed of them and thee,
And all that lewdness love, do hate the light to see.

1. From the River Styx, which mortals had to cross to enter the underworld.
2. Know.
3. Also.
4. Injured.

59

For day discovers all dishonest ways,
And showeth each thing, as it is indeed:
The praises of high God he fair displays,
40 And his large bounty rightly doth areed.[1]
Day's dearest children be the blessed seed,
Which darkness shall subdue, and heaven win:
Truth is his daughter; he her first did breed,
Most sacred virgin, without spot of sin.
Our life is day, but death with darkness doth begin.

1. Show.

from THE FAERIE QUEENE

BOOK III, CANTO VI

[*The Garden of Adonis*]

30

In that same Garden all the goodly flowers,
Wherewith dame Nature doth her beautify,
And decks the garlands of her paramours,[1]
Are fetched: there is the first seminary[2]
Of all things, that are born to live and die,
According to their kinds. Long work it were,
Here to account the endless progeny[3]
Of all the weeds, that bud and blossom there;
But so much as doth need, must needs be counted here.

1. Lovers.
2. Seed-plot.
3. Children.

3 1

10   It sited was in fruitful soil of old,
     And girt[1] in with two walls on either side;
     The one of iron, the other of bright gold,
     That none might thorough-break,[2] nor over-stride:
     And double gates it had, which opened wide,
     By which both in and out men moten[3] pass;
     Th'one fair and fresh, the other old and dried:
     Old *Genius*[4] the porter of them was,
     Old *Genius*, the which a double nature has.

3 2

     He letteth in, he letteth out to wend,
20   All that to come into the world desire;
     A thousand thousand naked babes attend
     About him day and night, which do require,
     That he with fleshly weeds[5] would them attire:
     Such as him list,[6] such as eternal fate
     Ordained hath, he clothes with sinful mire,
     And sendeth forth to live in mortal state,
     Till they again return back by the hinder[7] gate.

3 3

     After that they again returned been,
     They in the Garden planted be again;
30   And grow afresh as they had never seen
     Fleshly corruption, nor mortal pain.
     Some thousand years so do they there remain;

1. Encircled.
2. Break through.
3. Might.
4. The god responsible for bringing things into existence.
5. Clothes.
6. Wants.
7. Back.

And then of him are clad with other hue,
Or sent into the changeful world again,
Till thither they return, where first they grew:
So like a wheel around they run from old to new.

34
Nor needs there Gardener to set, or sow,
To plant or prune: for of their own accord
All things, as they created were, do grow,
40 And yet remember well the mighty word,
Which first was spoken by th'Almighty lord,
That bade them to increase and multiply:
Nor do they need with water of the ford,
Or of the clouds to moisten their roots dry;
For in themselves eternal moisture they imply.

35
Infinite shapes of creatures there are bred,
And uncouth forms, which none yet ever knew,
And every sort is in a sundry bed
Set by itself, and ranked in comely rew;[1]
50 Some fit for reasonable souls t'endue,[2]
Some made for beasts, some made for birds to wear,
And all the fruitful spawn of fishes hue
In endless ranks along enranged were,
That seem'd the *Ocean* could not contain them there.

36
Daily they grow and daily forth are sent
Into the world, it to replenish more;
Yet is the stock not lessened, nor spent,
But still remains in everlasting store,
As it at first created was of yore.[3]

1. Row.
2. Inhabit.
3. Long ago.

60 For in the wide womb of the world there lies,
In hateful darkness and in deep horror,
An huge eternal *Chaos*, which supplies
The substances of nature's fruitful progenies.

37

All things from thence do their first being fetch,
And borrow matter, whereof they are made,
Which when as form and feature it does catch,
Becomes a body, and doth then invade
The state of life, out of the grisly shade.
That substance is eternal, and bides so,
70 Nor when the life decays, and form does fade,
Doth it consume, and into nothing go,
But changed is, and often altered to and fro.

38

The substance is not changed, not altered,
But th'only form and outward fashion;
For every substance is conditioned
To change her hue and sundry forms to don,
Meet[1] for her temper and complexion:
Forms are variable and decay,
By course of kind, and by occasion;
80 And that fair flower of beauty fades away,
As doth the lily fresh before the sunny ray.

39

Great enemy to it, and to all the rest,
That in the *Garden of Adonis* springs,
Is wicked *Time*, who with his scythe addressed,
Does mow the flowering herbs and goodly things,
And all their glory to the ground down flings,
Where they do wither and are foully marred:
He flies about, and with his flaggy wings
Beats down both leaves and buds without regard,
90 Nor ever pity may relent his malice hard.

1. Suitable.

40

Yet pity often did the gods relent,
To see fair things marred, and spoiled quite:
And their great mother *Venus* did lament
The loss of her dear brood, her dear delight;
Her heart was pierced with pity at the sight,
When walking through the Garden, them she spied,
Yet no'te[1] she find redress for such despite.[2]
For all that lives is subject to that law;
All things decay in time, and to their end do draw.

41

100 But were it not that *Time* their troubler is,
All that in this delightful Garden grows
Should happy be, and have immortal bliss:
For here all plenty, and all pleasure flows,
And sweet love gentle fits amongst them throws,
Without fell rancour,[3] or fond jealousy;
Frankly each paramour his leman[4] knows,
Each bird his mate, nor any does envy
Their goodly merriment, and gay felicity.[5]

42

There is continual spring and harvest there
110 Continual, both meeting at one time:
For both the boughs do laughing blossoms bear,
And eke[6] at once the heavy trees they climb,
Which seem to labour under their fruits' load:
The whiles the joyous birds make their pastime
Amongst the shady leaves, their sweet abode,
And their true loves without suspicion tell abroad.

1. Could not.
2. Malice.
3. Spite.
4. Mistress.
5. Happiness.
6. Also.

from THE FAERIE QUEENE

MUTABILITY, CANTO VII

[*The Seasons and the Months*]

28

So, forth issued the Seasons of the year;
First, lusty *Spring*, all dight[1] in leaves of flowers
That freshly budded and new blooms did bear
(In which a thousand birds had built their bowers
That sweetly sung, to call forth paramours):[2]
And in his hand a javelin he did bear,
And on his head (as fit for warlike stours)[3]
A gilt-engraven morion[4] he did wear;
That as some did him love, so others did him fear.

29

10 Then came the jolly *Summer*, being dight
In a thin silken cassock[5] coloured green,
That was unlined all, to be more light:
And on his head a garland well beseen[6]
He wore, from which as he had chauffed[7] been
The sweat did drop; and in his hand he bore
A bow and shafts, as he in forest green
Had hunted late the Leopard and the Boar,
And now would bathe his limbs, with labour heated sore.

1. Decked.
2. Lovers.
3. Conflicts.
4. Helmet.
5. Robe.
6. Of good appearance.
7. Heated.

30

Then came the *Autumn* all in yellow clad,
As though he joyed in his plenteous store,
Laden with fruits that made him laugh, full glad
That he had banished hunger, which to-fore
Had by the belly oft him pinched sore.
Upon his head a wreath that was enrolled
With ears of corn, of every sort he bore:
And in his hand a sickle he did hold,
To reap the ripened fruits the which the earth had yold.[1]

31

Lastly, came *Winter* clothed all in frieze,[2]
Chattering his teeth for cold that did him chill,
While on his hoary beard his breath did freeze;
And the dull drops that from his purpled bill
As from a limbeck[3] did adown distil.
In his right hand a tipped staff he held
With which his feeble steps he stayed still:
For, he was faint with cold, and weak with eld;[4]
That scarce his loosed limbs he able was to weld.[5]

32

These, marching softly, thus in order went,
And after them, the Months all riding came;
First, sturdy *March* with brows full sternly bent,
And armed strongly, rode upon a Ram,
The same which over *Hellespontus*[6] swam:

1. Yielded.
2. A heavy, coarse material.
3. Alembic, apparatus used for distillation.
4. Age.
5. Wield.
6. Hellespontus, the 'sea of Helle' now called the Dardanelles, is the straits at the mouth of the Black Sea. In Greek mythology Helle and her brother Phryxus were fleeing through the air to Colchis on the back of a magical golden ram when she became giddy and fell into the sea.

Yet in his hand a spade he also hent[1]
And in a bag all sorts of seeds the same,
Which on the earth he strowed[2] as he went,
And filled her womb with fruitful hope of nourishment.

33
Next came *April* full of lustyhed,[3]
And wanton as a Kid whose horn new buds:
Upon a Bull he rode, the same which led
Europa[4] floating through the *Argolic* floods:
50 His horns were gilded all with golden studs
And garnished with garlands goodly dight
Of all the fairest flowers and freshest buds
Which th'earth brings forth, and wet he seemed in sight
With waves, through which he waded for his love's delight.

34
Then came fair *May*, the fairest maid on ground,
Decked all with dainties of her season's pride,
And throwing flowers out of her lap around:
Upon two brethren's shoulders she did ride,
The twins of *Leda*,[5] which on either side
60 Supported her like to their sovereign Queen.
Lord! how all creatures laughed, when her they spied,
And leapt and danced as they had ravished been!
And *Cupid's*[6] self about her fluttered all in green.

1. Held.
2. Scattered.
3. Energy, lustiness.
4. A beautiful girl in Greek mythology who was carried off by Zeus in the form of a white bull across the sea to Crete.
5. Leda was seduced by Zeus in the form of a swan and gave birth to two eggs.
6. Greek god of love.

35

And after her, came jolly *June*, arrayed
All in green leaves, as he a Player were:
Yet in his time, he wrought as well as played,
That by his plough-irons might right well appear:
Upon a Crab he rode, that him did bear
With crooked crawling steps an uncouth pace,
70 And backward yode,[1] as Bargemen wont to fare
Bending their force contrary to their face,
Like that ungracious crew which feigns demurest grace.[2]

36

Then came hot *July* boiling like to fire,
That all his garments he had cast away:
Upon a Lion, raging yet with ire[3]
He boldly rode and made him to obey:
It was the beast that whilom[4] did foray
The Nemean forest, till th'*Amphitrionide*[5]
Him slew, and with his hide did him array;
80 Behind his back a scythe, and by his side
Under his belt he bore a sickle circling wide.

37

The sixth was *August*, being rich arrayed
In garment all of gold down to the ground:
Yet rode he not, but led a lovely Maid
Forth by the lily hand, the which was crowned
With ears of corn, and full her hand was found;

1. Went.
2. Hypocritical courtiers who walk backwards away from the monarch to show respect.
3. Anger.
4. Formerly.
5. Heracles, who killed the Nemean lion as part of his twelve labours, was the foster-son of Amphitrion.

That was the righteous Virgin, which of old
Lived here on earth, and plenty made abound;
But, after Wrong was loved and Justice sold,
90 She left th'unrighteous world and was to heaven extolled.

38

Next him, *September* marched eke[1] on foot;
Yet was he heavy-laden with the spoil
Of harvest's riches, which he made his boot,
And him enriched with bounty of the soil:
In his one hand, as fit for harvest's toil,
He held a knife-hook; and in th'other hand
A pair of weights, with which he did assoil[2]
Both more and less, where it in doubt did stand,
And equal gave to each as Justice duly scanned.

39

100 Then came *October* full of merry glee:
For, yet his noul was totty of the must,[3]
Which he was treading in the wine-vats sea,
And of the joyous oil, whose gentle gust
Made him so frolic and so full of lust:
Upon a dreadful Scorpion he did ride,
The same which by *Diana's*[4] doom unjust
Slew great *Orion*:[5] and eke by his side
He had his ploughing share, and coulter[6] ready tied.

1. Also.
2. Acquit.
3. His head was dizzy with the new wine.
4. Goddess of the moon and the hunt. In anger at Orion's boasts of
his skills as a hunter, she sent a scorpion to kill him. In remorse, she
transformed both of them into stars.
5. A great hunter (see previous note).
6. The iron blade fixed in front of a ploughshare.

40

Next was *November*, he full gross and fat,
110   As fed with lard, and that right well might seem;
For, he had been a-fatting hogs of late,
That yet his brows with sweat, did reek and steam,
And yet the season was full sharp and breem,[1]
In planting eke he took no small delight:
Whereon he rode, not easy was to deem;
For it a dreadful *Centaur*[2] was in sight,
The seed of *Saturn*, and fair *Nais*, *Chiron* hight.

41

And after him, came next the chill *December*:
Yet he through merry feasting which he made,
120   And great bonfires, did not the cold remember;
His Saviour's birth his mind so much did glad:
Upon a shaggy-bearded Goat he rode,
The same wherewith *Dan Jove*[3] in tender years,
They say, was nourished by th'*Idaean*[4] maid;
And in his hand a broad deep bowl he bears;
Of which, he freely drinks an health to all his peers.

42

Then came old *January*, wrapped well
In many weeds to keep the cold away;
Yet did he quake and quiver like to quell,
130   And blow his nails to warm them if he may:

1. Harsh.
2. A centaur is a mythological creature with the top half of a man and the bottom half of a horse. Chiron was the centaur who taught Achilles and other heroes music, medicine and hunting. He is seen in the zodiac sign of Sagittarius.
3. Jove is another name for Jupiter, the Roman counterpart of the Greek Zeus, king of the gods.
4. From Mount Ida, a mountain near Troy.

For, they were numbed with holding all the day
An hatchet keen, with which he felled wood,
And from the trees did lop the needless spray:
Upon an huge great Earth-pot steane[1] he stood;
From whose wide mouth, there flowed forth the Roman flood.

43
And lastly, came cold *February*, sitting
In an old wagon, for he could not ride;
Drawn of two fishes for the season fitting,
Which through the flood before did softly slide
140 And swim away: yet had he by his side
His plough and harness fit to till the ground,
And tools to prune the trees, before the pride
Of hasting Prime did make them burgeon[2] round:
So passed the twelve Months forth, and their due places found.

44
And after these, there came the *Day*, and *Night*,
Riding together both with equal pace,
Th'one on a Palfrey black, the other white;
But *Night* had covered her uncomely face
With a black veil, and held in hand a mace,[3]
150 On top whereof the moon and stars were pight,[4]
And sleep and darkness round about did trace:
But *Day* did bear, upon his sceptre's height,
The goodly Sun, encompassed all with beames bright.

45
Then came the *Hours*, fair daughters of high *Jove*,
And timely *Night*, the which were all endued[5]
With wondrous beauty fit to kindle love;

1. Large urn.
2. Begin to grow rapidly.
3. Heavy club used as a staff of office.
4. Painted.
5. Endowed.

But they were Virgins all and love eschewed,[1]
That might forslack the charge to them fore-shewed
By mighty *Jove*; who did them Porters make
160 Of heaven's gate (whence all the gods issued)
Which they did daily watch, and nightly wake
By even turns, nor ever did their charge forsake.

46

And after all came *Life*, and lastly *Death*;
Death with most grim and grisly visage seen,
Yet is he nought but parting of his breath;
Nor ought to seen, but like a shade to ween,[2]
Unbodied, unsouled, unheard, unseen.
But *Life* was like a fair young lusty boy,
Such as they fain *Dan Cupid* to have been,
170 Full of delightful health and lively joy,
Decked all with flowers, and wings of gold fit to employ.

47

When these were past, thus 'gan[3] the *Titaness*;[4]
Lo, mighty mother,[5] now be judge and say,
Whether in all thy creatures more or less
CHANGE doth not reign and bear the greatest sway:
For, who sees not, that *Time* on all doth prey?
But *Times* do change and move continually.
So nothing here long standeth in one stay:
Wherefore, this lower world who can deny
180 But to be subject still to *Mutability*?[6]

1. Avoided or abstained from.
2. Think.
3. Began.
4. Mythological creature of enormous size and strength.
5. Mother Nature.
6. Changefulness.

William Shakespeare
(1564–1616)

We know very few details about Shakespeare's life. Church records tell us he was baptized on 24 April 1564, but we do not know his birthday. He was born in Stratford-upon-Avon, Warwickshire, the third of eight children. His father, John Shakespeare, was a merchant, and his mother, Mary Arden, the daughter of a Roman Catholic squire.

Shakespeare was probably educated at the local grammar school, which would have given him a thorough grounding in the classics, the heart of an Elizabethan education. As the eldest son, he may have been expected to join his father in business, but we do not know how he spent his time. However, the knowledge of sporting pursuits shown in his plays, and the fact that he was only eighteen years old when he married a pregnant Anne Hathaway, seven years older than himself, suggest that he was something of a tearaway. Local legend says that he left Stratford after being caught poaching deer, though he returned as a prosperous landowner late in life.

By 1592 he was known in London as an actor and a playwright. Some songs from his plays are printed here. Shakespeare's reputation rests mainly on the 38 plays that he either wrote or collaborated on, but he also wrote three long poems: *Venus and Adonis* (1593), *The Rape of Lucrece* (1594), and 'A Lover's Complaint', which was published in 1609 in the same volume as his sonnets.

It is likely that the sonnets had been circulated in manuscript form before they were published. They were printed with a dedication 'To the only begetter of these ensuing sonnets, Mr W.H.', and many names have been suggested that fit those initials. However, the historian A. L. Rowse has suggested that since the dedication was written by the publisher, Thomas Thorpe, rather than by Shakespeare, 'Mr W.H.' may have been Sir William Harvey, third husband of the Countess of Southampton. Rowse suggests that when the Countess died in 1607, Harvey inherited the manuscript and sold it to Thorpe. The Countess of Southampton's eldest son, the third Earl of Southampton, Henry Wriothesly, had become Shakespeare's patron in 1592. Southampton was the only person to whom Shakespeare ever dedicated any of his works publicly.

The first 126 sonnets in the book seem to be addressed to a beautiful young man. Many of them seem to be quite homosexually erotic, but they are often written in an ambiguous way that also suggests close friendship or love that is not physically expressed. Certainly, many of them urge the young man to marry and have children so that his line will be continued. This would fit with Southampton's known reluctance to marry, although he was the only son and had a duty to carry on the family name.

Sonnets 127 to 152 are addressed to a mysterious dark-haired, dark-eyed lady, about whom Shakespeare is often very uncomplimentary. She is described as seductive but faithless, and several of the sonnets suggest that she is not only his mistress but also the mistress of his friend. The sonnets end with two that suggest the poet has paid a visit to a healing spring in the hope of being cured of his infatuation.

Throughout all the sonnets there runs a sense of time passing, and of the need to record the poet's feelings so that, by committing them to paper, they will be preserved for later generations to read and understand the beauty of the young man or the faithlessness of the lady. This is certainly the case in Sonnet 18, 'Shall I compare thee to a summer's day?' A day is short and fleeting, even summer will pass soon. The course of nature, if it is left unchecked, means that everything that is beautiful will decay. However, the poet says that as long as there are people alive to read his poem, it will give life to its subject.

Sonnet 130 gives life to the dark lady when Shakespeare rejects, and makes fun of, poetic conventions. His mistress is a real woman, and he thinks her as beautiful as any that other poets have told lies about by falsely comparing them to ideal standards of beauty.

'Blow, blow thou winter wind'

Blow, blow, thou winter wind,
Thou art not so unkind
As man's ingratitude;
Thy tooth is not so keen
Because thou art not seen,
Although thy breath be rude.
Heigh ho! sing heigh ho! unto the green holly:
Most friendship is feigning, most loving mere folly:
Then, heigh ho! the holly!
10   This life is most jolly.

Freeze, freeze, thou bitter sky,
Thou dost not bite so nigh
As benefits forgot:
Though thou the waters warp,
Thy sting is not so sharp
As friend remember'd not.
Heigh ho! sing heigh ho! unto the green holly:
Most friendship is feigning, most loving mere folly:
Then, heigh ho! the holly!
20   This life is most jolly.

from: *As You Like It*

Carpe Diem

O Mistress mine, where are you roaming?
O stay and hear! your true-love's coming
That can sing both high and low;
Trip no further, pretty sweeting,
Journeys end in lovers meeting –
Every wise man's son doth know.

What is love? 'tis not hereafter;
Present mirth hath present laughter;
      What's to come is still unsure:
10   In delay there lies no plenty, –
Then come kiss me, Sweet-and-twenty,
      Youth's a stuff will not endure.
          from: *Twelfth Night*

Fidele

Fear no more the heat o' the sun
   Nor the furious winter's rages;
Thou thy worldly task hast done,
   Home art gone and ta'en [1] thy wages:
Golden lads and girls all must,
As chimney-sweepers, come to dust.

Fear no more the frown o' the great
   Thou art past the tyrant's stroke;
Care no more to clothe and eat;
10   To thee the reed is as the oak: [2]
The sceptre, [3] learning, physic, [4] must
All follow this and come to dust.

Fear no more the lightning-flash
   Nor the all-dreaded thunder-stone;
Fear not slander, censure rash;
   Thou hast finished joy and moan:
All lovers young, all lovers must
Consign to thee, and come to dust.
          from: *Cymbeline*

1. Taken.
2. One is as unimportant as the other.
3. Earthly power.
4. Medicine.

A Sea Dirge

Full fathom five thy father lies:
  Of his bones are coral made;
Those are pearls that were his eyes:
  Nothing of him that doth fade,
But doth suffer a sea-change
Into something rich and strange.
Sea-nymphs hourly ring his knell: [1]
  Hark! now I hear them –
    Ding, dong, bell.

from: *The Tempest*

1. The church bell that was rung when someone died.

SONNETS

18

Shall I compare thee to a summer's day?
Thou art more lovely and more temperate.
Rough winds do shake the darling buds of May,
And summer's lease hath all too short a date.
Sometime too hot the eye of heaven shines,
And often is his gold complexion dimmed;
And every fair from fair sometime declines,
By chance or nature's changing course untrimmed.[1]

1. Uncorrected, as a sailor would trim a sail to correct his course.

But thy eternal summer shall not fade,
10   Nor lose possession of that fair thou ow'st,[1]
Nor shall Death brag thou wand'rest in his shade,
When in eternal lines to time thou grow'st.
   So long as men can breathe or eyes can see,
   So long lives this, and this gives life to thee.

1. That beauty you own.

27

Weary with toil, I haste me to my bed,
The dear repose for limbs with travel tired;
But then begins a journey in my head
To work my mind when body's work's expired;
For then my thoughts, from far where I abide,
Intend a zealous pilgrimage to thee,
And keep my drooping eyelids open wide,
Looking on darkness which the blind do see;
Save[1] that my soul's imaginary sight
10   Presents thy shadow to my sightless view,
Which like a jewel hung in ghastly night
Makes black night beauteous and her old face new.
   Lo, thus by day my limbs, by night my mind,
   For thee, and for myself, no quiet find.

1. Except.

73

That time of year thou mayst in me behold
When yellow leaves, or none, or few, do hang
Upon those boughs which shake against the cold,
Bare ruined choirs where late[1] the sweet birds sang.

1. Formerly.

In me thou seest the twilight of such day
As after sunset fadeth in the west,
Which by and by black night doth take away,
Death's second self, that seals up all in rest.
In me thou seest the glowing of such fire
10   That on the ashes of his youth doth lie,
As the deathbed whereon it must expire,
Consumed with that which it was nourished by.
　　This thou perceiv'st, which makes thy love more strong,
　　To love that[1] well which thou must leave[2] ere long.

1. 'That' carries the double meaning of both 'the poet' and 'your life'.
2. 'Leave' carries the double meaning of both 'give up' and 'depart from'.

87

Farewell, thou art too dear[1] for my possessing,
And like enough thou know'st thy estimate.
The charter of thy worth gives thee releasing;[2]
My bonds in thee are all determinate.[3]
For how do I hold thee but by thy granting,
And for that riches where is my deserving?
The cause of this fair gift in me is wanting,
And so my patent back again is swerving.[4]
Thyself thou gav'st, thy own worth then not knowing,
10   Or me, to whom thou gav'st it, else mistaking;

1. 'Dear' carries several meanings here: 'too costly', 'too deeply loved by me' and 'too high in rank'.
2. Your rank (but also your value as a person) gives you freedom.
3. My claim over you is ended.
4. The right of ownership reverts to you.

So thy great gift, upon misprision[1] growing,
Comes home again, on better judgement making.
   Thus have I had thee as a dream doth flatter,
   In sleep a king, but waking no such matter.

1. Failure to appreciate, undervaluing

106

When in the chronicle of wasted time[1]
I see descriptions of the fairest wights,[2]
And beauty making beautiful old rhyme
In praise of ladies dead and lovely knights;
Then, in the blazon[3] of sweet beauty's best,
Of hand, of foot, of lip, of eye, of brow,
I see their antique pen would have expressed
Even such a beauty as you master now.
So all their praises are but prophecies
10 Of this our time, all you prefiguring,
And, for they looked but with divining[4] eyes,
They had not skill enough your worth to sing:
   For we, which now behold these present days,
   Have eyes to wonder, but lack tongues to praise.

1. The history of past times.
2. Persons. Shakespeare is deliberately using a word which was archaic even in his day.
3. Catalogue of good qualities.
4. Seeing into the future.

116

Let me not to the marriage of true minds
Admit impediments;[1] love is not love
Which alters when it alteration finds,
Or bends with the remover to remove.

1. Obstacles.

O no, it is an ever-fixèd mark[1]
That looks on tempests and is never shaken;
It is the star to every wandering bark,[2]
Whose worth's unknown, although his height be taken.[3]
Love's not Time's fool, though rosy lips and cheeks
10   Within his bending sickle's compass[4] come;
Love alters not with his brief hours and weeks,
But bears it out[5] even to the edge of doom.
    If this be error and upon me proved,
    I never writ, nor no man ever loved.

1. A beacon or a lighthouse. The image of love as a stormy sea and the lover as a sailor adrift was a common one.
2. A ship.
3. A ship heavily laden with goods would lie low in the water, but the value of the goods would be unknown.
4. Within the reach of the sickle, a tool with a sharp, curved blade used for reaping corn, carried by Old Father Time in pictures.
5. Continues.

130

My mistress' eyes are nothing like the sun;
Coral is far more red than her lips' red;
If snow be white, why then her breasts are dun;[1]
If hairs be wires, black wires grow on her head.[2]
I have seen roses damasked, red and white,
But no such roses see I in her cheeks,
And in some perfumes is there more delight
Than in the breath that from my mistress reeks.[3]
I love to hear her speak, yet well I know

1. Brown.
2. The conventional description of Elizabethan beauties compared their hair to the fine gold wires used in embroidery.
3. This meant 'exhales' in Shakespeare's time, without the modern sense of foul-smelling air.

10   That music hath a far more pleasing sound.
     I grant I never saw a goddess go;
     My mistress when she walks treads on the ground.
         And yet, by heaven, I think my love as rare[1]
         As any she belied with false compare.[2]

1. Extraordinary and precious.
2. 'False' here means both mistaken and artificial.

138

When my love swears that she is made of truth[1]
I do believe her, though I know she lies,
That[2] she might think me some untutored youth,
Unlearnèd in the world's false subtleties.
Thus vainly[3] thinking that she thinks me young,
Although she knows my days are past the best,
Simply I credit her false-speaking tongue;
On both sides thus is simple truth suppressed.
But wherefore[4] says she not she is unjust?
10   And wherefore say not I that I am old?
     O, love's best habit is in seeming trust,
     And age in love loves not to have years told.
         Therefore I lie with her, and she with me,[5]
         And in our faults by lies we flattered be.

1. Completely honest.
2. So that.
3. 'Vainly' here means several things: 'foolishly', 'ineffectually' and
'conceitedly'.
4. Why.
5. 'Lie with her' here means both 'make love with her' and 'tell her
lies'.

John Donne
(1572–1631)

John Donne was born in London. From the age of eleven he studied at Oxford, and some people think he later studied at Cambridge and then possibly travelled abroad. He began to study law in 1592, following a family tradition by joining Lincoln's Inn in London. Shortly afterwards, he joined the Anglican Church, although he had been brought up a Roman Catholic.

In 1596 Donne joined the expedition against Cadiz led by Raleigh and the Earl of Essex, and in 1597 sailed to the Azores. After his return to England he became the private secretary of Sir Thomas Egerton, Keeper of the Great Seal. When in 1601 he secretly married Ann More, Egerton's niece, he was dismissed from his post and briefly imprisoned until the validity of the marriage was proved.

Over the next few years he scraped a meagre living as a lawyer, depending on his wife's cousin to house him, his wife and their children. He made several unsuccessful attempts to find employment. However, in 1608 a reconciliation with his father-in-law brought the family some money from his wife's dowry.

During all these years he wrote satires, songs, sonnets and treatises, though many were not published until after his death. However, one pamphlet which argued that English Roman Catholics could pledge an oath of allegiance to James I, King of England, without betraying their faith, won him the King's favour, and he was appointed a royal chaplain after being ordained a deacon and a priest at St Paul's Cathedral in London. His sermons were famous for their brilliance.

In 1617 his wife died shortly after giving birth to a still-born baby, their twelfth child in sixteen years of marriage. Donne mourned her deeply and never remarried.

James I appointed Donne dean of St Paul's Cathedral in 1621, and he remained in that post until his death. As well as sermons, he continued to write poetry, especially the Holy Sonnets, and devotional works. Some of his most famous sermons were delivered during the year before his death in 1631.

The most striking thing about Donne's poetry is his use of complicated comparisons. These conceits, as they were known, set out to prove a likeness between two things which seem at first totally unlike. For example, in 'The Flea' Donne points out to his beloved that the flea which has bitten both of them mingles both their blood inside it. This, he says, means they are as good as married. Therefore, he argues, it is a greater sin to kill the flea than to give way to his wooing, since the flea represents them and their marriage temple.

Donne's poems are often phrased very dramatically, in colloquial language. In this way they are quite different from the smooth and courtly poems of the Elizabethan era. 'The Sun Rising' begins with the poet telling off in no uncertain terms the sun whose rays have disturbed him and his beloved by shining on them through gaps in the curtains. He tells the sun to go and disturb other people, since lovers have their own time and their bed is the whole world to them.

Other poets of the period, such as George Herbert and Henry Vaughan, drew inspiration from Donne's imagery, and poets who wrote in this complex and dramatic style with its intricate metaphors later became known as the 'metaphysical poets'.

Donne was almost forgotten during the eighteenth century when poetry was dominated by the elegant classical style of Milton, Dryden and Pope. To the Romantic poets of the early nineteenth century, who had no time for either the intricacy of his imagery or the irregularity of his style, he was, in Coleridge's words, 'Donne, whose muse on dromedary trots, / wreathe iron pokers into true-love knots.' However, poets of the early twentieth century, such as Ezra Pound and T. S. Eliot, revived his popularity and acknowledged his influence, and he is now generally regarded as one of the greatest English poets.

Song

Go, and catch a falling star,
    Get with child a mandrake root,
Tell me, where all past years are,
    Or who cleft the Devil's foot,
Teach me to hear mermaids singing,
    Or to keep off envy's stinging,
        And find
        What wind
Serves to advance an honest mind.

10 If thou be'est born to strange sights,
    Things invisible to see,
Ride ten thousand days and nights,
    Till age snow white hairs on thee,
Thou, when thou return'st, wilt tell me
All strange wonders that befell thee,
        And swear
        No where
Lives a woman true, and fair.[1]

If thou find'st one, let me know,
    Such a pilgrimage were sweet,
20 Yet do not, I would not go,
    Though at next door we might meet,
Though she were true, when you met her,
And last, till you write your letter,
        Yet she
        Will be
False, ere I come, to two, or three.

1. Faithful as well as beautiful.

The Good Morrow

I wonder by my troth, what thou, and I
    Did, till we loved? were we not weaned till then,
But sucked on country pleasures, childishly?[1]
    Or snorted we in the seven sleepers' den?[2]
'Twas so; but this, all pleasures fancies be.
If ever any beauty I did see,
Which I desired, and got, 'twas but a dream of thee.

And now good morrow to our waking souls,
    Which watch not one another out of fear;[3]
10   For love, all love of other sights controls,
    And makes one little room, an every where.
Let sea-discoverers to new worlds have gone,
Let maps to others, worlds on worlds have shown,
Let us possess one world, each hath one, and is one.[4]

My face in thine eye, thine in mine appears,
    And true plain hearts do in the faces rest,
Where can we find two better hemispheres
    Without sharp north, without declining west?[5]
What ever dies, was not mixed equally;
20   If our two loves be one, or, thou and I
Love so alike, that none do slacken, none can die.[6]

1. Before they met and loved, their pleasures were all childish.
2. A cave in Ephesus in which seven Christian youths walled up alive slept miraculously for nearly 200 years.
3. They do not gaze at each other from suspicion but because they are absorbed in love.
4. Possessing each other makes their two worlds one, like two hemispheres joined in a globe.
5. North symbolizes coldness, and west symbolizes decline.
6. Medical theory of the time said that illness and death were caused by an imbalance in the elements that made up the body ('humours'), therefore perfect balance meant eternal life.

The Sun Rising

Busy old fool, unruly sun,
    Why dost thou thus,
Through windows, and through curtains call on us?
Must to thy motions lovers' seasons run?
        Saucy pedantic wretch, go chide
        Late school-boys, and sour prentices,[1]
    Go tell court-huntsmen, that the King will ride,
    Call country ants to harvest offices;[2]
Love, all alike, no season knows, nor clime,[3]
Nor hours, days, months, which are the rags of time.

        Thy beams, so reverend, and strong
        Why shouldst thou think?
I could eclipse and cloud them with a wink,
But that I would not lose her sight so long:
        If her eyes have not blinded thine,
        Look, and tomorrow late, tell me,
    Whether both th'Indias of spice and mine[4]
    Be where thou left'st them, or lie here with me.
Ask for those kings whom thou saw'st yesterday,
And thou shalt hear, All here in one bed lay.

        She'is all states, and all princes, I,
        Nothing else is.
Princes do but play us; compared to this,

1. Apprentices.
2. Harvest duties.
3. Climate.
4. The East and West Indies, where spices grew and mines of precious
stones were found.

All honour's mimic;[1] all wealth alchemy.[2]
>Thou sun art half as happy as we,
>In that the world's contracted thus;
>Thine age asks ease, and since thy duties be
>To warm the world, that's done in warming us.
Shine here to us, and thou art everywhere;
30 This bed thy centre is, these walls, thy sphere.

1. Pretence.
2. Alchemists sought the Philosophers' Stone, an elusive substance that would turn anything to gold. Here, Donne means that all wealth would be an illusion compared to the reality of the richness the two lovers find in each other.

The Flea

Mark but this flea, and mark in this,
How little that which thou deny'st me is;
Me it sucked first, and now sucks thee,
And in this flea, our two bloods mingled be;
Confess it, this cannot be said
A sin, or shame, or loss of maidenhead,[1]
>Yet this enjoys before it woo,
>And pampered swells with one blood made of two,
>And this, alas, is more than we would do.

10 Oh stay, three lives in one flea spare,
Where we almost, nay more than married are.
This flea is you and I, and this
Our marriage bed, and marriage temple is;
Though parents grudge, and you, we'are met,
And cloistered in these living walls of jet.[2]
>Though use make you apt to kill me,
>Let not to this, self murder added be,
>And sacrilege, three sins in killing three.

1. Virginity.
2. A flea's body is black, like jet.

Cruel and sudden, hast thou since
20   Purpled thy nail, in blood of innocence?[1]
In what could this flea guilty be,
Except in that drop which it sucked from thee?
Yet thou triumph'st, and say'st that thou
Find'st not thyself, nor me the weaker now;
    'Tis true, then learn how false, fears be;
    Just so much honour, when thou yield'st to me,
    Will waste, as this flea's death took life from thee.

1. Fleas were usually killed by cracking them with a fingernail.

The Dream

Dear love, for nothing less than thee
Would I have broke this happy dream,
    It was a theme
For reason, much too strong for phantasy,
Therefore thou waked'st me wisely; yet
My dream thou brok'st not, but continued'st it;
Thou art so true, that thoughts of thee suffice,
To make dreams truths, and fables histories;
Enter these arms, for since thou thought'st it best,
10   Not to dream all my dream, let's act the rest.

As lightning, or a taper's light,
Thine eyes, and not thy noise waked me;
    Yet I thought thee
(For thou lov'st truth) an angel, at first sight,
But when I saw thou saw'st my heart,
And knew'st my thoughts, beyond an angel's art,
When thou knew'st what I dreamed, when thou knew'st when
Excess of joy would wake me, and cam'st then,
I must confess, it could not choose but be
20   Profane, to think thee anything but thee.

Coming and staying showed thee, thee,
But rising makes me doubt, that now,
        Thou art not thou.
That love is weak, where fear's as strong as he;
'Tis not all spirit, pure, and brave,
If mixture it of fear, shame, honour, have.
Perchance as torches which must ready be,
Men light and put out, so thou deal'st with me,
Thou cam'st to kindle, goest to come; then I
30 Will dream that hope again, but else would die.

The Apparition

When by thy scorn, O murderess, I am dead,
And that thou think'st thee free
From all solicitation from me,
Then shall my ghost come to thy bed,
And thee, feigned vestal, in worse arms shall see;
Then thy sick taper will begin to wink,
And he, whose thou art then, being tired before,

Will, if thou stir, or pinch to wake him, think
        Thou call'st for more,
10 And in false sleep will from thee shrink,
And then poor aspen wretch, neglected thou
Bathed in a cold quicksilver sweat wilt lie
        A verier ghost than I;
What I will say, I will not tell thee now,
Lest that preserve thee; and since my love is spent,
I had rather thou shouldst painfully repent,
Than by my threatenings rest still innocent.

A Hymn to God the Father

I

Wilt thou forgive that sin where I begun,
    Which was my sin, though it were done before?
Wilt thou forgive that sin, through which I run,
    And do run still: though still I do deplore?
        When thou hast done, thou hast not done,[1]
           For, I have more.

II

Wilt thou forgive that sin which I have won
    Others to sin? and, made my sin their door?
Wilt thou forgive that sin which I did shun
10   A year, or two: but wallowed in, a score?
        When thou hast done, thou hast not done,
           For I have more.

III

I have a sin of fear, that when I have spun
    My last thread, I shall perish on the shore;
But swear by thy self, that at my death thy son
    Shall shine as he shines now, and heretofore;
        And, having done that, thou hast done,
           I fear no more.

1. Notice the pun on done/Donne, which sound the same.

Robert Herrick
(1591–1674)

Robert Herrick was born in London, the fourth son of a gold-smith. His father died when he was very young, and his uncle William became his guardian. When he was sixteen, he became an apprentice goldsmith with his uncle, but did not complete his apprenticeship. Instead, his uncle supported him while he studied, from 1613, at Cambridge University.

After taking his BA and MA degrees, Herrick was ordained in 1623, but little is known of his life in the next six years, apart from his membership as a chaplain of the Duke of Buckingham's expedition to the Isle of Rhé in 1627. He seems to have been friendly with a group of poets associated with the dramatist Ben Jonson, and his poems were circulated among them in manuscript form, though most were not printed until 1648.

Shortly after his mother died in 1629, he was given the living of Dean Prior, a rural parish in Devon. The contrast to his life in London must have been great, but he was essentially a man with a happy and friendly temperament, and he was described by Anthony Wood as becoming 'much beloved by the Gentry in those parts for his florid and witty discourse'. His poem 'A Thanksgiving to God, for his House' describes an idyllic and placid life, surrounded by his animals and cared for devotedly by his maid, Prudence Baldwin.

Because of his Royalist sympathies, Herrick was deprived of his living in 1647 during the period after the Civil War and the execution of King Charles I, when Cromwell and the Parliamentarians ruled. During this time, he lived in Westminster, in London, depending on the charity of his friends and family. He spent some time preparing his poems for publication, and had them printed in

1648 with a dedication to the Prince of Wales.

When the monarchy was restored in 1660, Herrick petitioned for his own restoration to his living, which was granted to him by King Charles II in the summer of 1662. He lived in Dean Prior until his death in 1674, at the ripe age of 83.

His poems were not widely popular at the time when they were published. His style was strongly influenced by Jonson, by the classical Roman writers and by the poems of the late Elizabethan age. This must have seemed quite old-fashioned to an audience whose tastes were tuned to the complexities of the metaphysical poets such as Donne and Marvell. His works were rediscovered in the early nineteenth century, and have been regularly printed ever since.

Herrick sets out his subject matter in the poem 'The Argument of his Book', which he printed at the beginning of his collection. As well as complimentary poems to various ladies and his friends, he dealt with themes taken from classical writings and wrote about the seasons and customs of English country life. Underpinning all his work was a solid bedrock of unintellectualized Christian faith.

Despite his use of classical allusions and names, his poems are easier for modern readers to understand than those of many of his contemporaries. This is partly because they are less profound, and partly because he expresses his thoughts and feelings with such grace and precision. Herrick loved the richness of sensuality and the variety of life, and this is shown vividly in such poems as 'Cherry-ripe', 'Delight in Disorder' and 'Upon Julia's Clothes'. The overriding message of his work is that life is short, the world is beautiful, love is splendid and we must use the short time we have to make the most of it. This message can be seen clearly in 'To the Virgins, to make much of Time', 'To Daffodils', 'To Blossoms' and 'Corinna's going a-Maying', where the warmth and exuberance of what seems to have been a kindly and jovial personality come over strongly.

The Argument of his Book[1]

I sing of brooks, of blossoms, birds and bowers:
Of April, May, of June, and July-flowers.
I sing of maypoles, hock-carts, wassails, wakes,
Of bride-grooms, brides, and of their bridal-cakes.
I write of youth, of love, and have access
By these, to sing of cleanly-wantonness.
I sing of dews, of rains, and piece by piece
Of balm, of oil, of spice and ambergris.[2]
I sing of times trans-shifting; and I write
10 How roses first came red, and lilies white.
I write of groves, of twilights, and I sing
The court of Mab,[3] and of the fairy-king.
I write of Hell; I sing (and ever shall)
Of Heaven, and hope to have it after all.

1. 'Argument' here means the subject matter.
2. Ambergris is a substance secreted by sperm whales. It was expensive to buy, and used in perfumery and medicine.
3. Mab was the queen of the fairies, referred to by Mercutio in *Romeo and Juliet*.

Delight in Disorder

A sweet disorder in the dress
Kindles in clothes a wantonness:
A lawn[1] about the shoulders thrown
Into a fine distraction;
An erring lace, which here and there
Enthralls the crimson stomacher:[2]

1. A piece of fine, light material.
2. An ornamental covering for the breast and stomach worn by women in the fifteenth to seventeenth centuries.

A cuff neglectful and thereby
Ribands[1] to flow confusedly:
A winning wave (deserving note)
10 In the tempestuous petticoat:
A careless shoe-string, in whose tie
I see a wild civility:
Do more bewitch me, than when art
Is too precise in every part.

1. Ribbons.

Cherry-ripe

Cherry-ripe, ripe, ripe, I cry,
Full and fair ones; come and buy:
If so be, you ask me where
They do grow? I answer, there,
Where my Julia's lips do smile;
There's the land, or cherry-isle:
Whose plantations fully show
All the year, where cherries grow.

Corinna's going a-Maying

Get up, get up for shame, the blooming morn
Upon her wings presents the god unshorn.
See how Aurora[1] throws her fair
Fresh-quilted colours through the air:
Get up, sweet slug-a-bed, and see
The dew bespangling herb and tree.
Each flower has wept, and bowed toward the East
Above an hour since; yet you not dressed,

1. Goddess of the dawn.

Nay! not so much as out of bed?
When all the birds have matins[1] said,
And sung their thankful hymns: 'tis sin,
Nay, profanation to keep in,
When as a thousand virgins on this day,
Spring, sooner than the lark, to fetch in May.[2]

Rise, and put on your foliage, and be seen
To come forth, like the spring-time, fresh and green;
And sweet as Flora.[3] Take no care
For jewels for your gown, or hair:
Fear not, the leaves will strew
Gems in abundance upon you:
Besides, the childhood of the day has kept,
Against you come, some orient pearls unwept:
Come and receive them while the light
Hangs on the dew-locks of the night,
And Titan on the eastern hill[4]
Retires himself, or else stands still
Till you come forth. Wash, dress, be brief in praying:
Few beads[5] are best, when once we go a-Maying.

Come, my Corinna, come; and coming, mark
How each field turns a street; each street a park
Made green, and trimmed with trees: see how
Devotion gives each house a bough,
Or branch. Each porch, each door, ere this,
An ark, a tabernacle[6] is
Made up of white-thorn, neatly interwove,
As if here were those cooler shades of love.
Can such delights be in the street,
And open fields, and we not see't?

1. Very early morning church service.
2. Whitethorn blossom, known as May-blossom, was traditionally gathered on Mayday.
3. Goddess of flowers.
4. The sun.
5. Beads on a rosary counted the number of prayers said.
6. A religious shrine.

Come, we'll abroad, and let's obey
40   The proclamation made for May:
And sin no more, as we have done, by staying;
But my Corinna, come, let's go a-Maying.

There's not a budding boy, or girl, this day,
But is got up, and gone to bring in May.
        A deal of youth, ere this, is come
        Back, and with white-thorn laden home.
        Some have despatched their cakes and cream,
        Before that we have left to dream:
And some have wept, and wooed, and plighted troth,[1]
50   And chose their priest, ere we can cast off sloth.
        Many a green-gown has been given;
        Many a kiss, both odd and even:
        Many a glance too has been sent
        From out the eye, love's firmament:
Many a jest told of the keys betraying
This night, and locks picked, yet we're not a-Maying.

Come, let us go, while we are in our prime;
And take the harmless folly of the time.
        We shall grow old apace,[2] and die
60   Before we know our liberty.
        Our life is short; and our days run
        As fast away as does the sun:
And as a vapour, or a drop of rain
Once lost, can ne'er be found again:
        So when or you or I are made
        A fable, song, or fleeting shade;
        All love, all liking, all delight
        Lies drowned with us in endless night.
Then while time serves, and we are but decaying;
70   Come, my Corinna, come, let's go a-Maying.

1. Promised to marry each other.
2. Quickly.

To the Virgins, to make much of Time

Gather ye rose-buds while ye may,
    Old Time is still a-flying:
And this same flower that smiles today,
    Tomorrow will be dying.

The glorious Lamp of Heaven, the Sun,
    The higher he's a-getting;
The sooner will his race be run,
    And nearer he's to setting.

That age is best, which is the first,
10   When youth and blood are warmer;
But being spent, the worse, and worst
    Times, still succeed the former.

Then be not coy, but use your time;
    And while ye may, go marry:
For having lost but once your prime,
    You may for ever tarry.

How Roses came red

Roses at first were white,
    Till they could not agree,
Whether my Sappho's breast,
    Or they more white should be.

But being vanquished quite,
    A blush their cheeks bespread;
Since which (believe the rest)
    The roses first came red.

To Daffodils

Fair daffodils, we weep to see
  You haste away so soon:
As yet the early-rising sun
  Has not attained his noon.
    Stay, stay,
  Until the hasting day
    Has run
  But to the even-song;
And, having prayed together, we
10 Will go with you along.

We have short time to stay, as you,
  We have as short a spring;
As quick a growth to meet decay
  As you, or any thing.
    We die,
  As your hours do, and dry
    Away
  Like to the summer's rain;
Or as the pearls of morning's dew
20 Ne'er to be found again.

To Blossoms

Fair pledges of a fruitful tree,
  Why do ye fall so fast?
  Your date is not so past;
But you may stay yet here a while,
  To blush and gently smile;
    And go at last.

What, were ye born to be
   An hour or half's delight;
   And so to bid goodnight?
10 'Twas pity Nature brought ye forth
   Merely to show your worth,
     And lose you quite.

But you are lovely Leaves, where we
   May read how soon things have
   Their end, though ne'er so brave:
And after they have shown their pride,
   Like you a while: they glide
     Into the grave.

Upon his departure hence

Thus I
Pass by,
And die:
As one,
Unknown,
And gone:
I'm made
A shade,
And laid
10 I'th' grave,
There have
My cave.
Where tell
I dwell,
Farewell.

Upon Julia's clothes

When as in silks my Julia goes,
Then, then (me thinks) how sweetly flows
That liquefaction of her clothes.

Next, when I cast mine eyes and see
That brave vibration each way free;
O how that glittering taketh me!

A Thanksgiving to God, for his House

Lord, thou hast given me a cell
    Wherein to dwell;
And little house, whose humble roof
    Is weather-proof;
Under the spars of which I lie
    Both soft, and dry;
Where thou my chamber for to ward[1]
    Hast set a guard
Of harmless thoughts, to watch and keep
10   Me, while I sleep.
Low is my porch, as is my fate,
    Both void of state;
And yet the threshold of my door
    Is worn by th' poor,
Who thither come, and freely get
    Good words, or meat.
Like as my parlour, so my hall
    And kitchen's small:
A little buttery, [2] and therein
    A little bin,

1. Guard.
2. Room in which food and drink was kept.

Which keeps my little loaf of bread
    Unchipped, unflead;[1]
Some brittle sticks of thorn or briar
    Make me a fire,
Close by whose living coal I sit,
    And glow like it.
Lord, I confess too, when I dine,
    The pulse[2] is thine,
And all those other bits, that be
30   There placed by thee:
The worts, the purslain and the mess
    Of water-cress,[3]
Which of thy kindness thou hast sent;
    And my content
Makes those, and my beloved Beet,
    To be more sweet.
'Tis thou that crown'st my glittering heart
    With guiltless mirth,
And giv'st me wassail bowls to drink,
40   Spiced to the brink.
Lord, 'tis thy plenty-dropping hand,
    That soils[4] my land,
And giv'st me, for my bushel sown,
    Twice ten for one;
Thou mak'st my teeming hen to lay
    Her egg each day;
Besides my healthful ewes to bear
    Me twins each year;
The while the conduits of my kine[5]
50   Run cream, (for wine.)

1. Undamaged and away from flies.
2. Peas and beans.
3. These are all salad greens.
4. Fertilizes.
5. The udders of my cows.

All these, and better thou dost send
    Me, to this end,
That I should render, for my part
    A thankful heart,
Which, fired with incense, I resign,
    As wholly thine;
But the acceptance, that must be
    My Christ, by thee.

George Herbert
(?1593–1633)

George Herbert was born in Montgomeryshire in Wales. His father died when he was only three years old, and the family later moved to Oxford and then to London, where he went to Westminster School from 1604 until 1609. His mother married Sir John Danvers, a man much younger than herself, who supported Herbert in his studies at Trinity College, Cambridge.

Herbert was very successful at university, and became first a Fellow of Trinity College and then, from 1619 until 1627, the university's Public Orator. He began a political career by being briefly MP for Montgomeryshire from 1623 to 1624, but changed direction and was ordained a deacon in 1624. Later, in 1626, he became a canon of Lincoln Cathedral.

In March 1629 he married Jane Danvers, his stepfather's cousin, and the following year they moved to Bemerton in Wiltshire, where he became the rector. In 1633 Herbert died at the rectory in Bemerton shortly before his fortieth birthday.

A book of Herbert's poems was published after his death under the title of *The Temple*. Nearly all of them concern aspects of religious faith, particularly his own intense spiritual struggle to submit his will to God's, as Christ did.

Herbert's poetic style falls in the tradition of Donne and the other metaphysical poets of the early seventeenth century. His poems often take a central metaphor and turn it into a conceit by extending it and exploring every aspect of it. For example, in 'Love' the image is of God as a warm and loving host and the poet as a guest who feels unworthy to be in his house. The last two lines remind us that God not only feeds us, but is himself the food in the communion service. The simplicity and the warmth of tone of this poem emphasize the message that Herbert finds at the heart of his faith: that God is Love.

Another striking and unusual aspect of Herbert's poems is his use of tricks of layout and language to emphasize the meaning. In 'Easter-Wings', the shape of the lines takes us from the expansiveness of man created by God 'in wealth and store', declining by his own sin until he becomes 'Most poor' and rising again to fly towards heaven through Christ's atonement. The layout suggests wings, and the images are of birds and flight. 'The Altar', too, uses this technique.

Sometimes Herbert uses patterns of language which call on us to admire their cleverness while still clearly delivering their message. In 'Paradise', the last word of each line of a verse is shortened by one letter to give the last word of the next line, and the image is of God as a patient gardener, who not only protects his plants but cuts and prunes them to improve them. In 'Heaven' he uses the device of an echo repeating the last syllable of a question, and in so doing answering it.

For modern readers, one of the most difficult aspects of Herbert's poetry is his constant use of references to both the Old and New Testaments, and to the liturgy used in church services. His original readers would have been far more familiar with these things than readers today. They would also have been more likely to understand the connections he made between events in the Old and New Testaments, where those in the Old Testament were seen as foreshadowing those in the New.

Another difficulty is caused by words that have changed their meaning in the last four hundred years. 'Meat' for example, meant food in general and not just animal flesh.

Herbert also used puns extensively, though not for comic effect as they are generally used now. In his poems, they act as a kind of shorthand, condensing two meanings into one word. For example, in 'The Agony' he uses a pun on both 'press' and 'vice' to emphasize his meaning. These puns are sometimes part of paradoxes often found in the Christian faith: how sacrifice can be triumph; how death can be life; how God can be man.

The Altar

A broken ALTAR, Lord, thy servant rears,
Made of a heart, and cemented with tears:
  Whose parts are as thy hand did frame;
  No workman's tool hath touched the same.[1]
        A HEART[2] alone
        Is such a stone,
        As nothing but
        Thy pow'r doth cut.
        Wherefore each part
        Of my hard heart
        Meets in this frame,
        To praise thy name:
  That if I chance to hold my peace,
  These stones to praise thee may not cease.
O let thy blessed SACRIFICE[3] be mine,
And sanctify this ALTAR to be thine.

1. The Israelites in the Old Testament were instructed to use only whole stones to build their altars, and not to cut them with tools.
2. The old laws were written on stone tablets, but St Paul tells us that the new law brought by Christ is written 'in the fleshy tables of the heart'.
3. The prayer after communion includes words which offer 'our souls and bodies, to be a living sacrifice'.

The Agony

Philosophers have measured mountains,
Fathomed the depths of seas, of states, and kings,
Walked with a staff[1] to heav'n, and traced fountains:
 But there are two vast, spacious things,
The which to measure it doth more behove:
Yet few there are that sound them; Sin and Love.

Who would know Sin, let him repair
Unto Mount Olivet;[2] there shall he see
A man so wrung with pains, that all his hair,
 His skin, his garments bloody be.
Sin is that press and vice,[3] which forceth pain
To hunt his cruel food through ev'ry vein.

Who knows not Love, let him assay
And taste that juice, which on the cross a pike
Did set again abroach;[4] then let him say
 If ever he did taste the like.
Love is that liquor sweet and most divine,
Which my God feels as blood; but I, as wine.

1. A staff can be both a measuring rod and a support.
2. The Mount of Olives was the place of Christ's emotional torment (agony) before the crucifixion, in which he contemplated his coming death and prayed that he might not have to undergo it, but resigned his will to God's.
3. The press was an instrument of torture in which limbs and bodies were squeezed. Grapes are also squeezed in a wine-press, to make the juice run. A vice is also a device for squeezing, and vice is another word for wickedness.
4. To broach something is to open it, as a spear opened a hole in Christ's side during the crucifixion and let his blood flow out.

The Sinner

Lord, how I am all ague,[1] when I seek
    What I have treasured in my memory!
    Since, if my soul make even with the week,
Each seventh note by right is due to thee.
I find there quarries of piled vanities,
    But shreds of holiness, that dare not venture
    To show their face, since cross to thy decrees:
There the circumference earth is, heav'n the centre.[2]
In so much dregs the quintessence is small:[3]
    The spirit and good extract of my heart
    Comes to about the many hundredth part.
Yet Lord restore thine image,[4] hear my call:
    And though my hard heart scarce to thee can groan,
    Remember that thou once didst write in stone.[5]

1. Ague was an illness involving fever and shivering.
2. So much of life is taken up by worldliness and sin, and heaven is only a tiny point at the centre.
3. The quintessence is the purest part of something.
4. Man is made in the image of God, but mars it by sin.
5. The ten commandments given to Moses on Mount Sinai were written on stone tablets.

Redemption[1]

Having been tenant long to a rich Lord,
    Not thriving, I resolved to be bold,
    And make a suit unto him, to afford
A new small-rented lease, and cancel th' old.[2]
In heaven at his manor I him sought:
    They told me there, that he was lately gone
    About some land, which he had dearly bought
Long since on earth, to take possession.
I straight returned, and knowing his great birth,
10   Sought him accordingly in great resorts;
        In cities, theatres, gardens, parks, and courts:
At length I heard a ragged noise and mirth
    Of thieves and murderers: there I him espied,
    Who straight, *Your suit is granted*, said, and died.

1. 'Redemption' means buying back or ransoming, as Christ redeemed
the sin of humankind.
2. The old agreement (covenant) between God and humanity, as shown
in the Old Testament, was replaced by the new covenant brought
about by the death of Christ.

Easter-Wings

Lord, who createdst man in wealth and store,
  Though foolishly he lost the same,
    Decaying more and more,
      Till he became
        Most poor:
        With thee
      O let me rise
    As larks, harmoniously,
  And sing this day thy victories:
Then shall the fall further the flight in me.[1]

My tender age in sorrow did begin:
  And still with sicknesses and shame
    Thou didst so punish sin,
      That I became
        Most thin.
        With thee
      Let me combine,
    And feel this day thy victory:
  For, if I imp my wing on thine,[2]
Affliction shall advance the flight in me.

1. The fall of humankind from grace paradoxically leads them closer to heaven because it made the birth and death of Christ necessary to atone for their sins.

2. Imping was a technique used by falconers, in which they grafted feathers into the wings of birds to repair damage and so restore or improve their flying ability. Here, Herbert says that the weaker we are, the more we need Christ's help, and so the higher our spirits fly towards God.

Colossians 3:3

Our life is hid with Christ in God.

My words and thoughts do both express this notion,
That **Life** hath with the sun a double motion.
The first **Is** straight, and our diurnal[1] friend,
    The other **Hid** and doth obliquely[2] bend.
One life is wrapped **In** flesh, and tends to earth:
The other winds towards **Him**, whose happy birth
   Taught me to live here so, **That** still one eye.
Should aim and shoot at that which **Is** on high:
        Quitting with daily labour all **My** pleasure,
          To gain at harvest an eternal **Treasure**.

1. Daily.
2. Diagonally, like the verse of the subtitle that runs through the poem.

Peace

Sweet Peace, where dost thou dwell? I humbly crave,
        Let me once know.
    I sought thee in a secret cave,
        And asked, if Peace were there.
A hollow wind did seem to answer, No:
        Go seek elsewhere.

I did; and going did a rainbow note:
        Surely, thought I,
    This is the lace of Peace's coat:
        I will search out the matter.
But while I looked, the clouds immediately
        Did break and scatter.

Then went I to a garden, and did spy
        A gallant flower,
    The Crown Imperial:[1] Sure, said I,
        Peace at the root must dwell.
But when I digged, I saw a worm devour
        What showed so well.

At length I met a rev'rend good old man,
20   Whom when for Peace
    I did demand, he thus began:
        There was a Prince of old[2]
At Salem dwelt, who lived with good increase
        Of flock and fold.[3]

He sweetly lived; yet sweetness did not save
        His life from foes.
    But after death out of his grave
        There sprang twelve stalks of wheat:[4]
Which many wond'ring at, got some of those
30   To plant and set.

It prospered strangely, and did soon disperse
        Through all the earth:
    For they that taste it do rehearse,
        That virtue lies therein,
A secret virtue bringing peace and mirth
        By flight of sin.

Take of this grain, which in my garden grows,
        And grows for you;
    Make bread of it: and that repose
40   And peace which ev'rywhere
With so much earnestness you do pursue,
        Is only there.

1. A large and beautiful flower.
2. The old man is telling the story of Melchizedek, a priest of Salem, who brought bread and wine to Abraham in the Old Testament. In representing both king and priest he also represents Christ.
3. A flock of sheep in a sheep-pen.
4. The twelve stalks of wheat represent the twelve disciples, who because of Christ's death were able to spread his message throughout the world.

Paradise

I bless thee, Lord, because I GROW
Among thy trees, which in a ROW
To thee both fruit and order OW.

What open force, or hidden CHARM
Can blast my fruit, or bring me HARM,
While the inclosure is thine ARM?

Inclose me still for fear I START.
Be to me rather sharp and TART,
Than let me want thy hand and ART.

10   When thou dost greater judgements SPARE,
And with thy knife but prune and PARE,
Ev'n fruitful trees more fruitful ARE.

Such sharpness shows the sweetest FREND:
Such cuttings rather heal than REND:
And such beginnings touch their END.

Heaven

O who will show me those delights on high?
        Echo.   *I.*
Thou Echo, thou art mortal, all men know.
        Echo.   *No.*
Wert thou not born among the trees and leaves?
        Echo.   *Leaves.*
And are there any leaves, that still abide?
        Echo.   *Bide.*
What leaves are they? impart the matter wholly.
10   *Echo.*   *Holy.*
Are holy leaves the Echo then of bliss?
        Echo.   *Yes*
Then tell me, what is that supreme delight?
        Echo.   *Light.*
Light to the mind: what shall the will enjoy?
        Echo.   *Joy.*
But are there cares and business with the pleasure?
        Echo.   *Leisure.*
Light, joy, and leisure; but shall they persever?
20   *Echo.*   *Ever.*

Love

Love bade me welcome: yet my soul drew back,
      Guilty of dust and sin.
But quick-eyed Love, observing me grow slack
      From my first entrance in,
Drew nearer to me, sweetly questioning,
      If I lacked anything.

A guest, I answered, worthy to be here:
      Love said, You shall be he.
I the unkind, ungrateful? Ah my dear,
      I cannot look on thee.
Love took my hand, and smiling did reply,
      Who made the eyes but I?

Truth Lord, but I have marred them: let my shame
      Go where it doth deserve.
And know you not, says Love, who bore the blame?
      My dear, then I will serve.
You must sit down, says Love, and taste my meat:[1]
      So I did sit and eat.

FINIS.

Glory be to God on high, and on earth
peace, good will towards men.

1. Here, 'meat' means not just food but also the body of Christ, eaten
symbolically during the communion service.

John Milton
(1608–1674)

John Milton was born in London, the son of a wealthy man whose business involved drafting contracts and acting as a financial agent. Later, he claimed that his father had destined him from childhood to 'the pursuits of literature'. His education at St Paul's School was unusual for the period, because his headmaster taught the English language and the works of English poets as well as Latin and Greek. He also had private lessons in Hebrew.

When Milton went to Christ's College, Cambridge, in 1625, he protested that the curriculum was old-fashioned, and asked for lessons in subjects like history, geography, physics and astronomy. He was already a skilful poet in both Latin and English, and also produced sonnets in Italian. His first really important poem, 'On the morning of Christ's Nativity', was written at Christmas 1629, while he was still at Cambridge.

Although he had intended to become a clergyman, Milton was dissatisfied with the state of the Church of England, and retired to his father's estate in Horton, Buckinghamshire, from 1632 until 1638. Here, he started an ambitious programme of reading classical literature and Church and political history. His short poem 'On Time', written during this period, shows the influence of the Italian literature he read. He also wrote the masque *Comus*, extracts from which are printed here. Masques were aristocratic entertainments involving both acting and music, and this one was presented at the Earl of Bridgewater's inauguration as Lord President of Wales. Some critics see the evil enchanter Comus as a first sketch for the Satan of *Paradise Lost*.

A tour of France and Italy in 1638 was cut short because the Civil War broke out in England. The war changed Milton's career completely. He settled in London and wrote a series of religious, social and political pamphlets, some of which were sparked off by the failure of his marriage to a seventeen-year-old girl, Mary Powell, in 1642. They soon discovered that they were incompatible, and she went home to her parents after a few weeks. They were reconciled in 1645, but she died in 1652.

Milton's writings supported the Parliamentary cause during the Civil War, and in 1649 he was appointed Latin Secretary to the Council of States. The nearest equivalent to this in today's government is the post of Foreign Secretary. His sight was already failing, and he was completely blind by 1652. After this time, he had a secretary to help with his literary work, and he was assisted in his political work by his friend, the poet Andrew Marvell. One of his most moving sonnets was written on the subject of his blindness, and the opening section of his later work, *Samson Agonistes*, in which Samson considers his blindness and strives to understand God's purpose in inflicting it on him, is obviously heartfelt.

After the restoration of the monarchy in 1660, Milton was punished for his support of the Parliamentary cause by a fine and a short term of imprisonment, but after that he was allowed to retire and live in seclusion. His second marriage in 1656 had been cut short by the death of his wife, and he married for a third time in 1663.

During his later years, he completed and revised his great epic work, *Paradise Lost*, which was published in 1674. The twelve volumes tell the story of the fall of Adam and humanity's banishment from paradise in scenes of great cosmic drama and profound moral and philosophical speculations. He also published in his later years *Paradise Regain'd*, the theme of which was Satan's temptation of Christ. *Samson Agonistes*, published in 1671, used the biblical story of Samson to show the defeated English Puritans a model of moral courage triumphing through sacrifice in the face of apparent defeat.

Although his earlier works use several forms, the style of poetry most closely associated with Milton is the unrhymed blank verse of *Paradise Lost*. The Latinized style of his language, with its long complex sentences and abstract terms, needs patience and perseverance to follow, although there are passages of startling beauty. The grandeur and gravity of Milton's style deeply influenced the work of the poets who followed him.

On Shakespeare

What needs my Shakespeare for his honoured bones
The labour of an age in piled stones
Or that his hallowed relics should be hid
Under a star-ypointing pyramid?[1]
Dear son of memory, great heir of fame,
What needst thou such weak witness of thy name?
Thou in our wonder and astonishment
Hast built thyself a livelong monument.
For whilst to th'shame of slow-endeavouring art,
10   Thy easy numbers flow, and that each heart
Hath from the leaves of thy unvalued book
Those Delphic[2] lines with deep impression took,
Then thou our fancy of itself bereaving,
Dost make us marble with too much conceiving;
And so sepulchered[3] in such pomp dost lie,
That kings for such a tomb would wish to die.

1. A pyramid pointing at the stars.
2. Delphi was the home of the future-foretelling oracle in ancient Greece.
3. Entombed.

On Time

Fly envious Time, till thou run out[4] thy race,
Call on the lazy leaden-stepping hours,
Whose speed is but the heavy plummet's[5] pace;
And glut thyself with what thy womb devours,[6]

4. Finish.
5. A weight attached to a line to make it hang straight, a plumbob.
6. Time, as well as giving birth to events, also devours them.

Which is no more than what is false and vain,
And merely mortal dross;[1]
So little is our loss,
So little is thy gain.
For when as each thing bad thou hast entombed,
10 And last of all, thy greedy self consumed,
Then long eternity shall greet our bliss
With an individual kiss;
And joy shall overtake us as a flood,
When everything that is sincerely good
And perfectly divine,
With truth, and peace, and love shall ever shine
About the supreme throne
Of him t'whose happy-making sight alone,
When once our heavenly-guided soul shall climb,
20 Then all this earthly grossness quit,
Attired with stars, we shall for ever sit,
    Triumphing over death, and chance, and thee O Time.

1. Useless left-overs.

Sonnets

I

O Nightingale, that on yon bloomy spray
    Warbl'st at eve, when all the woods are still,
    Thou with fresh hope the lover's heart dost fill,
    While the jolly hours lead on propitious May;
Thy liquid notes that close the eye of day,
    First heard before the shallow cuckoo's bill
    Portend success in love; O if Jove's will
    Have linked that amorous power to thy soft lay,[1]
Now timely sing, ere the rude bird of hate
10   Foretell my hopeless doom in some grove nigh:

1. Song.

As thou from year to year hast sung too late
For my relief; yet hadst no reason why,
    Whether the Muse, or Love, call thee his mate,
    Both them I serve, and of their train am I.

VII

How soon hath time, the subtle thief of youth,
    Stol'n on his wing my three and twentieth year!
    My hasting days fly on with full career,
    But my late spring no bud or blossom shew'th.[1]
Perhaps my semblance might deceive the truth,
    That I to manhood am arrived so near,
    And inward ripeness doth much less appear,
    That some more timely-happy spirits indu'th.[2]
Yet be it less or more, or soon or slow,
    It shall be still in strictest measure even,
10   To that same lot, however mean or high,
Toward which time leads me, and the will of Heaven;
    All is, if I have grace to use it so,
    As ever in my great Taskmaster's eye.

1. Shows.
2. Puts on.

XVI

When I consider how my light is spent
    Ere half my days in this dark world and wide,
    And that one talent which is death to hide,
    Lodged with me useless, though my soul more bent
To serve therewith my Maker, and present
    My true account, lest he returning chide,
    Doth God exact day-labour, light denied?
    I fondly ask; but Patience to prevent

That murmur, soon replies, God doth not need
10   Either man's work or his own gifts; who best
    Bear his mild yoke, they serve him best. His state
Is kingly. Thousands at his bidding speed
    And post o'er land and ocean without rest:
    They also serve who only stand and wait.

TO THE LORD GENERAL CROMWELL

Cromwell, our chief of men, who through a cloud
    Not of war only, but detractions rude,
    Guided by faith and matchless fortitude
    To peace and truth thy glorious way hast ploughed,
And on the neck of crowned fortune proud
    Hast reared God's trophies, and his work pursued,
    While Darwen stream with blood of Scots imbrued,[1]
    And Dunbar field resounds thy praises loud,
And Worcester's laureate wreath; yet much remains
10   To conquer still; peace hath her victories
    No less renowned than war; new foes arise
Threatening to bind our souls with secular[2] chains:
    Help us to save free conscience from the paw
    Of hireling wolves whose gospel is their maw.[3]

1. Dyed.
2. Worldly.
3. Mouth or stomach.

from COMUS

Bacchus that first from out the purple grape,
Crushed the sweet poison of misused wine,
After the Tuscan mariners transformed,
Coasting the Tyrrhene shore, as the winds listed,

On Circe's island fell (who knows not Circe
The daughter of the sun? Whose charmed cup
Whoever tasted, lost his upright shape,
And downward fell into a grovelling swine).
This nymph that gazed upon his clustering locks,
10 With ivy berries wreathed, and his blithe youth,
Had by him, ere he parted thence, a son
Much like his father, but his mother more,
Whom therefore she brought up and Comus named,
Who ripe, and frolic of his full grown age,
Roving the Celtic and Iberian fields,
At last betakes him to this ominous wood,
And in thick shelter of black shades imbowered,
Excels his mother at her mighty art,
Offering to every weary traveller
20 His orient liquor in a crystal glass,
To quench the drouth[1] of Phoebus, [2] which as they taste
(For most do taste through fond intemperate thirst)
Soon as the potion works, their human countenance,
Th'express resemblance of the gods, is changed
Into some brutish form of wolf, or bear,
Or ounce, or tiger, hog, or bearded goat,
All other parts remaining as they were,
And they, so perfect is their misery,
Not once perceive their foul disfigurement,
30 But boast themselves more comely than before,
And all their friends, and native home forget
To roll with pleasure in a sensual sty.

1. Drought.
2. The sun.

from COMUS

SONG

Sabrina fair
   Listen where thou art sitting
Under the glassy, cool, translucent wave,
   In twisted braids of lilies knitting
The loose train of thy amber-dropping[1] hair;
   Listen for dear honour's sake,
   Goddess of the silver lake,
     Listen and save.

   Listen and appear to us
10 In name of great Oceanus,[2]
By the earth-shaking Neptune's mace,
And Tethys' grave majestic pace,
By hoary Nereus' wrinkled look,
And the Carpathian wizard's hook,
By scaly Triton's winding shell,
And old sooth-saying Glaucus' spell,
By Leucothea's lovely hands,
And her son that rules the strands,
By Thetis' tinsel-slippered feet,
20 And the songs of sirens sweet,
By dead Parthenope's dear tomb,
And fair Ligea's golden comb,
Wherewith she sits on diamond rocks
Sleeking her soft alluring locks,
By all the nymphs that nightly dance
Upon thy streams with wily glance,

1. Perfumed.
2. All the names in the following passage are those of mythological gods, goddesses, sirens and nymphs connected with the sea.

Rise, rise, and heave thy rosy head
From thy coral-paven bed,
And bridle in thy headlong wave,
30 Till thou our summons answered have.
        Listen and save.

SABRINA RISES, ATTENDED BY WATER – NYMPHS,
AND SINGS
By the rushy-fringed bank,
Where grows the willow and the osier dank,
    My sliding chariot stays,
Thick set with agate, and the azurn sheen
Of turquois blue, and emerald green
    That in the channel strays;
Whilst from off the waters fleet
Thus I set my printless feet
40 O'er the cowslip's velvet head,
That bends not as I tread;
Gentle swain, at thy request
    I am here.

from PARADISE LOST

BOOK I

        Say first, for Heav'n hides nothing from thy view
    Nor the deep Tract of Hell, say first what cause
    Mov'd our Grand Parents in that happy State,
    Favour'd of Heav'n so highly, to fall off
    From their Creator, and transgress his Will
    For one restraint, Lords of the World besides?
    Who first seduc'd them to that foul revolt?
    Th'infernal Serpent; he it was, whose guile
    Stirr'd up with Envy and Revenge, deceiv'd
10 The Mother of Mankind, what time his Pride
    Had cast him out from Heav'n, with all his Host
    Of Rebel Angels, by whose aid aspiring
    To set himself in Glory above his Peers,

He trusted to have equall'd the most High,
If he oppos'd; and with ambitious aim
Against the Throne and Monarchy of God
Rais'd impious War in Heav'n and Battle proud
With vain attempt. Him the Almighty Power
Hurl'd headlong flaming from th'Ethereal Sky
20 With hideous ruin and combustion down
To bottomless perdition, there to dwell
In Adamantine[1] Chains and penal Fire,
Who durst defy th'Omnipotent to Arms.
Nine times the Space that measures Day and Night
To mortal men, he with his horrid crew
Lay vanquisht, rolling in the fiery Gulf
Confounded[2] though immortal: But his doom
Reserv'd him to more wrath; for now the thought
Both of lost happiness and lasting pain
30 Torments him; round he throws his baleful[3] eyes
That witness'd[4] huge affliction and dismay
Mixt with obdúrate pride and steadfast hate:
At once as far as Angel's ken[5] he views
The dismal Situation waste and wild,
A Dungeon horrible, on all sides round
As one great Furnace flam'd, yet from those flames
No light, but rather darkness visible
Serv'd only to discover sights of woe,
Regions of sorrow, doleful shades, where peace
40 And rest can never dwell, hope never comes
That comes to all; but torture without end
Still urges, and a fiery Deluge, fed
With ever-burning Sulphur unconsum'd:
Such place Eternal Justice had prepar'd

1. The hardest rocks and minerals.
2. Defeated.
3. Full of evil and woe.
4. Showed his.
5. Knowledge.

For those rebellious, here their Prison ordain'd
In utter[1] darkness, and their portion set
As far remov'd from God and light of Heav'n
As from the Center thrice to th'utmost Pole.[2]
O how unlike the place from whence they fell!

*   *   *

50   Thus Satan talking to his nearest Mate
With Head uplift above the wave, and Eyes
That sparkling blaz'd, his other Parts besides
Prone on the Flood, extended long and large
Lay floating many a rood,[3] in bulk as huge
As whom the Fables name of monstrous size,
Titanian, or Earth-born, that warr'd on Jove,
Briareos or Typhon,[4] whom the Den
By ancient Tarsus held, or that Sea-beast
60   Leviathan,[5] which God of all his works
Created hugest that swim th'Ocean stream:
Him haply[6] slumb'ring on the Norway foam
The Pilot of some small night-founder'd Skiff,
Deeming some Island, oft, as Sea-men tell,
With fixed Anchor in his scaly rind
Moors by his side under the Lee, while Night
Invests[7] the Sea, and wished Morn delays:
So stretcht out huge in length the Arch-fiend lay
Chain'd on the burning Lake, nor ever thence
70   Had ris'n or heav'd his head, but that the will
And high permission of all-ruling Heaven
Left him at large to his own dark designs,

1. Total.
2. Three times the distance from the earth to the outermost point of
the universe.
3. A quarter of an acre.
4. Titans and Giants who warred against Jove.
5. Biblical sea-monster, usually a whale.
6. Perhaps.
7. Enfolds.

That with reiterated crimes he might
Heap on himself damnation, while he sought
Evil to others, and enrag'd might see
How all his malice serv'd but to bring forth
Infinite goodness, grace and mercy shown
On Man by him seduc't, but on himself
Treble confusion, wrath and vengeance pour'd.
80 Forthwith upright he rears from off the Pool
His mighty Stature; on each hand the flames
Driv'n backward slope their pointing spires, and roll'd
In billows, leave i' th'midst a horrid Vale.
Then with expanded wings he steers his flight
Aloft, incumbent on[1] the dusky Air
That felt unusual weight, till on dry Land
He 'lights, if it were Land that ever burn'd
With solid, as the Lake with liquid fire;
And such appear'd in hue, as when the force
90 Of subterranean wind transports a Hill
Torn from Pelorus,[2] or the shatter'd side
Of thund'ring Etna, whose combustible
And fuell'd entrails thence conceiving Fire,
Sublim'd with Mineral fury, aid the Winds,
And leave a singed bottom all involv'd[3]
With stench and smoke: Such resting found the sole
Of unblest feet. Him follow'd his next Mate,
Both glorying to have 'scap't the Stygian[4] flood
As Gods, and by their own recover'd strength,
100 Not by the sufferance of supernal[5] Power.
    'Is this the Region, this the Soil, the Clime,'[6]
Said then the lost Arch Angel, 'this the seat

1. Weighing upon.
2. Near Etna.
3. Rolled around.
4. From Styx, the river of Hell.
5. Heavenly.
6. Climate.

That we must change for Heav'n, this mournful gloom
For that celestial light? Be it so, since he
Who now is Sovran[1] can dispose and bid
What shall be right: farthest from him is best
Whom reason hath equall'd, force hath made supreme
Above his equals. Farewell happy Fields
Where Joy for ever dwells: Hail horrors, hail
110   Infernal world, and thou profoundest Hell
Receive thy new Possessor: One who brings
A mind not to be chang'd by Place or Time.
The mind is its own place, and in itself
Can make a Heav'n of Hell, a Hell of Heav'n.
What matter where, if I be still the same,
And what I should be, all but less than he
Whom Thunder hath made greater? Here at least
We shall be free; th'Almighty hath not built
Here for his envy, will not drive us hence:
120   Here we may reign secure, and in my choice
To reign is worth ambition though in Hell:
Better to reign in Hell, than serve in Heav'n.

1. Sovereign (lord).

from   PARADISE LOST

BOOK IV

Evening in Eden

Now came still evening on, and twilight gray
Had in her sober livery all things clad;
Silence accompanied, for beast and bird,
They to their grassy couch, these to their nests
Were slunk, all but the wakeful nightingale;
She all night long her amorous descant sung:
Silence was pleased: now glowed the firmament

With living sapphires. Hesperus[1] that led
The starry host, rode brightest, till the moon
10   Rising in clouded majesty, at length
Apparent queen unveiled her peerless light,
And o'er the dark her silver mantle threw.

1. The planet Venus when it shines in the evening sky.

from SAMSON AGONISTES

Samson. A little onward lend thy guiding hand
To these dark steps, a little further on.
For yonder bank hath choice of sun or shade;
There I am wont to sit, when any chance
Relieves me from my task of servile toil,
Daily in the common prison else enjoined me,[1]
Where I a prisoner chained, scarce freely draw[2]
The air imprisoned also, close and damp,
Unwholesome draught: but here I feel amends,
10   The breath of Heaven fresh-blowing, pure and sweet,
With dayspring[3] born; here leave me to respire.
This day a solemn feast the people hold
To Dagon their sea-idol, and forbid
Laborious works, unwillingly this rest
Their superstition yields me; hence with leave
Retiring from the popular noise, I seek
This unfrequented place to find some ease,
Ease to the body some, none to the mind
From restless thoughts, that like a deadly swarm
20   Of hornets armed, no sooner found alone,
But rush upon me thronging, and present
Times past, what once I was, and what am now.

1. Imposed on me.
2. Breathe.
3. Dawn.

O wherefore[1] was my birth from Heaven foretold
Twice by an angel, who at last in sight
Of both my parents all in flames ascended
From off the altar, where an offering burned,
As in a fiery column charioting
His godlike presence, and from some great act
Or benefit revealed to Abraham's race?
30 Why was my breeding ordered and prescribed
As of a person separate to God,
Designed for great exploits; if I must die
Betrayed, captived, and both my eyes put out,
Made of my enemies the scorn and gaze;
To grind in brazen fetters[2] under task
With this Heaven-gifted strength? O glorious strength
Put to the labour of a beast, debased
Lower than bondslave! Promise was that I
Should Israel from Philistian yoke deliver;
40 Ask for this great deliverer now, and find him
Eyeless in Gaza at the mill with slaves,
Himself in bonds under Philistian yoke;
Yet stay, let me not rashly call in doubt
Divine prediction; what if all foretold
Had been fulfilled but through mine own default,
Whom have I to complain of but my self?
Who this high gift of strength committed to me,
In what part lodged, how easily bereft me,
Under the seal of silence could not keep,
50 But weakly to a woman must reveal it
O'ercome with importunity and tears.
O impotence of mind, in body strong!
But what is strength without a double share
Of wisdom, vast, unwieldy, burdensome,
Proudly secure, yet liable to fall
By weakest subtleties, not made to rule,

1. Why.
2. Brass chains.

But to subserve where wisdom bears command.
God, when he gave me strength, to shew withal
How slight the gift was, hung it in my hair.
60   But peace, I must not quarrel with the will
Of highest dispensation, which herein
Hap'ly[1] had ends above my reach to know.
Suffices that to me strength is my bane,[2]
And proves the source of all my miseries;
So many and so huge, that each apart
Would ask a life to wail, but chief of all,
O loss of sight, of thee I most complain!
Blind among enemies, O worse than chains,
Dungeon, or beggary, or decrepit age!
70   Light the prime work of God to me is extinct,
And all her various objects of delight
Annulled, which might in part my grief have eased,
Inferior to the vilest now become
Of man or worm; the vilest here excel me,
They creep, yet see, I dark in light exposed
To daily fraud, contempt, abuse and wrong,
Within doors, or without, still as a fool,
In power of others, never in my own;
Scarce half I seem to live, dead more than half.
80   O dark, dark, dark, amid the blaze of noon,
Irrecoverably dark, total eclipse
Without all hope of day!
O first created beam, and thou great Word,
Let there be light, and light was over all;
Why am I thus bereaved thy prime decree?
The sun to me is dark
And silent as the moon,
When she deserts the night
Hid in her vacant interlunar cave.
90   Since light so necessary is to life,

1. Perhaps.
2. Ruin.

And almost life itself, if it be true
That light is in the soul,
She all in every part; why was the sight
To such a tender ball as th'eye confined?
So obvious and so easy to be quenched,
And not as feeling through all parts diffused,
That she might look at will through every pore?
Then had I not been thus exiled from light;
As in the land of darkness yet in light,
100 To live a life half dead, a living death,
And buried; but O yet more miserable!
Myself, my sepulchre, a moving grave,
Buried, yet not exempt
By privilege of death and burial
From worst of other evils, pains and wrongs,
But made hereby obnoxious more
To all the miseries of life,
Life in captivity
Among inhuman foes.

Andrew Marvell
(1621–1678)

Andrew Marvell was born at Winestead in East Yorkshire. The family moved to Hull when his father was appointed Lecturer at Holy Trinity Church there, and Marvell was educated at Hull Grammar School. At the age of twelve, he went to Cambridge University and received his BA degree when he was eighteen. After leaving Cambridge in 1641, he travelled in Holland, France, Italy and Spain until 1647.

His first poems were published when he was only sixteen years old and still at Cambridge. They were written in Latin and Greek, and celebrated the birth of a child to King Charles I and his Queen, Henrietta Maria. However, his political sympathies later on lay with the Parliamentarian side during the Civil War. He was a tutor to the daughter of a Roundhead military leader, General Fairfax, from 1650 to 1652, during which time he wrote a long ode in a Latin style celebrating Cromwell's return from Ireland. He also wrote many of his best known lyric poems, including 'To His Coy Mistress', during this period.

He became a tutor to Cromwell's ward, William Dutton, in 1653, and travelled to France with him. Later, when they were in England, he lived at the house of John Oxenbridge in Eton. Oxenbridge had made two trips to Bermuda, and it is thought that this inspired Marvell to write his poem 'Bermudas'. He also wrote several poems in praise of Cromwell, who was by this time Lord Protector of England.

Marvell was friendly with the poet John Milton, who was Latin Secretary to the Council of State. Milton recommended his appointment as Assistant Secretary with a salary of £200 a year, which represented financial security at that time. From 1659 until his death, Marvell served as MP for Hull, which had been stoutly Parliamentarian during the Civil War.

Oliver Cromwell died in 1658. He was succeeded as Lord Protector by his son Richard, but within two years the monarchy was restored by popular demand, and Charles II was crowned in 1661. Marvell wrote several long and bitter verses against the corruption of the monarchy.

Marvell's poetry is written in the elegant and sinewy style of the metaphysical school. His poems are full of elaborate, often witty comparisons. For example, in 'To His Coy Mistress', he considers all the ways he and the lady who will not yield to his persuasions could spend their time if only they were immortal, but points out that life is short, and there is no place for love beyond the grave, so they must make the most of the time they have.

Many poems were inspired by events of the time, public or personal. 'The Picture of Little T.C. in a Prospect of Flowers' was written about the daughter of a friend of his. Her name was Theophila Cornwell, and she had been named after an elder sister who had died as a baby. Marvell uses the picture of her surrounded by flowers in a garden to convey thoughts of the transience of spring and the fragility of childhood. Flowers, too, die after a brief blossoming.

Others were written in the pastoral style beloved of many poets who learned their style of writing by reading the great poets of ancient Rome. Even here, Marvell tends to place a particular picture before us. In 'The Nymph Complaining for the Death of Her Fawn', the nymph weeps for the little animal as its life-blood ebbs away, and tells us how it consoled her for her betrayal in love.

Although Marvell was a Parliamentarian and a strong supporter of Cromwell, he was not a Puritan. He had flirted briefly with the Catholic Church as a youth, and was a rather worldly man, described in his thirties as 'a notable English Italo-Machiavellian'. During his lifetime, his prose satires were better known and considered wittier than his verse, and many of his poems were not published until 1681, three years after his death, from a collection owned by his wife, Mary.

To His Coy Mistress

Had we but world enough, and time,
This coyness, Lady, were no crime.
We would sit down, and think which way
To walk, and pass our long love's day.
Thou by the Indian Ganges' side
Shouldst rubies find: I by the tide
Of Humber[1] would complain. I would
Love you ten years before the flood:
And you should, if you please, refuse
10 Till the conversion of the Jews.[2]
My vegetable[3] love should grow
Vaster than empires, and more slow.
An hundred years should go to praise
Thine eyes, and on thy forehead gaze.
Two hundred to adore each breast:
But thirty thousand to the rest.
An age at least to every part,
And the last age should show your heart:
For, Lady, you deserve this state;
20 Nor would I love at lower rate.
    But at my back I always hear
Time's wingèd chariot hurrying near:
And yonder all before us lie
Deserts of vast eternity.
Thy beauty shall no more be found;
Nor, in thy marble vault, shall sound
My echoing song: then worms shall try
That long-preserved virginity:

1. Marvell's home city was Hull, on the River Humber.
2. An event so far in the future as to be thought impossible.
3. Characterized only by growth, without feeling or thought.

And your quaint honour turn to dust;
30 And into ashes all my lust.
The grave's a fine and private place,
But none, I think, do there embrace.
  Now, therefore, while the youthful glue[1]
Sits on thy skin like morning dew,
And while thy willing soul transpires
At every pore with instant fires,
Now let us sport us while we may;
And now, like amorous birds of prey,
Rather at once our time devour,
40 Than languish in his slow-chapped[2] power.
Let us roll all our strength, and all
Our sweetness, up into one ball:
And tear our pleasures with rough strife,
Thorough the iron grates of life.
Thus, though we cannot make our sun
Stand still,[3] yet we will make him run.

1. Some editions give this word as 'hue'.
2. Slowly devouring, particularly by a bird of prey's beak.
3. Joshua made the sun stand still in the war against Gideon (Joshua, chapter 10: v. 12).

The Picture of Little T.C. in a Prospect[1] of Flowers

I

See with what simplicity
This nymph begins her golden days!
In the green grass she loves to lie,
And there with her fair aspect tames
The wilder flowers, and gives them names:
But only with the roses plays;
          And them does tell
What colour best becomes them, and what smell.

1. 'Prospect' here can mean either a 'landscape' or a 'mental survey'.

2

Who can foretell for what high cause
10   This Darling of the Gods was born!
Yet this is she whose chaster laws
The wanton Love shall one day fear,
And, under her command severe,
See his bow broke and ensigns torn.
          Happy, who can
Appease this virtuous enemy of man!

3

O, then let me in time compound,[1]
And parley with those conquering eyes;
Ere they have tried their force to wound,
20   Ere, with their glancing wheels, they drive
In triumph over hearts that strive,
And them that yield but more despise.
          Let me be laid,
Where I may see thy glories from some shade.

4

Meantime, whilst every verdant thing
Itself does at thy beauty charm,
Reform the errors of the spring;
Make that the tulips may have share
Of sweetness, seeing they are fair;
30   And roses of their thorns disarm:
          But most procure
That violets may a longer age endure.

1. Negotiate.

5

But, O young beauty of the woods,
Whom Nature courts with fruits and flowers,
Gather the flowers, but spare the buds;
Lest Flora[1] angry at thy crime,
To kill her infants in their prime,
Do quickly make the example yours;
          And, ere we see,
Nip in the blossom all our hopes and thee.

1 Goddess of flowers.

The Nymph Complaining for the Death of Her Fawn

The wanton troopers riding by
Have shot my fawn, and it will die.
Ungentle men! They cannot thrive –
To kill thee! Thou ne'er didst alive
Them any harm: alas, nor could
Thy death yet do them any good.
I'm sure I never wished them ill;
Nor do I for all this; nor will:
But if my simple prayers may yet
10   Prevail with heaven to forget
Thy murder, I will join my tears
Rather than fail. But, O my fears!
It cannot die so.[1] Heaven's King
Keeps register of everything:
And nothing may we use in vain.
E'en beasts must be with justice slain,
Else men are made their deodands.[2]

1. It cannot die with its murder unavenged.
2. Legally, any personal possession which caused someone's death was
forfeited. It is suggested here that if animals are not killed with justice,
then the killers are forfeited.

Though they should wash their guilty hands
In this warm life-blood, which doth part
20 From thine, and wound me to the heart,
Yet could they not be clean: their stain
Is dyed in such a purple grain,
There is not such another in
The world, to offer for their sin.

  Unconstant Sylvio, when yet
I had not found him counterfeit,
One morning (I remember well),
Tied in this silver chain and bell
Gave it to me: nay, and I know
30 What he said then; I'm sure I do.
Said he, 'Look how your huntsman here
Hath taught a fawn to hunt his *dear*.'
But Sylvio soon had me beguiled.
This waxèd tame, while he grew wild,
And quite regardless of my smart,
Left me his fawn, but took his heart.

  Thenceforth I set myself to play
My solitary time away
With this: and very well content,
40 Could so mine idle life have spent.
For it was full of sport; and light
Of foot, and heart; and did invite
Me to its game; it seemed to bless
Itself in me. How could I less
Than love it? O I cannot be
Unkind, t'a beast that loveth me.

  Had it lived long, I do not know
Whether it too might have done so
As Sylvio did: his gifts might be
50 Perhaps as false or more than he.
But I am sure, for ought that I
Could in so short a time espy,
Thy love was far more better than
The love of false and cruel men.

With sweetest milk, and sugar, first
I it at mine own fingers nursed.
And as it grew, so every day
It waxed more white and sweet than they.
It had so sweet a breath! And oft
60   I blushed to see its foot more soft,
And white (shall I say than my hand?)
Nay, any lady's of the land.
    It is a wondrous thing, how fleet
'Twas on those little silver feet.
With what a pretty skipping grace,
It oft would challenge me the race:
And when 't had left me far away,
'Twould stay, and run again, and stay.
For it was nimbler much than hinds;
70   And trod, as on the four winds.
    I have a garden of my own
But so with roses overgrown,
And lilies, that you would it guess
To be a little wilderness.
And all the springtime of the year
It only lovèd to be there.
Among the beds of lilies, I
Have sought it oft, where it should lie;
Yet could not, till itself would rise,
80   Find it, although before mine eyes.
For, in the flaxen lilies' shade,
It like a bank of lilies laid.
Upon the roses it would feed,
Until its lips e'en seemed to bleed:
And then to me 'twould boldly trip,
And print those roses on my lip.
But all its chief delight was still
On roses thus itself to fill:
And its pure virgin limbs to fold
90   In whitest sheets of lilies cold.
Had it lived long, it would have been

Lilies without, roses within.
   O help! O help! I see it faint:
And die as calmly as a saint.
See how it weeps. The tears do come
Sad, slowly dropping like a gum.
So weeps the wounded balsam: so
The holy frankincense doth flow.
The brotherless Heliades
100   Melt in such amber tears as these.[1]
   I in a golden vial will
Keep these two crystal tears; and fill
It till it do o'erflow with mine;
Then place it in Diana's[2] shrine.
   Now my sweet fawn is vanished to
Whither the swans and turtles[3] go:
In fair Elysium to endure,
With milk-white lambs, and ermines pure.
O do not run too fast: for I
110   Will but bespeak thy grave, and die.
   First my unhappy statue shall
Be cut in marble; and withal,
Let it be weeping too – but there
The engraver sure his art may spare,
For I so truly thee bemoan,
That I shall weep though I be stone:
Until my tears (still dropping) wear
My breast, themselves engraving there.
There at my feet shalt thou be laid,
120   Of purest alabaster made:
For I would have thine image be
White as I can, though not as thee.

1. When Phaethon died in Greek mythology, his sisters were turned
into poplar trees and their tears into amber.
2. Diana was the goddess of chastity as well as of the hunt.
3. Turtledove.

The Garden

1

How vainly[1] men themselves amaze
To win the palm, the oak, or bays,[2]
And their uncessant labours see
Crowned from some single herb or tree,
Whose short and narrow vergèd shade
Does prudently their toils upbraid,
While all flow'rs and all trees do close
To weave the garlands of repose.

2

Fair Quiet, have I found thee here,
And Innocence, thy sister dear!
Mistaken long, I sought you then
In busy companies of men.
Your sacred plants, if here below,
Only among the plants will grow.
Society is all but rude,[3]
To this delicious solitude.

3

No white nor red was ever seen[4]
So am'rous as this lovely green.
Fond[5] lovers, cruel as their flame,
Cut in these trees their mistress' name.

1. 'Vainly' here can mean both 'futilely' and 'arrogantly', and 'amaze'
carries the two meanings of 'perplex' and 'drive themselves mad'.
2. Awards for military, civic or poetic achievement.
3. Almost uncivil.
4. White and red were associated with ladies.
5. Both 'doting' and 'foolish'.

Little, alas, they know, or heed,
How far these beauties hers exceed!
Fair trees! wheres'e'er your barks I wound,
No name shall but your own be found.

4
When we have run our passion's heat,
Love hither makes his best retreat.
The gods, that mortal beauty chase,
Still in a tree did end their race.
Apollo hunted Daphne so,
30 Only that she might laurel grow.
And Pan did after Syrinx speed,
Not as a nymph, but for a reed.

5
What wondrous life is this I lead!
Ripe apples drop about my head;
The luscious clusters of the vine
Upon my mouth do crush their wine;
The nectarene, and curious[1] peach,
Into my hands themselves do reach;
Stumbling on melons, as I pass,
40 Ensnared with flowers, I fall on grass.

6
Meanwhile the mind, from pleasures less,
Withdraws into its happiness:
The mind, that ocean where each kind
Does straight its own resemblance find,
Yet it creates, transcending these,
Far other worlds, and other seas,
Annihilating all that's made
To a green thought in a green shade.

1. Choice.

7
Here at the fountain's sliding foot,
50 Or at some fruit-tree's mossy root,
Casting the body's vest aside,
My soul into the boughs does glide:
There like a bird it sits, and sings,
Then whets, and combs its silver wings;
And, till prepared for longer flight,
Waves in its plumes the various light.

8
Such was that happy garden-state,
While man there walked without a mate:
After a place so pure, and sweet,
60 What other help could yet be meet!
But 'twas beyond a mortal's share
To wander solitary there:
Two paradises 'twere in one
To live in paradise alone.

9
How well the skilful gardener drew
Of flowers and herbs this dial new,[1]
Where from above the milder sun
Does through a fragrant zodiac run;
And, as it works, the industrious bee
70 Computes its time as well as we.
How could such sweet and wholesome hours
Be reckoned but[2] with herbs and flowers!

1. Gardens, like a sundial made of flowers, serve as a clock for both
days and seasons.
2. Except.

On a Drop of Dew

See how the orient dew,
Shed from the bosom of the morn
　　Into the blowing roses,
Yet careless of its mansion new,
For the clear region where 'twas born
　　Round in itself incloses:
　　And in its little globe's extent,
Frames as it can its native element.
　　How it the purple flow'r does slight,
10　　　Scarce touching where it lies,
　　But gazing back upon the skies,
　　　Shines with a mournful light,
　　　　Like its own tear,
Because so long divided from the sphere.
　　Restless it rolls and unsecure,
　　　Trembling less it grow impure,
　　Till the warm sun pity its pain,
And to the skies exhale it back again.
　　　So the soul, that drop, that ray
20　Of the clear fountain of eternal day,
Could it within the human flow'r be seen,
　　Remembering still its former height,
　　Shuns the sweet leaves and blossoms green,
　　And recollecting[1] its own light,
Does, in its pure and circling thoughts, express
The greater heaven in an heaven less.
　　　In how coy[2] a figure wound,
　　　Every way it turns away:
　　So the world excluding round,
30　　　Yet receiving in the day,

1. Both 'remembering' and 'collecting again'.
2. Modest.

Dark beneath, but bright above,
Here disdaining, there in love.
How loose and easy hence to go,
How girt[1] and ready to ascend,
Moving but on a point below,
It all about does upwards bend.
Such did the manna's[2] sacred dew distill,
White and entire, though congealed and chill,
Congealed on earth: but does, dissolving, run
40   Into the glories of th' almighty sun.

1. Prepared.
2. The miraculous food which fell with the dew for the Israelites in the
wilderness.

Bermudas

Where the remote Bermudas ride
In the ocean's bosom unespied,
From a small boat, that rowed along,
The listening winds received this song.
    'What should we do but sing his praise
That led us through the watery maze,
Unto an isle so long unknown,[1]
And yet far kinder than our own?
Where he the huge sea-monsters wracks,[2]
10   That lift the deep upon their backs,
He lands us on a grassy stage,
Safe from the storms, and prelate's rage.
He gave us this eternal spring,
Which here enamels everything,
And sends the fowl to us in care,
On daily visits through the air.

1. The Bermudas were discovered in 1515.
2. An earlier poem by Waller refers to a fight between Bermudans and
two stranded whales.

He hangs in shades the orange bright,
Like golden lamps in a green night,
And does in the pom'granates close
20   Jewels more rich than Ormus[1] shows.
He makes the figs our mouths to meet,
And throws the melons at our feet,
But apples[2] plants of such a price,
No tree could ever bear them twice.
With cedars, chosen by his hand,
From Lebanon, he stores the land,
And makes the hollow seas, that roar,
Proclaim the ambergris[3] on shore.
He cast (of which we rather boast)
30   The gospel's pearl upon our coast,
And in these rocks for us did frame
A temple, where to sound his name.
Oh let our voice his praise exalt,
Till it arrive at heaven's vault:
Which thence (perhaps) rebounding, may
Echo beyond the Mexique Bay.'
    Thus sung they, in the English boat,
An holy and a cheerful note,
And all the way, to guide their chime,
40   With falling oars they kept the time.

1. Hormuz in the Persian Gulf.
2. Pineapples.
3. A substance secreted by sperm whales, used in perfumery and medicine.

On Mr Milton's 'Paradise Lost'

When I beheld the poet blind, yet bold,
In slender book his vast design unfold,
Messiah crowned, God's reconciled decree,
Rebelling Angels, the Forbidden Tree,
Heaven, Hell, Earth, Chaos, all; the argument
Held me a while, misdoubting his intent
That he would ruin (for I saw him strong)
The sacred truths to fable and old song,
(So Sampson groped the temple's posts in spite)[1]
10   The world o'erwhelming to revenge his sight.

     Yet as I read, soon growing less severe,
I liked his project, the success did fear;
Through that wide field how he his way should find
O'er which lame faith leads understanding blind;
Lest he perplexed the things he would explain,
And what was easy he should render vain.

     Or if a work so infinite he spanned,
Jealous I was that some less skilful hand
(Such as disquiet always what is well,
20   And by ill imitating would excel)
Might hence presume the whole Creation's day
To change in scenes, and show it in a play.

     Pardon me, Mighty Poet, nor despise
My causeless, yet not impious, surmise.
But I am now convinced that none will dare
Within thy labours to pretend a share.
Thou hast not missed one thought that could be fit,
And all that was improper dost omit:
So that no room is here for writers left,
30   But to detect their ignorance or theft.

1. Alluding to Milton's earlier work *Samson Agonistes*, which appeared
in 1671.

That majesty which through thy work doth reign
Draws the devout, deterring the profane.
And things divine thou treat'st of in such state
As them preserves, and thee, inviolate.
At once delight and horror on us seize,
Thou sing'st with so much gravity and ease;
And above human flight dost soar aloft,
With plume so strong, so equal, and so soft.
The bird named from that paradise you sing
40 So never flags, but always keeps on wing.[1]
    Where couldst thou words of such a compass find?
Whence furnish such a vast expense of mind?
Just heaven thee, like Tiresias,[2] to requite,
Rewards with prophecy thy loss of sight.
    Well mightst thou scorn thy readers to allure
With tinkling rhyme, of thine own sense secure;
While the *Town-Bayes*[3] writes all the while and spells,
And like a pack-horse tires without his bells.
Their fancies like our bushy points[4] appear,
50 The poets tag them; we for fashion wear.
I too, transported by the mode, offend,
And while I meant to *praise* thee must *commend*.[5]
Thy verse created like thy theme sublime,
In number, weight, and measure, needs not rhyme.

1. The bird of paradise was supposed to be perpetually in flight.
2. Tiresias was given the gift of prophecy by the gods to compensate for the loss of his sight.
3. Referring to Dryden, who had a character called Bayes based on him in a comedy.
4. Laces with tassels used to secure the hose to the doublet.
5. He must use the word 'commend' for the sake of his rhyme.

Henry Vaughan

(1622–1695)

Henry Vaughan was born in Wales and lived most of his life there, except for a few years after 1638. His twin brother Thomas is known to have begun his studies at Jesus College, Oxford, in that year, and Henry is thought to have gone with him, though there is no record of him there. In 1640 he moved to London to study law, and returned to Wales two years later as secretary to Judge Lloyd.

Shortly after this, Vaughan married Catherine Wise, and they had four children. After his wife died, he married her younger sister, Elizabeth, by whom he had another four children. He became interested in medicine after translating and then writing works on the subject, and is thought to have practised as a physician.

During the 1640s and 1650s he published several translations from Latin of works by classical writers, and also some collections of his own poems. Several of these collections had titles in Latin, although they were written in English. The best known of these is probably *Silex Scintillans* (*The Glittering Flint*).

Vaughan's poems deal with secular as well as sacred subjects, but his fame as a poet rests mainly on his imaginative perceptions of religious themes and his often mystical expression of the hand of God as it appears in the natural world. In 'The World', for example, he begins with an image of eternity seen as a ring of pure and endless light. Around and beneath it, he sees time moving and images of people caught and deluded by the material world so that they do not see, as the poet does, that the things of this world are no more than shadows and that eternity is reserved for those in the presence of God. In 'The Water-fall' a familiar and very real cataract leads him to meditate on comparisons between the flow of a stream through a landscape and the flow of his spiritual life, and also on all the ways water symbolizes 'sublime truths and wholesome themes'.

A Rhapsody

OCCASIONALLY WRITTEN UPON A MEETING WITH SOME
OF HIS FRIENDS AT THE GLOBE TAVERN, IN A CHAMBER
PAINTED OVER HEAD WITH A CLOUDY SKY AND SOME
FEW DISPERSED STARS AND ON THE SIDES WITH LAND-
SCAPES, HILLS, SHEPHERDS, AND SHEEP

Darkness, & stars i' the mid day! they invite
Our active fancies to believe it night:
For taverns need no sun, but for a sign,
Where rich tobacco, and quick tapers shine;
And royal, witty sack,[1] the poets' soul,
With brighter suns than he doth gild the bowl;
As though the pot, and poet did agree,
Sack should to both illuminator be.
That artificial cloud with its curled brow,
10 Tells us 'tis late; and that blue space below
Is fired with many stars; mark, how they break
In silent glances o'er the hills, and speak
The evening to the plains; where shot from far,
They meet in dumb salutes, as one great star.
    The room (me thinks) grows darker; & the air
Contracts a sadder colour, and less fair:
Or is't the drawer's[2] skill, hath he no arts
To blind us so, we can't know pints from quarts?
No, no, 'tis night; look where the jolly clown[3]
20 Musters his bleating herd, and quits the down.
Hark! how his rude pipe frets the quiet air,
Whilst every hill proclaims *Lycoris*[4] fair.

1. Wine imported from Spain.
2. Barman.
3. Countryman.
4. Lycoris was a girl's name taken from the classics.

Rich, happy man! that canst thus watch, and sleep,
Free from all cares; but thy wench, pipe & sheep.
    But see the Moon is up; view where she stands
Sentinel o'er the door, drawn by the hands
Of some base painter, that for gain hath made
Her face the landmark to the tippling trade.
This cup to her, that to *Endymion*[1] give;

30 'Twas wit at first, and wine that made them live:
Choke may the painter! and his box disclose
No other colours than his fiery nose;
And may we no more of his pencil see,
Than two churchwardens, and mortality.
    Should we go now a wandering, we should meet
With catchpoles,[2] whores, & carts in every street:
Now when each narrow lane, each nook & cave,
Sign-posts, & shop-doors, pimp for every knave,
When riotous sinful plush, and tell-tale spurs

40 Walk Fleet street, & the Strand, when the soft stirs
Of bawdy, ruffled silks, turn night to day;
And the loud whip, and coach scolds all the way;
When lust of all sorts, and each itchy blood
From the Tower-wharf to Cymbeline, and Lud,
Hunts for a mate, and the tired footman reels
'Twixt chair-men,[3] torches, & the hackney wheels:
    Come, take the other dish; it is to him[4]
That made his horse a Senator: each brim
Look big as mine; the gallant, jolly beast

50 Of all the herd (you'll say) was not the least.
    Now crown the second bowl, rich as his worth
I'll drink it to; he! that like fire broke forth

---

1. Endymion was a shepherd loved by the moon in Greek myth.
2. Catchpoles were officers who arrested people for debt.
3. Men who carried sedan-chairs.
4. Vaughan is using references to events in Roman times to make allusions to events of his own time and emphasize his support for Charles I against Parliament.

Into the Senate's face, crossed Rubicon,
And the State's pillars, with their laws thereon:
And made the dull grey beards, & furred gowns fly
Into *Brundusium* to consult, and lie:
   This to brave *Sylla*! why should it be said,
We drink more to the living, than the dead?
Flatterers, and fools do use it: let us laugh
60 At our own honest mirth; for they that quaff
To honour others, do like those that sent
Their gold and plate to strangers to be spent:
   Drink deep; this cup be pregnant;[1] & the wine
Spirit of wit, to make us all divine,
That big with sack, and mirth we may retire
Possessors of more souls, and nobler fire;
And by the influx of this painted sky
And laboured[2] forms, to higher matters fly;
So, if a nap shall take us, we shall all,
70 After full cups have dreams poetical.

Let's laugh now, and the pressed grape drink,
Till the drowsy Day-Star wink;
And in our merry, mad mirth run
Faster, and further than the Sun;
And let none his cup forsake,
Till that Star again doth wake;
So we men below shall move
   Equally with the gods above.

1. Fruitful.
2. Highly elaborate. This is probably an insult to the artist.

The Retreat

Happy those early days! when I
Shined in my Angel-infancy.
Before I understood this place
Appointed for my second race,

Or taught my soul to fancy aught
But a white, celestial thought,
When yet I had not walked above
A mile, or two, from my first love,[1]
And looking back (at that short space,)
10　Could see a glimpse of his bright-face;
When on some gilded cloud, or flower
My gazing soul would dwell an hour,
And in those weaker glories spy
Some shadows of eternity;
Before I taught my tongue to wound
My conscience with a sinful sound,
Or had the black art to dispense
A several sin to every sense,
But felt through all this fleshly dress
20　Bright shoots of everlastingness.
　　O how I long to travel back
And tread again that ancient track!
That I might once more reach that plain,
Where first I left my glorious train,
From whence the enlightened spirit sees
That shady city of palm trees,[2]
But (ah!) my soul with too much stay
Is drunk, and staggers in the way.
Some men a forward motion love,
30　But I by backward steps would move,
And when this dust falls to the urn
In that state I came return.

1. God.
2. A reference to the scene in Deuteronomy, chapter 34: v.1–4, where God shows Moses the plain of the valley of Jericho, the city of palm trees, and gives it to him and his descendants.

Peace

My soul, there is a country
   Far beyond the stars,
Where stands a winged sentry
   All skilful in the wars,
There above noise, and danger
   Sweet peace sits crowned with smiles,
And one born in a manger
   Commands the beauteous files,
He is thy gracious friend,
10   And (O my soul awake!)
Did in pure love descend
   To die here for thy sake,
If thou canst get but thither,
   There grows the flower of peace,
The rose that cannot wither,
   Thy fortress, and thy ease;
Leave then thy foolish ranges;
   For none can thee secure,
But one, who never changes,
20   Thy God, thy life, thy cure.

The World (I)

1

I saw Eternity the other night
Like a great *Ring* of pure and endless light,[1]
    All calm, as it was bright,
And round beneath it, Time in hours, days, years
     Driven by the spheres
Like a vast shadow moved, in which the world
    And all her train were hurled;

1. A circle has no end, like eternity.

The doting lover in his quaintest strain
    Did there complain,
10 Near him, his lute, his fancy, and his flights,
    Wit's sour delights,
With gloves, and knots the silly snares of pleasure
    Yet his dear treasure
All scattered lay, while he his eyes did pour[1]
    Upon a flower.

2

The darksome states-man hung with weights and woe
Like a thick midnight-fog moved there so slow
    He did nor stay, nor go;
Condemning thoughts (like sad eclipses) scowl
20   Upon his soul,
And clouds of crying witnesses without
    Pursued him with one shout.
Yet digged the mole, and lest his ways be found
    Worked under ground,
Where he did clutch his prey, but one did see
    That policy,[2]
Churches and altars fed him, perjuries
    Were gnats and flies,
It rained about him blood and tears, but he
30   Drank them as free.

3

The fearful miser on a heap of rust
Sat pining all his life there, did scarce trust
    His own hands with the dust,
Yet would not place one piece above, but lives
    In fear of thieves.[3]

1. A pun on pour/pore.
2. The cunning statesman works secretly, like a mole working under-
ground, to conceal his wickedness, but is blind like a mole to the fact
that God sees what he does.
3. 'Lay up for yourselves treasure in heaven, where neither moth nor
rust doth corrupt, and where thieves do not break through nor steal'
(Matthew, chapter 6: v. 20).

Thousands there were as frantic as himself
    And hugged each one his pelf,
The down-right epicure placed heaven in sense
    And scorned pretence
40 While others slipped into a wide excess
    Said little less;
The weaker sort slight, trivial wares enslave
    Who think them brave,
And poor, despised truth sat counting by
    Their victory.

4

Yet some, who all this while did weep and sing,
And sing, and weep, soared up into the *Ring*,
    But most would use no wing.
O fools (said I,) thus to prefer dark night
50   Before true light,
To live in grots, and caves, and hate the day
    Because it shows the way,[1]
The way which from this dead and dark abode
    Leads up to God,
A way where you might tread the Sun, and be
    More bright than he.
But as I did their madness so discuss
    One whispered thus,
This ring the bride-groom did for none provide
60   *But for his bride.*[2]

John ii 16–17
*All that is in the world, the lust of the flesh, the lust of the eyes, and
the pride of life, is not of the father but is of the world.*

    *And the world passeth away, and the lusts thereof, but he that
doth the will of God abideth for ever.*

1. Vaughan is possibly thinking of the myth of the cave in Plato's
Republic, where prisoners chained in a cave facing a wall can only
know what goes on by seeing shadows moving on the wall. They
confuse the shadows with the real world.
2. Only those who find salvation with God will live in eternity.

The Water-fall

With what deep murmurs through time's silent stealth
Doth thy transparent, cool and watery wealth
      Here flowing fall,
      And chide, and call,
As if his liquid, loose retinue stayed
Ling'ring, and were of this steep place afraid,
      The common pass
      Where, clear as glass,
      All must descend
10   Not to an end:
But quickened by this deep and rocky grave,
Rise to a longer course more bright and brave.[1]
Dear stream! dear bank, where often I
Have sat, and pleased my pensive eye,
Why, since each drop of thy quick store
Runs thither, whence it flowed before,
Should poor souls fear a shade or night,
Who came (sure) from a sea of light?[2]
Or since those drops are all sent back
20 So sure to thee, that none doth lack,
Why should frail flesh doubt any more
That what God takes, he'll not restore?
O useful element and clear!
My sacred wash and cleanser here,[3]
My first consigner unto those
Fountains of life, where the Lamb goes?

1. Beautiful.
2. The movement of water from sea to clouds, to rain, to rivers and again to sea was seen as an example of God's order in the world, ensuring nothing is wasted. As a metaphor, it is applied here to the life of man, coming from God and returning there again.
3. The water of baptism.

What sublime truths, and wholesome themes,
Lodge in thy mystical, deep streams!
Such as dull man can never find
30 Unless that Spirit lead his mind,
Which first upon thy face did move,[1]
And hatched all with his quickening love.
As this loud brook's incessant fall
In streaming rings restagnates all,
Which reach by course the bank, and then
Are no more seen, just so pass men.
O my invisible estate,
My glorious liberty, still late!
Thou art the channel my soul seeks,
40 Not this with cataracts and creeks.

1. 'The earth was without form, and void ... and the spirit of God moved on the face of the waters' (Genesis, chapter 1: v. 2).

The Shower (II)

Waters above! eternal springs!
The dew, that silvers the *Dove's*[1] wings!
O welcome, welcome to the sad:
Give dry dust drink; drink that makes glad!
Many fair *evenings*, many *flowers*
Sweetened with rich and gentle showers
Have I enjoyed, and down have run
Many a fine and shining *sun*;
But never till this happy hour
10 Was blest with such an *evening-shower*!

1. The Holy Spirit.

The True Christmas

So stick up *ivy* and the *bays*,[1]
And then restore the *heathen* ways.
Green will remind you of the spring,
Though this great day denies the thing,
And mortifies the earth and all
But your wild *revels*, and loose *hall*.
Could you wear *flowers*, and *roses* strow
Blushing upon your breasts' *warm snow*,
That very *dress* your lightness will
10   Rebuke, and wither at the ill.
The brightness of this day we owe
Not unto *music*, *masque* nor *show*:
Nor gallant *furniture*, nor *plate*;
But to the *manger's* mean estate.
His *life* while here, as well as *birth*,
Was but a check to *pomp* and *mirth*;
And all man's *greatness* you may see
Condemned by his *humility*.

    Then leave your open *house* and *noise*,
20   To welcome him with *holy joys*,
And the poor *shepherd's* watchfulness:
Whom *light* and *hymns* from Heaven did bless.
What you *abound* with, cast abroad[1]
To those that *want*, and ease your load.
Who empties thus, will bring more in;
But riot is both *loss* and *sin*.
Dress finely what comes not in sight,
And then you keep your *Christmas* right.

1. Ivy and bay leaves were associated with pagan festivals.
2. 'Cast your bread upon the waters and it shall be returned to you'
(Ecclesiastes, chapter 9:v.1).

from *The Chemist's Key*

The greedy cheat with impure hands may not
Attempt this Art,[1] nor is it ever got
By the unlearned and rude: the vicious mind
To lust and softness given, it strikes stark blind,
So the sly, wandering factor . . .[2]
But the sage, pious man, who still adores
And loves his Maker, and his love implores,
Whoever joys to search the secret cause
And series of his works, their love and laws,
10   Let him draw near, and joining will with strength,
Study this Art in all her depth and length;
Then grave experience shall his consort[3] be
Skilled in large nature's inmost mystery.
The knots and doubts his busy course and cares
Will oft disturb, till time the truth declares,
And stable patience, through all trials passed,
Brings the glad end and long hoped for, at last.

1. The art of chemistry. In those days, chemistry was part of the science of alchemy, which drew comparisons between spiritual transformation and chemical operations, in that both sought to change one substance into another one more greatly desired.

2. A factor was a commission merchant.

3. Partner.

John Dryden

(1631–1700)

Dryden was born into a Puritan family in Northamptonshire and educated at Westminster School and Trinity College, Cambridge. In about 1657 he is thought to have gone to London as clerk to his cousin, Cromwell's chamberlain. His first important poem was written in memory of Cromwell, but after the Restoration he wrote poems celebrating the return of Charles II and was rewarded by being made Poet Laureate in 1668 and Historiographer Royal in 1670.

The theatres had been closed during the period between the execution of Charles I and the restoration of Charles II, because the Puritans in Parliament disapproved of play-going. However, when they re-opened in 1661, Dryden began to write plays. His first comedy appeared in 1663, the year in which Dryden married Lady Elizabeth Howard, the sister of his patron Sir Robert Howard. For twenty years he was the foremost playwright in England, producing comedies, tragedies and heroic plays, full of style and pageantry. He also collaborated with Sir Robert Howard and with the composer Henry Purcell to write plays containing songs and music.

Although he had written in defence of his Protestant faith, Dryden converted to Catholicism in 1685 when the Catholic King James II came to the throne, and wrote a long poem defending this decision. However, when James II was ousted in 1688 and the Protestant William III became King, Dryden lost both his laureateship and his pension because of his views.

Dryden's later plays were much less successful, and he turned to translation as a source of income. His translations of the classics and of Chaucer, together with other poetry and some celebrated critical essays, were published during the ten years before his death in May 1700. He was buried in Westminster Abbey.

Other writers of the period acknowledged Dryden's contribution to English poetry. Pope wrote of him:

> Dryden taught to join
> The varying verse, the full resounding line,
> The long majestic march, and energy divine.

What Dryden achieved in his poetry was not the emotional excitement we find in the Romantic poets of the early nineteenth century, nor the intellectual complexities of the metaphysical poets. His subject matter was often factual, and he aimed at expressing his thoughts in the most precise and concentrated way possible. Although he uses formal poetic structures such as heroic stanzas and heroic couplets, he tried to achieve the rhythms of speech. However, he knew that different subjects need different kinds of verse, and in one essay he wrote: 'the expressions of a poem designed purely for instruction ought to be plain and natural, yet majestic . . . The florid, elevated and figurative way is for the passions; for [these] are begotten in the soul by showing the objects out of their true proportion . . . A man is to be cheated into passion, but to be reasoned into truth.'

Dryden's long satires, which depend on a thorough understanding of the political events of his day, are perhaps less accessible without a great deal of explanation to modern readers than to those of his own time. However, even though Shadwell, the victim of his satire 'Mac Flecknoe', is now largely forgotten, we can still admire the elegance of Dryden's insults to him.

The poems of public celebration and the songs and elegies can be enjoyed for the vigour of their expression. In *Annus Mirabilis, The Year of Wonders 1666*, for example, he praises England's greatness in commerce, science and in naval power while describing both the naval war between the British and the Dutch and the Great Fire of London. In the passage printed here, he describes the battle and compares the crippled ships of both fleets, lying helplessly alongside each other with masts shot away and battered sides taking in water, to an exhausted hare, helpless before the dog that has been chasing her, who is himself too exhausted for the kill.

from ANNUS MIRABILIS

THE YEAR OF
WONDERS
1666

The cheerful soldiers, with new stores supplied,
    Now long to execute their spleenful will;
And in revenge for those three days they tried,
    Wish one, like Joshua's, when the sun stood still.

Thus re-inforced, against the adverse fleet
    Still doubling ours, brave Rupert leads the way.[1]
With the first blushes of the morn they meet,
    And bring night back upon the new-born day.

His presence soon blows up the kindling fight,
10   And his loud guns speak thick like angry men;
It seemed as slaughter had been breathed all night,
    And death new pointed his dull dart agen.

The Dutch, too well his mighty conduct knew,
    And matchless courage since the former fight;
Whose navy like a stiff stretched cord did show
    Till he bore in and bent them into flight.

The wind he shares while half their fleet offends
    His open side, and high above him shows;
Upon the rest at pleasure he descends,
20   And, doubly harmed, he double harms bestows.

Behind, the Gen'ral mends his weary pace,[2]
    And sullenly to his revenge he sails;
So glides some trodden serpent on the grass,
    And long behind his wounded volume trails.

1. Prince Rupert (1619–1682), joint-commander of the English fleet.
2. George Monk, the Duke of Albemarle, (1608–1670) was the joint-
commander with Prince Rupert of the English fleet.

Th' increasing sound is borne to either shore,
  And for their stakes the throwing nations fear.
Their passions double with the cannons' roar,
  And with warm wishes each man combats there.

Plied thick and close as when the fight begun,
30 Their huge unwieldy navy wastes away;
So sicken waning moons too near the sun,
  And blunt their crescents on the edge of day.

And now reduced on equal terms to fight,
  Their ships like wasted patrimonies show:
Where the thin scatt'ring trees admit the light,
  And shun each other's shadows as they grow.

The warlike Prince had severed from the rest
  Two giant ships, the pride of all the main;
Which, with his one, so vigorously he pressed
40 And flew so home they could not rise again.

Already battered, by his lee they lay,
  In vain upon the passing winds they call;
The passing winds through their torn canvas play,
  And flagging sails on heartless sailors fall.

Their opened sides receive a gloomy light,
  Dreadful as day let in to shades below;
Without, grim death rides bare-faced in their sight,
  And urges ent'ring billows as they flow.

When one dire shot, the last they could supply,
50 Close by the board the Prince's main-mast bore.[1]
All three now, helpless, by each other lie,
  And this offends not, and those fear no more.

1. The shot carried away the Prince's main-mast where it joined the deck, making it helpless to move.

So have I seen some fearful hare maintain
　　A course till tired before the dog she lay;
Who, stretched behind her, pants upon the plain,
　　Past pow'r to kill as she to get away.

With his lolled tongue he faintly licks his prey,
　　His warm breath blows her flix[1] up as she lies;
She, trembling, creeps upon the ground away,
60　　And looks back to him with beseeching eyes.

The Prince unjustly does his stars accuse,
　　Which hindered him to push his fortune on;
For what they to his courage did refuse,
　　By mortal valour never must be done.

This lucky hour the wise Batavian[2] takes,
　　And warns his tattered fleet to follow home;
Proud to have so got off with equal stakes,
　　Where 'twas a triumph not to be o'ercome.

1. Fur.
2. The Dutch commander.

Song

Fairest isle, all isles excelling,
　　Seat of pleasures and of loves;
Venus here will choose her dwelling,
　　And forsake her Cyprian groves.

Cupid, from his fav'rite nation,
　　Care and envy will remove;
Jealousy, that poisons passion,
　　And despair that dies for love.

Gentle murmurs, sweet complaining
10   Sighs that blow the fire of love;
Soft repulses, kind disdaining,
    Shall be all the pains you prove

Every swain shall pay his duty,
    Grateful every nymph shall prove:
And as these excel in beauty,
    Those shall be renowned for love.

To the memory of Mr Oldham[1]

Farewell, too little and too lately known,
Whom I began to think and call my own;
For sure our souls were near allied, and thine
Cast in the same poetic mould with mine.
One common note on either lyre did strike,
And knaves and fools we both abhorred alike.
To the same goal did both our studies drive;
The last set out the soonest did arrive.
Thus Nisus fell upon the slippery place,
10   While his young friend performed and won the race.
O early ripe! to thy abundant store
What could advancing age have added more?
It might (what nature never gives the young)
Have taught the numbers of thy native tongue;
But satire needs not those, and wit will shine
Through the harsh cadence of a rugged line.
A noble error, and but seldom made
When poets are by too much force betrayed.
Thy generous fruits though gathered ere their prime
20   Still showed a quickness; and maturing time
But mellows what we write to the dull sweets of rhyme.

1. John Oldham (1653–1683), the satirist.

Once more, hail and farewell! farewell thou young
But ah! too short Marcellus of our tongue.
Thy brows with ivy and with laurels bound;
But Fate and gloomy night encompass thee around.

Song

Can life be a blessing,
Or worth the possessing,
Can life be a blessing if love were away?
Ah no! though our love all night keep us waking,
And though he torment us with cares all the day,
Yet he sweetens, he sweetens our pains in the taking;
There's an hour at the last, there's an hour to repay.

In every possessing,
The ravishing blessing,
10   In every possessing the fruit of our pain,
Poor lovers forget long ages of anguish,
Whate'er they have suffered and done to obtain;
'Tis a pleasure, a pleasure to sigh and to languish,
When we hope, when we hope to be happy again.

from Mac Flecknoe

OR A SATIRE UPON THE
TRUE-BLUE PROTESTANT POET
T.S.

All human things are subject to decay,
And when Fate summons monarchs must obey.
This Flecknoe[1] found, who, like Augustus, young
Was called to Empire and had governed long;

1. Richard Flecknoe, who died in 1678, was an Irish poet whose work
Dryden disliked.

In prose and verse was owned, without dispute
Through all the realms of Nonsense, absolute.
This aged prince, now flourishing in peace
And blest with issue of a large increase,
Worn out with business, did at length debate
10   To settle the succession of the state;
And pond'ring which of all his sons was fit
To reign and wage immortal war with wit,
Cried: ''Tis resolved; for nature pleads that he
Should only rule who most resembles me.
Shadwell[1] alone my perfect image bears,
Mature in dullness from his tender years.
Shadwell alone, of all my sons, is he
Who stands confirmed in full stupidity.
The rest to some faint meaning make pretence,
20   But Shadwell never deviates into sense.
Some beams of wit on other souls may fall,
Strike through and make a lucid interval,
But Shadwell's genuine night admits no ray,
His rising fogs prevail upon the day.
Besides his goodly fabric fills the eye,
And seems designed for thoughtless majesty:
Thoughtless as monarch oaks that shade the plain
And, spread in solemn state, supinely reign.

from AURENG-ZEBE

When I consider life, 'tis all a cheat;
Yet, fooled with hope, men favour the deceit:
Trust on, and think tomorrow will repay;

1. Thomas Shadwell (1642–1692) was a dramatist, considered second-rate by Dryden. 'Mac' means 'son of', so the poem suggests he is the poetic son of Flecknoe. Dryden partly attacked Shadwell because of political disagreements with him, but also because of professional jealousy.

Tomorrow's falser than the former day;
Lies worse, and while it says, we shall be blest
With some new joys, cuts off what we possessed.
Strange cozenage![1] none would live past years again,
Yet all hope pleasure in what yet remain;
And from the dregs of life, think to receive
10   What the first sprightly running could not give.
I'm tired of waiting for this chymick gold,[2]
Which fools us young, and beggars us when old.

1. Cheating.
2. The alchemists searched for a substance that would turn all things to gold.

On the death of Mr Purcell[1]

I

Mark how the lark and linnet sing,
    With rival notes
They strain their warbling throats
    To welcome in the spring.
    But in the close of night,
When Philomel[2] begins her heavenly lay,
    They cease their mutual spite,
    Drink in her music with delight,
And list'ning and silent, and silent and list'ning,
10   And list'ning and silent obey.

1. Henry Purcell, (1659–1695), English composer who became organist of the Chapel Royal and composer to Charles II.
2. Poetic name for the nightingale.

II

So ceased the rival crew, when Purcell came,
They sung no more, or only sung his fame.
   Struck dumb, they all admired
     The godlike man,
   Alas, too soon retired,
     As he too late began.
We beg not hell our Orpheus[1] to restore;
     Had he been there,
     Their sovereign's fear
20   Had sent him back before.
The power of harmony too well they knew;
He long e'er this had tuned their jarring sphere,
     And left no hell below.

III

The heavenly quire, who heard his notes from high,
Let down the scale of music from the sky:
     They handed him along,
And all the way he taught, and all the way they sung.
Ye brethren of the lyre and tuneful voice,
Lament his lot: but at your own rejoice.
30 Now live secure, and linger out your days,
The gods are pleased alone with Purcell's lays,
     Nor know to mend their choice.

1. Musician in Greek legend

Alexander Pope

(1688–1744)

Alexander Pope was born in London, the son of a Roman Catholic tradesman in the linen business. In 1700 the family left London to live at Binfield in Windsor Forest, because a law brought in after the Protestant William III became King prohibited Catholics from living within ten miles of London. Catholics were also barred from attending Protestant universities, and so Pope was educated mainly at home. He had some lessons from priests, but taught himself Greek, picked up French and Italian, and read widely in English and Latin poetry. A serious illness when he was about twelve left him with a curved spine. He never grew taller than 4ft 6in and suffered from frequent headaches and bouts of illness all his life.

Pope was encouraged in his writing as a teenager by several retired writers who lived near by and introduced him to other fashionable London wits and writers. He made some warm friendships, particularly with Jonathan Swift and John Gay, but was also quarrelsome and attacked other writers viciously in print. Although he never married, he had many women friends and wrote them witty letters.

In 1718 Pope bought a house in Twickenham, where he lived for the rest of his life, entertaining many famous literary and political people of the day. He loved the garden and spent much time improving it and building an elaborate geological grotto.

Pope translated works by great classical writers such as Horace, Virgil and Homer, and wrote his own satires in their style. Literary criticism, autobiography and politics are the theme of many of the satires. His *Essay on Criticism* considers both the best ways of judging a poem and indirectly the best ways of writing one. Some parts of it make witty use of the defects he is criticizing to illustrate his meaning. For example, at one point he points out that poetry written with predictable rhymes is boring to read:

Where'er you find 'the cooling western breeze',
In the next line, it 'whispers through the trees';
If crystal streams 'with pleasing murmurs creep',
The reader's threaten'd (not in vain) with 'sleep'.

One of Pope's most famous works is *The Rape of the Lock*. He was asked to write a humorous poem to mend a quarrel that had developed between two wealthy families after Robert, Lord Petre, cut off a lock of Arabella Fermor's hair. Pope's poem mocks the traditions of classical epics: the rape of Helen of Troy becomes here the theft of a lock of hair; the gods become minute sylphs; Aeneas's voyage up the Tiber becomes Belinda's voyage up the Thames, and the description of Achilles's shield becomes one of Belinda's petticoat. He also uses the epic style of invocations, lamentations, exclamations and similes, and in some cases adds parody to imitation by following the framework of actual speeches in Homer's *Iliad*. Although the poem is extremely funny at times, Pope always keeps a sense that beauty is fragile, and that the loss of a lock of hair touches Belinda deeply. As his introductory letter makes clear, women in that period were essentially supposed to be decorative rather than rational, and the loss of beauty was a serious matter.

In his later work, his poems took the form of moral essays. The *Essay on Man*, for example, is concerned with the part evil plays in the world and with the social order God has decreed for man. Because man cannot know God's purposes, he cannot complain about the existence of evil and must accept that 'Whatever is, is right.'

Pope's style uses the heroic couplets perfected by Dryden with extraordinary power. His expression is concise and forceful, conveying emotion as well as reason and wit. Many quotations from Pope, such as 'A little learning is a dangerous thing,' 'Hope springs eternal in the human breast,' and 'The proper study of mankind is man,' have passed so deeply into the English language

that they are taken as proverbial. This would have greatly pleased
Pope, who wrote:

> True Wit is Nature to advantage dress'd;
> What oft was thought, but ne'er so well express'd.

Ode on Solitude

Happy the man, whose wish and care
    A few paternal acres bound,
Content to breathe his native air,
            In his own ground.

Whose herds with milk, whose fields with bread,
    Whose flocks supply him with attire,
Whose trees in summer yield him shade,
            In winter fire.

Blest, who can unconcern'dly find
10   Hours, days, and years slide soft away,
In health of body, peace of mind,
            Quiet by day,

Sound sleep by night; study and ease,
    Together mixt; sweet recreation;
And innocence, which most does please
            With meditation.

Thus let me live, unseen, unknown,
    Thus unlamented let me die,
Steal from the world, and not a stone
            Tell where I lie.

The Dying Christian to his Soul

I

Vital spark of heav'nly flame!
Quit, oh quit this mortal frame:
Trembling, hoping, ling'ring, flying,
Oh the pain, the bliss of dying!
Cease, fond Nature, cease thy strife,
And let me languish into life.

II

    Hark! they whisper; Angels say,
    'Sister Spirit, come away!'
    What is this absorbs me quite?
10   Steals my senses, shuts my sight,
Drowns my spirits, draws my breath?
Tell me, my Soul, can this be Death?

III

The world recedes; it disappears!
Heav'n opens on my eyes! my ears
    With sounds seraphic ring:
Lend, lend your wings! I mount! I fly!
O Grave! where is thy Victory?
    O Death! where is thy Sting?

from AN ESSAY ON MAN

ADDRESSED TO HENRY ST JOHN,
LORD BOLINGBROKE[1]

I. PROEM

Awake, my St John! leave all meaner things
To low ambition, and the pride of Kings.
Let us (since Life can little more supply
Than just to look about us and to die)
Expatiate free o'er all this scene of Man;
A mighty maze! but not without a plan;
A Wild, where weeds and flow'rs promiscuous shoot;
Or Garden, tempting with forbidden fruit.
Together let us beat this ample field,
10 Try what the open, what the covert yield;
The latent tracts, the giddy heights, explore
Of all who blindly creep, or sightless soar;

1. Viscount Bolingbroke (1678–1751), statesman and philosopher.

Eye Nature's walks, shoot Folly as it flies,
And catch the Manners living as they rise;
Laugh where we must, be candid where we can;
But vindicate the ways of God to Man.

*   *   *

II. HOPE ETERNAL

Heav'n from all creatures hides the book of Fate.
All but the page prescrib'd, their present state:
From brutes what men, from men what spirits know:
20   Or who could suffer Being here below?
The lamb thy riot dooms to bleed to-day,
Had he thy Reason, would he skip and play?
Pleas'd to the last, he crops the flow'ry food,
And licks the hand just rais'd to shed his blood.
Oh blindness to the future! kindly giv'n,
That each may fill the circle mark'd by Heav'n:
Who sees with equal eye, as God of all,
A hero perish, or a sparrow fall,
Atoms or systems into ruin hurl'd,
30   And now a bubble burst, and now a world.
    Hope humbly then; with trembling pinions soar;
Wait the great teacher Death; and God adore.
What future bliss, he gives not thee to know,
But gives that Hope to be thy blessing now.
Hope springs eternal in the human breast:
Man never Is, but always To be blest:
The soul uneasy, and confin'd from home,
Rests and expatiates in a life to come.
    Lo, the poor Indian! whose untutor'd mind
40   Sees God in clouds, or hears him in the wind;
His soul, proud Science never taught to stray
Far as the solar walk, or milky way;
Yet simple Nature to his hope has giv'n,
Behind the cloud-topt hill, an humbler heav'n;

Some safer world in depth of woods embrac'd,
Some happier island in the wat'ry waste,
Where slaves once more their native land behold,
No fiends torment, no Christians thirst for gold.
To Be, contents his natural desire,
50 He asks no Angel's wing, no Seraph's fire;
But thinks, admitted to that equal sky,
His faithful dog shall bear him company.[1]

III. THE PROPER STUDY

Know then thyself, presume not God to scan,
The proper study of Mankind is Man.
Plac'd on this isthmus of a middle state,
A Being darkly wise, and rudely great:
With too much knowledge for the Sceptic side,
With too much weakness for the Stoic's pride,
He hangs between; in doubt to act, or rest;
60 In doubt to deem himself a God, or Beast;
In doubt his Mind or Body to prefer;
Born but to die, and reas'ning but to err;
Alike in ignorance, his reason such,
Whether he thinks too little, or too much:
Chaos of Thought and Passion, all confus'd;
Still by himself abus'd, or disabus'd;
Created half to rise, and half to fall;
Great Lord of all things, yet a prey to all;
Sole judge of Truth, in endless Error hurl'd:
70 The glory, jest, and riddle of the world!

*   *   *

1. Christian theology teaches that animals do not have souls.

IV. OPINION'S VARYING RAYS

Whate'er the Passion, knowledge, fame, or pelf,[1]
Not one will change his neighbour with himself.
The learn'd is happy nature to explore;
The fool is happy that he knows no more;
The rich is happy in the plenty giv'n,
The poor contents him with the care of Heav'n.
See the blind beggar dance, the cripple sing,
The sot[2] a hero, lunatic a king;
The starving chemist in his golden views
80   Supremely bless'd, the poet in his Muse.
    See some strange comfort ev'ry state attend.
And pride bestow'd on all, a common friend;
See some fit Passion ev'ry age supply,
Hope travels through, nor quits us when we die.
    Behold the child, by Nature's kindly law,
Pleas'd with a rattle, tickled with a straw:
Some livelier play-thing gives his youth delight,
A little louder, but as empty quite:
Scarfs, garters, gold, amuse his riper stage,
90   And beads and pray'r-books are the toys of age:
Pleas'd with this bauble still, as that before;
Till tir'd he sleeps, and Life's poor play is o'er.
    Mean-while Opinion gilds with varying rays
Those painted clouds that beautify our days;
Each want of happiness by Hope supply'd,
And each vacuity of sense by Pride:
These build as fast as knowledge can destroy;
In Folly's cup still laughs the bubble, joy;
One prospect lost, another still we gain;
100   And not a vanity is giv'n in vain;

1. Money.
2. Drunkard.

Ev'n mean Self-love becomes, by force divine,
The scale to measure others' wants by thine.
See! and confess, one comfort still must rise,
'Tis this, Tho' Man's a fool, yet GOD IS WISE.

*   *   *

VII. EPILOGUE

Come then, my Friend, my Genius! come along;
O master of the poet, and the song!
And while the Muse now stoops, or now ascends,
To Man's low passions, or their glorious ends,
Teach me, like thee, in various nature wise,
110 To fall with dignity, with temper rise;
Form'd by thy converse, happily to steer
From grave to gay, from lively to severe;
Correct with spirit, eloquent with ease,
Intent to reason, or polite to please.
Oh! while along the stream of Time thy name
Expanded flies, and gathers all its fame,
Say, shall my little bark attendant sail,
Pursue the triumph, and partake the gale?
When statesmen, heroes, kings, in dust repose,
120 Whose sons shall blush their fathers were thy foes,
Shall then this verse to future age pretend
Thou wert my guide, philosopher, and friend?
That, urg'd by thee, I turn'd the tuneful art
From sounds to things, from fancy to the heart;
For Wit's false mirror held up Nature's light;
Show'd erring Pride, WHATEVER IS, IS RIGHT;
That REASON, PASSION, answer one great aim;
That true SELF-LOVE and SOCIAL are the same;
That VIRTUE only makes our Bliss below;
130 And all our Knowledge is, OURSELVES TO KNOW.

from EPISTLE TO DR ARBUTHNOT[1]

BEING THE PROLOGUE TO THE SATIRES

P. Shut, shut the door, good John![2] fatigu'd I said,
Tye up the knocker, say I'm sick, I'm dead.
The Dog-star rages! nay, 'tis past a doubt,
All Bedlam, or Parnassus, is let out:
Fire in each eye, and papers in each hand,
They rave, recite, and madden round the land.
    What walls can guard me, or what shades can hide?
They pierce my Thickets, through my Grot[3] they glide,
By land, by water, they renew the charge,
They stop the chariot, and they board the barge.
No place is sacred, not the Church is free,
Ev'n Sunday shines no Sabbath-day to me:
Then from the Mint[4] walks forth the Man of rhyme,
Happy! to catch me, just at Dinner-time.
    Is there a Parson, much be-mus'd in beer,
A maudlin Poetess, a rhyming Peer,
A Clerk, foredoom'd his father's soul to cross,
Who pens a Stanza, when he should *engross*?
Is there, who, lock'd from ink and paper, scrawls
With desp'rate charcoal round his darken'd walls?
All fly to TWIT'NAM,[5] and in humble strain
Apply to me, to keep them mad or vain.
Arthur, whose giddy son neglects the laws,
Imputes to me and my damn'd works the cause:
Poor Cornus sees his frantic wife elope,
And curses Wit, and Poetry, and Pope.

1. Pope's doctor and friend.
2. Pope's servant was called John Searle.
3. Pope built an ornamental grotto at his house in Twickenham.
4. A sanctuary for bankrupts in Southwark.
5. Twickenham.

Friend to my life! (which did not you prolong,
The world had wanted many an idle song)
What *Drop* or *Nostrum*[1] can this plague remove?
30 Or which must end me, a Fool's wrath or love?
A dire dilemma! either way I'm sped,
If foes, they write, if friends, they read me dead.
Seiz'd and ty'd down to judge, how wretched I?
Who can't be silent, and who will not lie:
To laugh, were want of goodness and of grace,
And to be grave, exceeds all Pow'r of face.
I sit with sad civility, I read
With honest anguish, and an aching head;
And drop at last, but in unwilling ears,
40 This saving counsel, 'Keep your piece nine years.'
'Nine years!' cries he, who high in Drury-lane,
Lull'd by soft Zephyrs[2] through the broken pane,
Rhymes ere he wakes, and prints before *Term* ends,
Oblig'd by hunger, and request of friends:
'The piece, you think, is incorrect? why take it,
I'm all submission, what you'd have it, make it.'
Three things another's modest wishes bound,
My Friendship, and a Prologue, and ten pound.
Pitholeon[3] sends to me: 'You know his Grace,
50 I want a Patron; ask him for a Place.'
Pitholeon libell'd me – 'But here's a letter
Informs you, Sir, 'twas when he knew no better.
Dare you refuse him? Curl invites to dine,[4]
He'll write a *Journal*, or he'll turn Divine.'
Bless me! a packet. – ''Tis a stranger sues,
A Virgin Tragedy, an Orphan Muse.'

1. Medicine.
2. Breezes.
3. Pope's own note on this name tells us that it was 'taken from a
foolish poet of Rhodes who pretended much to Greek'.
4. Edmund Curll (1675–1747) was a printer and bookseller and an
enemy of Pope's.

If I dislike it, 'Furies, death and rage!'
If I approve, 'Commend it to the Stage.'
There (thank my stars) my whole commission ends,
60   The Play'rs and I are, luckily, no friends.
Fir'd that the house reject him, ''Sdeath! I'll print it,
And shame the fools – Your int'rest, Sir, with Lintot.'[1]
Lintot, dull rogue! will think your price too much:
'Not, Sir, if you revise it, and retouch.'
All my demurs but double his attacks;
At last he whispers, 'Do; and we go snacks.'[2]
Glad of a quarrel, straight I clap the door,
Sir, let me see your works and you no more.

1. Another bookseller.
2. Half-shares.

from THE RAPE[1] OF THE LOCK

AN HEROI-COMICAL POEM
CANTO I

[*Belinda wakes up*]

What dire offence from am'rous causes springs,
What mighty contests rise from trivial things,
I sing – This verse to CARYL,[2] Muse! is due:
This, ev'n Belinda may vouchsafe to view:
Slight is the subject, but not so the praise,
If She inspire, and He approve my lays.
    Say what strange motive, Goddess! could compel
A well-bred Lord t' assault a gentle Belle?
O say what stranger cause, yet unexplor'd,
10   Could make a gentle Belle reject a Lord?

1. The word is used here in the sense of 'theft'. Lord Petre, the Baron of the poem, cut off a lock of Miss Arabella Fermor's hair, and so brought about a quarrel between their two families.
2. John Caryll, a mutual friend of both the families concerned and Pope, asked him to write this poem to heal the breach.

In tasks so bold, can little men engage,
And in soft bosoms, dwells such mighty Rage?
    Sol, through white curtains shot a tim'rous ray,
And ope'd those eyes that must eclipse the day:
Now lap-dogs give themselves the rousing shake.
And sleepless lovers, just at twelve, awake:
Thrice rung the bell, the slipper knock'd the ground,
And the press'd watch return'd a silver sound.
Belinda still her downy pillow prest,
20 Her guardian SYLPH prolong'd the balmy rest:
'Twas He had summon'd to her silent bed
The morning-dream that hover'd o'er her head,
A Youth more glitt'ring than a Birth-night Beau,
(That ev'n in slumber caus'd her cheek to glow)
Seem'd to her ear his winning lips to lay,
And thus in whispers said, or seem'd to say.
    'Fairest of mortals, thou distinguish'd care
Of thousand bright Inhabitants of Air!
If e'er one Vision touch thy infant thought,
30 Of all the Nurse and all the Priest have taught;
Of airy Elves by moonlight shadows seen,
The silver token, and the circled green,
Or virgins visited by Angel-pow'rs
With golden crowns and wreaths of heav'nly flow'rs;
Hear and believe! thy own importance know,
Nor bound thy narrow views to things below.
Some secret truths, from learned pride conceal'd,
To Maids alone and Children are reveal'd:
What tho' no credit doubting Wits may give?
40 The Fair and Innocent shall still believe.
Know then, unnumber'd Spirits round thee fly,
The light Militia of the lower sky:
These, tho' unseen, are ever on the wing,
Hang o'er the Box, and hover round the Ring.[1]

*   *   *

1. A fashionable parade in Hyde Park.

[*Belinda prepares for the day*]

'Of these am I, who thy protection claim,
A watchful sprite, and Ariel is my name.
Late, as I rang'd the crystal wilds of air,
In the clear Mirror of thy ruling Star
I saw, alas! some dread event impend,
50   Ere to the main this morning sun descend,
But heav'n reveals not what, or how, or where:
Warn'd by the Sylph, oh pious maid, beware!
This to disclose is all thy guardian can:
Beware of all, but most beware of Man!'
    He said; when Shock,[1] who thought she slept too long,
Leap'd up, and wak'd his mistress with his tongue.
'Twas then, Belinda, if report say true,
Thy eyes first open'd on a Billet-doux;[2]
Wounds, Charms, and Ardours, were no sooner read,
60   But all the Vision vanish'd from thy head.
    And now, unveil'd, the Toilet stands display'd,
Each silver Vase in mystic order laid.
First, rob'd in white, the Nymph intent adores,
With head uncover'd, the Cosmetic pow'rs.
A heav'nly Image in the glass appears,
To that she bends, to that her eyes she rears;
Th' inferior Priestess, at her altar's side,
Trembling begins the sacred rites of Pride
Unnumber'd treasures ope at once, and here
70   The various off'rings of the world appear;
From each she nicely culls with curious toil,
And decks the Goddess with the glitt'ring spoil.
This casket India's glowing gems unlocks,
And all Arabia breathes from yonder box.

1. Belinda's lap-dog.
2. Love-letter.

The Tortoise here and Elephant unite,
Transform'd to combs, the speckled, and the white.
Here files of pins extend their shining rows,
Puffs, Powders, Patches, Bibles, Billet-doux.
Now awful Beauty puts on all its arms;
80 The fair each moment rises in her charms,
Repairs her smiles, awakens ev'ry grace,
And calls forth all the wonders of her face;
Sees by degrees a purer blush arise,
And keener lightnings quicken in her eyes.
The busy Sylphs surround their darling care,
These set the head, and those divide the hair,
Some fold the sleeve, whilst others plait the gown;
And Betty's[1] prais'd for labours not her own.

CANTO II

[The Baron is tempted by the Locks]

Not with more glories, in th' ethereal plain,
90 The Sun first rises o'er the purpled main,
Than, issuing forth, the rival of his beams
Launch'd on the bosom of the silver Thames.
Fair Nymphs, and well-drest Youths around her shone,
But ev'ry eye was fix'd on her alone.
On her white breast a sparkling Cross she wore,
Which Jews might kiss, and Infidels adore.
Her lively looks a sprightly mind disclose,
Quick as her eyes, and as unfix'd as those:
Favours to none, to all she smiles extends;
100 Oft she rejects, but never once offends.
Bright as the sun, her eyes the gazers strike,
And, like the sun, they shine on all alike.

1. Belinda's maid.

Yet graceful ease, and sweetness void of pride,
Might hide her faults, if Belles had faults to hide:
If to her share some female errors fall,
Look on her face, and you'll forget 'em all.

    This Nymph, to the destruction of mankind,
Nourish'd two Locks, which graceful hung behind
In equal curls, and well conspir'd to deck
110 With shining ringlets the smooth iv'ry neck.
Love in these labyrinths his slaves detains,
And mighty hearts are held in slender chains.
With hairy springes[1] we the birds betray,
Slight lines of hair surprise the finny prey,
Fair tresses Man's imperial race ensnare,
And Beauty draws us with a single hair.

    The adventurous Baron the bright Locks admir'd,
He saw, he wish'd, and to the Prize aspir'd
Resolv'd to win, he meditates the way,
120 By force to ravish, or by fraud betray.
For when success a lover's toil attends,
Few ask, if fraud or force attain'd his ends.

*   *   *

[*Ariel puts the sprites on guard*]

    'Our humbler province is to tend the Fair,
Not a less pleasing, tho' less glorious care.
To save the powder from too rude a gale,
Nor let th' imprison'd essences exhale,
To draw fresh colours from the vernal flow'rs;
To steal from rainbows, e'er they drop in show'rs
A brighter wash; to curl their waving hairs,
130 Assist their blushes, and inspire their airs;
Nay oft, in dreams, invention we bestow,
To change a Flounce, or add a Furbelow.

    1. Traps.

'This day, black Omens threat the brightest Fair
That e'er deserv'd a watchful spirit's care;
Some dire disaster, or by force, or slight;
But what, or where, the fates have wrapt in night.
Whether the nymph shall break Diana's law,[1]
Or some frail China jar receive a flaw;
Or stain her honour, or her new brocade;
140   Forget her pray'rs, or miss a masquerade;
Or lose her heart, or necklace, at a ball;
Or whether Heav'n has doom'd that Shock must fall.
Haste then, ye spirits! to your charge repair:
The flutt'ring fan be Zephyretta's care;
The drops to thee, Brillante, we consign;
And, Momentilla, let the watch be thine;
Do thou, Crispissa, tend her fav'rite Lock;
Ariel himself shall be the guard of Shock.

'To fifty chosen Sylphs, of special note,
150   We trust th' important charge, the Petticoat:
Oft have we known that seven-fold fence to fail,
Tho' stiff with hoops, and arm'd with ribs of whale;
Form a strong line about the silver bound,
And guard the wide circumference around.

'Whatever spirit, careless of his charge,
His post neglects, or leaves the fair at large,
Shall feel sharp vengeance soon o'ertake his sins,
Be stop'd in vials, or transfix'd with pins;
Or plung'd in lakes of bitter washes lie,
160   Or wedg'd whole ages in a bodkin's[2] eye:
Gums and Pomatums[3] shall his flight restrain,
While, clog'd, he beats his silken wings in vain;
Or Alum styptics with contracting pow'r
Shrink his thin essence like a rivel'd flow'r:

1. Become unchaste.
2. Needle.
3. Creams.

Or, as Ixion fix'd, the wretch shall feel
The giddy motion of the whirling Mill,
In fumes of burning Chocolate shall glow,
And tremble at the sea that froths below!'
    He spoke; the spirits from the sails descend;
170 Some, orb in orb, around the nymph extend;
Some thrid the mazy ringlets of her hair;
Some hang upon the pendants of her ear;
With beating hearts the dire event they wait,
Anxious, and trembling for the birth of Fate.

CANTO III

[*The game of cards*]

Close by those meads, for ever crown'd with flow'rs,
Where Thames with pride surveys his rising tow'rs,
There stands a structure of majestic frame,
Which from the neighb'ring Hampton takes its name.
Here Britain's statesmen oft the fall foredoom
180 Of foreign Tyrants, and of Nymphs at home;
Here thou, great ANNA![1] whom three realms obey,
Dost sometimes counsel take – and sometimes Tea.
    Hither the Heroes and the Nymphs resort,
To taste awhile the pleasures of a Court;
In various talk th' instructive hours they past,
Who gave the ball, or paid the visit last;
One speaks the glory of the British Queen,
And one describes a charming Indian screen;
A third interprets motions, looks, and eyes;
190 At ev'ry word a reputation dies.
Snuff, or the fan, supply each pause of chat,
With singing, laughing, ogling, *and all that*.

1. Queen Anne.

Mean while, declining from the noon of day,
The sun obliquely shoots his burning ray;
The hungry Judges soon the sentence sign,
And wretches hang that Jury-men may dine;
The merchant from th' Exchange returns in peace,
And the long labours of the Toilet cease.
Belinda now, whom thirst of fame invites,
200 Burns to encounter two advent'rous Knights,
At Ombre[1] singly to decide their doom;
And swells her breast with conquests yet to come.
Straight the three bands prepare in arms to join,
Each band the number of the sacred Nine.
Soon as she spreads her hand, th' aërial guard
Descend, and sit on each important card:
First Ariel perch'd upon a Matadore,[2]
Then each according to the rank they bore;
For Sylphs, yet mindful of their ancient race,
210 Are, as when women, wond'rous fond of place.
    Behold, four Kings in majesty rever'd,
With hoary whiskers and a forky beard;
And four fair Queens whose hands sustain a flow'r,
Th' expressive emblem of their softer pow'r;
Four Knaves in garbs succinct, a trusty band,
Caps on their heads, and halberts in their hand;
And particolour'd troops, a shining train,
Draw forth to combat on the velvet plain.
    The skilful Nymph reviews her force with care:
220 'Let Spades be trumps!' she said, and trumps they were.
    Now move to war her sable Matadores,
In show like leaders of the swarthy Moors.
Spadillio[3] first, unconquerable Lord!
Led off two captive trumps, and swept the board.

1. A card game for three players using a pack of forty cards and
dealing nine cards each to begin.
2. Spades.
3. Ace of Spades.

As many more Manillio[1] forc'd to yield,
And march'd a victor from the verdant field.
Him Basto[2] follow'd, but his fate more hard
Gain'd but one trump and one Plebeian card.
With his broad sabre next, a chief in years,
230   The hoary Majesty of Spades appears,
Puts forth one manly leg, to sight reveal'd,
The rest, his many-colour'd robe conceal'd.
The rebel Knave, who dares his prince engage,
Proves the just victim of his royal rage.
Ev'n mighty Pam,[3] that Kings and Queens o'er-threw
And mow'd down armies in the fights of Loo,[4]
Sad chance of war! now destitute of aid,
Falls undistinguish'd by the victor Spade!
    Thus far both armies to Belinda yield;
240   Now to the Baron fate inclines the field.
His warlike Amazon her host invades,
Th' imperial consort of the crown of Spades.
The Club's black Tyrant first her victim dy'd,
Spite of his haughty mien, and barb'rous pride:
What boots the regal circle on his head,
His giant limbs, in state unwieldy spread;
That long behind he trails his pompous robe,
And, of all monarchs, only grasps the globe?
    The Baron now his Diamonds pours apace;
250   Th' embroider'd King who shows but half his face,
And his refulgent Queen, with pow'rs combin'd,
Of broken troops an easy conquest find.
Clubs, Diamonds, Hearts, in wild disorder seen,
With throngs promiscuous strow the level green.
Thus when dispers'd a routed army runs,
Of Asia's troops, and Afric's sable sons,

1. Two of Spades.
2. Ace of Clubs.
3. Knave of Clubs.
4. Another card game in which the Knave of Clubs was a powerful card.

With like confusion different nations fly,
Of various habit and of various dye;
The pierc'd battalions disunited fall,
In heaps on heaps; one fate o'erwhelms them all.
    The Knave of Diamonds tries his wily arts,
And wins (oh shameful chance!) the Queen of Hearts.
At this, the blood the virgin's cheek forsook,
A livid paleness spreads o'er all her look;
She sees, and trembles at th' approaching ill,
Just in the jaws of ruin, and Codille.[1]
And now, (as oft in some distemper'd State)
On one nice Trick depends the gen'ral fate:
An Ace of Hearts steps forth: the King unseen
Lurk'd in her hand, and mourn'd his captive Queen:
He springs to vengeance with an eager pace,
And falls like thunder on the prostrate Ace.
The nymph, exulting, fills with shouts the sky;
The walls, the woods, and long canals reply.
    O thoughtless mortals! ever blind to fate,
Too soon dejected, and too soon elate.
Sudden these honours shall be snatch'd away,
And curs'd for ever this victorious day.
    For lo! the board with cups and spoons is crown'd,
The berries crackle, and the mill turns round;
On shining altars of Japan they raise
The silver lamp; the fiery spirits blaze:
From silver spouts the grateful liquors glide,
While China's earth receives the smoking tide:
At once they gratify their sense and taste,
And frequent cups prolong the rich repast.
Straight hover round the Fair her airy band;
Some, as she sipp'd, the fuming liquor fann'd,
Some o'er her lap their careful plumes display'd,
Trembling, and conscious of the rich brocade.

1. Loss of the game.

Coffee (which makes the politician wise,
And see through all things with his half-shut eyes)
Sent up in vapours to the Baron's brain
New stratagems, the radiant Lock to gain.
Ah cease, rash youth! desist ere 'tis too late,
Fear the just Gods, and think of Scylla's Fate!
Chang'd to a bird, and sent to flit in air,
She dearly pays for Nisus' injur'd hair!
    But when to mischief mortals bend their will,
300 How soon they find fit instruments of ill?
Just then, Clarissa drew with tempting grace
A two-edg'd weapon from her shining case:
So Ladies in Romance assist their Knight,
Present the spear, and arm him for the fight.
He takes the gift with rev'rence, and extends
The little engine on his fingers' ends;
This just behind Belinda's neck he spread,
As o'er the fragrant steams she bends her head.
Swift to the Lock a thousand Sprites repair,
310 A thousand wings, by turns, blow back the hair;
And thrice they twitch'd the diamond in her ear;
Thrice she look'd back, and thrice the foe drew near.
Just in that instant, anxious Ariel sought
The close recesses of the Virgin's thought;
As on the nosegay in her breast reclin'd,
He watch'd th' ideas rising in her mind,
Sudden he view'd, in spite of all her art,
An earthly Lover lurking at her heart.
Amaz'd, confus'd, he found his pow'r expir'd,
320 Resign'd to fate, and with a sigh retir'd.
    The Peer now spreads the glitt'ring Forfex wide,
T' inclose the Lock; now joins it, to divide.
Ev'n then, before the fatal engine clos'd,
A wretched Sylph too fondly interpos'd;
Fate urg'd the shears, and cut the Sylph in twain,
(But airy substance soon unites again)
The meeting points the sacred hair dissever

From the fair head, for ever, and for ever!
   Then flash'd the living lightning from her eyes,
330 And screams of horror rend th' affrighted skies.
Not louder shrieks to pitying heav'n are cast,
When husbands, or when lap-dogs breathe their last;
Or when rich China vessels, fall'n from high,
In glitt'ring dust and painted fragments lie!
   'Let wreaths of triumph now my temples twine,
(The Victor cry'd) the glorious Prize is mine!
While fish in streams, or birds delight in air,
Or in a coach-and-six the British Fair,
As long as *Atalantis*[1] shall be read,
340 Or the small pillow grace a Lady's bed,
While visits shall be paid on solemn days,
When num'rous wax-lights in bright order blaze,
While nymphs take treats, or assignations give,
So long my honour, name, and praise shall live!'
   What Time would spare, from Steel receives its date,
And monuments, like men, submit to fate!
Steel could the labour of the Gods destroy,
And strike to dust th' imperial tow'rs of Troy;
Steel could the works of mortal pride confound,
350 And hew triumphal arches to the ground.
What wonder then, fair nymph! thy hairs should feel
The conqu'ring force of unresisted Steel?

CANTO IV

[*Belinda laments the loss of the Lock*]

        *   *   *

Then see! the nymph in beauteous grief appears,
Her eyes half-languishing, half-drown'd in tears;

1. A scandalous novel.

On her heav'd bosom hung her drooping head,
Which, with a sigh, she rais'd; and thus she said.
    'For ever curs'd be this detested day,
Which snatch'd my best, my fav'rite curl away!
Happy! ah ten times happy had I been,
360 If Hampton-Court these eyes had never seen!
Yet am not I the first mistaken maid,
By love of Courts to num'rous ills betray'd.
Oh had I rather un-admir'd remain'd
In some lone isle, or distant Northern land;
Where the gilt chariot never marks the way,
When none learn Ombre, none ere taste Bohea![1]
There kept my charms conceal'd from mortal eye,
Like roses, that in deserts bloom and die.
What mov'd my mind with youthful Lords to roam?
370 O had I stay'd, and said my pray'rs at home!
'Twas this, the morning omens seem'd to tell;
Thrice from my trembling hand the patch-box[2] fell;
The tott'ring China shook without a wind,
Nay Poll sat mute, and Shock was most unkind!
A Sylph too warn'd me of the threats of fate,
In mystic visions, now believ'd too late!
See the poor remnants of these slighted hairs!
My hands shall rend what ev'n thy rapine spares:
These in two sable ringlets taught to break,
380 Once gave new beauties to the snowy neck;
The sister-lock now sits, uncouth, alone,
And in its fellow's fate foresees its own;
Uncurl'd it hangs, the fatal shears demands,
And tempts, once more, thy sacrilegious hands.
Oh hadst thou, cruel! been content to seize
Hairs less in sight, or any hairs but these!

1. The best quality tea.
2. Decorative patches were a popular ornament for the face.

CANTO V

[*The battle of the beaux and the belles*]

She said: the pitying audience melt in tears,
But Fate and Jove had stopp'd the Baron's ears.
In vain Thalestris with reproach assails,
390   For who can move when fair Belinda fails?

       *   *   *

'To arms, to arms!' the fierce Virago cries,
And swift as lightning to the combat flies.
All side in parties and begin th' attack;
Fans clap, silks rustle, and tough whalebones crack;
Heroes' and Heroines' shouts confus'dly rise,
And bass and treble voices strike the skies.
No common weapons in their hands are found,
Like Gods they fight, nor dread a mortal wound.

       *   *   *

   See fierce Belinda on the Baron flies,
400   With more than usual lightning in her eyes:
Nor fear'd the chief th' unequal fight to try,
Who sought no more than on his foe to die.
But this bold Lord, with manly strength endued,
She with one finger and a thumb subdued:
Just where the breath of life his nostrils drew,
A charge of snuff the wily virgin threw;
The Gnomes direct, to ev'ry atom just,
The pungent grains of titillating dust.
Sudden, with starting tears each eye o'erflows,
410   And the high dome re-echoes to his nose.
   'Now meet thy fate!' incens'd Belinda cry'd,
And drew a deadly bodkin from her side.

       *   *   *

'Restore the Lock!' she cries; and all around
'Restore the Lock!' the vaulted roofs rebound.
Not fierce Othello in so loud a strain
Roar'd for the handkerchief that caus'd his pain.
But see how oft ambitious aims are cross'd,
And chiefs contend till all the prize is lost!
The Lock, obtain'd with guilt and kept with pain,
420   In ev'ry place is sought, but sought in vain:
With such a prize no mortal must be blest,
So Heav'n decrees! with Heav'n who can contest?

*   *   *

But trust the Muse – she saw it upward rise,
Tho' mark'd by none but quick, poetic eyes:

*   *   *

A sudden Star, it shot through liquid air,
And drew behind a radiant trail of hair.
Not Berenice's Locks[1] first rose so bright,
The heav'ns bespangling with dishevel'd light.
The Sylphs behold it kindling as it flies,
430   And pleas'd pursue its progress through the skies.

*   *   *

Then cease, bright Nymph! to mourn thy ravish'd hair,
Which adds new glory to the shining sphere!
Not all the tresses that fair head can boast,
Shall draw such envy as the Lock you lost.
For, after all the murders of your eye,
When, after millions slain, yourself shall die;

1. The wife of an Egyptian king who vowed to sacrifice her hair to
the gods if her husband returned home victorious. She hung it in the
temple, but it was stolen and the king was told that the winds had
wafted it to heaven and turned it into a group of stars.

When those fair suns shall set, as set they must,
And all those tresses shall be laid in dust,
This Lock, the Muse shall consecrate to fame,
440 And 'midst the stars inscribe Belinda's name.

from AN ESSAY ON CRITICISM

I

'Tis hard to say, if greater want' of skill
Appear in writing or in judging ill;
But, of the two, less dang'rous is th' offence
To tire our patience, than mislead our sense.
Some few in that, but numbers err in this;
Ten censure wrong for one who writes amiss;
A fool might once himself alone expose,
Now one in verse makes many more in prose.
     'Tis with our judgments as our watches, none
10 Go just alike, yet each believes his own.
In Poets as true genius is but rare,
True Taste as seldom is the Critic's share;
Both must alike from Heav'n derive their light,
These born to judge, as well as those to write.
Let such teach others who themselves excel,
And censure freely who have written well.
Authors are partial to their wit, 'tis true,
But are not Critics to their judgment too?

*   *   *

II

Of all the causes which conspire to blind
20 Man's erring judgment, and misguide the mind,
What the weak head with strongest bias rules,
Is *Pride*, the never-failing vice of fools.
Whatever Nature has in worth deny'd,
She gives in large recruits of needful Pride;

For as in bodies, thus in souls, we find
What wants in blood and spirits, swell'd with wind:
Pride, where Wit fails, steps in to our defence,
And fills up all the mighty Void of sense:
If once right reason drives that cloud away,
30   Truth breaks upon us with resistless day.
Trust not yourself; but your defects to know,
Make use of ev'ry friend – and ev'ry foe.
      A *little learning* is a dang'rous thing;
Drink deep, or taste not the Pierian spring:[1]
There shallow draughts intoxicate the brain,
And drinking largely sobers us again.
Fir'd at first sight with what the Muse imparts,
In fearless youth we tempt the heights of Arts,
While from the bounded level of our mind,
40   Short views we take, nor see the lengths behind;
But, more advanc'd, behold with strange surprise,
New distant scenes of endless science rise!
So pleas'd at first the tow'ring Alps we try,
Mount o'er the vales, and seem to tread the sky,
Th' eternal snows appear already past,
And the first clouds and mountains seem the last:
But, those attain'd, we tremble to survey
The growing labours of the lengthen'd way,
Th' increasing prospect tires our wand'ring eyes,
50   Hills peep o'er hills, and Alps on Alps arise!
      A perfect Judge will read each work of Wit
With the same spirit that its author writ:
Survey the WHOLE, nor seek slight faults to find
Where nature moves, and rapture warms the mind;
Nor lose, for that malignant dull delight,
The gen'rous pleasure to be charm'd with wit.
But in such lays as neither ebb nor flow,
Correctly cold, and regularly low,

1. The fountain of knowledge.

That shunning faults, one quiet tenor keep,
60 We cannot blame indeed – but we may sleep.
In Wit, as Nature, what affects our hearts
Is not th' exactness of peculiar parts;
'Tis not a lip, or eye, we beauty call,
But the joint force and full result of all.
Thus when we view some well-proportion'd dome,
(The world's just wonder, and ev'n thine, O Rome!)
No single parts unequally surprise,
All comes united to th' admiring eyes;
No monstrous height, or breadth, or length appear;
70 The Whole at once is bold, and regular.
        Whoever thinks a faultless piece to see,
Thinks what ne'er was, nor is, nor e'er shall be.
In ev'ry work regard the writer's End,
Since none can compass more than they intend;
And if the means be just, the conduct true,
Applause, in spight of trivial faults, is due.
As men of breeding, sometimes men of wit,
T' avoid great errors, must the less commit:
Neglect the rules each verbal Critic lays,
80 For not to know some trifles is a praise.
Most Critics, fond of some subservient art,
Still make the Whole depend upon a Part:
They talk of principles, but notions prize,
And all to one lov'd Folly sacrifice.

                *   *   *

Some to *Conceit*[1] alone their taste confine,
And glitt'ring thoughts struck out at ev'ry line;
Pleas'd with a work where nothing's just or fit;
One glaring Chaos and wild heap of wit.
Poets, like painters, thus, unskill'd to trace
90 The naked nature and the living grace,

1. Complicated metaphor

With gold and jewels cover ev'ry part,
And hide with ornaments their want of art.
True Wit is Nature to advantage dress'd;
What oft was thought, but ne'er so well express'd;
Something, whose truth convinc'd at sight we find,
That gives us back the image of our mind.
As shades more sweetly recommend the light,
So modest plainness sets off sprightly wit.
For works may have more wit than does 'em good,
100 As bodies perish through excess of blood.

    Others for *Language* all their care express,
And value books, as women men, for dress:
Their praise is still, – 'The Style is excellent';
The Sense, they humbly take upon content.
Words are like leaves, and where they most abound,
Much fruit of sense beneath is rarely found.
False Eloquence, like the prismatic glass,
Its gaudy colours spreads on ev'ry place;
The face of Nature we no more survey,
110 All glares alike, without distinction gay;
But true Expression, like th' unchanging Sun,
Clears, and improves whate'er it shines upon;
It gilds all objects, but it alters none.
Expression is the dress of thought, and still
Appears more decent, as more suitable;
A vile conceit in pompous words express'd,
Is like a clown in regal purple dress'd:
For diff'rent styles with diff'rent subjects sort,
As sev'ral garbs with country, town, and court.
120 Some by old words to fame have made pretence,
Ancients in phrase, mere moderns in their sense;
Such labour'd nothings, in so strange a style,
Amaze th' unlearn'd, and make the learned smile.

*   *   *

In words, as fashions, the same rule will hold;
Alike fantastic, if too new, or old:
Be not the first by whom the new are try'd,
Nor yet the last to lay the old aside.
    But most by Numbers judge a Poet's song;
And smooth or rough, with them, is right or wrong:
130 In the bright Muse, tho' thousand charms conspire,
Her voice is all these tuneful fools admire;
Who haunt Parnassus but to please their ear,
Not mend their minds; as some to church repair,
Not for the doctrine, but the music there.
These equal syllables alone require,
Tho' oft the ear the open vowels tire;
While expletives their feeble aid do join,
And ten low words oft creep in one dull line:
While they ring round the same unvary'd chimes,
140 With sure returns of still expected rhymes;
Where'er you find 'the cooling western breeze',
In the next line, it 'whispers through the trees':
If crystal streams 'with pleasing murmurs creep',
The reader's threaten'd (not in vain) with 'sleep':
Then, at the last and only couplet fraught
With some unmeaning thing they call a thought,
A needless Alexandrine[1] ends the song,
That, like a wounded snake, drags its slow length along.
Leave such to tune their own dull rhymes, and know
150 What's roundly smooth, or languishingly slow;
And praise the easy vigour of a line,
Where Denham's[2] strength and Waller's[3] sweetness join.
True ease in writing comes from art, not chance,
As those move easiest who have learn'd to dance.
'Tis not enough no harshness gives offence,
The sound must seem an Echo to the sense;

1. A twelve-syllable line.
2. Sir John Denham, a contemporary poet.
3. Edmund Waller, a favourite poet of Pope's.

Soft is the strain when Zephyr gently blows,
And the smooth stream in smoother numbers flows:
But when loud surges lash the sounding shore,
160   The hoarse, rough verse should like the torrent roar.
When Ajax strives some rock's vast weight to throw,
The line too labours, and the words move slow;
Not so, when swift Camilla scours the plain,
Flies o'er th' unbending corn, and skims along the main.
Hear how Timotheus' vary'd lays surprize,[1]
And bid alternate passions fall and rise!
While at each change, the son of Lybian Jove
Now burns with glory, and then melts with love;
Now his fierce eyes with sparkling fury glow,
170   Now sighs steal out, and tears begin to flow:
Persians and Greeks like turns of nature found,
And the World's victor stood subdued by Sound!
The power of Music all our hearts allow,
And what Timotheus was, is DRYDEN now.
     Avoid Extremes; and shun the fault of such
Who still are pleas'd too little or too much.
At ev'ry trifle scorn to take offence:
That always shows great pride, or little sense;
Those heads, as stomachs, are not sure the best
180   Which nauseate all, and nothing can digest.
Yet let not each gay Turn thy rapture move,
For fools admire, but men of sense approve:
As things seem large which we through mists descry,
Dulness is ever apt to magnify.
     Some foreign writers, some our own despise;
The Ancients only, or the Moderns prize.
Thus Wit, like Faith, by each man is apply'd
To one small sect, and all are damn'd beside.
Meanly they seek the blessing to confine,
190   And force that sun but on a part to shine,

     1. See 'Alexander's Feast' by Dryden, where Timotheus is the musician
described playing before Alexander the Great.

Which not alone the southern wit sublimes,
But ripens spirits in cold northern climes;
Which from the first has shone on ages past,
Enlights the present, and shall warm the last;
Tho' each may feel increases and decays,
And see now clearer and now darker days.
Regard not then if Wit be old or new,
But blame the false, and value still the true.

Thomas Gray

(1716–1771)

Thomas Gray was born in London. His family was not particularly wealthy, and he was the only one of their twelve children to survive infancy. When he was nine, he went to Eton College, where his uncle was one of the masters. His schooldays were a time he recalled with great happiness, as is evident in his 'Ode on a Distant Prospect of Eton College'. Gray was a naturally scholarly boy who spent his time reading great literature and avoiding athletics. He made three close friends: Horace Walpole, Thomas Ashton and Richard West, and the four of them prided themselves on their sense of style, their sense of humour and their appreciation of beauty.

In 1734 Gray went to Cambridge, but found the curriculum dull and wrote disparagingly to his friends of the masters ('mad with Pride') and the Fellows ('sleepy, drunken, dull, illiterate Things'). He spent his time as an undergraduate reading classical and modern literature and playing Vivaldi and Scarlatti on the harpsichord for relaxation.

Gray toured Europe with Walpole, his old school friend, in 1739, but they fell out because Walpole wanted to attend fashionable parties and Gray wanted to visit all the antiquities. He began seriously writing poems in 1742 after his friend Richard West died. He moved to Cambridge and began a self-imposed programme of literary study, becoming one of the most learned men of his time. A very shy man, he declined the poet laureateship when it was offered to him. He was rather eccentric, and subject to much teasing from undergraduates. Eventually, he was made Regius Professor of Modern History, but never delivered any lectures.

Gray was so self-critical and fearful of failure that he only published thirteen poems during his lifetime, and once wrote that he feared his collected works would be 'mistaken for the works of a flea'. Gray's friend Walpole said: 'He never wrote anything easily but things of Humour,' and this is evident in the mock elegy he wrote to commemorate the death by drowning of Walpole's cat Selima, 'On a favourite Cat, drowned in a tub of Gold fishes'. Walpole later displayed the fatal china vase on a pedestal at his house in Strawberry Hill. Gray's surviving letters also show his sharp observation and his playful sense of humour.

Much to Gray's distress, because he hated publicity, 'Elegy written in a Country Churchyard' became a literary sensation when it was published in 1751. Its reflective, calm and stoic tone was greatly admired, and it was pirated, imitated, quoted and translated into Latin and Greek. It remains a popular poem to this day.

Gray himself considered that his two Pindaric odes, 'The Progress of Poesy' and 'The Bard' were his best works. Pindaric odes are written with great fire and passion, unlike the calmer and more reflective Horatian odes such as 'Ode on a Distant Prospect of Eton College'. 'The Bard' tells of a wild Welsh poet prophesying in detail the downfall of the house of Plantagenet to Edward I after the conquest of Wales. It is very melodramatic, and ends with the bard hurling himself to his death from the top of a mountain.

In the intervals between his scholastic duties, Gray travelled widely throughout Britain in search of picturesque scenery and ancient monuments. These things were not generally valued in the early eighteenth century, when the popular taste ran to classical styles in architecture and literature and people liked their scenery tame and well tended. Some people have seen Gray's writings on this topic, and the Gothic details that appear in his 'Elegy', as the first foreshadowing of the Romantic movement that dominated the early nineteenth century, when Wordsworth and the other Lake poets had taught people to value the picturesque, the sublime and the Gothic.

When Gray died in 1771, he was buried beside his mother in the graveyard of the church in Stoke Poges which was the setting for his 'Elegy', and his grave can be seen there to this day.

Ode on a Distant Prospect of Eton College

Ye distant spires, ye antique towers
    That crown the watery glade,
Where grateful Science[1] still adores
    Her Henry's[2] holy shade;
And ye, that from the stately brow
Of Windsor's heights th' expanse below
Of grove, of lawn, of mead survey,
Whose turf, whose shade, whose flowers among
Wanders the hoary Thames along
10   His silver-winding way:

Ah happy hills! ah pleasing shade!
    Ah fields beloved in vain!
Where once my careless childhood stray'd,
    A stranger yet to pain!
I feel the gales that from ye blow
A momentary bliss bestow,
As waving fresh their gladsome wing
My weary soul they seem to soothe,
And, redolent of joy and youth,
20   To breathe a second spring.

Say, Father Thames, for thou hast seen
    Full many a sprightly race[3]
Disporting on thy margent[4] green
    The paths of pleasure trace;
Who foremost now delight to cleave

1. Knowledge.
2. Henry VI founded Eton in 1440.
3. Generation.
4. Margin (river bank).

With pliant arm, thy glassy wave?
The captive linnet which enthral?
What idle progeny succeed
To chase the rolling circle's speed
30   Or urge the flying ball?

While some on earnest business bent
   Their murmuring labours ply
'Gainst graver hours that bring constraint
   To sweeten liberty:
Some bold adventurers disdain
The limits of their little reign
And unknown regions dare descry:
Still as they run they look behind,
They hear a voice in every wind,
40   And snatch a fearful joy.

Gay hope is theirs by fancy fed,
   Less pleasing when possessed
The tear forgot as soon as shed,
   The sunshine of the breast:
Theirs buxom health, of rosy hue,
Wild wit, invention ever new,
And lively cheer, of vigour born;
The thoughtless day, the easy night,
The spirits pure, the slumbers light
50   That fly th' approach of morn.

Alas! regardless of their doom
   The little victims play;
No sense have they of ills to come
   Nor care beyond to-day:
Yet see how all around 'em wait
The ministers of human fate
And black Misfortune's baleful train!
Ah show them where in ambush stand
To seize their prey, the murderous band!
60   Ah, tell them they are men!

These shall the fury Passions tear,
   The vultures of the mind,
Disdainful Anger, pallid Fear,
   And Shame that sculks behind;
Or pining Love shall waste their youth,
Or Jealousy with rankling tooth
That inly gnaws the secret heart,
And Envy wan, and faded Care,
Grim-visaged comfortless Despair,
70   And Sorrow's piercing dart.

Ambition this shall tempt to rise,
   Then whirl the wretch from high
To bitter Scorn a sacrifice
   And grinning Infamy.
The stings of Falsehood those shall try
And hard Unkindness' alter'd eye,
That mocks the tear it forced to flow;
And keen Remorse with blood defiled,
And moody Madness laughing wild
80   Amid severest woe.

Lo, in the vale of years beneath
   A grisly troop are seen,
The painful family of Death,
   More hideous than their queen:
This racks the joints, this fires the veins,
That every labouring sinew strains,
Those in the deeper vitals rage:
Lo! Poverty, to fill the band,
That numbs the soul with icy hand,
90   And slow-consuming Age.

To each his sufferings: all are men,
   Condemn'd alike to groan;
The tender for another's pain,
   Th' unfeeling for his own.
Yet, ah! why should they know their fate,

Since sorrow never comes too late,
And happiness too swiftly flies?
Thought would destroy their paradise.
No more; – where ignorance is bliss,
100   'Tis folly to be wise.

On a favourite Cat, drowned in a tub of Gold fishes

'Twas on a lofty vase's side,
Where China's gayest art had dyed
The azure flowers that blow,
Demurest of the tabby kind
The pensive Selima, reclined,
Gazed on the lake below.

Her conscious tail her joy declared:
The fair round face, the snowy beard,
The velvet of her paws,
10   Her coat that with the tortoise vies,
Her ears of jet, and emerald eyes –
She saw, and purr'd applause.

Still had she gazed, but 'midst the tide
Two angel forms were seen to glide,
The Genii of the stream:
Their scaly armour's Tyrian[1] hue
Through richest purple, to the view
Betray'd a golden gleam.

The hapless Nymph with wonder saw:
20   A whisker first, and then a claw
With many an ardent wish
She stretch'd, in vain, to reach the prize –
What female heart can gold despise?
What Cat's averse to fish?

1. Purple, after the dye made in ancient Tyre.

Presumptuous maid! with looks intent
Again she stretch'd, again she bent,
Nor knew the gulf between –
Malignant Fate sat by and smiled –
The slippery verge her feet beguiled;
30 She tumbled headlong in!

Eight times emerging from the flood
She mew'd to every watery God
Some speedy aid to send: –
No Dolphin came, no Nereid[1] stirr'd,
Nor cruel Tom nor Susan[2] heard –
A favourite has no friend!

From hence, ye Beauties! undeceived
Know one false step is ne'er retrieved,
And be with caution bold:
40 Not all that tempts your wandering eyes
And heedless hearts, is lawful prize,
Nor all that glisters, gold!

1. Sea nymph.
2. Servants.

Elegy written in a Country Churchyard

The curfew tolls the knell of parting day,
The lowing herd wind slowly o'er the lea,
The ploughman homeward plods his weary way,
And leaves the world to darkness and to me.

Now fades the glimmering landscape on the sight,
And all the air a solemn stillness holds,
Save where the beetle wheels his droning flight,
And drowsy tinklings lull the distant folds:

Save that from yonder ivy-mantled tower
10   The moping owl does to the moon complain
Of such as, wandering near her secret bower,
Molest her ancient solitary reign.

Beneath those rugged elms, that yew-tree's shade
Where heaves the turf in many a mouldering heap,
Each in his narrow cell for ever laid,
The rude forefathers of the hamlet sleep.

The breezy call of incense-breathing morn,
The swallow twittering from the straw-built shed,
The cock's shrill clarion, or the echoing horn,
20   No more shall rouse them from their lowly bed.

For them no more the blazing hearth shall burn
Or busy housewife ply her evening care:
No children run to lisp their sire's return,
Or climb his knees the envied kiss to share.

Oft did the harvest to their sickle yield,
Their furrow oft the stubborn glebe[1] has broke;
How jocund[2] did they drive their team afield!
How bow'd the woods beneath their sturdy stroke!

Let not ambition mock their useful toil,
30   Their homely joys, and destiny obscure;
Nor grandeur hear with a disdainful smile
The short and simple annals[3] of the poor.

The boast of heraldry, the pomp of power,
And all that beauty, all that wealth e'er gave,
Awaits alike th' inevitable hour: –
The paths of glory lead but to the grave.

1. Soil.
2. Cheerful.
3. Stories.

Nor you, ye proud, impute to these the fault
If memory o'er their tomb no trophies raise,
Where through the long-drawn aisle and fretted[1] vault
40   The pealing anthem swells the note of praise.

Can storied urn or animated bust
Back to its mansion call the fleeting breath?
Can honour's voice provoke the silent dust,
Or flattery soothe the dull cold ear of death?

Perhaps in this neglected spot is laid
Some heart once pregnant with celestial fire;
Hands, that the rod of empire might have sway'd,
Or waked to extasy the living lyre:

But knowledge to their eyes her ample page
50   Rich with the spoils of time, did ne'er unroll;
Chill penury repress'd their noble rage,
And froze the genial current of the soul.

Full many a gem of purest ray serene
The dark unfathom'd caves of ocean bear:
Full many a flower is born to blush unseen,
And waste its sweetness on the desert air.

Some village-Hampden,[2] that with dauntless breast
The little tyrant of his fields withstood,
Some mute inglorious Milton here may rest,
60   Some Cromwell, guiltless of his country's blood.

Th' applause of listening senates to command,
The threats of pain and ruin to despise,
To scatter plenty o'er a smiling land,
And read their history in a nation's eyes

1. Covered with carvings in relief.
2. John Hampden (1594–1643), English politician and patriot known
for his resistance to Charles I during the Civil War.

Their lot forbad: nor circumscribed alone
Their growing virtues, but their crimes confined;
Forbad to wade thro' slaughter to a throne,
And shut the gates of mercy on mankind;

70 The struggling pangs of conscious truth to hide,
To quench the blushes of ingenuous shame,
Or heap the shrine of luxury and pride
With incense kindled at the Muse's flame.

Far from the madding crowd's ignoble strife
Their sober wishes never learn'd to stray;
Along the cool sequester'd vale of life
They kept the noiseless tenour of their way.

Yet e'en these bones from insult to protect
Some frail memorial still erected nigh,
With uncouth rhymes and shapeless sculpture deck'd,
80 Implores the passing tribute of a sigh.

Their name, their years, spelt by th' unletter'd Muse,
The place of fame and elegy supply:
And many a holy text around she strews,
That teach the rustic moralist to die.

For who, to dumb forgetfulness a prey,
This pleasing anxious being e'er resign'd,
Left the warm precincts of the cheerful day,
Nor cast one longing lingering look behind?

On some fond breast the parting soul relies,
90 Some pious drops the closing eye requires;
E'en from the tomb the voice of nature cries,
E'en in our ashes live their wonted fires.

For thee, who, mindful of th' unhonour'd dead,
Dost in these lines their artless tale relate;
If chance, by lonely contemplation led,
Some kindred spirit shall enquire thy fate, –

Haply some hoary-headed swain may say,
'Oft have we seen him at the peep of dawn
Brushing with hasty steps the dews away,
To meet the sun upon the upland lawn;

'There at the foot of yonder nodding beech
That wreathes its old fantastic roots so high,
His listless length at noon-tide would he stretch,
And pore upon the brook that babbles by.

'Hard by yon wood, now smiling as in scorn,
Muttering his wayward fancies he would rove;
Now drooping, woeful-wan, like one forlorn,
Or crazed with care, or cross'd in hopeless love.

'One morn I miss'd him on the custom'd hill,
Along the heath, and near his favourite tree;
Another came; nor yet beside the rill,
Nor up the lawn, nor at the wood was he;

'The next with dirges due in sad array
Slow through the church-way path we saw him borne, –
Approach and read (for thou canst read) the lay
Graved on the stone beneath yon aged thorn.'

THE EPITAPH
Here rests his head upon the lap of earth
A youth, to fortune and to fame unknown;
Fair science frown'd not on his humble birth
And melancholy mark'd him for her own.

Large was his bounty, and his soul sincere;
Heaven did a recompense as largely send:
He gave to misery (all he had) a tear,
He gain'd from Heaven ('twas all he wish'd) a friend.

No farther seek his merits to disclose,
Or draw his frailties from their dread abode,
(There they alike in trembling hope repose,)
The bosom of his Father and his God.

The Bard

PINDARIC ODE[1]

    'Ruin seize thee, ruthless King!
  Confusion on thy banners wait;
Tho' fann'd by Conquest's crimson wing
  They mock the air with idle state.
Helm, nor hauberk's twisted mail,
Nor e'en thy virtues, Tyrant, shall avail
To save thy secret soul from nightly fears,
From Cambria's[2] curse, from Cambria's tears!'
 – Such were the sounds that o'er the crested pride
10   Of the first Edward[3] scatter'd wild dismay,
As down the steep of Snowdon's shaggy side
  He wound with toilsome march his long array: –
Stout Glo'ster stood aghast in speechless trance;
'To arms!' cried Mortimer, and couch'd his quivering lance.

    On a rock, whose haughty brow
Frowns o'er old Conway's foaming flood,
  Robed in the sable garb of woe
With haggard eyes the Poet stood:
(Loose his beard and hoary hair
20 Stream'd like a meteor to the troubled air)
And with a master's hand and prophet's fire
Struck the deep sorrows of his lyre:
    'Hark, how each giant-oak and desert-cave
Sighs to the torrent's awful voice beneath!
O'er thee, oh King! their hundred arms they wave,

1. Pindar (522–442 BC) was a Greek lyric poet.
2. Wales.
3. King Edward I of England, conqueror of Wales.

Revenge on thee in hoarser murmurs breathe;
Vocal no more, since Cambria's fatal day,
To high-born Hoel's harp, or soft Llewellyn's lay.

30   'Cold is Cadwallo's tongue,
           That hush'd the stormy main:
Brave Urien sleeps upon his craggy bed:
           Mountains, ye mourn in vain
           Modred, whose magic song
Made huge Plinlimmon bow his cloud-topt head.
           On dreary Arvon's shore they lie
Smear'd with gore and ghastly pale:
Far, far aloof the affrighted ravens sail;
           The famish'd eagle screams, and passes by.
Dear lost companions of my tuneful art,
40   Dear as the light that visits these sad eyes,
Dear as the ruddy drops that warm my heart,
           Ye died amidst your dying country's cries –
No more I weep; They do not sleep;
           On yonder cliffs, a grisly band,
I see them sit; They linger yet,
           Avengers of their native land:
With me in dreadful harmony they join,
And weave with bloody hands the tissue of thy line.

           'Weave the warp and weave the woof
50   The winding sheet of Edward's race:
           Give ample room and verge enough
               The characters of hell to trace.
Mark the year, and mark the night,
When Severn[1] shall re-echo with affright
The shrieks of death thro' Berkley's[2] roof that ring,
Shrieks of an agonizing king!

1. The River Severn, marking the southern border of Wales.
2. Edward I's son, Edward II, proclaimed by him the first Prince of
Wales, was murdered in a particularly gruesome way in Berkeley
Castle.

She-wolf of France,[1] with unrelenting fangs
That tear'st the bowels of thy mangled mate,
   From thee be born, who o'er thy country hangs
60 The scourge of heaven.[2] What terrors round him wait!
   Amazement in his van, with flight combined,
   And sorrow's faded form, and solitude behind.

'Mighty victor, mighty lord,
   Low on his funeral couch he lies!
No pitying heart, no eye, afford
   A tear to grace his obsequies.
Is the sable warrior fled?[3]
Thy son is gone. He rests among the dead.
The swarm that in thy noon-tide beam were born?
70 – Gone to salute the rising morn.
Fair laughs the Morn, and soft the zephyr blows,
   While proudly riding o'er the azure realm
In gallant trim the gilded vessel goes:
   Youth on the prow, and Pleasure at the helm:
Regardless of the sweeping whirlwind's sway,
That hush'd in grim repose expects his evening prey.

'Fill high the sparkling bowl,
The rich repast prepare;
   Reft of a crown, he yet may share the feast:[4]
80 Close by the regal chair
   Fell Thirst and Famine scowl
   A baleful smile upon their baffled guest,
Heard ye the din of battle bray,
   Lance to lance, and horse to horse?
   Long years of havock urge their destined course,[5]
And thro' the kindred squadrons mow their way.

1. Isabella of Angoulême, estranged wife of Edward II.
2. Edward III.
3. The Black Prince, eldest son of Edward III.
4. Richard II, deposed and murdered.
5. The Wars of the Roses.

Ye towers of Julius, London's lasting shame,[1]
With many a foul and midnight murder fed,
   Revere his consort's faith, his father's fame,

90   And spare the meek usurper's holy head![2]
Above, below, the rose of snow,
   Twined with her blushing foe, we spread:[3]
The bristled boar in infant-gore[4]
   Wallows beneath the thorny shade.
Now, brothers, bending o'er the accurséd loom,
Stamp we our vengeance deep, and ratify his doom.

'Edward, lo! to sudden fate
   (Weave we the woof; The thread is spun;)
Half of thy heart we consecrate.

100   (The web is wove; The work is done.)
— Stay, oh stay! nor thus forlorn
Leave me unbless'd, unpitied, here to mourn:
In yon bright track that fires the western skies
They melt, they vanish from my eyes.
But oh! what solemn scenes on Snowdon's height
   Descending slow their glittering skirts unroll?
Visions of glory, spare my aching sight,
Ye unborn ages, crowd not on my soul!
No more our long-lost Arthur we bewail: —

110 All hail, ye genuine kings! Britannia's issue, hail!
   'Girt with many a baron bold
Sublime their starry fronts they rear;
   And gorgeous dames, and statesmen old
In bearded majesty, appear.

1. The Tower of London.
2. Henry VI, murdered at prayer in the Tower of London.
3. The red and white roses were the symbols of the houses of Lancaster and York who opposed each other during the Wars of the Roses.
4. The symbol of Richard III, last of the Plantagenet kings, killed at the battle of Bosworth.

In the midst a form divine!
Her eye proclaims her of the Briton-line:
Her lion-port, her awe-commanding face
Attemper'd sweet to virgin-grace.[1]
What strings symphonious tremble in the air,
120   What strains of vocal transport round her play?
Hear from the grave, great Taliessin,[2] hear;
    They breathe a soul to animate thy clay.
Bright Rapture calls, and soaring as she sings,
Waves in the eye of heaven her many-colour'd wings.

'The verse adorn again
    Fierce war, and faithful love,
And truth severe, by fairy fiction drest.
    In buskin'd measures move
Pale grief, and pleasing pain,
130   With horror, tyrant of the throbbing breast.
A voice as of the cherub-choir
    Gales from blooming Eden bear,
    And distant warblings lessen on my ear
That lost in long futurity expire.
Fond impious man, think'st thou yon sanguine cloud
    Raised by thy breath, has quench'd the orb of day?
To-morrow he repairs the golden flood
    And warms the nations with redoubled ray.
Enough for me: with joy I see
140   The different doom our fates assign:
Be thine despair and sceptred care,
    To triumph and to die are mine.'
– He spoke, and headlong from the mountain's height
Deep in the roaring tide he plunged to endless night.

1. Elizabeth I.
2. Welsh bard.

William Blake

(1757–1827)

William Blake was born in London and lived there most of his life. Although he was largely self-taught, he was widely read. As a child, he had a strong visual imagination and wanted to become a painter. His father first sent him to drawing school and then at the age of fourteen apprenticed him to an engraver. After he had finished his apprenticeship, he studied at the Royal Academy but soon left because he did not agree with the doctrines of Sir Joshua Reynolds, who was then its president.

After Blake married Catherine Boucher in 1782, she helped him to print his poems, which he etched on small copper plates with pictures in the margin. These were laborious to produce, since they were printed one at a time and coloured – largely by hand. They were not particularly successful, since Blake made no attempt to fit into the popular style of the time. In both a literary and a political sense, he was a rebel, supporting both the American and French Revolutions and writing against the monarchy of both England and France.

Blake's most popular poems have always been his *Songs of Innocence*. These poems are short and lyrical with a joyful freshness of observation. They were published in 1789, at the height of Blake's optimism about the effects of the Age of Revolutions on humanity. By the time of the outbreak of war between England and France in 1794, disillusion had set in, and this is reflected in a companion volume of poems entitled *Songs of Experience*. Although these were written in the same deceptively simple style as the *Songs of Innocence*, and often about the same subjects, they represent what Blake called 'the two contrary states of the human soul'. Some poems from each volume are paired by being given the same title, and some by the nature of their subjects, such as 'The Lamb' and 'The Tyger'. They develop Blake's view that true innocence is not the same as ignorance but consists of experience transformed by human creativity and imagination. 'Without Contraries', Blake wrote, 'is no progression.'

The Christian tone of many of his poems has given Blake the reputation of a Christian mystic, but this is far from the truth. He identified Christ with all spiritual goodness and the human character, but saw God the Father as personifying absolute authority and ruling with terror and tyranny. Blake the rebel was always against authority, and he saw the authority of the Church as stifling true spirituality. This is shown particularly in his poems 'The Garden of Love' and 'The Vagabond'.

During the war with France, Blake's radical politics affected his income, and he moved for three years to Felpham in Sussex under the patronage of William Hayley, a liberal poet whose works he was illustrating. There, he experienced some profound spiritual insights that led him to write his later visionary epic poems. These expressed Blake's consistent view that man's true nature is distorted and imprisoned by laws and conventions, including those of science and reason, and that he can only liberate himself by freeing his own energies. He opposes the oppressive God of the Old Testament with the youthful Christ of the New, overthrowing established orders by the sword. His words to the well-known hymn, 'Jerusalem', express this clearly.

Blake's later years were dogged by poverty, but he attracted many friends with similar radical ideals, and they enabled him to survive financially by commissioning engravings from him. He was deeply suspicious of the Industrial Revolution, the effects of which he saw all around him, destroying the landscape with its 'dark satanic mills' and eventually destroying his own craft of engraving. The ideals of social justice and views on ecology and the relationship between humanity and Nature he expressed in *Auguries of Innocence* are probably more meaningful in today's world than they were in his own time.

The Little Black Boy

My mother bore me in the southern wild,
And I am black, but O! my soul is white;
White as an angel is the English child:
But I am black as if bereav'd of light.

My mother taught me underneath a tree
And sitting down before the heat of day,
She took me on her lap and kissed me,
And pointing to the east began to say.

Look on the rising sun: there God does live
10 And gives his light, and gives his heat away.
And flowers and trees and beasts and men receive
Comfort in morning joy in the noon day.

And we are put on earth a little space,
That we may learn to bear the beams of love,
And these black bodies and this sun-burnt face
Is but a cloud, and like a shady grove.

For when our souls have learn'd the heat to bear
The cloud will vanish we shall hear his voice.
Saying: come out from the grove my love & care,
20 And round my golden tent like lambs rejoice.

Thus did my mother say and kissed me,
And thus I say to little English boy.
When I from black and he from white cloud free,
And round the tent of God like lambs we joy:

I'll shade him from the heat till he can bear,
To lean in joy upon our father's knee.
And then I'll stand and stroke his silver hair,
And be like him and he will then love me.

from: *Songs of Innocence*

Nurse's Song

When the voices of children are heard on the green
And laughing is heard on the hill,
My heart is at rest within my breast
And every thing else is still

Then come home my children, the sun is gone down
And the dews of night arise
Come come leave off play, and let us away
Till the morning appears in the skies

No no let us play, for it is yet day
10 And we cannot go to sleep
Besides in the sky, the little birds fly
And the hills are all covered with sheep

Well well go & play till the light fades away
And then go home to bed
The little ones leaped & shouted & laugh'd
And all the hills ecchoed

from: *Songs of Innocence*

Nurse's Song

When the voices of children, are heard on the green
And whisperings are in the dale:
The days of my youth rise fresh in my mind,
My face turns green and pale.

Then come home my children, the sun is gone down
And the dews of night arise
Your spring & your day, are wasted in play
And your winter and night in disguise.

from: *Songs of Experience*

The Chimney Sweeper

When my mother died I was very young,
And my father sold me while yet my tongue,
Could scarcely cry weep weep weep weep.
So your chimneys I sweep & in soot I sleep.

There's little Tom Dacre, who cried when his head
That curl'd like a lambs back, was shav'd, so I said.
Hush Tom never mind it, for when your head's bare,
You know that the soot cannot spoil your white hair.

And so he was quiet, & that very night,
10   As Tom was a sleeping he had such a sight,
That thousands of sweepers Dick, Joe Ned & Jack
Were all of them lock'd up in coffins of black

And by came an Angel who had a bright key,
And he open'd the coffins & set them all free.
Then down a green plain leaping laughing they run
And wash in a river and shine in the Sun.

Then naked & white, all their bags left behind,
They rise upon clouds, and sport in the wind.
And the Angel told Tom if he'd be a good boy,
20   He'd have God for his father & never want joy.

And so Tom awoke and we rose in the dark
And got with our bags & our brushes to work.
Tho' the morning was cold, Tom was happy & warm,
So if all do their duty, they need not fear harm.

from: *Songs of Innocence*

The Chimney Sweeper

A little black thing among the snow:
Crying 'weep! weep!' in notes of woe!
Where are thy father & mother? say?
They are both gone up to the church to pray.

Because I was happy upon the heath.
And smil'd among the winters snow:
They clothed me in the clothes of death.
And taught me to sing the notes of woe.

And because I am happy & dance & sing.
10 They think they have done me no injury:
And are gone to praise God & his Priest & King
Who make up a heaven of our misery.

from: *Songs of Experience*

The Lamb

Little Lamb who made thee
Dost thou know who made thee
Gave thee life & bid thee feed.
By the stream & o'er the mead;
Gave thee clothing of delight,
Softest clothing wooly bright;
Gave thee such a tender voice,
Making all the vales rejoice:
Little Lamb who made thee
10 Dost thou know who made thee

Little Lamb I'll tell thee,
Little Lamb I'll tell thee:
He is called by thy name,
For he calls himself a Lamb:
He is meek & he is mild,
He became a little child:
I a child & thou a lamb,

We are called by his name.
    Little Lamb God bless thee.
20 Little Lamb God bless thee.

from: *Songs of Innocence*

The Tyger

Tyger Tyger, burning bright,
In the forests of the night:
What immortal hand or eye,
Could frame thy fearful symmetry?

In what distant deeps or skies
Burnt the fire of thine eyes!
On what wings dare he aspire?
What the hand, dare seize the fire?

And what shoulder, & what art,
10 Could twist the sinews of thy heart?
And when thy heart began to beat,
What dread hand? & what dread feet?

What the hammer? what the chain,
In what furnace was thy brain?
What the anvil? what dread grasp,
Dare its deadly terrors clasp?

When the stars threw down their spears
And water'd heaven with their tears:
Did he smile his work to see?
20 Did he who made the Lamb make thee?

Tyger, Tyger burning bright,
In the forests of the night:
What immortal hand or eye,
Dare frame thy fearful symmetry?

from: *Songs of Experience*

Infant Joy

I have no name
I am but two days old. –
What shall I call thee?
I happy am
Joy is my name, –
Sweet joy befall thee!

Pretty joy!
Sweet joy but two days old.
Sweet joy I call thee:
10   Thou dost smile.
I sing the while
Sweet joy befall thee.

       from: *Songs of Innocence*

Infant Sorrow

My mother groand! my father wept.
Into the dangerous world I leapt:
Helpless, naked, piping loud;
Like a fiend hid in a cloud.

Struggling in my fathers hands:
Striving against my swadling bands:
Bound and weary I thought best
To sulk upon my mothers breast.

       from: *Songs of Experience*

The School Boy

I love to rise in a summer morn,
When the birds sing on every tree;
The distant huntsman winds his horn,
And the sky-lark sings with me.
O! what sweet company.

But to go to school in a summer morn
O! it drives all joy away;
Under a cruel eye outworn,
The little ones spend the day,
10 In sighing and dismay.

Ah! then at times I drooping sit,
And spend many an anxious hour.
Nor in my book can I take delight,
Nor sit in learnings bower,
Worn thro' with the dreary shower

How can the bird that is born for joy,
Sit in a cage and sing.
How can a child when fears annoy,
But droop his tender wing,
20 And forget his youthful spring.

O! father & mother, if buds are nip'd,
And blossoms blown away,
And if the tender plants are strip'd
Of their joy in the springing day,
By sorrow and cares dismay,

How shall the summer arise in joy
Or the summer fruits appear
Or how shall we gather what griefs destroy
Or bless the mellowing year,
30 When the blasts of winter appear.

from: *Songs of Experience*

The Sick Rose

O Rose thou art sick.
The invisible worm,
That flies in the night
In the howling storm:

Has found out thy bed
Of crimson joy:
And his dark secret love
Does thy life destroy.

from *Songs of Experience*

Ah! Sun-flower

Ah Sun-flower! weary of time.
Who countest the steps of the Sun:
Seeking after that sweet golden clime
Where the travellers journey is done.

Where the Youth pined away with desire,
And the pale Virgin shrouded in snow:
Arise from their graves and aspire,
Where my Sun-flower wishes to go.

from: *Songs of Experience*

London

I wander thro' each charter'd street,
Near where the charter'd Thames does flow.
And mark in every face I meet
Marks of weakness, marks of woe.

In every cry of every Man,
In every Infants cry of fear,
In every voice: in every ban,
The mind-forg'd manacles I hear.

How the Chimney-sweeper's cry
10 Every blackning Church appalls,
And the hapless Soldier's sigh,
Runs in blood down Palace walls.

But most thro' midnight streets I hear
How the youthful Harlots curse
Blasts the new-born Infants tear
And blights with plagues the Marriage hearse.

from: *Songs of Experience*

The Fly

Little Fly
Thy summers play,
My thoughtless hand
Has brush'd away.

Am not I
A fly like thee?
Or art not thou
A man like me?

For I dance
10   And drink & sing;
Till some blind hand
Shall brush my wing.

If thought is life
And strength & breath;
And the want
Of thought is death;

Then am I
A happy fly,
If I live,
20   Or if I die.

from: *Songs of Experience*

The Garden of Love

I went to the Garden of Love.
And saw what I never had seen:
A Chapel was built in the midst,
Where I used to play on the green.

And the gates of this Chapel were shut,
And 'Thou shalt not' writ over the door;
So I turn'd to the Garden of Love,
That so many sweet flowers bore.

And I saw it was filled with graves,
10   And tomb-stones where flowers should be:
And Priests in black gowns, were walking their rounds,
And binding with briars, my joys & desires.

from: *Songs of Experience*

The Little Vagabond

Dear Mother, dear Mother, the Church is cold.
But the Ale-house is healthy & pleasant & warm;
Besides I can tell where I am used well,
Such usage in heaven will never do well.

But if at the Church they would give us some Ale.
And a pleasant fire, our souls to regale;
We'd sing and we'd pray, all the live-long day;
Nor ever once wish from the Church to stray,

Then the Parson might preach & drink & sing.
10   And we'd be as happy as birds in the spring:
And modest dame Lurch, who is always at Church,
Would not have bandy children nor fasting nor birch.

And God like a father rejoicing to see,
His children as pleasant and happy as he:
Would have no more quarrel with the Devil or the Barrel
But kiss him & give him both drink and apparel.

from: *Songs of Experience*

Auguries of Innocence

To see a World in a Grain of Sand
And a Heaven in a Wild Flower
Hold Infinity in the palm of your hand
And Eternity in an hour
A Robin Red breast in a Cage
Puts all Heaven in a Rage
A dove house filld with doves & Pigeons
Shudders Hell thro all its regions
A dog starvd at his Masters Gate
10   Predicts the ruin of the State
A Horse misusd upon the Road
Calls to Heaven for Human blood
Each outcry of the hunted Hare
A fibre from the Brain does tear
A Skylark wounded in the wing
A Cherubim does cease to sing
The Game Cock clipd & armd for fight
Does the Rising Sun affright
Every Wolfs & Lions howl
20   Raises from Hell a Human Soul
The wild deer wandring here & there
Keeps the Human Soul from Care
The Lamb misusd breeds Public strife
And yet forgives the Butchers Knife
The Bat that flits at close of Eve
Has left the Brain that wont Believe
The Owl that calls upon the Night
Speaks the Unbelievers fright

He who shall hurt the little Wren
30 Shall never be belovd by Men
He who the Ox to wrath has movd
Shall never be by Woman lovd
The wanton Boy that kills the Fly
Shall feel the Spiders enmity
He who torments the Chafers sprite
Weaves a Bower in endless Night
The Catterpiller on the Leaf
Repeats to thee thy Mothers grief
Kill not the Moth nor Butterfly
40 For the Last Judgment draweth nigh
He who shall train the Horse to War
Shall never pass the Polar Bar
The Beggers Dog & Widows Cat
Feed them & thou wilt grow fat
The Gnat that sings his Summers song
Poison gets from Slanders tongue
The poison of the Snake & Newt
Is the sweat of Envys Foot
The Poison of the Honey Bee
50 Is the Artists Jealousy
The Princes Robes & Beggars Rags
Are Toadstools on the Misers Bags
A truth thats told with bad intent
Beats all the Lies you can invent
It is right it should be so
Man was made for Joy & Woe
And when this we rightly know
Thro the World we safely go
Joy & Woe are woven fine
60 A Clothing for the Soul divine
Under every grief & pine
Runs a joy with silken twine
The Babe is more than swadling Bands
Throughout all these Human Lands
Tools were made & Born were hands

Every Farmer Understands
Every Tear from Every Eye
Becomes a Babe in Eternity
This is caught by Females bright
70   And returnd to its own delight
The Bleat the Bark Bellow & Roar
Are Waves that Beat on Heavens Shore
The Babe that weeps the Rod beneath
Writes Revenge in realms of death
The Beggars Rags fluttering in Air
Does to Rags the Heavens tear
The Soldier armd with Sword & Gun
Palsied strikes the Summers Sun
The poor Mans Farthing is worth more
80   Than all the Gold on Africs Shore
One Mite wrung from the Labrers hands
Shall buy & sell the Misers Lands
Or if protected from on high
Does that whole Nation sell & buy
He who mocks the Infants Faith
Shall be mock'd in Age & Death
He who shall teach the Child to Doubt
The rotting Grave shall neer get out
He who respects the Infants faith
90   Triumphs over Hell & Death
The Childs Toys & the Old Mans Reasons
Are the Fruits of the Two seasons
The Questioner who sits so sly
Shall never know how to Reply
He who replies to words of Doubt
Doth put the Light of Knowledge out
The Strongest Poison ever known
Came from Caesars Laurel Crown
Nought can deform the Human Race
100   Like to the Armours iron brace
When Gold & Gems adorn the Plow
To peaceful Arts shall Envy Bow

A Riddle or the Crickets Cry
Is to Doubt a fit Reply
The Emmets Inch & Eagles Mile
Make Lame Philosophy to smile
He who Doubts from what he sees
Will neer Believe do what you Please
If the Sun & Moon should doubt
110 Theyd immediately Go out
To be in a Passion you Good may do
But no Good if a Passion is in you
The Whore & Gambler by the State
Licencd build that Nations Fate
The Harlots cry from Street to Street
Shall weave Old Englands winding Sheet
The Winners Shout the Losers Curse
Dance before dead Englands Hearse
Every Night & every Morn
120 Some to Misery are Born
Every Morn & every Night
Some are Born to sweet delight
Some are Born to sweet delight
Some are Born to Endless Night
We are led to Believe a Lie
When we see [with] not Thro the Eye
Which was Born in a Night to perish in a Night
When the Soul Slept in Beams of Light
God Appears & God is Light
130 To those poor Souls who dwell in Night
But does a Human Form Display
To those who Dwell in Realms of day

Robert Burns
(1759–1796)

Burns was born in Alloway, Ayrshire, the eldest of seven children in a family of tenant farmers. Although his education was very limited, his parents encouraged him to read, and he learned many traditional songs and stories from them. He had to work on his father's farm from his early teens, and the hard work and lack of good food led to rheumatic heart disease. His father encouraged him to read the Bible and English literature, and Burns taught himself to read French. He began to write poetry when he was fifteen.

In 1784 Burns's father died, and the family moved to Mossgiel, a farm near Mauchline. During the next two years, he realized the possibilities of using his own Scottish dialect to express himself in verse, and wrote many of his best known poems.

Several of Burns's early poems satirized the Church and Calvinist theology, making him unpopular with the church authorities. They were also angered by the number of his casual love affairs. His mother's servant girl bore him a daughter in 1785, and he next had an affair with Jean Armour, the daughter of a builder in Mauchline. Although she bore him twins in 1786, her father forbade her to marry him, and Burns planned to emigrate. However, this plan was abandoned when his first book, *Poems, chiefly in the Scottish Dialect*, was an instant success.

Burns went to Edinburgh and earned some money from the second edition of his poems. He was lionized by fashionable society, but his resentment when he felt that he was being patronized alienated some people. Eventually, he returned to Ayrshire and took up his affair with Jean Armour again, and they married after another set of twins was born in 1788. To support his family, Burns reluctantly took a post as an excise man. For some time, he struggled to combine this work with running a farm, but his health began to suffer. In 1791 he gave up the farm and settled in Dumfries.

James Johnson, an engraver, worked with Burns to collect traditional songs and ballads in *The Scots Musical Museum*, for which Burns acted as unpaid editor. He also wrote verse for *Select Collection of Original Scottish Airs*, compiled by George Thomson. Included in these two collections are such popular pieces as 'A red red Rose', 'Ae fond kiss', 'John Anderson my jo' and 'Comin' Thro' the Rye'. Many were collected from the oral tradition, and although Burns often adapted and improved existing lyrics, he wrote many original lyrics for traditional tunes.

Burns's political opinions were radical, and he championed the cause of Republicanism after the French Revolution. His views on democracy are well expressed in his famous poem 'For a' that and a that', which was translated into many languages in later years, and learned by heart by a generation of Russian schoolchildren. His Republican views did not stop him from celebrating the Jacobite cause in such poems as 'Charlie he's my darling'; even though the last Jacobite rebellion had died fourteen years before Burns's birth, the Hanoverian English kings remained deeply unpopular in Scotland. However, he often had to tone his views down because of his employment by the government.

The strain of his work and his literary pursuits took its toll of his health, and Burns died of his long-standing rheumatic heart condition at the age of 37. The editor of a memorial book of his poems took a disapproving view of Burns's life, and presented him as a drunkard and a rake, a reputation which clung for many years. However, this could not destroy the enduring power of his poetry. He was one of the first poets to use effectively the language of ordinary people and the details of their lives. 'To a Mouse' superbly combines a meditation on destiny with sharp observation of farming life. His eye for sham, hypocrisy and cruelty was derisive, but he was also the master of romantic songs that are powerful in their simplicity and perfectly fit the tunes for which he wrote them. His glorious verse narrative, 'Tam o'Shanter', is a comic masterpiece.

Burns's poetry needs very little explanation, but a glossary of Scottish dialect words is printed after these poems.

John Barleycorn.* A Ballad

I
There was three kings into the east,
    Three kings both great and high,
And they hae sworn a solemn oath
    John Barleycorn¹ should die.

II
They took a plough and plough'd him down,
    Put clods upon his head,
And they hae sworn a solemn oath
    John Barleycorn was dead.

III
But the chearful Spring came kindly on,
10   And show'rs began to fall;
John Barleycorn got up again,
    And sore surpris'd them all.

IV
The sultry suns of Summer came,
    And he grew thick and strong,
His head weel arm'd wi' pointed spears,
    That no one should him wrong.

V
The sober Autumn enter'd mild,
    When he grew wan and pale;
His bending joints and drooping head
20   Show'd he began to fail.

*This is partly composed on the plan of an old song by the same name.
1. Barley is the grain from which whisky is made.

VI

His colour sicken'd more and more,
    He faded into age;
And then his enemies began
    To show their deadly rage.

VII

They've taen a weapon, long and sharp,
    And cut him by the knee;
Then ty'd him fast upon a cart,
    Like a rogue for forgerie.

VIII

They laid him down upon his back,
30   And cudgell'd him full sore;
They hung him up before the storm,
    And turn'd him o'er and o'er.

IX

They filled up a darksome pit
    With water to the brim,
They heaved in John Barleycorn,
    There let him sink or swim.

X

They laid him out upon the floor,
    To work him farther woe,
And still, as signs of life appear'd,
40   They toss'd him to and fro.

XI

They wasted, o'er a scorching flame,
    The marrow of his bones;
But a Miller us'd him worst of all,
    For he crush'd him between two stones.

XII

And they hae taen his very heart's blood,
    And drank it round and round;
And still the more and more they drank,
    Their joy did more abound.

XIII

John Barleycorn was a hero bold,
50   Of noble enterprise,
For if you do but taste his blood,
    'Twill make your courage rise.

XIV

'Twill make a man forget his woe;
    'Twill heighten all his joy:
'Twill make the widow's heart to sing,
    Tho' the tear were in her eye.

XV

Then let us toast John Barleycorn,
    Each man a glass in hand;
And may his great posterity
60   Ne'er fail in old Scotland!

Up in the Morning Early

Cauld blaws the wind frae east to west,
    The drift is driving sairly;
Sae loud and shill 's I hear the blast,
    I'm sure it 's winter fairly.
Up in the morning 's no for me,
    Up in the morning early;
When a' the hills are cover'd wi' snaw,
    I'm sure it is winter fairly.

The birds sit chittering in the thorn,
10   A' day they fare but sparely;
And lang 's the night frae e'en to morn,
    I'm sure it 's winter fairly.
        Up in the morning 's, &c.

My bony Mary

Go fetch to me a pint o' wine,
  And fill it in a silver tassie;
That I may drink, before I go,
  A service to my bonie lassie:
The boat rocks at the Pier o' Lieth,
  Fu' loud the wind blaws frae the Ferry,
The ship rides by the Berwick-law,
  And I maun leave my bony Mary.

The trumpets sound, the banners fly,
10   The glittering spears are ranked ready,
The shouts o' war are heard afar,
  The battle closes deep and bloody.
It 's not the roar o' sea or shore,
  Wad make me langer wish to tarry,
Nor shouts o' war that 's heard afar –
  It 's leaving thee, my bony Mary!

O whistle, and I'll come to ye, my lad

O whistle, and I'll come to ye, my lad,
O whistle, and I'll come to ye, my lad;
Tho' father, and mother, and a' should gae mad,
  Thy JEANIE will venture wi' ye, my lad.

But warily tent, when ye come to court me,
And come nae unless the back-yett be a-jee;
Syne up the back-style and let naebody see,
  And come as ye were na comin to me –
  And come as ye were na comin to me –
10   O whistle &c.

At kirk, or at market whene'er ye meet me,
Gang by me as tho' that ye car'd nae a flie;
But steal me a blink o' your bonie black e'e,
    Yet look as ye were na lookin at me –
    Yet look as ye were na lookin at me –
        O whistle &c.

Ay vow and protest that ye care na for me,
And whyles ye may lightly my beauty a wee;
But court nae anither, tho' jokin ye be,
20   For fear that she wyle your fancy frae me –
    For fear that she wyle your fancy frae me –

Ae fond kiss

TUNE, RORY DALL'S PORT

Ae fond kiss and then we sever;
Ae fareweel, and then for ever!
Deep in heart-wrung tears I'll pledge thee,
Warring sighs and groans I'll wage thee. –

Who shall say that Fortune grieves him,
While the star of hope she leaves him:
Me, nae chearful twinkle lights me;
Dark despair around benights me. –

I'll ne'er blame my partial fancy,
10 Naething could resist my Nancy:
But to see her, was to love her;
Love but her, and love for ever. –

Had we never lov'd sae kindly,
Had we never lov'd sae blindly!
Never met – or never parted,
We had ne'er been broken hearted. –

Fare-thee-weel, thou first and fairest!
Fare-thee-weel thou best and dearest!
Thine be ilka joy and treasure,
20 Peace, Enjoyment, Love and Pleasure! –

Ae fond kiss and then we sever!
Ae fareweel! Alas, for ever:
Deep in heart-wrung tears I'll pledge thee,
Warring sighs and groans I'll wage thee. –

John Anderson my jo

John Anderson my jo, John,
  When we were first acquent;
Your locks were like the raven,
  Your bony bow was brent;
But now your brow is beld, John,
  Your locks are like the snaw;
But blessings on your frosty pow,
John Anderson my jo.

John Anderson my jo, John,
10   We clamb the hill the gither;
And mony a canty day, John,
  We've had wi' ane anither:
Now we maun totter down, John,
  And hand in hand we'll go;
And sleep the gither at the foot,
John Anderson my jo.

A red red Rose

O my Luve 's like a red, red rose,
  That's newly sprung in June;
O my Luve 's like the melodie
  That 's sweetly play'd in tune –

As fair art thou, my bonie lass,
    So deep in luve am I;
And I will love thee still, my Dear,
    Till a' the seas gang dry –

Till a' the seas gang dry, my Dear,
10   And the rocks melt wi' the sun:
I will love thee still, my Dear,
    While the sands o' life shall run –

And fare thee weel, my only Luve!
    And fare thee weel, a while!
And I will come again, my Luve,
    Tho' it were ten thousand mile!

For a' that and a' that

Is there, for honest Poverty
    That hings his head, and a' that;
The coward-slave, we pass him by,
    We dare be poor for a' that!
    For a' that, and a' that,
        Our toils obscure, and a' that,
    The rank is but the guinea's stamp,[1]
        The Man 's the gowd for a' that. –

What though on hamely fare we dine,
10   Wear hoddin grey, and a' that.
Gie fools their silks, and knaves their wine,
    A Man 's a Man for a' that.
    For a' that, and a' that;
        Their tinsel[2] show, and a' that;
    The honest man, though e'er sae poor,
        Is king o' men for a' that. –

1. A man's rank is only like the stamp that turns gold into a guinea coin,
with a value accepted in society, but the true value lies in the gold itself, not
the stamp.
2 Cheap and flashy.

Ye see yon birkie ca'd, a lord,
    Wha struts, and stares, and a' that,
Though hundreds worship at his word,
20   He's but a coof for a' that.
  For a' that, and a' that,
    His ribband, star and a' that,
  The man of independent mind,
    He looks and laughs at a' that. –

A prince can mak a belted knight,
    A marquis, duke, and a' that;
But an honest man 's aboon his might,
    Gude faith he mauna fa' that!
  For a' that, and a' that,
30   Their dignities, and a' that,
  The pith o' Sense, and pride o' Worth,
    Are higher rank than a' that. –

Then let us pray that come it may,
    As come it will for a' that,
That Sense and Worth, o'er a' the earth
    Shall bear the gree, and a' that.
  For a' that, and a' that,
    It's comin yet for a' that,
  That Man to Man the warld o'er,
40   Shall brothers be for a' that. –

Charlie he's my darling

      'Twas on a monday morning,
        Right early in the year,
      That Charlie cam to our town,
        The young Chevalier. –

CHORUS

An' Charlie he 's my darling, my darling, my darling,
Charlie he 's my darling, the young Chevalier. –

As he was walking up the street,
    The city for to view,
O there he spied a bonie lass
10   The window looking thro'. –
        An Charlie &c.

Sae light 's he jimped up the stair,
    And tirled at the pin;
And wha sae ready as hersel
    To let the laddie in. –
        An Charlie &c.

He set his Jenny on his knee,
    All in his Highland dress;
For brawlie weel he ken'd the way
20   To please a bonie lass. –
        An Charlie &c.

It's up yon hethery mountain,
    And down yon scroggy glen,
We daur na gang a milking,
    For Charlie and his men. –
        An Charlie &c.[1]

1. Charles Edward Stuart, 1720–1788, claimant to the British throne,
also called The Young Chevalier, Bonny Prince Charlie and The
Young Pretender. He was the grandson of King James II, who had
been deposed because of his Catholic sympathies in 1688 and replaced
by the Protestant William of Orange. His father, known as the Old
Pretender, had led a failed Jacobite rebellion in 1715. In 1745 Charles
Stuart arrived in Scotland, where several Highland clans came to his
assistance. He had several military successes and advanced as far south
as Derby before being forced to retreat and finally defeated at Culloden
Moor. He was hunted as a fugitive for five months, sheltered by
Highlanders, before escaping to France in 1746. He was a handsome
man and a popular hero in Scotland, especially among women.

To a Mouse, On turning her up in her Nest, with the Plough, November, 1785

Wee, sleeket, cowran, tim'rous *beastie*,
O, what a panic's in thy breastie!
Thou need na start awa sae hasty,
        Wi' bickering brattle!
I wad be laith to run an' chase thee,
        Wi' murd'ring *pattle*!

I'm truly sorry Man's dominion
Has broken Nature's social union,
An' justifies that ill opinion,
10   Which makes thee startle,
At me, thy poor, earth-born companion,
        An' *fellow-mortal*!

I doubt na, whyles, but thou may *thieve*;
What then? poor beastie, thou maun live!
A *daimen-icker* in a *thrave*
        'S a sma' request:
I'll get a blessin wi' the lave,
        An' never miss 't!

Thy wee-bit *housie*, too, in ruin!
20 Its silly wa's the win's are strewin!
An' naething, now, to big a new ane,
        O' foggage green!
An' bleak *December's winds* ensuin,
        Baith snell an' keen!

Thou saw the fields laid bare an' wast,
An' weary *Winter* comin fast,
An' cozie here, beneath the blast,
   Thou thought to dwell,
Till crash! the cruel *coulter* past
30   Out thro' thy cell.

That wee-bit heap o' leaves an' stibble,
Has cost thee monie a weary nibble!
Now thou 's turn'd out, for a' thy trouble,
   But house or hald,
To thole the Winter's *sleety dribble*,
    An' *cranreuch* cauld!

But Mousie, thou art no thy-lane,
In proving *foresight* may be vain:
The best laid schemes o' *Mice* an' *Men*,
40   Gang aft agley,
An' lea'e us nought but grief an' pain,
    For promis'd joy!

Still, thou art blest, compar'd wi' *me*!
The *present* only toucheth thee:
But Och! I *backward* cast my e'e,
   On prospects drear!
An' *forward*, tho' I canna *see*,
    I *guess* an' *fear*!

Tam o' Shanter. A Tale

Of Brownyis and of Bogillis full is this buke.

GAWIN DOUGLAS

When chapman billies leave the street,
And drouthy neebors, neebors meet,
As market-days are wearing late,
An' folk begin to tak the gate;
While we sit bousing at the nappy,
And getting fou and unco happy,
We think na on the lang Scots miles,
The mosses, waters, slaps, and styles,
That lie between us and our hame,
10 Whare sits our sulky sullen dame,
Gathering her brows like gathering storm,
Nursing her wrath to keep it warm.

    This truth fand honest *Tam o' Shanter*,
As he frae Ayr ae night did canter,
(Auld Ayr, wham ne'er a town surpasses,
For honest men and bonny lasses).

    O *Tam*! hadst thou but been sae wise,
As ta'en thy ain wife *Kate*'s advice!
She tauld thee weel thou was a skellum,
20 A blethering, blustering, drunken blellum;
That frae November till October,
Ae market-day thou was nae sober;
That ilka melder, wi' the miller,
Thou sat as lang as thou had siller;
That every naig was ca'd a shoe on,
The smith and thee gat roaring fou on;
That at the L—d's house, even on Sunday,
Thou drank wi' Kirkton Jean till Monday.

She prophesied that late or soon,
30 Thou would be found deep drown'd in Doon;
Or catch'd wi' warlocks in the mirk,
By *Alloway*'s auld haunted kirk.

Ah, gentle dames! it gars me greet,
To think how mony counsels sweet,
How mony lengthen'd sage advices,
The husband frae the wife despises!

But to our tale: Ae market-night,
Tam had got planted unco right;
Fast by an ingle, bleezing finely,
40 Wi' reaming swats, that drank divinely;
And at his elbow, Souter *Johnny*,
His ancient, trusty, drouthy crony;
Tam lo'ed him like a vera brither;
They had been fou for weeks thegither.
The night drave on wi' sangs and clatter;
And ay the ale was growing better:
The landlady and *Tam* grew gracious,
Wi' favours, secret, sweet, and precious:
The Souter tauld his queerest stories;
50 The landlord's laugh was ready chorus:
The storm without might rair and rustle,
Tam did na mind the storm a whistle.
Care, mad to see a man sae happy,
E'en drown'd himsel amang the nappy:
As bees flee hame wi' lades o' treasure,
The minutes wing'd their way wi' pleasure:
Kings may be blest, but *Tam* was glorious,
O'er a' the ills o' life victorious!

But pleasures are like poppies spread,
60 You seize the flower, its bloom is shed;
Or like the snow falls in the river,
A moment white – then melts for ever;
Or like the borealis race,
That flit ere you can point their place;

Or like the rainbow's lovely form
Evanishing amid the storm. –
Nae man can tether time or tide;
The hour approaches *Tam* maun ride;
That hour, o' night's black arch the key-stane,
70 That dreary hour he mounts his beast in;
And sic a night he taks the road in,
As ne'er poor sinner was abroad in.

    The wind blew as 'twad blawn its last;
The rattling showers rose on the blast;
The speedy gleams the darkness swallow'd;
Loud, deep, and lang, the thunder bellow'd:
That night, a child might understand,
The Deil had business on his hand.

    Weel mounted on his gray mare, *Meg*,
80 A better never lifted leg,
Tam skelpit on thro' dub and mire,
Despising wind, and rain, and fire;
Whiles holding fast his gude blue bonnet;
Whiles crooning o'er some auld Scots sonnet;
Whiles glowring round wi' prudent cares,
Lest bogles catch him unawares:
Kirk-Alloway was drawing nigh,
Whare ghaists and houlets nightly cry. –

    By this time he was cross the ford,
90 Whare, in the snaw, the chapman smoor'd;
And past the birks and meikle stane,
Whare drunken *Charlie* brak 's neck-bane;
And thro' the whins, and by the cairn,
Whare hunters fand the murder'd bairn;
And near the thorn, aboon the well,
Whare *Mungo*'s mither hang'd hersel. –
Before him *Doon* pours all his floods;
The doubling storm roars thro' the woods;
The lightnings flash from pole to pole;

100   Near and more near the thunders roll:
When, glimmering thro' the groaning trees,
Kirk-Alloway seem'd in a bleeze;
Thro' ilka bore the beams were glancing,
And loud resounded mirth and dancing. –

      Inspiring bold *John Barleycorn*!
What dangers thou canst make us scorn!
Wi' tippeny, we fear nae evil;
Wi' usquabae, we'll face the devil! –
The swats sae ream'd in *Tammie*'s noddle,
110   Fair play, he car'd na deils a boddle.
But *Maggie* stood right sair astonish'd,
Till, by the heel and hand admonish'd,
She ventured forward on the light;
And, vow! *Tam* saw an unco sight!
Warlocks and witches in a dance;
Nae cotillion brent new frae *France*,
But hornpipes, jigs, strathspeys, and reels,
Put life and mettle in their heels.
A winnock-bunker in the east,
120   There sat auld Nick, in shape o' beast;
A towzie tyke, black, grim, and large,
To gie them music was his charge:
He screw'd the pipes and gart them skirl,
Till roof and rafters a' did dirl. –
Coffins stood round, like open presses,
That shaw'd the dead in their last dresses;
And by some devilish cantraip slight
Each in its cauld hand held a light. –
By which heroic *Tam* was able
130   To note upon the haly table,
A murderer's banes in gibbet airns;
Twa span-lang, wee, unchristen'd bairns;
A thief, new-cutted frae a rape,
Wi' his last gasp his gab did gape;
Five tomahawks, wi' blude red-rusted;

Five scymitars, wi' murder crusted;
A garter, which a babe had strangled;
A knife, a father's throat had mangled,
Whom his ain son o' life bereft,
140 The grey hairs yet stack to the heft;
Wi' mair o' horrible and awefu',
Which even to name wad be unlawfu'.

Three Lawyers' tongues, turn'd inside out,
Wi' lies seam'd like a beggar's clout;
And Priests' hearts, rotten, black as muck,
Lay stinking, vile, in every neuk. –

As *Tammie* glowr'd, amaz'd, and curious,
The mirth and fun grew fast and furious:
The piper loud and louder blew;
150 The dancers quick and quicker flew;
They reel'd, they set, they cross'd, they cleekit,
Till ilka carlin swat and reekit,
And coost her duddies to the wark,
And linket at it in her sark!

Now, *Tam*, O *Tam*! had thae been queans,
A' plump and strapping in their teens,
Their sarks, instead o' creeshie flannen,
Been snaw-white seventeen hunder linnen!
Thir breeks o' mine, my only pair,
160 That ance were plush, o' gude blue hair,
I wad hae gi'en them off my hurdies,
For ae blink o' the bonie burdies!

But wither'd beldams, auld and droll,
Rigwoodie hags wad spean a foal,
Lowping and flinging on a crummock,
I wonder didna turn thy stomach.

But *Tam* kend what was what fu' brawlie,
There was ae winsome wench and wawlie,
That night enlisted in the core,

170   (Lang after kend on *Carrick* shore;
     For mony a beast to dead she shot,
     And perish'd mony a bony boat,
     And shook baith meikle corn and bear,
     And kept the country-side in fear:)
     Her cutty sark, o' Paisley harn,
     That while a lassie she had worn,
     In longitude tho' sorely scanty,
     It was her best, and she was vauntie. —
     Ah! little kend thy reverend grannie,
180   That sark she coft for her wee Nannie,
     Wi' twa pund Scots, ('twas a' her riches),
     Wad ever grac'd a dance of witches!

     But here my Muse her wing maun cour;
     Sic flights are far beyond her pow'r;
     To sing how Nannie lap and flang,
     (A souple jade she was, and strang),
     And how *Tam* stood, like ane bewitch'd,
     And thought his very een enrich'd;
     Even Satan glowr'd, and fidg'd fu' fain,
190   And hotch'd and blew wi' might and main:
     Till first ae caper, syne anither,
     Tam tint his reason a' thegither,
     And roars out, 'Weel done, Cutty-sark!'
     And in an instant all was dark:
     And scarcely had he Maggie rallied,
     When out the hellish legion sallied.

     As bees bizz out wi' angry fyke,
     When plundering herds assail their byke;
     As open pussie's mortal foes,
200   When, pop! she starts before their nose;
     As eager runs the market-crowd,
     When 'Catch the thief!' resounds aloud;
     So Maggie runs, the witches follow,
     Wi' mony an eldritch skreech and hollow.

Ah, *Tam*! Ah, *Tam*! thou'll get thy fairin!
In hell they'll roast thee like a herrin!
In vain thy *Kate* awaits thy comin!
Kate soon will be a woefu' woman!
Now, do thy speedy utmost, Meg,
210 And win the key-stane* of the brig;
There at them thou thy tail may toss,
A running stream they dare na cross.
But ere the key-stane she could make,
The fient a tail she had to shake!
For Nannie, far before the rest,
Hard upon noble Maggie prest,
And flew at *Tam* wi' furious ettle;
But little wist she Maggie's mettle –
Ae spring brought off her master hale,
220 But left behind her ain gray tail:
The carlin claught her by the rump,
And left poor Maggie scarce a stump.

Now, wha this tale o' truth shall read,
Ilk man and mother's son, take heed:
Whene'er to drink you are inclin'd,
Or cutty-sarks run in your mind,
Think, ye may buy the joys o'er dear,
Remember Tam o'Shanter's mare.

* *It is a well known fact that witches, or any evil spirits, have no power to
follow a poor wight any farther than the middle of the next running stream. – It
may be proper likewise to mention to the benighted traveller, that when he falls
in with* bogles, *whatever danger may be in his going forward, there is much more
hazard in turning back.*

Glossary

a', all
aboon, above, over
ae, one, only
aft, often
agley, wrong, awry
ain, own
airns, irons
a-jee, ajar
ance, once
ane, one
anither, another
auld, old
auld Nick, the Devil
awa, away
awefu', awful
ay, ever
back-jett, back-style, back gate
bairn, child
baith, both
bane, banes, bone, bones
beastie, beast
beld, bald
beldams, old woman, hag, witch
bickering, scurrying
birkie, lively fellow
bizz, buzz, flurry
bleeze, bleezing, blaze, blazing
blellum, idle babbler, blusterer
blethering, talking foolishly
blude, blood
boddle, small copper coin
bogles, ghosts, goblins
bony, bonie, bonny, pretty
bore, crevice or narrow passage
borealis, the Northern Lights
bousing, boozing, drinking
  heavily
brae, braes, hillside by a river
brak 's, broke his
brattle, hurry, scamper
brawlie, splendidly
breastie, little creature
breeks, trousers, breeches
brent, branded, new; smooth,

unwrinkled
brither, brother
burdies, girls
but, except, without
byke, hive, crowd
ca'd, called
cairn, pile of stones, a marker
cam, came
canna, cannot
cantraip, magic, witching
canty, lively, pleasant, cheerful
carlin, old woman, witch, old
  fellow
cauld, cold
chapman billies, pedlars
clatter, chatter, uproar
claught, cleekit, caught, linked
clout, patch
coft, bought
coof, fool, clown
coost, cast, threw off
core, band, team
cot, cottage
coulter, ploughshare
cour, lower, fold
cowran, timid
cozie, cosy
cranreuch, hoar-frost
creeshie, greasy, filthy
crony, friend
crummock, stick with crook
cutty, short
daimen-icker, occasional ear of
  corn
daur, dare
Deil, Devil
didna, didn't
dirl, shake, rattle
drave, drove
drouthy, thirsty
dub, mire, muddy puddle
duddies, clothes, rags
e'e, e'en, eye, eyes
eldritch, ghastly, haunted

ettle, purpose, aim
fa', fall, fortune
fain, glad, content
fairin, present from a fair, reward
fairly, clearly, indeed
fand, found
fidg'd, fidgeted
fient, fiend, devil
flang, flung
flannen, flannel
flie, fly
foggage, coarse grass
fou, full, drunk, quite
frae, from
fu', full
fyke, fiddle, fuss
gab, talk, mouth
gae, gave
gang, go, depart, walk
gars, gart, make, made
gat, got
ghaists, ghosts
gibbet, scaffold
gie, give
gi'en, given
glowring, scowling
gowd, gold
gree, social degree or class, agree
greet, cry, weep
gude, good
hae, ha', have
hald, hold, dwelling, refuge
hale, whole, healthy
haly, holy
hame, hamely, home, homely
harn, coarse material
herrin, herring
hersel, herself
hethery, heathery
hoddin, coarse homespun cloth
hollow, halloo
hotch'd, hitched, jerked about
howlets, owls
hunder, hundred
hurdies, backside, buttocks
ilk, ilka, each, every

ingle, hearth in which a fire burns
jade, wench, hussy, mare
jimped, jumped
jo, sweetheart
ken, kens, ken'd, know, knows, knew
key-stane, key-stone
kirk, church
lades, loads
laith, unwilling, reluctant
lang, langer, long, longer
lap, leapt
lea'e, leave
linket, skipped
linnen, linen
lo'ed, loved
lowping, leaping, jumping
luve, love
mair, more
mak, make, do
maun, mauna, must, must not
meikle, much
melder, cornmeal, or grinding corn
mire, mud
mirk, darkness
mither, mother
monie, mony, many
na, nae, not, by no means
naig, small horse, nag
nappy, ale
neebors, neighbours
neuk, nook, corner
noddle, head, brain
o'er, over
pattle, spade
pow, head
queans, young girls
rair, roar
ream'd, reaming, cream, froth, foaming
reekit, smoked, smoky
ribband, ribbon
rigwoodie, withered, coarse
rills, streams
sae, so

sair, sairly, sore, sorry, hard, harsh
sangs, songs
sark, shirt, chemise, shift
scroggy, covered with stunted bushes
shaw'd, showed, revealed
shill, shrill
sic, such
siller, silver, money
skellum, rascal, scoundrel
skelpit, beaten or rushed
skirl, shriek, yell
slaps, *n.* gap in a fence; *adv.* suddenly
sleeket, smooth, glossy, sly
sma', small
snaw, snow
snell, keen, bitter
souple, soft, pliant, supple
souter, shoemaker, cobbler
span-lang, small, the width of a handspan
spean, wean
stack, stuck
stane, stone
stibble, stubble
strang, strong
strathspeys, traditional dances or tunes
strewin', scattering
styles, stiles
swats, *n.* new small beer; *v.* sweats
syne, then, since
taen, taken
tassie, goblet, cup
tauld, told

tent, care, careful
thegither, together
thir, these
thole, endure, suffer
thrave, two stooks of corn
thy-lane, by yourself, alone
tim'rous, fearful
tint, lost
tippeny, ale
tirled, rattled the latch of a door
towzie, shaggy, unkempt
'twad, it would have
tyke, mongrel, dog
unco, odd, strange, very
usquabae, whisky
vauntie, vain, proud
vera, very, actual, true, real
wa's, walls
wad, would
wark, work, business
warlocks, wizards
wast, waste
wawlie, handsome, fine, ample
wee-bit, tiny
weel, well
wha, wham, who, whom
whare, where
whene'er, whenever
whins, thorns, gorse or furze bushes
whyles, at times, sometimes
wi', with
win's, winds, breaths
winnock-bunker, window-seat
winsome, attractive
wyle, lure, beguile
yon, yonder, that

William Wordsworth

(1770–1850)

William Wordsworth was born at Cockermouth in Cumberland and educated first at Hawkshead school and later at St John's College, Cambridge. He developed a keen love of nature, and his memories of an idyllic childhood among the mountains and lakes of Cumbria were the wellspring of much of his later poetry, particularly *The Prelude*. He often spent his holidays visiting places famous for their scenic beauty.

In 1790 he spent the long summer vacation on a walking tour in France and Switzerland with a college friend. After returning to England to finish his BA degree he returned to France for a year, where he fell in love with Annette Vallon of Orleans, who bore him a daughter in December 1792. He also fell in love with the ideals of the French Revolution, which he saw as a revolution to free the individual. Despite the outbreak of war between France and Great Britain in 1793, Wordsworth remained sympathetic to the French cause for many years.

Wordsworth had earned little money from his writing, but a legacy of £900 inherited from a friend in 1795 enabled him to move with his sister Dorothy to Dorset and then to Somerset. There he met the poet Samuel Taylor Coleridge. The two became friends, and together published a volume of poems called *Lyrical Ballads* in 1798. This work is usually taken to mark the beginning of the Romantic movement in English poetry. In his preface to the second edition, Wordsworth expressed his feeling that the language used by poets of his day was too literary and dead, and that poetry should be written in language 'really used by men' on subjects which reflected real life and experiences. Poetry, he said, sprang from 'emotion recollected in tranquillity'.

The late eighteenth century has often been called the 'Age of Revolutions'. Changes in agriculture and the rapid growth of industry caused enormous upheavals in society. A revolution in scientific thought sprang up in the wake of Sir Isaac Newton's discoveries. Political thought about the rights of ordinary people and the relationship between people and government was deeply affected by the French Revolution and the American War of Independence.

Naturally, these upheavals were reflected in changes in literature. The most obvious is the feeling for nature expressed in the poetry of the time. Earlier poets saw nature as something to be conquered and tamed. Man (in the sense of humanity) and his thoughts were their central themes. Wordsworth and the other Romantic poets saw nature as a kind of spiritual healer, with a personality of its own. Perhaps the destruction of the landscape by the effects of the Industrial Revolution led them to value what they were losing. The mood they create in writing about the natural world is often one of nostalgia or regret.

The most noticeable change in poetry, though, is shown by the change in emphasis from humanity to the individual. It is significant that one of the subtitles of *The Prelude* was *A poem on the growth of an individual mind*. Many of Wordsworth's poems show a solitary figure in a landscape.

Earlier poetry did not place the same value on childhood as the Romantic poets. Children were seen either as miniature adults, or (because so many died young) as symbolic of the fragility of life. In Wordsworth's ode 'Intimations of Immortality', he says that children and their instincts are closest to the God seen in nature in their youth. They come into the world 'trailing clouds of glory', with knowledge they forget as they grow into the 'prison-house' of adult life. However, he concludes that although the splendid visions of childhood are gone, they remain deep in the heart as thoughts 'too deep for tears'.

Wordsworth married a friend from childhood in 1802, and lived in the Lake District for the rest of his life. In old age, disillusioned with the outcome of the French Revolution, he became very reactionary and his poetry far less inspired. His greatest poems sprang from his early joy in nature, his interest in the lives of real people, and his belief that the imagination can reach truths that cannot be grasped by reason.

'A slumber did my spirit seal'

A slumber did my spirit seal;
   I had no human fears:
She seemed a thing that could not feel
   The touch of earthly years.

No motion has she now, no force;
   She neither hears nor sees;
Rolled round in earth's diurnal[1] course,
   With rocks, and stones, and trees.

1. Daily.

'She dwelt among the untrodden ways'

She dwelt among the untrodden ways
   Beside the springs of Dove,[1]
A Maid whom there were none to praise
   And very few to love:

A violet by a mossy stone
   Half hidden from the eye!
– Fair as a star, when only one
   Is shining in the sky.

She lived unknown, and few could know
10   When Lucy ceased to be;
But she is in her grave, and, oh,
   The difference to me!

1. The River Dove.

Ode: Intimations of Immortality from Recollections of Early Childhood

The Child is Father of the Man;
And I could wish my days to be
Bound each to each by natural piety.

I

There was a time when meadow, grove, and stream,
The earth, and every common sight,
    To me did seem
    Apparelled[1] in celestial light,
The glory and the freshness of a dream.
It is not now as it hath been of yore; –
    Turn wheresoe'er I may,
      By night or day,
The things which I have seen I now can see no more.

II

10   The Rainbow comes and goes,
    And lovely is the Rose;
    The Moon doth with delight
Look round her when the heavens are bare;
    Waters on a starry night
    Are beautiful and fair;
  The sunshine is a glorious birth;
  But yet I know, where'er I go,
That there hath past away a glory from the earth.

III

Now, while the birds thus sing a joyous song,
20   And while the young lambs bound
    As to the tabor's[2] sound,

1. Clothed.
2. Small drum.

To me alone there came a thought of grief:
A timely utterance gave that thought relief,
 And I again am strong:
The cataracts blow their trumpets from the steep;
No more shall grief of mine the season wrong;
I hear the Echoes through the mountains throng,
The Winds come to me from the fields of sleep,
 And all the earth is gay;
30 Land and sea
 Give themselves up to jollity,
 And with the heart of May
 Doth every Beast keep holiday; –
 Thou Child of Joy,
Shout round me, let me hear thy shouts, thou happy
 Shepherd-boy!

IV

Ye blessèd Creatures, I have heard the call
 Ye to each other make; I see
The heavens laugh with you in your jubilee;
 My heart is at your festival,
40 My head hath its coronal,[1]
The fulness of your bliss, I feel – I feel it all.
 Oh evil day! if I were sullen
 While Earth herself is adorning,
 This sweet May-morning,
 And the Children are culling[2]
 On every side,
 In a thousand valleys far and wide,
 Fresh flowers; while the sun shines warm,
And the Babe leaps up on his Mother's arm: –
50 I hear, I hear, with joy I hear!
 – But there's a Tree, of many, one,
A single Field which I have looked upon,
Both of them speak of something that is gone:

1. Garland.
2. Gathering.

        The Pansy at my feet
        Doth the same tale repeat:
Whither is fled the visionary gleam?
Where is it now, the glory and the dream?

V

Our birth is but a sleep and a forgetting:
The Soul that rises with us, our life's Star,
60   Hath had elsewhere its setting,
            And cometh from afar:
        Not in entire forgetfulness,
        And not in utter nakedness,
But trailing clouds of glory do we come
        From God, who is our home:
Heaven lies about us in our infancy!
Shades of the prison-house begin to close
        Upon the growing Boy,
            But He
70 Beholds the light, and whence it flows,
        He sees it in his joy;
The Youth, who daily farther from the east
        Must travel, still is Nature's Priest,
        And by the vision splendid
        Is on his way attended;
At length the Man perceives it die away,
And fade into the light of common day.

VI

Earth fills her lap with pleasures of her own;
Yearnings she hath in her own natural kind,
80 And, even with something of a Mother's mind,
        And no unworthy aim,
        The homely Nurse doth all she can
To make her Foster-child, her Inmate Man,
        Forget the glories he hath known,
And that imperial palace whence he came.

VII

Behold the Child among his new-born blisses,
A six years' Darling of a pigmy size!
See, where 'mid work of his own hand he lies,
Fretted by sallies of his mother's kisses,
90   With light upon him from his father's eyes!
See, at his feet, some little plan or chart,
Some fragment from his dream of human life,
Shaped by himself with newly-learnèd art;
      A wedding or a festival,
      A mourning or a funeral;
        And this hath now his heart,
      And unto this he frames his song:
        Then will he fit his tongue
To dialogues of business, love, or strife;
100   But it will not be long
      Ere this be thrown aside,
      And with new joy and pride
The little Actor cons another part;
Filling from time to time his 'humorous stage'
With all the Persons, down to palsied Age,
That Life brings with her in her equipage;
      As if his whole vocation
      Were endless imitation.

VIII

Thou, whose exterior semblance doth belie
110   Thy Soul's immensity;
Thou best Philosopher, who yet dost keep
Thy heritage, thou Eye among the blind,
That, deaf and silent, read'st the eternal deep,
Haunted for ever by the eternal mind, –
      Mighty Prophet! Seer blest!
      On whom those truths do rest,
Which we are toiling all our lives to find,
In darkness lost, the darkness of the grave;
Thou, over whom thy Immortality

120 Broods like the Day, a Master o'er a Slave,
    A Presence which is not to be put by;
    Thou little Child, yet glorious in the might
    Of heaven-born freedom on thy being's height,
    Why with such earnest pains dost thou provoke
    The years to bring the inevitable yoke,
    Thus blindly with thy blessedness at strife?
    Full soon thy Soul shall have her earthly freight,
    And custom lie upon thee with a weight,
    Heavy as frost, and deep almost as life!

    IX

130   O joy! that in our embers
           Is something that doth live,
           That nature yet remembers
           What was so fugitive!
    The thought of our past years in me doth breed
    Perpetual benediction:[1] not indeed
    For that which is most worthy to be blest;
    Delight and liberty, the simple creed
    Of Childhood, whether busy or at rest,
    With new-fledged hope still fluttering in his breast: —
140   Not for these I raise
           The song of thanks and praise;
         But for those obstinate questionings
         Of sense and outward things,
         Fallings from us, vanishings;
         Blank misgivings of a Creature
    Moving about in worlds not realized,
    High instincts before which our mortal Nature
    Did tremble like a guilty Thing surprised:
           But for those first affections,
150   Those shadowy recollections,
         Which, be they what they may,
    Are yet the fountain light of all our day,

    1. Blessing.

Are yet a master light of all our seeing;
    Uphold us, cherish, and have power to make
Our noisy years seem moments in the being
Of the eternal Silence: truths that wake,
        To perish never;
Which neither listlessness, nor mad endeavour,
        Nor Man nor Boy,
160 Nor all that is at enmity with joy,
Can utterly abolish or destroy!
            Hence in a season of calm weather
            Though inland far we be,
Our Souls have sight of that immortal sea
            Which brought us hither,
        Can in a moment travel thither,
And see the Children sport upon the shore,
And hear the mighty waters rolling evermore.

x
Then sing, ye Birds, sing, sing a joyous song!
170   And let the young Lambs bound
            As to the tabor's sound!
We in thought will join your throng,
            Ye that pipe and ye that play,
            Ye that through your hearts today
            Feel the gladness of the May!
What though the radiance which was once so bright
Be now for ever taken from my sight,
            Though nothing can bring back the hour
Of splendour in the grass, of glory in the flower;
180   We will grieve not, rather find
            Strength in what remains behind;
            In the primal sympathy
            Which having been must ever be;
            In the soothing thoughts that spring
            Out of human suffering;
            In the faith that looks through death,
In years that bring the philosophic mind.

XI

And O, ye Fountains, Meadows, Hills, and Groves,
Forebode not any severing of our loves!
190   Yet in my heart of hearts I feel your might;
I only have relinquished one delight
To live beneath your more habitual sway.
I love the Brooks which down their channels fret,
Even more than when I tripped lightly as they;
The innocent brightness of a new-born Day
      Is lovely yet;
The Clouds that gather round the setting sun
Do take a sober colouring from an eye
That hath kept watch o'er man's mortality;
200   Another race hath been, and other palms[1] are won.
Thanks to the human heart by which we live,
Thanks to its tenderness, its joys, and fears,
To me the meanest flower that blows can give
Thoughts that do often lie too deep for tears.

1. Prizes.

To a Butterfly

I've watched you now a full half-hour,
Self-poised upon that yellow flower;
And, little Butterfly! indeed
I know not if you sleep or feed.
How motionless! – not frozen seas
More motionless! and then
What joy awaits you, when the breeze
Hath found you out among the trees,
And calls you forth again!

10   This plot of orchard-ground is ours;
My trees they are, my Sister's flowers;

Here rest your wings when they are weary;
Here lodge as in a sanctuary!
Come often to us, fear no wrong;
Sit near us on the bough!
We'll talk of sunshine and of song,
And summer days, when we were young;
Sweet childish days, that were as long
As twenty days are now.

To the Small Celandine

Pansies, lilies, kingcups, daisies,
Let them live upon their praises;
Long as there's a sun that sets,
Primroses will have their glory;
Long as there are violets,
They will have a place in story:
There's a flower that shall be mine,
'Tis the little Celandine.

Composed upon Westminster Bridge, September 3, 1802

Earth has not anything to show more fair:
Dull would he be of soul who could pass by
A sight so touching in its majesty:
This City now doth, like a garment, wear
The beauty of the morning; silent, bare,
Ships, towers, domes, theatres, and temples lie
Open unto the fields, and to the sky;
All bright and glittering in the smokeless air.
Never did sun more beautifully steep[1]

1. Soak.

10   In his first splendour, valley, rock, or hill;
  Ne'er saw I, never felt, a calm so deep!
  The river glideth at his own sweet will:
  Dear God! the very houses seem asleep;
  And all that mighty heart is lying still!

London, 1802

  Milton! thou shouldst be living at this hour:
  England hath need of thee: she is a fen
  Of stagnant waters: altar, sword, and pen,
  Fireside, the heroic wealth of hall and bower,
  Have forfeited their ancient English dower
  Of inward happiness. We are selfish men;
  Oh! raise us up, return to us again;
  And give us manners, virtue, freedom, power.
  Thy soul was like a Star, and dwelt apart:
10   Thou hadst a voice whose sound was like the sea:
  Pure as the naked heavens, majestic, free,
  So didst thou travel on life's common way,
  In cheerful godliness; and yet thy heart
  The lowliest duties on herself did lay.

'I wandered lonely as a cloud'

  I wandered lonely as a cloud
  That floats on high o'er vales and hills,
  When all at once I saw a crowd,
  A host, of golden daffodils;
  Beside the lake, beneath the trees,
  Fluttering and dancing in the breeze.

Continuous as the stars that shine
And twinkle on the milky way,
They stretched in never-ending line
10 Along the margin of a bay:
Ten thousand saw I at a glance,
Tossing their heads in sprightly dance.

The waves beside them danced; but they
Out-did the sparkling waves in glee:
A poet could not but be gay,
In such a jocund company:
I gazed – and gazed – but little thought
What wealth the show to me had brought:

For oft, when on my couch I lie
20 In vacant or in pensive mood,
They flash upon that inward eye
Which is the bliss of solitude;
And then my heart with pleasure fills,
And dances with the daffodils.

'Surprised by joy – impatient as the Wind'

Surprised by joy – impatient as the Wind
I turned to share the transport – Oh! with whom
But Thee, deep buried in the silent tomb,
That spot which no vicissitude can find?
Love, faithful love, recalled thee to my mind –
But how could I forget thee? Through what power,
Even for the least division of an hour,
Have I been so beguiled as to be blind
To my most grievous loss! – That thought's return
10 Was the worst pang that sorrow ever bore,
Save one, one only, when I stood forlorn,
Knowing my heart's best treasure was no more;
That neither present time, nor years unborn
Could to my sight that heavenly face restore.

To a Skylark

Ethereal[1] minstrel! pilgrim of the sky!
Dost thou despise the earth where cares abound?
Or, while the wings aspire,[2] are heart and eye
Both with thy nest upon the dewy ground?
Thy nest which thou canst drop into at will,
Those quivering wings composed, that music still!

Leave to the nightingale her shady wood;
A privacy of glorious light is thine;
Whence thou dost pour upon the world a flood
10   Of harmony, with instinct more divine;
Type of the wise who soar, but never roam;
True to the kindred points of Heaven and Home!

1. Heavenly.
2. Aim upwards.

from THE PRELUDE

BOOK FIRST

One summer evening (led by her) I found
A little boat tied to a willow tree
Within a rocky cave, its usual home.
Straight I unloosed her chain, and stepping in
Pushed from the shore. It was an act of stealth
And troubled pleasure, nor without the voice
Of mountain-echoes did my boat move on,
Leaving behind her still on either side,
Small circles glittering idly in the moon,
10   Until they melted all into one track
Of sparkling light. But now, like one who rows
(Proud of his skill) to reach a chosen point

With an unswerving line, I fixed my view
Upon the summit of a craggy ridge,
The horizon's utmost boundary; far above
Was nothing but the stars and the grey sky.
She was an elfin pinnace,[1] lustily
I dipped my oars into the silent lake
And, as I rose upon the stroke, my boat
20 Went heaving through the water like a swan;
When, from behind that craggy steep till then
The horizon's bound, a huge peak, black and huge,
As if with voluntary power instinct[2]
Upreared its head. I struck and struck again
And growing still in stature the grim shape
Towered up between me and the stars, and still,
For so it seemed, with purpose of its own
And measured motion like a living thing
Strode after me. With trembling oars I turned
30 And through the silent water stole my way
Back to the covert,[3] of the willow tree;
There in her mooring-place I left my bark, –
And through the meadows homeward went in grave
And serious mood, but after I had seen
That spectacle, for many days, my brain
Worked with a dim and undetermined sense
Of unknown modes of being; o'er my thoughts
There hung a darkness, call it solitude
Or blank desertion. No familiar shapes
40 Remained, no pleasant images of trees,
Of sea or sky, no colours of green fields;
But huge and mighty forms, that do not live
Like living men, moved slowly through the mind
By day, and were a trouble to my dreams.

*   *   *

1. A small dinghy.
2. Filled.
3. Shelter.

And in the frosty season, when the sun
Was set, and visible for many a mile
The cottage windows blazed through twilight gloom,
I heeded not their summons – happy time
It was indeed for all of us, for me
50 It was a time of rapture! Clear and loud
The village clock tolled six – I wheeled about,
Proud and exulting like an untired horse
That cares not for his home. All shod with steel
We hissed along the polished ice in games
Confederate,[1] imitative of the chase
And woodland pleasures, – the resounding horn,
The pack loud chiming, and the hunted hare.
So through the darkness and the cold we flew,
And not a voice was idle; with the din
60 Smitten, the precipices rang aloud;
The leafless trees and every icy crag
Tinkled like iron; while far distant hills
Into the tumult sent an alien sound
Of melancholy, not unnoticed, while the stars
Eastward were sparkling clear, and in the west
The orange sky of evening died away.
Not seldom from the uproar I retired
Into a silent bay, or sportively
Glanced sideway, leaving the tumultuous throng
70 To cut across the reflex[2] of a star
That fled and flying still before me gleamed
Upon the glassy plain; and oftentimes
When we had given our bodies to the wind
And all the shadowy banks on either side
Came sweeping through the darkness, spinning still
The rapid line of motion, then at once
Have I, reclining back upon my heels,
Stopped short, yet still the solitary cliffs
Wheeled by me – even as if the earth had rolled

1. Games played in a group.
2. Reflection.

80   With visible motion her diurnal[1] round!
      Behind me did they stretch in solemn train,
      Feebler and feebler, and I stood and watched
      Till all was tranquil as a dreamless sleep.

      1. Daily.

Samuel Taylor Coleridge
(1772–1834)

Coleridge was born in Ottery St Mary, Devonshire, the youngest child of ten of a clergyman and schoolmaster. He was educated at Christ's Hospital, London. According to his own account, he was a temperamental child, an oddity, bad at sports but an avid reader. In 1791 he went to Jesus College, Cambridge, but got into debt and, in order to escape from it, joined the army under a false name. His family bought him out of that mistake and he returned to Cambridge, but left in 1794 without taking his degree.

By this time, he had met and befriended Robert Southey, who later became the Poet Laureate. They planned a 'Pantisocracy', an ideal community on the banks of the Susquehanna River in Pennsylvania consisting of twelve young men and their wives. Coleridge and Southey married two sisters, but that was the only practical outcome of the Pantisocracy project, and in Coleridge's case the marriage proved unhappy. Southey left for Portugal, and Coleridge remained in England to write and lecture.

In 1796 Coleridge published *Poems on Various Subjects*. The following year he met William Wordsworth, who was living not far away with his sister Dorothy. A great friendship grew up; they went on long walks and visits, and even travelled to Germany together. At this time, Coleridge wrote among other works his conversational poems 'Frost at Midnight' and 'The Nightingale', and his long narrative poem 'The Rime of the Ancient Mariner'. These were published with some of Wordsworth's poems in their 1798 volume *Lyrical Ballads*, which is generally taken to be the first major work of the English Romantic movement.

One particularly striking poem written during this period was 'Kubla Khan'. Coleridge's health had never been good, and he had taken to using a form of opium for relief of pain from rheumatism and other ailments. His addiction to the drug became a curse that he struggled against for the rest of his life. His account of the drug-induced dream that inspired him to turn a sentence in a history book into a mystical poem, and how an interruption caused him to forget the ending, is printed here.

Coleridge never settled into steady work. He lived in the Lake District on the charity of various friends and family for a while, and then went to Malta for two years as secretary to the governor. He was a journalist, and also wrote and lectured on various aspects of literary criticism, politics, philosophy and theology, and of course continued to write poetry. His literary criticism had a great influence on later writers and critics.

In 1816, with his health wrecked by opium, Coleridge went to live at the house of Dr James Gillman, a physician of Highgate who admired his work. Gillman's care improved his health, and Coleridge spent the rest of his life there, receiving many visits from friends and from young writers who came to hear him deliver long and learned monologues on literature. He continued to write and publish until his death.

Coleridge was one of the most gifted and learned men of his time. He was prone to make grand forecasts about his work which were never quite fulfilled, a failure which he put down to his 'constitutional indolence'. However, the volume and depth of his writings on various subjects, and the lyricism of his poetry, would be beyond the reach of most people.

The dreamlike imagery of his poetry, nightmarish in places in 'The Rime of the Ancient Mariner', blends the natural and the supernatural with profound concepts derived from his reading of philosophy and mysticism. At the same time he can write of his delight in his child and capture with precision his own thoughts, feelings and reactions to the natural world. This is particularly well shown in 'Frost at Midnight', where he depicts himself awake and gazing into the flickering fire on a frosty night when everybody else in the house is asleep, and reflects on his solitude, on memories of his childhood, and on his joy in and hopes for the son who lies asleep in the cradle next to him.

The Rime of the Ancient Mariner

ARGUMENT

How a Ship having passed the Line was driven by storms to the cold Country towards the South Pole; and how from thence she made her course to the tropical Latitude of the Great Pacific Ocean; and of the strange things that befell; and in what manner the Ancyent Marinere came back to his own Country.

PART I

An ancient Mariner meeteth three Gallants bidden to a wedding-feast, and detaineth one.

It is an ancient Mariner
And he stoppeth one of three.
'By thy long grey beard and glittering eye,
Now wherefore stopp'st thou me?

The Bridegroom's doors are opened wide,
And I am next of kin;
The guests are met, the feast is set:
May'st hear the merry din.'

The Wedding Guest is spellbound by the eye of the old seafaring man, and constrained to hear his tale.

He holds him with his skinny hand,
'There was a ship,' quoth he.   10
'Hold off! unhand me, grey-beard loon!'[1]
Eftsoons[2] his hand dropt he.

He holds him with his glittering eye –
The Wedding-Guest stood still,
And listens like a three years' child:
The Mariner hath his will.

The Wedding-Guest sat on a stone:
He cannot choose but hear;
And thus spake on that ancient man,
The bright-eyed Mariner.   20

1. Rogue or worthless person.
2. Soon.

The Mariner
tells how the
ship sailed
southward
with a good
wind and fair
weather, till it
reached the
line.

'The ship was cheered, the harbour cleared,
Merrily did we drop
Below the kirk, below the hill,
Below the lighthouse top.

The Sun came up upon the left,
Out of the sea came he!
And he shone bright, and on the right
Went down into the sea.

Higher and higher every day,
Till over the mast at noon –'   30
The Wedding-Guest here beat his breast,
For he heard the loud bassoon.

The Wedding-
Guest heareth
the bridal
music; but
the Mariner
continueth
his tale.

The bride hath paced into the hall,
Red as a rose is she;
Nodding their heads before her goes
The merry minstrelsy.

The Wedding-Guest he beat his breast,
Yet he cannot choose but hear;
And thus spake on that ancient man,
The bright-eyed Mariner.   40

The ship
driven by a
storm toward
the south pole.

'And now the STORM-BLAST came, and he
Was tyrannous and strong:
He struck with his o'ertaking wings,
And chased us south along.

With sloping masts and dipping prow,
As who pursued with yell and blow
Still treads the shadow of his foe,
And forward bends his head,
The ship drove fast, loud roared the blast,
And southward aye we fled.   50

And now there came both mist and snow,
And it grew wondrous cold:
And ice, mast-high, came floating by,
As green as emerald.

The land of
ice, and of
fearful sounds
where no
living thing
was to be seen.

And through the drifts the snowy clifts
Did send a dismal sheen:
Nor shapes of men nor beasts we ken —
The ice was all between.

The ice was here, the ice was there,
The ice was all around: 60
It cracked and growled, and roared and
    howled,
Like noises in a swound![1]

Till a great
sea-bird,
called the
Albatross,
came through
the snow-fog,
and was
received with
great joy and
hospitality.

At length did cross an Albatross,
Thorough the fog it came;
As if it had been a Christian soul,
We hailed it in God's name.

It ate the food it ne'er had eat,
And round and round it flew.
The ice did split with a thunder-fit;
The helmsman steered us through!   70

And lo! the
Albatross
proveth a bird
of good omen,
and followeth
the ship as it
returned
northward
through fog
and floating ice.

And a good south wind sprung up behind;
The Albatross did follow,
And every day, for food or play,
Came to the mariners' hollo!

In mist or cloud, on mast or shroud,
It perched for vespers nine;
Whiles all the night, through fog-smoke
    white,
Glimmered the white Moon-shine.'

1. Swoon.

The ancient Mariner inhospitably killeth the pious bird of good omen.

'God save thee, ancient Mariner!
From the fiends, that plague thee thus! –
Why look'st thou so?' – With my cross-bow
I shot the ALBATROSS.

80

PART II

The Sun now rose upon the right:
Out of the sea came he,
Still hid in mist, and on the left
Went down into the sea.

And the good south wind still blew behind,
But no sweet bird did follow,
Nor any day for food or play
Came to the mariners' hollo!

90

His shipmates cry out against the ancient Mariner, for killing the bird of good luck.

And I had done a hellish thing,
And it would work 'em woe:
For all averred, I had killed the bird
That made the breeze to blow.
Ah wretch! said they, the bird to slay,
That made the breeze to blow!

But when the fog cleared off, they justify the same, and thus make themselves accomplices in the crime.

Nor dim nor red, like God's own head,
The glorious Sun uprist:
Then all averred, I had killed the bird
That brought the fog and mist.
'Twas right, said they, such birds to slay,
That bring the fog and mist.

100

The fair breeze
continues; the
ship enters the
Pacific Ocean,
and sails
northward,
even till it
reaches the Line.

The fair breeze blew, the white foam flew,
The furrow followed free;
We were the first that ever burst
Into that silent sea.

The ship hath
been suddenly
becalmed.

Down dropt the breeze, the sails dropt down,
'Twas sad as sad could be;
And we did speak only to break
The silence of the sea!   110

All in a hot and copper sky,
The bloody Sun, at noon,
Right up above the mast did stand,
No bigger than the Moon.

Day after day, day after day,
We stuck, nor breath nor motion;
As idle as a painted ship
Upon a painted ocean.

And the
Albatross begins
to be avenged.

Water, water, every where,
And all the boards did shrink;   120
Water, water, every where,
Nor any drop to drink.

The very deep did rot: O Christ!
That ever this should be!
Yea, slimy things did crawl with legs
Upon the slimy sea.

About, about, in a reel and rout
The death-fires danced at night;
The water, like a witch's oils,
Burnt green, and blue and white.   130
And some in dreams assuréd were

A Spirit had
followed them;
one of the
invisible
inhabitants of

Of the spirit that plagued us so;
Nine fathom deep he had followed us
From the land of mist and snow.

this planet, neither departed souls nor angels; concerning whom the learned
Jew, Josephus, and the Platonic Constantinopolitan, Michael Psellus, may be
consulted. They are very numerous, and there is no climate or element without
one or more.

And every tongue, through utter drought,
Was withered at the root;
We could not speak, no more than if
We had been choked with soot.

The shipmates,
in their sore
distress, would
fain throw the
whole guilt on
the ancient

Ah! well a-day! what evil looks
Had I from old and young!   140
Instead of the cross, the Albatross
About my neck was hung.

Mariner: in sign whereof they hang the dead sea-bird round his neck.

PART III

There passed a weary time. Each throat
Was parched, and glazed each eye.
A weary time! a weary time!
How glazed each weary eye,

The ancient
Mariner be-
holdeth a sign
in the element
afar off.

When looking westward, I beheld
A something in the sky.

At first it seemed a little speck,
And then it seemed a mist;   150
It moved and moved, and took at last
A certain shape, I wist.[1]

A speck, a mist, a shape, I wist!
And still it neared and neared:
As if it dodged a water-sprite,
It plunged and tacked and veered.

1. Knew.

With throats unslaked, with black lips baked,
We could nor laugh nor wail;
Through utter drought all dumb we stood!
I bit my arm, I sucked the blood,   160
And cried, A sail! a sail!

With throats unslaked, with black lips baked,
Agape they heard me call:
Gramercy!¹ they for joy did grin,
And all at once their breath drew in,
As they were drinking all.

See! see! (I cried) she tacks no more!
Hither to work us weal;²
Without a breeze, without a tide,
She steadies with upright keel!   170

The western wave was all a-flame.
The day was well nigh done!
Almost upon the western wave
Rested the broad bright Sun;
When that strange shape drove suddenly
Betwixt us and the Sun.

And straight the Sun was flecked with bars,
(Heaven's Mother send us grace!)
As if through a dungeon-grate he peered
With broad and burning face.   180

1. Thanks.
2. Good.

At its nearer approach, it seemeth him to be a ship; and at a dear ransom he freeth his speech from the bonds of thirst.

A flash of joy;

and horror follows. For can it be a ship that comes onward without wind or tide?

It seemeth him but the skeleton of a ship.

And its ribs
are seen as
bars on the
face of the
setting Sun.
The Spectre-
Woman and
her Death-
mate, and no
other on
board the
skeleton ship.

Alas! (thought I, and my heart beat loud)
How fast she nears and nears!
Are those *her* sails that glance in the Sun,
Like restless gossameres?

Are those *her* ribs through which the Sun
Did peer, as through a grate?
And is that Woman all her crew?
Is that a DEATH? and are there two?
Is DEATH that woman's mate?

Like vessel,
like crew!
Death and
Life-in-Death
have diced for
the ship's
crew, and she
(the latter)
winneth the
ancient
Mariner.

Her lips were red, *her* looks were free,   190
Her locks were yellow as gold:
Her skin was as white as leprosy,
The Night-mare LIFE-IN-DEATH was she,
Who thicks man's blood with cold.

The naked hulk alongside came,
And the twain were casting dice;
'The game is done! I've won! I've won!'
Quoth she, and whistles thrice.

No twilight
within the
courts of the
Sun.

The Sun's rim dips; the stars rush out:
At one stride comes the dark;   200
With far-heard whisper, o'er the sea,
Off shot the spectre-bark.

At the rising
of the Moon,

We listened and looked sideways up!
Fear at my heart, as at a cup,
My life-blood seemed to sip!
The stars were dim, and thick the night,
The steersman's face by his lamp gleamed
     white;

From the sails the dew did drip –
Till clomb[1] above the eastern bar
The hornéd Moon, with one bright star   210
Within the nether[2] tip.

*one after
another,*

One after one, by the star-dogged Moon,
Too quick for groan or sigh,
Each turned his face with a ghastly pang,
And cursed me with his eye.

*his shipmates
drop down
dead.*

Four times fifty living men,
(And I heard nor sigh nor groan)
With heavy thump, a lifeless lump,
They dropped down one by one.

*But Life-in-
Death begins
her work on
the ancient
Mariner.*

The souls did from their bodies fly, –   220
They fled to bliss or woe!
And every soul, it passed me by,
Like the whizz of my cross-bow!

PART IV

*The Wedding-
Guest feareth
that a Spirit
is talking to
him;*

'I fear thee, ancient Mariner!
I fear thy skinny hand!
And thou art long, and lank, and brown,
As is the ribbed sea-sand.

I fear thee and thy glittering eye,
And thy skinny hand, so brown.' –

*but the ancient
Mariner assureth
him of his
bodily life, and
proceedeth to
relate his
horrible penance.*

Fear not, fear not, thou Wedding-Guest!   230
This body dropt not down.

1. Climbed.
2. Lower.

Alone, alone, all, all alone,
Alone on a wide wide sea!
And never a saint took pity on
My soul in agony.

He despiseth
the creatures
of the calm,

The many men, so beautiful!
And they all dead did lie:
And a thousand thousand slimy things
Lived on; and so did I.

and envieth
that *they*
should live,
and so many
lie dead.

I looked upon the rotting sea,   240
And drew my eyes away;
I looked upon the rotting deck,
And there the dead men lay.

I looked to heaven, and tried to pray;
But or ever a prayer had gusht,
A wicked whisper came, and made
My heart as dry as dust.

I closed my lids, and kept them close,
And the balls like pulses beat;
For the sky and the sea, and the sea and the   250
   sky
Lay like a load on my weary eye,
And the dead were at my feet.

But the curse
liveth for him
in the eye of
the dead men.

The cold sweat melted from their limbs,
Nor rot nor reek did they:
The look with which they looked on me
Had never passed away.

An orphan's curse would drag to hell
A spirit from on high;
But oh! more horrible than that
Is the curse in a dead man's eye!   260
Seven days, seven nights, I saw that curse,
And yet I could not die.

In his lone-
liness and
fixedness he
yearneth to-
wards the
journeying
Moon, and the
stars that still
sojourn, yet
still move
onward; and
every where
the blue sky
belongs to

The moving Moon went up the sky,
And no where did abide:
Softly she was going up,
And a star or two beside –

Her beams bemocked the sultry main,
Like April hoar-frost spread;
But where the ship's huge shadow lay,
The charméd water burnt alway   270
A still and awful red.

them, and is their appointed rest, and their native country and their own natural
homes, which they enter unannounced, as lords that are certainly expected and
yet there is a silent joy at their arrival.

By the light
of the Moon he
beholdeth
God's crea-
tures of the
great calm.

Beyond the shadow of the ship,
I watched the water-snakes:
They moved in tracks of shining white,
And when they reared, the elfish light
Fell off in hoary flakes.

Within the shadow of the ship
I watched their rich attire:
Blue, glossy green, and velvet black,   280
They coiled and swam; and every track
Was a flash of golden fire.

Their beauty
and their
happiness.

O happy living things! no tongue
Their beauty might declare:
A spring of love gushed from my heart,

He blesseth
them in his
heart.

And I blessed them unaware:
Sure my kind saint took pity on me,
And I blessed them unaware.

The spell
begins to
break.

The self-same moment I could pray;
And from my neck so free
The Albatross fell off, and sank   290
Like lead into the sea.

PART V

Oh sleep! it is a gentle thing,
Beloved from pole to pole!
To Mary Queen the praise be given!
She sent the gentle sleep from Heaven,
That slid into my soul.

By grace of the holy Mother, the ancient Mariner is refreshed with rain.

The silly buckets on the deck,
That had so long remained,
I dreamt that they were filled with dew;
And when I awoke, it rained.   300

My lips were wet, my throat was cold,
My garments all were dank;
Sure I had drunken in my dreams,
And still my body drank.

I moved, and could not feel my limbs:
I was so light – almost
I thought that I had died in sleep,
And was a blessèd ghost.

He heareth sounds and seeth strange sights and commotions in the sky and the element.

And soon I heard a roaring wind:
It did not come anear;   310
But with its sound it shook the sails,
That were so thin and sere.[1]

The upper air burst into life!
And a hundred fire-flags sheen,
To and fro they were hurried about!
And to and fro, and in and out,
The wan stars danced between.

And the coming wind did roar more loud,
And the sails did sigh like sedge;
And the rain poured down from one black   320
    cloud;
The Moon was at its edge.

1. Worn.

The thick black cloud was cleft, and still
The Moon was at its side:
Like waters shot from some high crag,
The lightning fell with never a jag,
A river steep and wide.

The bodies of the ship's crew are inspirited, and the ship moves on;

The loud wind never reached the ship,
Yet now the ship moved on!
Beneath the lightning and the Moon
The dead men gave a groan.   330

They groaned, they stirred, they all uprose,
Nor spake, nor moved their eyes;
It had been strange, even in a dream,
To have seen those dead men rise.

The helmsman steered, the ship moved on;
Yet never a breeze up-blew;
The mariners all 'gan work the ropes,
Where they were wont to do;
They raised their limbs like lifeless tools –
We were a ghastly crew.   340

The body of my brother's son
Stood by me, knee to knee:
The body and I pulled at one rope,
But he said nought to me.

'I fear thee, ancient Mariner!'
Be calm, thou Wedding-Guest!
'Twas not those souls that fled in pain,
Which to their corses¹ came again,
But a troop of spirits blest:

1. Corpses.

but not by the
souls of the
men, nor by
daemons of
earth or
middle air, but
by a blessed
troop of
angelic spirits,
sent down by
the invocation
of the
guardian saint.

For when it dawned – they dropped their   350
   arms,
And clustered round the mast;
Sweet sounds rose slowly through their
   mouths,
And from their bodies passed.

Around, around, flew each sweet sound,
Then darted to the Sun;
Slowly the sounds came back again,
Now mixed, now one by one.

Sometimes a-dropping from the sky
I heard the sky-lark sing;
Sometimes all little birds that are,   360
How they seemed to fill the sea and air
With their sweet jargoning!

And now 'twas like all instruments,
Now like a lonely flute;
And now it is an angel's song,
That makes the heavens be mute.

It ceased; yet still the sails made on
A pleasant noise till noon,
A noise like of a hidden brook
In the leafy month of June,   370
That to the sleeping woods all night
Singeth a quiet tune.

Till noon we quietly sailed on,
Yet never a breeze did breathe:
Slowly and smoothly went the ship,
Moved onward from beneath.

The lonesome Spirit from the south-pole carries on the ship as far as the Line, in obedience to the angelic troop, but still requireth vengeance.

Under the keel nine fathom deep,
From the land of mist and snow,
The spirit slid: and it was he
That made the ship to go.   380
The sails at noon left off their tune,
And the ship stood still also.

The Sun, right up above the mast,
Had fixed her to the ocean:
But in a minute she 'gan stir,
With a short uneasy motion –
Backwards and forwards half her length
With a short uneasy motion.

Then like a pawing horse let go,
She made a sudden bound: 390
It flung the blood into my head,
And I fell down in a swound.

The Polar Spirit's fellow-daemons, the invisible inhabitants of the element, take part in his wrong; and two of them relate, one to the other, that penance long and heavy for the ancient Mariner hath been accorded to the Polar Spirit, who returneth southward.

How long in that same fit I lay,
I have not to declare;
But ere my living life returned,
I heard and in my soul discerned
Two voices in the air.

'Is it he?' quoth one, 'Is this the man?
By him who died on cross,
With his cruel bow he laid full low   400
The harmless Albatross.

The spirit who bideth by himself
In the land of mist and snow,
He loved the bird that loved the man
Who shot him with his bow.'

The other was a softer voice,
As soft as honey-dew:
Quoth he, 'The man hath penance done,
And penance more will do.'

PART VI

First Voice

'But tell me, tell me! speak again,
Thy soft response renewing —   410
What makes that ship drive on so fast?
What is the ocean doing?'

Second Voice

'Still as a slave before his lord,
The ocean hath no blast;
His great bright eye most silently
Up to the Moon is cast —

If he may know which way to go:
For she guides him smooth or grim.
See, brother, see! how graciously   420
She looketh down on him.'

First Voice

'But why drives on that ship so fast,
Without or wave or wind?'

Second Voice

'The air is cut away before,
And closes from behind.

Fly, brother, fly! more high, more high!
Or we shall be belated:
For slow and slow that ship will go,
When the Mariner's trance is abated.'

I woke, and we were sailing on   430
As in a gentle weather:
'Twas night, calm night, the moon was high;
The dead men stood together.

The Mariner hath been cast into a trance; for the angelic power causeth the vessel to drive northward faster than human life could endure.

The supernatural motion is retarded; the Mariner awakes, and his penance begins anew.

All stood together on the deck,
For a charnel[1]-dungeon fitter:
All fixed on me their stony eyes,
That in the Moon did glitter.

The pang, the curse, with which they died,
Had never passed away:
I could not draw my eyes from theirs,   440
Nor turn them up to pray.

The curse is
finally ex-
piated.

And now this spell was snapt: once more
I viewed the ocean green,
And looked far forth, yet little saw
Of what had else been seen –

Like one, that on a lonesome road
Doth walk in fear and dread,
And having once turned round walks on,
And turns no more his head;
Because he knows, a frightful fiend   450
Doth close behind him tread.

But soon there breathed a wind on me,
Nor sound nor motion made:
Its path was not upon the sea,
In ripple or in shade.

It raised my hair, it fanned my cheek
Like a meadow-gale of spring –
It mingled strangely with my fears,
Yet it felt like a welcoming.

Swiftly, swiftly flew the ship,   460
Yet she sailed softly too:
Sweetly, sweetly blew the breeze –
On me alone it blew.

1. Place where dead bodies or bones were kept.

And the
ancient
Mariner be-
holdeth his
native
country.

Oh! dream of joy! is this indeed
The light-house top I see?
Is this the hill? is this the kirk?
Is this mine own countree?

We drifted o'er the harbour-bar,
And I with sobs did pray –
O let me be awake, my God!
Or let me sleep alway.

470

The harbour-bar was clear as glass,
So smoothly it was strewn!
And on the bay the moonlight lay,
And the shadow of the Moon.

The rock shone bright, the kirk no less,
That stands above the rock:
The moonlight steeped in silentness
The steady weathercock.

And the bay was white with silent light,
Till rising from the same,
Full many shapes, that shadows were,
In crimson colours came.

480

The angelic
spirits leave
the dead
bodies,
and appear in
their own
forms of light.

A little distance from the prow
Those crimson shadows were:
I turned my eyes upon the deck –
Oh, Christ! what I saw there!

Each corse lay flat, lifeless and flat,
And, by the holy rood!
A man all light, a seraph-man,
On every corse there stood.

490

This seraph-band, each waved his hand:
It was a heavenly sight!
They stood as signals to the land,
Each one a lovely light;

This seraph-band, each waved his hand,
No voice did they impart –
No voice; but oh! the silence sank
Like music on my heart

But soon I heard the dash of oars,   500
I heard the Pilot's cheer;
My head was turned perforce away
And I saw a boat appear.

The Pilot and the Pilot's boy,
I heard them coming fast:
Dear Lord in Heaven! it was a joy
The dead men could not blast.

I saw a third – I heard his voice:
It is the Hermit good!
He singeth loud his godly hymns   510
That he makes in the wood.
He'll shrieve[1] my soul, he'll wash away
The Albatross's blood.

PART VII

The Hermit of
the Wood,
This Hermit good lives in that wood
Which slopes down to the sea.
How loudly his sweet voice he rears!
He loves to talk with marineres
That come from a far countree.

He kneels at morn, and noon, and eve –
He hath a cushion plump: 520
It is the moss that wholly hides
The rotted old oak-stump.

The skiff-boat neared: I heard them talk,
'Why, this is strange, I trow!
Where are those lights so many and fair,
That signal made but now?'

1. Hear confession, give penance and pronounce absolution for sins.

the ship with
wonder.

'Strange, by my faith!' the Hermit said –
'And they answered not our cheer!
The planks looked warped! and see those
   sails,
How thin they are and sere!   530
I never saw aught like to them,
Unless perchance it were

Brown skeletons of leaves that lag
My forest-brook along;
When the ivy-tod is heavy with snow,
And the owlet whoops to the wolf below,
That eats the she-wolf's young.'

'Dear Lord! it hath a fiendish look –
(The Pilot made reply)
I am a-feared' – 'Push on, push on!'   540
Said the Hermit cheerily.

The boat came closer to the ship,
But I nor spake nor stirred;
The boat came close beneath the ship,
And straight a sound was heard.

The ship
suddenly
sinketh.

Under the water it rumbled on,
Still louder and more dead:
It reached the ship, it split the bay;
The ship went down like lead.

The ancient
Mariner is
saved in the
Pilot's boat.

Stunned by that loud and dreadful sound,   550
Which sky and ocean smote,
Like one that hath been seven days drowned
My body lay afloat;
But swift as dreams, myself I found
Within the Pilot's boat.

Upon the whirl, where sank the ship,
The boat spun round and round;
And all was still, save that the hill
Was telling of the sound.

I moved my lips – the Pilot shrieked   560
And fell down in a fit;
The holy Hermit raised his eyes,
And prayed where he did sit.

I took the oars: the Pilot's boy,
Who now doth crazy go,
Laughed loud and long, and all the while
His eyes went to and fro.
'Ha! ha!' quoth he, 'full plain I see,
The Devil knows how to row.'

And now, all in my own countree,   570
I stood on the firm land!
The Hermit stepped forth from the boat,
And scarcely he could stand.

The ancient Mariner earnestly entreateth the Hermit to shrieve him; and the penance of life falls on him.

'Oh shrieve me, shrieve me, holy man!'
The Hermit crossed his brow.
'Say quick,' quoth he, 'I bid thee say –
What manner of man art thou?'

Forthwith this frame of mine was wrenched
With a woful agony,
Which forced me to begin my tale;   580
And then it left me free.

And ever and anon throughout his future life an agony constraineth

Since then, at an uncertain hour,
That agony returns:
And till my ghastly tale is told,
This heart within me burns.

him to travel from land to land;

I pass, like night, from land to land;
I have strange power of speech;
That moment that his face I see,
I know the man that must hear me:
To him my tale I teach.   590

What loud uproar bursts from that door!
The wedding-guests are there:
But in the garden-bower the bride
And bride-maids singing are:
And hark the little vesper bell,
Which biddeth me to prayer!

O Wedding-Guest! this soul hath been
Alone on a wide wide sea:
So lonely 'twas, that God himself
Scarce seeméd there to be.   600

O sweeter than the marriage-feast,
'Tis sweeter far to me,
To walk together to the kirk
With a goodly company! –

To walk together to the kirk,
And all together pray,
While each to his great Father bends,
Old men, and babes, and loving friends
And youths and maidens gay!

and to teach,   Farewell, farewell! but this I tell   610
by his own   To thee, thou Wedding-Guest!
example, love   He prayeth well, who loveth well
and reverence   Both man and bird and beast.
to all things
that God made
and loveth.

He prayeth best, who loveth best
All things both great and small;
For the dear God who loveth us,
He made and loveth all.

The Mariner, whose eye is bright,
Whose beard with age is hoar,
Is gone: and now the Wedding-Guest   620
Turned from the bridegroom's door.

He went like one that hath been stunned,
And is of sense forlorn:
A sadder and a wiser man,
He rose the morrow morn.

Frost at Midnight

The Frost performs its secret ministry,
Unhelped by any wind. The owlet's cry
Came loud – and hark, again! loud as before.
The inmates of my cottage, all at rest,
Have left me to that solitude, which suits
Abstruser[1] musings: save that at my side
My cradled infant slumbers peacefully.
'Tis calm indeed! so calm, that it disturbs
And vexes meditation with its strange
10 And extreme silentness. Sea, hill, and wood,
This populous village! Sea, and hill, and wood,
With all the numberless goings-on of life,
Inaudible as dreams! the thin blue flame
Lies on my low-burnt fire, and quivers not;
Only that film, which fluttered on the grate,
Still flutters there, the sole unquiet thing.
Methinks, its motion in this hush of nature
Gives it dim sympathies with me who live,
Making it a companionable form,
20 Whose puny flaps and freaks the idling Spirit
By its own moods interprets, every where
Echo or mirror seeking of itself,
And makes a toy of Thought.

                              But O! how oft,
How oft, at school, with most believing mind,

1. Profound, out of the ordinary range of human thought.

Presageful,[1] have I gazed upon the bars,
To watch that fluttering *stranger*! and as oft
With unclosed lids, already had I dreamt
Of my sweet birth-place, and the old church-tower,
Whose bells, the poor man's only music, rang
30 From morn to evening, all the hot Fair-day,
So sweetly, that they stirred and haunted me
With a wild pleasure, falling on mine ear
Most like articulate sounds of things to come!
So gazed I, till the soothing things, I dreamt,
Lulled me to sleep, and sleep prolonged my dreams!
And so I brooded all the following morn,
Awed by the stern preceptor's[2] face, mine eye
Fixed with mock study on my swimming book:
Save if the door half opened, and I snatched
40 A hasty glance, and still my heart leaped up,
For still I hoped to see the *stranger's* face,
Townsman, or aunt, or sister more beloved,
My play-mate when we both were clothed alike!

   Dear Babe, that sleepest cradled by my side,
Whose gentle breathings, heard in this deep calm,
Fill up the intersperséd vacancies
And momentary pauses of the thought!
My babe so beautiful! it thrills my heart
With tender gladness, thus to look at thee,
50 And think that thou shalt learn far other lore,
And in far other scenes! For I was reared
In the great city, pent 'mid cloisters dim,
And saw nought lovely but the sky and stars.
But *thou*, my babe! shalt wander like a breeze
By lakes and sandy shores, beneath the crags
Of ancient mountain, and beneath the clouds,
Which image in their bulk both lakes and shores
And mountain crags: so shalt thou see and hear

1. Foreseeing.
2. Teacher's.

The lovely shapes and sounds intelligible
60 Of that eternal language, which thy God
Utters, who from eternity doth teach
Himself in all, and all things in himself.
Great universal Teacher! he shall mould
Thy spirit, and by giving make it ask.

Therefore all seasons shall be sweet to thee,
Whether the summer clothe the general earth
With greenness, or the redbreast sit and sing
Betwixt the tufts of snow on the bare branch
Of mossy apple-tree, while the high thatch
70 Smokes in the sun-thaw; whether the eave-drops fall
Heard only in the trances of the blast,
Or if the secret ministry of frost
Shall hang them up in silent icicles,
Quietly shining to the quiet Moon.

A Beck in Winter

Over the broad, the shallow, rapid stream,
The Alder, a vast hollow Trunk, and ribb'd –
All mossy green with mosses manifold,
And ferns still waving in the river-breeze
Sent out, like fingers, five projecting trunks –
The shortest twice 6 (?) of a tall man's strides. –
One curving upward in its middle growth
Rose straight with grove of twigs – a pollard[1] tree: –
The rest more backward, gradual in descent –
10 One in the brook and one befoamed its waters:
One ran along the bank in the elk-like head
And pomp of antlers –

1. A tree whose branches have been cut and used, leaving the trunk to grow new branches.

Sonnet

TO THE RIVER OTTER

Dear native Brook! wild Streamlet of the West!
  How many various-fated years have past,
  What happy and what mournful hours, since last
I skimm'd the smooth thin stone along thy breast,
Numbering its light leaps! yet so deep imprest
Sink the sweet scenes of childhood, that mine eyes
  I never shut amid the sunny ray,
But straight with all their tints thy waters rise,
  Thy crossing plank, thy marge[1] with willows grey,
And bedded sand that vein'd with various dyes
Gleam'd through thy bright transparence! On my way,
  Visions of Childhood! oft have ye beguil'd[2]
Lone manhood's cares, yet waking fondest sighs:
  Ah! that once more I were a careless Child!

1. Bank.
2. Often have you whiled away the time agreeably when I was oppressed by the cares of adult life.

Fragment

Sea-ward, white gleaming thro' the busy scud[1]
With arching Wings, the sea-mew[2] o'er my head
Posts on, as bent on speed, now passaging
Edges the stiffer Breeze, now, yielding, drifts,
Now floats upon the air, and sends from far
A wildly-wailing Note.

1. Ocean spray driven swiftly by the wind.
2. A type of gull.

Fragment

The spruce and limber yellow-hammer
In the dawn of spring and sultry summer,
In hedge or tree the hours beguiling
With notes as of one who brass is filing.

Kubla Khan

OR, A VISION IN A DREAM, A FRAGMENT

The following fragment is here published at the request of a poet of great and deserved celebrity [Lord Byron], and, as far as the Author's own opinions are concerned, rather as a psychological curiosity, than on the ground of any supposed *poetic* merits.

In the summer of the year 1797, the Author, then in ill health, had retired to a lonely farm-house between Porlock and Linton, on the Exmoor confines of Somerset and Devonshire. In consequence of a slight indisposition, an anodyne had been prescribed, from the effects of which he fell asleep in his chair at the moment that he was reading the following sentence, or words of the same substance, in 'Purchas's Pilgrimage': 'Here the Khan Kubla commanded a palace to be built, and a stately garden thereunto. And thus ten miles of fertile ground were inclosed with a wall.' The Author continued for about three hours in a profound sleep, at least of the external senses, during which time he has the most vivid confidence, that he could not have composed less than from two to three hundred lines; if that indeed can be called composition in which all the images rose up before him as *things*, with a parallel production of the correspondent expressions, without any sensation or consciousness of effort. On awaking he appeared to himself to have a distinct recollection of the whole, and taking his pen, ink, and paper, instantly and eagerly wrote down the lines that are here preserved. At this moment he was unfortunately called out by a person on business from Porlock, and detained by him above an hour, and on his return to his room, found, to his no small surprise and mortification, that though he still retained some vague and dim recollection of the general purport of the vision, yet, with the exception of some eight or ten scattered lines and images, all the rest had passed away like the images on the surface of a stream into which a stone has been cast, but, alas! without the after restoration of the latter!

In Xanadu did Kubla Khan
A stately pleasure-dome decree:
Where Alph, the sacred river, ran
Through caverns measureless to man
   Down to a sunless sea.
So twice five miles of fertile ground
With walls and towers were girdled round:
And there were gardens bright with sinuous rills,[1]
Where blossomed many an incense-bearing tree;
And here were forests ancient as the hills,
10 Enfolding sunny spots of greenery.

But oh! that deep romantic chasm which slanted
Down the green hill athwart a cedarn cover![2]
A savage place! as holy and enchanted
As e'er beneath a waning moon was haunted
By woman wailing for her demon-lover!
And from this chasm, with ceaseless turmoil seething,
As if this earth in fast thick pants were breathing,
A mighty fountain momently[3] was forced:
Amid whose swift half-intermitted burst

1. Small streams that wind in a serpentine way.
2. Across a thicket of cedar trees.
3. From moment to moment.

20 Huge fragments vaulted like rebounding hail,
Or chaffy grain beneath the thresher's flail:
And 'mid these dancing rocks at once and ever
It flung up momently the sacred river.
Five miles meandering with a mazy motion
Through wood and dale the sacred river ran,
Then reached the caverns measureless to man,
And sank in tumult to a lifeless ocean:
And 'mid this tumult Kubla heard from far
Ancestral voices prophesying war!

30   The shadow of the dome of pleasure
        Floated midway on the waves;
        Where was heard the mingled measure
        From the fountain and the caves.
It was a miracle of rare device,
A sunny pleasure-dome with caves of ice!

        A damsel with a dulcimer[1]
        In a vision once I saw:
        It was an Abyssinian maid,
        And on her dulcimer she played,
40   Singing of Mount Abora.
        Could I revive within me
        Her symphony and song,
        To such a deep delight 'twould win me,
That with music loud and long,
I would build that dome in air,
That sunny dome! those caves of ice!
And all who heard should see them there,
And all should cry, Beware! Beware!
50 His flashing eyes, his floating hair!
Weave a circle round him thrice,
And close your eyes with holy dread,
For he on honey-dew hath fed,
And drunk the milk of Paradise.

1. A musical instrument with wire strings that are struck with rods.

Cologne

In Köhln, a town of monks and bones,
And pavements fang'd with murderous stones
And rags, and hags, and hideous wenches;
I counted two and seventy stenches,
All well defined, and several stinks!
Ye Nymphs that reign o'er sewers and sinks,
The river Rhine, it is well known,
Doth wash your city of Cologne;
But tell me, Nymphs, what power divine
10   Shall henceforth wash the river Rhine?

The Netherlands

Water and windmills, greenness, Islets green; –
Willows whose Trunks beside the shadows stood
Of their own higher half, and willowy swamp: –
Farmhouses that at anchor seem'd – in the inland sky
The fog-transfixing Spires –
Water, wide water, greenness and green banks,
And water seen –

Answer to a child's question

Do you ask what the birds say? The Sparrow, the Dove,
The Linnet and Thrush say, 'I love and I love!'
In the winter they're silent – the wind is so strong;
What it says, I don't know, but it sings a loud song.
But green leaves, and blossoms, and sunny warm weather,
And singing, and loving – all come back together.
But the Lark is so brimful of gladness and love,
The green fields below him, the blue sky above,
That he sings, and he sings; and for ever sings he –
10   'I love my Love, and my Love loves me!'

On Donne's poetry

With Donne, whose muse on dromedary trots,
Wreathe iron pokers into true-love knots;
Rhyme's sturdy cripple, fancy's maze and clue,
Wit's forge and fire-blast, meaning's press and screw.

George Gordon Noel, Sixth Baron Byron
(1788–1824)

Byron was born in London in January 1788, but spent his early childhood in Scotland. His father died when he was three. The household was disorderly and poor, and Byron suffered at the hands of a vain and violent mother and a drunken nurse. He had a club foot, and although he worked hard at becoming athletic, his handicap often made him unhappy.

When Byron was ten, he inherited a title and the estate of Newstead Abbey in Nottinghamshire from his great-uncle. In 1800 he went to Harrow School and in 1805 to Trinity College, Cambridge. He was popular, and spent as much time swimming, playing cricket, gambling and going to parties as he did studying. Determined to stand out from the crowd, he kept a pet bear. While he was still at university, his first book of poems, *Hours of Idleness*, was published.

After leaving Cambridge, Byron spent two years travelling in Europe and the Middle East. In the first two cantos of *Childe Harold's Pilgrimage*, which he published when he came back, he described the wonderful things and places he had seen, particularly in his beloved Greece. His hero, Childe Harold, was the first in a succession of young men with stormy emotions, shunning humanity and tormented by mysterious sins from a guilty past, who became known as 'Byronic heroes'. Gothic chillers were very popular then, and this kind of hero was immediately appealing.

The poem was a tremendous success, and Byron became famous. The whole of fashionable London, particularly the female part, wanted to meet the handsome, witty poet, whom they saw as the personification of the romantic heroes of his poems, 'mad, bad, and dangerous to know'. His poems sold out as fast as he could write them: *The Giaour* and *The Bride of Abydos* in 1813, *The Corsair* and *Lara* in 1814, and *Hebrew Melodies* in 1815.

Byron married Anna Isabella Milbanke in 1815, but she left him shortly after their daughter Augusta Ada was born. Rumours and scandals circulated about his private life, and the fashionable society he loved shunned him. In 1816 he left England for ever.

After writing the third canto of *Childe Harold's Pilgrimage* and the narrative poem *The Prisoner of Chillon* in Geneva, Byron moved to Italy, where he spent most of the rest of his life. He continued to write poetry, particularly the long satire *Don Juan*, often considered his best work, and also made less successful attempts at writing poetic drama. At this time, he befriended two other English poets living in Italy: Percy Bysshe Shelley and Leigh Hunt. Shelley's early death in 1822 hit him hard.

An ardent supporter of the Greek revolt against the Turks, Byron joined the Greek forces at Missolonghi in 1823, despite poor health. He not only recruited a regiment to fight for Greek independence, but contributed his own money to the cause. In return, the Greeks made him commander-in-chief of their forces in January 1824. However, he caught rheumatic fever and died at the age of 36. His heart was kept in Greece, but his body was brought back and buried near his English home.

The most striking thing about Byron's poetry is its strength and masculinity. Trenchantly witty, Byron saw himself in the satiric tradition of Pope and Dryden and vividly expressed his detestation for the popular Lake Poets in the section from Canto III of *Don Juan* printed here. He used unflowery and colloquial language in many poems, such as 'Written after swimming from Sestos to Abydos'. He had a turn for drama, expressed in the vibrantly galloping rhythms of 'The Destruction of Sennacherib'. However, he could also write poems such as 'When we two parted' and 'So we'll go no more a-roving', which express strong feelings in simple and touching language. He made little use of imagery and did not aspire to write of things beyond this world; the Victorian critic John Ruskin wrote of him that he 'spoke only of what he had seen and known; and spoke without exaggeration, without mystery, without enmity, and without mercy'.

She walks in beauty

She walks in beauty, like the night
    Of cloudless climes and starry skies;
And all that's best of dark and bright
    Meet in her aspect and her eyes:
Thus mellowed to that tender light
    Which heaven to gaudy day denies.

One shade the more, one ray the less,
    Had half impaired the nameless grace,
Which waves in every raven tress,
10   Or softly lightens o'er her face;
Where thoughts serenely sweet express,
    How pure, how dear their dwelling-place.

And on that cheek, and o'er that brow,
    So soft, so calm, yet eloquent,
The smiles that win, the tints that glow,
    But tell of days in goodness spent,
A mind at peace with all below,
    A heart whose love is innocent!

The Destruction of Sennacherib[1]

The Assyrian came down like the wolf on the fold,
And his cohorts were gleaming in purple and gold;
And the sheen of their spears was like stars on the sea,
When the blue wave rolls nightly on deep Galilee.

1. This poem concerns the siege of Jerusalem by the Assyrian king
Sennacherib, the story of which is told in the second book of Kings,
chapter 19: v. 35: 'And it came to pass that night that the angel of the Lord
went out and smote in the camp of the Assyrians an hundred fourscore and
five thousand: and when they arose early in the morning, behold, they were
all dead corpses.'

Like the leaves of the forest when summer is green,
That host with their banners at sunset were seen;
Like the leaves of the forest when autumn hath blown,
That host on the morrow lay withered and strown.[1]

For the Angel of Death spread his wings on the blast,
And breathed in the face of the foe as he passed;
And the eyes of the sleepers waxed deadly and chill,
And their hearts but once heaved, and for ever grew still!

And there lay the steed with his nostril all wide,
But through it there rolled not the breath of his pride;
And the foam of his gasping lay white on the turf,
And cold as the spray of the rock-beating surf.

And there lay the rider distorted and pale,
With the dew on his brow, and the rust on his mail:
And the tents were all silent, the banners alone,
The lances unlifted, the trumpet unblown.

And the widows of Ashur[2] are loud in their wail,
And the idols are broke in the temple of Baal;[3]
And the might of the Gentile, unsmote by the sword,
Hath melted like snow in the glance of the Lord!

1. Scattered.
2. A major city of Assyria.
3. The god of the Assyrians.

When we two parted

When we two parted
  In silence and tears,
Half broken-hearted
  To sever for years,
Pale grew thy cheek and cold,
  Colder thy kiss;
Truly that hour foretold
  Sorrow to this.

The dew of the morning
10 Sunk chill on my brow —
It felt like the warning
  Of what I feel now.
Thy vows are all broken,
  And light is thy fame;
I hear thy name spoken,
  And share in its shame.

They name thee before me,
  A knell to mine ear;
A shudder comes o'er me —
20 Why wert thou so dear?
They know not I knew thee,
  Who knew thee too well: —
Long, long shall I rue thee,
  Too deeply to tell.

In secret we met —
  In silence I grieve,
That thy heart could forget,
  Thy spirit deceive.
If I should meet thee
30 After long years,
How should I greet thee? —
  With silence and tears.

Written after swimming from Sestos to Abydos

If, in the month of dark December,
   Leander, who was nightly wont
(What maid will not the tale remember?)
   To cross thy stream, broad Hellespont![1]

If, when the wintry tempest roared,
   He sped to Hero, nothing loth,
And thus of old thy current poured,
   Fair Venus! how I pity both!

For *me*, degenerate modern wretch,
10   Though in the genial month of May,
My dripping limbs I faintly stretch,
   And think I've done a feat today.

But since he crossed the rapid tide,
   According to the doubtful story,
To woo, – and – Lord knows what beside.
   And swam for Love, as I for Glory;

'Twere hard to say who fared the best:
   Sad mortals! thus the Gods still plague you!
He lost his labour, I my jest;
20   For he was drowned, and I've the ague.[2]

1. The Greek myth tells that Hero, a priestess of Venus, fell in love with Leander, who swam across the Hellespont, a four-mile-wide strait in what is now called the Dardanelles, every night to visit her. One night, he drowned, and the broken-hearted Hero drowned herself in the same sea. Byron with his friend Lieutenant Ekenhead repeated this trip in 1810 and accomplished it in an hour and ten minutes.
2. A fever with shivering fits.

Stanzas for Music

There be none of beauty's daughters
　　With a magic like thee;
And like music on the waters
　　Is thy sweet voice to me:
When, as if its sound were causing
The charmèd ocean's pausing,
The waves lie still and gleaming,
And the lulled winds seem dreaming:

And the midnight moon is weaving
10　　Her bright chain o'er the deep;
Whose breast is gently heaving,
　　As an infant's asleep:
So the spirit bows before thee,
To listen and adore thee;
With a full but soft emotion,
Like the swell of summer's ocean.

Remember thee! Remember thee!

Remember thee! remember thee!
　　Till Lethe[1] quench life's burning stream
Remorse and Shame shall cling to thee,
　　And haunt thee like a feverish dream!

Remember thee! Aye, doubt it not.
　　Thy husband too shall think of thee:[2]
By neither shalt thou be forgot,
　　Thou *false* to him, thou *fiend* to me!

1. Lethe was the river of Hades, the Greek underworld where dead souls went. To swim in it caused everything to be forgotten.
2. This poem was written after an unhappy love affair with Lady Caroline Lamb, wife of Lord Melbourne.

So we'll go no more a-roving

So we'll go no more a-roving
  So late into the night,
Though the heart be still as loving,
  And the moon be still as bright.

For the sword outwears its sheath,
  And the soul wears out the breast,
And the heart must pause to breathe,
  And love itself have rest.

Though the night was made for loving,
10   And the day returns too soon,
Yet we'll go no more a-roving
  By the light of the moon.

from CHILDE[1] HAROLD'S PILGRIMAGE

CANTO III

The Eve of Waterloo

XXI
There was a sound of revelry by night,
And Belgium's capital had gathered then
Her Beauty and her Chivalry – and bright
The lamps shone o'er fair women and brave men;[2]
A thousand hearts beat happily; and when
Music arose with its voluptuous swell,

1. A youth of knightly family before attaining knighthood.
2. The British army was quartered in Brussels, where the Duchess of
Richmond gave a ball on the eve of the battle.

Soft eyes looked love to eyes which spake again,
And all went merry as a marriage bell;
But hush! hark! a deep sound strikes like a rising knell!

XXII

Did ye not hear it? – No; 'twas but the wind,
10 Or the car rattling o'er the stony street;
On with the dance! let joy be unconfined;
No sleep till morn, when youth and pleasure meet
To chase the glowing hours with flying feet –
But hark! – that heavy sound breaks in once more,
As if the clouds its echo would repeat;
And nearer, clearer, deadlier than before!
Arm! arm! it is – it is – the cannon's opening roar!

XXIII

Within a windowed niche of that high hall
20 Sate Brunswick's fated chieftain;[1] he did hear
That sound the first amidst the festival,
And caught its tone with death's prophetic ear;
And when they smiled because he deemed it near,
His heart more truly knew that peal too well
Which stretched his father on a bloody bier,
And roused the vengeance blood alone could quell:
He rushed into the field, and, foremost fighting, fell.

XXIV

Ah! then and there was hurrying to and fro,
And gathering tears, and tremblings of distress,
30 And cheeks all pale, which but an hour ago
Blushed at the praise of their own loveliness;
And there were sudden partings, such as press
The life out from young hearts, and choking sighs
Which ne'er might be repeated; who could guess
If ever more should meet those mutual eyes,
Since upon night so sweet such awful morn could rise!

1. The Duke of Brunswick, deprived of his dukedom by Napoleon,
was killed in the battle.

XXV

And there was mounting in hot haste – the steed,
The mustering squadron, and the clattering car,
Went pouring forward with impetuous speed,
40 And swiftly forming in the ranks of war;
And the deep thunder peal on peal afar;
And near, the beat of the alarming drum
Roused up the soldier ere the morning star;
While thronged the citizens with terror dumb,
Or whispering with white lips – 'The foe! They come! They
    come!'

XXVI

And wild and high the 'Cameron's gathering' rose!
The war-note of Lochiel, which Albyn's hills
Have heard, and heard, too, have her Saxon foes: –
How in the noon of night that pibroch[1] thrills,
50 Savage and shrill! But with the breath which fills
Their mountain-pipe, so fill the mountaineers
With the fierce native daring which instils
The stirring memory of a thousand years,
And Evan's, Donald's fame rings in each clansman's ears!

XXVII

And Ardennes waves above them her green leaves,
Dewy with nature's tear-drops, as they pass,
Grieving, if aught inanimate e'er grieves,
Over the unreturning brave, – alas!
Ere evening to be trodden like the grass
60 Which now beneath them, but above shall grow
In its next verdure, when this fiery mass
Of living valour, rolling on the foe,
And burning with high hope, shall moulder cold and low.

1. A warlike tune played on a bagpipe.

XXVIII

Last noon beheld them full of lusty life,
Last eve in beauty's circle proudly gay,
The midnight brought the signal-sound of strife,
The morn the marshalling in arms, – the day
Battle's magnificently stern array!
The thunder-clouds close o'er it, which when rent
70 The earth is covered thick with other clay,
Which her own clay shall cover, heaped and pent,
Rider and horse, – friend, foe, – in one red burial blent! . . .

from DON JUAN

CANTO III

XCI

Milton's the prince of poets – so we say;
    A little heavy, but no less divine:
An independent being in his day –
    Learned, pious, temperate, in love and wine;
But, his life falling into Johnson's way,
    We're told this great high priest of all the Nine[1]
Was whipt at college – a harsh sire – odd spouse,
For the first Mrs Milton left his house.

XCII

All these are, *certes*, entertaining facts,
10   Like Shakespeare's stealing deer, Lord Bacon's bribes;
Like Titus' youth, and Caesar's earliest acts;
        Like Burns (whom Doctor Currie well describes);
Like Cromwell's pranks; – but although truth exacts
        These amiable descriptions from the scribes,
As most essential to their hero's story,
They do not much contribute to his glory.

1. The nine muses were the goddesses of the arts in Greek mythology.

XCIII

All are not moralists, like Southey, when
    He prated to the world of 'Pantisocrasy';[1]
Or Wordsworth unexcised, unhired, who then
20   Seasoned his pedlar poems with democracy:
Or Coleridge, long before his flighty pen
    Let to the Morning Post its aristocracy;
When he and Southey, following the same path,
Espoused two partners (milliners of Bath).

XCIV

Such names at present cut a convict figure,
    The very Botany Bay in moral geography;
Their loyal treason, renegado rigour,
    Are good manure for their more bare biography;
Wordsworth's last quarto, by the way, is bigger
30   Than any since the birthday of typography;
A drowsy frowsy poem, called the 'Excursion',
Writ in a manner which is my aversion.

*   *   *

XCVIII

We learn from Horace, 'Homer sometimes sleeps';
    We feel without him, Wordsworth sometimes wakes, –
To show with what complacency he creeps,
    With his dear '*Waggoners*', around his lakes.
He wishes for 'a boat' to sail the deeps –
    Of ocean? – No, of air; and then he makes
Another outcry for 'a little boat',
40   And drivels seas to set it well afloat.

1. Southey was the Poet Laureate at the time this was written. He and Coleridge married two sisters and made unfulfilled plans to found a utopian community in Pennsylvania.

XCIX

If he must fain sweep o'er the ethereal plain,
    And Pegasus runs restive in his 'Waggon',
Could he not beg the loan of Charles's Wain?
    Or pray Medea for a single dragon?
Or if too classic for his vulgar brain,
    He feared his neck to venture such a nag on,
And he must needs mount nearer to the moon,
Could not the blockhead ask for a balloon?

C

'Pedlars', and 'Boats', and 'Waggons'! Oh! ye shades
50   Of Pope and Dryden, are we come to this?
That trash of such sort not alone evades
    Contempt, but from the bathos' vast abyss
Floats scumlike uppermost, and these Jack Cades
    Of sense and song above your graves may hiss –
The 'little boatman' and his 'Peter Bell'
Can sneer at him who drew 'Achitophel'!

Percy Bysshe Shelley
(1792–1822)

Shelley was born in Warnham, in Sussex. His family were landed gentry: his father was a Member of Parliament, and his grandfather a rich baronet. His parents disapproved of both his opinions and his poetry, and after Shelley died, his father opposed the publication of his works.

At the age of twelve, Shelley was sent to Eton, which in those days was notoriously tough. His refusal to conform meant he was victimized in 'Shelley-hunts' and known as 'mad Shelley'. He loved reading the fashionable Gothic horror novels, and experimented with devil-raising and alchemy. He started writing early, and had published a novel before he left school. Some early poems were published in a volume with others written by his sister.

When Shelley arrived at Oxford in 1810, he befriended another undergraduate, Jefferson Hogg, but five months later both were expelled for publishing a pamphlet entitled *The Necessity of Atheism*. His parents disowned him, and he lived for a short time on money which his sisters sent him secretly, sometimes by the hand of their schoolfriend Harriet Westbrook. Shelley felt sorry for Harriet, because she was unhappy at school, and in 1811 they eloped to Scotland.

Shelley wrote one long poem, *Queen Mab*, and a number of prose political works in the next three years. His politics were idealistic, and he longed for an age when people would put aside selfishness and live in love and freedom. He corresponded with the philosopher William Godwin, whose views he found sympathetic, and in 1814 he left Harriet and their two children and went to Europe with Godwin's daughter Mary and her half-sister Claire Claremont. Two years later Harriet drowned herself in the Serpentine. This tragedy prejudiced many people against him.

Mary Godwin was a more serious and intellectual person than Harriet, and Shelley found her far more compatible. One of her main virtues for him, though, was that she continued to love him despite his many relationships with other women. In the spring of 1818 they went to live in Italy, at that time a home to many English poets, including Byron, who became a great friend. Shelley called Italy a 'paradise of exiles'. Once, he and Mary and Byron and Claire Claremont spent an evening telling chilling stories, but only Mary Shelley's *Frankenstein* was ever written down and published. One of Shelley's works from this period, *Adonais*, was written in mourning for the poet John Keats, who died in Rome of tuberculosis in 1821.

During the last weeks of his life Shelley and Mary lived with their friends Jane and Edward Williams in a house on the Italian coast. While Shelley and Edward Williams were returning on their yacht from a visit to Byron in Pisa, they were caught in a sudden violent storm. Their bodies were washed ashore ten days later, on 18 July 1822. Byron, the poet Leigh Hunt and Shelley's friend Trelawney burned the body on the beach and took the ashes to the Protestant cemetery in Rome, where Keats was also buried.

Shelley's poetry was very much part of the spirit of his age. It was an age of revolutions in all spheres of life: industry, agriculture, politics and literature. Wordsworth's definition of poetry as 'the spontaneous overflow of powerful feelings' seems natural to us, but the classical school of Dryden and Pope would have found such a statement astounding. Shelley read very little earlier poetry, and his poetic ideas were formed by reading Wordsworth, Coleridge and Southey.

Shelley had the gift of music in his writing, and is most often remembered for lyric poems such as 'To Night', 'Ode to the West Wind' and 'To a Skylark'. He could also evoke brilliant visual imagery, as in 'The Cloud'. However, as well as the Shelley who is the most Romantic of poets in these poems, there is the Shelley whose intense political feelings are displayed in poems such as 'Song to the Men of England' and 'England in 1819'. There is also the Shelley who could produce that masterpiece of the imagination 'Ozymandias', a poem as relevant to the age that produced the atom bomb as to any other age in history.

Ozymandias

I met a traveller from an antique land
Who said: Two vast and trunkless legs of stone
Stand in the desert . . . Near them, on the sand,
Half sunk, a shattered visage[1] lies, whose frown,
And wrinkled lip, and sneer of cold command,
Tell that its sculptor well those passions read
Which yet survive, stamped on these lifeless things,
The hand that mocked them, and the heart that fed:
And on the pedestal these words appear:
10 'My name is Ozymandias, king of kings:
Look on my works, ye Mighty, and despair!'
Nothing beside remains. Round the decay
Of that colossal wreck, boundless and bare
The lone and level sands stretch far away.

1. Face.

Stanzas written in dejection, near Naples

1

The sun is warm, the sky is clear,
    The waves are dancing fast and bright,
Blue isles and snowy mountains wear
    The purple noon's transparent might,
    The breath of the moist earth is light,
Around its unexpanded buds;
    Like many a voice of one delight,
The winds, the birds, the ocean floods,
The City's voice itself, is soft like Solitude's.

II

10 I see the Deep's untrampled floor
        With green and purple seaweeds strown;
    I see the waves upon the shore,
        Like light dissolved in star-showers, thrown:
        I sit upon the sands alone, –
    The lightning of the noontide ocean
        Is flashing round me, and a tone
    Arises from its measured motion,
How sweet! did any heart now share in my emotion.

III

    Alas! I have not hope nor health,
20   Nor peace within nor calm around,
    Nor that content surpassing wealth
        The sage in meditation found,
        And walked with inward glory crowned –
    Nor fame, nor power, nor love, nor leisure.
        Others I see whom these surround –
    Smiling they live, and call life pleasure; –
To me that cup has been dealt in another measure.

IV

    Yet now despair itself is mild,
        Even as the winds and waters are;
30 I could lie down like a tired child,
        And weep away the life of care
        Which I have borne and yet must bear,
    Till death like sleep might steal on me,
        And I might feel in the warm air
    My cheek grow cold, and hear the sea
Breathe o'er my dying brain its last monotony.

V

Some might lament that I were cold,
    As I, when this sweet day is gone,
Which my lost heart, too soon grown old,
    Insults with this untimely moan;
    They might lament – for I am one
Whom men love not, – and yet regret,
    Unlike this day, which, when the sun
    Shall on its stainless glory set,
Will linger, though enjoyed, like joy in memory yet.

40

Sonnet: England in 1819

An old, mad, blind, despised, and dying king,[1] –
Princes, the dregs of their dull race, who flow
Through public scorn, – mud from a muddy spring, –
Rulers who neither see, nor feel, nor know,
But leechlike to their fainting country cling,
Till they drop, blind in blood, without a blow, –
A people starved and stabbed in the untilled field, –
An army, which liberticide[2] and prey
Makes as a two-edged sword to all who wield, –
Golden and sanguine[3] laws which tempt and slay;
Religion Christless, Godless – a book sealed;
A Senate, – Time's worst statute unrepealed, –
Are graves, from which a glorious Phantom may
Burst, to illumine our tempestuous day.

10

1. George III.
2. The murder of liberty.
3. Carries the meanings of both optimistic and bloody.

Song to the Men of England

Men of England, wherefore[1] plough
For the lords who lay ye low?
Wherefore weave with toil and care
The rich robes your tyrants wear?

Wherefore feed, and clothe, and save,
From the cradle to the grave,
Those ungrateful drones[2] who would
Drain your sweat – nay, drink your blood?

Wherefore, Bees of England, forge
10   Many a weapon, chain and scourge,[3]
That these stingless drones may spoil
The forced produce of your toil?

Have ye leisure, comfort, calm,
Shelter, food, love's gentle balm?[4]
Or what is it ye buy so dear
With your pain and with your fear?

The seed ye sow, another reaps:
The wealth ye find, another keeps;
The robes ye weave, another wears;
20   The arms ye forge, another bears.

Sow seed, – but let no tyrant reap;
Find wealth, – let no imposter heap;
Weave robes, – let not the idle wear;
Forge arms, – in your defence to bear.

1. Why.
2. Male bee, larger than the worker bee who makes the honey, so a lazy person who lives on the work of others.
3. Whip.
4. Soothing ointment.

Shrink to your cellars, holes, and cells;
In halls ye deck another dwells.
Why shake the chains ye wrought? Ye see
The steel ye tempered[1] glance on ye.

With plough and spade, and hoe and loom,
30   Trace your grave and build your tomb,
And weave your winding-sheet,[2] till fair
England be your sepulchre.[3]

1. To temper steel is to bring it to the right state of hardness.
2. Shroud.
3. Tomb.

Ode to the West Wind

I

O wild West Wind, thou breath of Autumn's being,
Thou, from whose unseen presence the leaves dead
Are driven, like ghosts from an enchanter fleeing,

Yellow, and black, and pale, and hectic red,
Pestilence-stricken multitudes: O thou,
Who chariotest[1] to their dark wintry bed

The wingèd seeds, where they lie cold and low,
Each like a corpse within its grave, until
Thine azure sister of the Spring shall blow

10   Her clarion[2] o'er the dreaming earth, and fill
(Driving sweet buds like flocks to feed in air)
With living hues and odours plain and hill:

Wild Spirit, which art moving everywhere;
Destroyer and preserver; hear, oh, hear!

1. Drives swiftly as in a chariot.
2. Trumpet.

II

Thou on whose stream, mid the deep sky's commotion,
Loose clouds like earth's decaying leaves are shed,
Shook from the tangled boughs of Heaven and Ocean,

Angels of rain and lightning: there are spread
On the blue surface of thine aëry surge,
20 Like the bright hair uplifted from the head

Of some fierce Maenad,[1] even from the dim verge
Of the horizon to the zenith's height,
The locks of the approaching storm. Thou dirge[2]

Of the dying year, to which this closing night
Will be the dome of a vast sepulchre,[3]
Vaulted with all thy congregated might

Of vapours, from whose solid atmosphere
Black rain, and fire, and hail will burst: oh, hear!

III

Thou who didst waken from his summer dreams
30 The blue Mediterranean, where he lay,
Lulled by the coil of his crystalline streams,

Beside a pumice isle in Baiae's[4] bay,
And saw in sleep old palaces and towers
Quivering within the wave's intenser day,

All overgrown with azure moss and flowers
So sweet, the sense faints picturing them! Thou
For whose path the Atlantic's level powers

1. Literally, a frenzied woman. Maenads were female attendants of
Bacchus, the ancient Greek god of wine, who performed savage rituals
in his honour.
2. Funeral song, lament.
3. Tomb, or monument to the dead.
4. Resort on the Italian coast near Naples.

Cleave themselves into chasms, while far below
The sea-blooms and the oozy woods which wear
40 The sapless foliage of the ocean, know

Thy voice, and suddenly grow gray with fear,
And tremble and despoil themselves: oh, hear!

IV
If I were a dead leaf thou mightest bear;
If I were a swift cloud to fly with thee;
A wave to pant beneath thy power, and share

The impulse of thy strength, only less free
Than thou, O uncontrollable! If even
I were as in my boyhood, and could be

The comrade of thy wanderings over Heaven,
50 As then, when to outstrip thy skiey speed
Scarce seemed a vision; I would ne'er have striven

As thus with thee in prayer in my sore need.
Oh, lift me as a wave, a leaf, a cloud!
I fall upon the thorns of life! I bleed!

A heavy weight of hours has chained and bowed
One too like thee: tameless, and swift, and proud.

V
Make me thy lyre,[1] even as the forest is:
What if my leaves are falling like its own!
The tumult of thy mighty harmonies

60 Will take from both a deep, autumnal tone,
Sweet though in sadness. Be thou, Spirit fierce,
My spirit! Be thou me, impetuous one!

1. Ancient stringed musical instrument, like a harp.

Drive my dead thoughts over the universe
Like withered leaves to quicken a new birth!
And, by the incantation of this verse,

Scatter, as from an unextinguished hearth
Ashes and sparks, my words among mankind!
Be through my lips to unawakened earth

The trumpet of a prophecy! O, Wind,
70   If Winter comes, can Spring be far behind?

The Cloud

I bring fresh showers for the thirsting flowers,
        From the seas and the streams;
I bear light shade for the leaves when laid
        In their noonday dreams.
From my wings are shaken the dews that waken
        The sweet buds every one,
When rocked to rest on their mother's breast,
        As she dances about the sun.
I wield the flail of the lashing hail,
10   And whiten the green plains under,
And then again I dissolve it in rain,
        And laugh as I pass in thunder.

I sift the snow on the mountains below,
        And their great pines groan aghast;
And all the night 'tis my pillow white,
        While I sleep in the arms of the blast.
Sublime on the towers of my skiey bowers,
        Lightning my pilot sits;
In a cavern under is fettered the thunder,
20   It struggles and howls at fits;
Over earth and ocean, with gentle motion,
        This pilot is guiding me,

Lured by the love of the genii that move
    In the depths of the purple sea;
Over the rills, and the crags, and the hills,
    Over the lakes and the plains,
Wherever he dream, under mountain or stream,
    The Spirit he loves remains;
And I all the while bask in Heaven's blue smile,
30   Whilst he is dissolving in rains.

The sanguine[1] Sunrise, with the meteor eyes,
    And his burning plumes outspread,
Leaps on the back of my sailing rack,
    When the morning star shines dead:
As on the jag of a mountain crag,
    Which an earthquake rocks and swings,
An eagle alit one moment may sit
    In the light of its golden wings.
And when Sunset may breathe, from the lit sea beneath,
40   It ardours of rest and of love,
And the crimson pall[2] of eve may fall
    from the depth of Heaven above,
With wings folded I rest, on mine aëry nest,
    As still as a brooding dove.

That orbèd maiden with white fire laden,
    Whom mortals call the Moon,
Glides glimmering o'er my fleece-like floor,
    By the midnight breezes strewn;
And wherever the beat of her unseen feet,
50   Which only the angels hear,
May have broken the woof of my tent's thin roof,
    The stars peep behind her and peer;
And I laugh to see them whirl and flee,
    Like a swarm of golden bees,

1. Coloured red, like blood.
2. Can be a cloth used to drape over a coffin, or a cloak.

When I widen the rent in my wind-built tent,
    Till the calm rivers, lakes, and seas,
Like strips of the sky fallen through me on high,
    Are each paved with the moon and these.

I bind the Sun's throne with a burning zone,
60   And the Moon's with a girdle of pearl;
The volcanoes are dim, and the stars reel and swim,
    When the whirlwinds my banner unfurl.
From cape to cape, with a bridge-like shape,
    Over a torrent sea,
Sunbeam-proof, I hang like a roof, –
    The mountains its columns be.
The triumphal arch through which I march
    With hurricane, fire, and snow,
When the Powers of the air are chained to my chair,
70   Is the million-coloured bow;
The sphere-fire above its soft colours wove,
    While the moist Earth was laughing below.

I am the daughter of Earth and Water,
    And the nursling of the Sky;
I pass through the pores of the ocean and shores;
    I change, but I cannot die.
For after the rain when with never a stain
    The pavilion of Heaven is bare,
And the winds and sunbeams with their convex gleams
80   Build up the blue dome of air,
I silently laugh at my own cenotaph,[1]
    And out of the caverns of rain,
Like a child from the womb, like a ghost from the tomb,
    I arise and unbuild it again.

1. A monument built to a person buried elsewhere.

To a Skylark

Hail to thee, blithe Spirit!
   Bird thou never wert,
That from Heaven, or near it,
   Pourest thy full heart
In profuse strains of unpremeditated art.

Higher still and higher
   From the earth thou springest
Like a cloud of fire;
   The blue deep thou wingest,
10 And singing still dost soar, and soaring ever singest.

In the golden lightning
   Of the sunken sun,
O'er which clouds are bright'ning,
   Thou dost float and run;
Like an unbodied joy whose race is just begun.

The pale purple even[1]
   Melts around thy flight;
Like a star of Heaven,
   In the broad daylight
20 Thou art unseen, but yet I hear thy shrill delight,

Keen as are the arrows
   Of that silver sphere,
Whose intense lamp narrows
   In the white dawn clear
Until we hardly see – we feel that it is there.

1. Evening.

All the earth and air
  With thy voice is loud,
As, when night is bare,
  From one lonely cloud
30 The moon rain out her beams, and Heaven is over-flowed.

What thou art we know not;
  What is most like thee?
From rainbow clouds there flow not
  Drops so bright to see
As from thy presence showers a rain of melody.

Like a Poet hidden
  In the light of thought,
Singing hymns unbidden,
  Till the world is wrought
40 To sympathy with hopes and fears it heeded not:

Like a high-born maiden
  In a palace-tower,
Soothing her love-laden
  Soul in secret hour
With music sweet as love, which overflows her bower:

Like a glow-worm golden
  In a dell of dew,
Scattering unbeholden
  Its aëreal hue
50 Among the flowers and grass, which screen it from the view!

Waking or asleep,
  Thou of death must deem[1]
Things more true and deep
  Than we mortals dream,
Or how could thy notes flow in such a crystal stream?

1. Judge or consider.

We look before and after,
    And pine for what is not:
Our sincerest laughter
    With some pain is fraught;
60 Our sweetest songs are those that tell of saddest thought.

Yet if we could scorn
    Hate, and pride, and fear;
If we were things born
    Not to shed a tear,
I know not how thy joy we ever should come near.

Better than all measures
    Of delightful sound,
Better than all treasures
    That in books are found,
70 Thy skill to poet were, thou scorner of the ground!

Teach me half the gladness
    That thy brain must know,
Such harmonious madness
    From my lips would flow
The world should listen then – as I am listening now.

Like a rose embowered
    In its own green leaves,
By warm winds deflowered,
    Till the scent it gives
80 Makes faint with too much sweet those heavy-wingèd thieves:

Sound of vernal[1] showers
    On the twinkling grass,
Rain-awakened flowers,
    All that ever was
Joyous, and clear, and fresh, thy music doth surpass:

1. Spring.

Teach us, Sprite or Bird,
    What sweet thoughts are thine:
I have never heard
    Praise of love or wine
90 That panted forth a flood of rapture so divine.

Chorus Hymeneal,[1]
    Or triumphal chant,
Matched with thine would be all
    But an empty vaunt,[2]
A thing wherein we feel there is some hidden want.

What objects are the fountains
    Of thy happy strain?
What fields, or waves, or mountains?
    What shapes of sky or plain?
100 What love of thine own kind? what ignorance of pain?

With thy clear keen joyance
    Languor[3] cannot be:
Shadow of annoyance
    Never came near thee:
Thou lovest – but ne'er knew love's sad satiety.[4]

1. Marriage-song.
2. Boast.
3. Weariness, lack of energy.
4. The excess of pleasure that produces disgust.

To Night

I

Swiftly walk o'er the western wave,
    Spirit of Night!
Out of the misty eastern cave,
Where, all the long and lone daylight,
Thou wovest dreams of joy and fear,
Which make thee terrible and dear, —
    Swift be thy flight!

II

Wrap thy form in a mantle gray,
    Star-inwrought![1]
10 Blind with thine hair the eyes of Day;
Kiss her until she be wearied out,
Then wander o'er city, and sea, and land,
Touching all with thine opiate[2] wand —
    Come, long-sought!

III

When I arose and saw the dawn,
    I sighed for thee;
When light rode high, and the dew was gone,
And noon lay heavy on flower and tree,
And the weary Day turned to his rest,
20 Lingering like an unloved guest,
    I sighed for thee.

1. Embroidered.
2. Sedative drug.

IV

Thy brother Death came, and cried,
     Wouldst thou me?
Thy sweet child Sleep, the filmy-eyed,
Murmured like a noontide bee,
Shall I nestle near thy side?
Wouldst thou me? – And I replied,
     No, not thee!

V

Death will come when thou art dead,
30   Soon, too soon –
Sleep will come when thou art fled;
Of neither would I ask the boon
I ask of thee, belovèd Night –
Swift be thine approaching flight,
     Come soon, soon!

from ADONAIS

I

I weep for Adonais – he is dead!
O, weep for Adonais! though our tears
Thaw not the frost which binds so dear a head!
And thou, sad Hour, selected from all years
To mourn our loss, rouse thy obscure compeers,
And teach them thine own sorrow, say: 'With me
Died Adonais; till the Future dares
Forget the Past, his fate and fame shall be
An echo and a light unto eternity!'

*   *   *

XL

10   He has outsoared the shadow of our night;
Envy and calumny and hate and pain,
And that unrest which men miscall delight,
Can touch him not and torture not again;
From the contagion of the world's slow stain
He is secure, and now can never mourn
A heart grown cold, a head grown gray in vain;
Nor, when the spirit's self has ceased to burn,
With sparkless ashes load an unlamented urn.

*   *   *

LII

The One remains, the many change and pass;
20   Heaven's light forever shines, Earth's shadows fly;
Life, like a dome of many-coloured glass,
Stains the white radiance of Eternity,
Until Death tramples it to fragments. – Die,
If thou wouldst be with that which thou dost seek!
Follow where all is fled – Rome's azure sky,
Flowers, ruins, statues, music, words, are weak
The glory they transfuse with fitting truth to speak.

*   *   *

LV

The breath whose might I have invoked in song
Descends on me; my spirit's bark is driven,
30   Far from the shore, far from the trembling throng
Whose sails were never to the tempest given;
The massy earth and spherèd skies are riven!
I am borne darkly, fearfully, afar;
Whilst, burning through the inmost veil of Heaven,
The soul of Adonais, like a star,
Beacons from the abode where the Eternal are.

John Clare

(1793–1864)

John Clare was born in Helpstone, Northamptonshire, into a family of poor agricultural labourers. His parents were practically illiterate, although his father knew many folk songs. Unusually for a time when education was not thought important for working-class children, Clare became a keen reader early in life, and began writing poems at the age of thirteen after reading a book of poems called *The Seasons* by the Scottish poet James Thomson.

Because of his family's poverty, Clare had to work in the fields when he was still very young. He fell in love with a farmer's daughter named Mary Joyce, though her father ended the relationship in 1816. Clare never forgot her.

By a stroke of good luck, Clare's first book, *Poems Descriptive of Rural Life and Scenery*, was published in 1820. He visited London, and his publisher John Taylor introduced him to many other writers. The book brought him fame and a degree of financial security for a while, and he married Patty Turner, who was already pregnant with his first child.

Clare's second book of poems, *The Village Minstrel*, appeared in 1821, and he began to plan a long poem called *The Shepherd's Calendar*, though he had many arguments with his publisher before it was published in 1827. However, despite his critical success, he could not earn enough money from writing to support his growing family and had to continue with casual labouring work. He was constantly torn between the two worlds of literary London and his often illiterate neighbours, between the need to write poetry and the need for money to feed and clothe his children. His health began to suffer, and he had bouts of severe depression, which became worse after his sixth child was born in 1830 and his poetry sold less well.

Clare's friends and his London patrons clubbed together to move the family to a larger cottage with a smallholding in the village of Northborough, not far from Helpstone, thinking that would help him. However, this only made him feel more alienated, and although *The Rural Muse* was published in 1835, his mental state declined.

In 1837 Clare was taken to Dr Matthew Allen's private asylum in Epping Forest. He was there for over four years, but escaped in 1841 and walked home. First of all he went to look for Mary Joyce, his first love, and did not believe her family when they told him she had died three years earlier. Then he went home and spent five unhappy months with his family. Eventually, he was taken to Northampton General Lunatic Asylum where he stayed, continuing to write poetry and letters, until he died in 1864.

Clare lived during a period of massive changes in both town and countryside. The Industrial Revolution was blackening urban areas. Many former agricultural workers went to work in factories because of the rural poverty caused by the war with France, which kept wages down but forced prices up. The Agricultural Revolution saw pastures ploughed up, trees and hedges uprooted, the nearby fens drained and the common land enclosed. This destruction of a centuries-old way of life distressed Clare deeply.

His early work delights both in nature and the cycle of the rural year. Poems such as 'Winter Evening', 'Haymaking' and 'Wood Pictures in Summer' celebrate the beauty of the world and the certainties of rural life, where animals must be fed and crops harvested. Poems such as 'Little Trotty Wagtail' show his sharp observation of wildlife, though 'The Badger' is unsentimental about the place of animals in the countryside. At this time, he often used poetic forms such as the sonnet and the rhyming couplet. His later poetry tends to be more meditative and use forms similar to the folks songs and ballads of his youth. A good example of this is 'Evening'.

Clare's spelling and punctuation were irregular. For example, he always wrote 'hugh' for 'huge', and tended not to punctuate at all.

Many dialect expressions add to the richness of his work. He often used old words in new and powerfully descriptive ways, as in his description of the squirrel that 'sputters up the powdered oak' in 'First Sight of Spring'.

Haymaking

'Tis haytime and the red-complexioned sun
Was scarcely up ere blackbirds had begun
Along the meadow hedges here and there
To sing loud songs to the sweet-smelling air
Where breath of flowers and grass and happy cow
Fling o'er one's senses streams of fragrance now
While in some pleasant nook the swain[1] and maid
Lean o'er their rakes and loiter in the shade
Or bend a minute o'er the bridge and throw
Crumbs in their leisure to the fish below
10 – Hark at that happy shout – and song between
'Tis pleasure's birthday in her meadow scene.
What joy seems half so rich from pleasure won
As the loud laugh of maidens in the sun?

1. Lover.

Wood Pictures in Summer

The one delicious green that now prevades[1]
The woods and fields in endless lights and shades
And that deep softness of delicious hues
That overhead blends – softens – and subdues
The eye to extacy and fills the mind
With views and visions of enchanting kind
While on the velvet down beneath the swail[2]
I sit on mossy stulp[3] and broken rail

1. Pervades (saturates).
2. Shade.
3. Tree-stump.

Or lean o'er crippled gate by hugh[1] old tree
10   Broken by boys disporting there at swee[2]
While sunshine spread from an exaustless sky
Gives all things extacy as well as I
And all wood-swaily places, even they
Are joy's own tennants, keeping holiday

1. Huge.
2. Swinging.

Autumn Morning

The autumn morning waked by many a gun
Throws o'er the fields her many-coloured light
Wood wildly touched close-tanned and stubbles dun
A motley[1] paradise for earth's delight
Clouds ripple as the darkness breaks to light
And clover fields are hid with silver mist
One shower of cobwebs o'er the surface spread
And threads of silk in strange disorder twist
Round every leaf and blossom's bottly[2] head.
10   Hares in the drowning herbage scarcely steal
But on the battered pathway squats abed
And by the cart-rut nips her morning meal
Look where we may the scene is strange and new
And every object wears a changing hue

1. Many-coloured.
2. Bottle-shaped.

Winter Evening

The crib-stock fothered,[1] horses suppered-up
And cows in sheds all littered-down in straw
The threshers gone, the owls are left to whoop
The ducks go waddling with distended craw[2]
Through little hole made in the henroost door
And geese with idle gabble never o'er
Bate[3] careless hog untill he tumbles down
Insult provoking spite to noise the more
While fowl high-perched blink with contemptuous frown
On all the noise and bother heard below
Over the stable ridge in crowds the crow
With jackdaws intermixed known by their noise
To the warm woods behind the village go
And whistling home for bed go weary boys

1. Foddered (fed).
2. Stretched gullet.
3. Torment.

Snow Storm

What a night the wind howls hisses and but stops
To howl more loud while the snow volly keeps
Insessant batter at the window pane
Making our comfort feel as sweet again
And in the morning when the tempest drops
At every cottage-door mountainious heaps
Of snow lies drifted that all entrance stops
Untill the beesom[1] and the shovel gains
The path – and leaves a wall on either side –
The shepherd rambling valleys white and wide

1. Broom.

With new sensations his old memorys fills
When hedges left at night, no more descried,[1]
Are turned to one white sweep of curving hills
And trees, turned bushes, half their bodys hide

The boy that goes to fodder with supprise
Walks o'er the gate he opened yesternight
The hedges all have vanished from his eyes
E'en some tree tops the sheep could reach to bite
The novel scene emboldens new delight
20 And though with cautious steps his sports begin
He bolder shuffles the hugh[2] hills of snow
Till down he drops and plunges to the chin
And struggles much and oft escape to win
Then turns and laughs but dare not further go
For deep the grass and bushes lie below
Where little birds that soon at eve went in
With heads tucked in their wings now pine for day
And little feel boys o'er their heads can stray

1. Made out, espied.
2. Huge.

First Sight of Spring

The hazel blooms, in threads of crimson hue,
Peep through the swelling buds and look for spring
Ere yet a whitethorn leaf appears in view
Or March finds throstles[1] pleased enough to sing
On the old touchwood tree woodpeckers cling
A moment and their harsh-toned notes renew.
In happier mood the stockdove claps his wing
The squirrel sputters up the powdered oak
With tail cocked o'er his head and ears errect
10 Startled to hear the woodman's understroke

1. Thrushes.

And with the courage that his fears collect
He hisses fierce, half malice and half glee,
Leaping from branch to branch about the tree
In winter's foliage moss and lichens drest[1]

1. Dressed.

Night Wind

Darkness like midnight from the sobbing woods
Clamours with dismal tidings of the rain
Roaring as rivers breaking loose in floods
To spread and foam and deluge all the plain
The cotter[1] listens at his door again
Half doubting whether it be floods or wind
And through the thickening darkness looks affraid
Thinking of roads that travel has to find
Through night's black depths in danger's garb arrayed
10   And the loud glabber[2] round the flaze[3] soon stops
When hushed to silence by the lifted hand
Of fearing dame who hears the noise in dread
And thinks a deluge comes to drown the land
Nor dares she go to bed untill the tempest drops

1. Peasant.
2. Chatter.
3. Smoking fire.

Evening Schoolboys

Harken that happy shout – the school-house door
Is open thrown and out the younkers[1] teem
Some run to leapfrog on the rushy moor
And others dabble in the shallow stream
Catching young fish and turning pebbles o'er

1. Youngsters.

For mussel clams – Look in that mellow gleam
Where the retiring sun that rests the while
Streams through the broken hedge – How happy seem
Those schoolboy friendships leaning o'er the stile
10   Both reading in one book – anon a dream
Rich with new joys doth their young hearts beguile
And the book's pocketed most hastily
Ah happy boys well may ye turn and smile
When joys are yours that never cost a sigh

Evening

'Tis evening, the black snail has got on his track,
And gone to its nest is the wren;
And the packman-snail too, with his home on his back,
Clings on the bowed bents[1] like a wen.[2]

The shepherd has made a rude[3] mark with his foot
Where his shaddow reached when he first came;
And it just touched the tree where his secret love cut
Two letters that stand for love's name

The evening comes in with the wishes of love
10   And the shepherd he looks on the flowers
And thinks who would praise the soft song of the dove,
And meet joy in these dewfalling hours

For nature is love, and the wishes of love,
When nothing can hear or intrude;
It hides from the eagle, and joins with the dove
In beautiful green solitude.

1. Grass-stems.
2. Wart.
3. Rough.

The Wren

Why is the cuckoo's melody preferred
And nightingale's rich song so fondly praised
In poets' rhymes? Is there no other bird
Of nature's minstrelsy that oft hath raised
One's heart to extacy and mirth as well?
I judge not how another's taste is caught:
With mine, there's other birds that bear the bell
Whose song hath crowds of happy memories brought.
Such the wood-robin singing in the dell[1]
10 And little wren that many a time hath sought
Shelter from showers in huts where I did dwell
In early spring the tennant of the plain
Tenting my sheep and still they come to tell
The happy stories of the past again

1. Glade or clearing.

Little Trotty Wagtail

Little trotty wagtail he went in the rain
And tittering tottering sideways he ne'er got straight again
He stooped to get a worm and looked up to catch a fly
And then he flew away ere his feathers they were dry

Little trotty wagtail he waddled in the mud
And left his little foot marks trample where he would
He waddled in the water-pudge and waggle went his tail
And chirrup up his wings to dry upon the garden rail

Little trotty wagtail you nimble all about
10 And in the dimpling water-pudge[1] you waddle in and out
Your home is nigh at hand and in the warm pigsty
So little Master Wagtail I'll bid you a 'Good bye'

1. Puddle.

The Sky Lark

The rolls and harrows lie at rest beside
The battered road and spreading far and wide
Above the russet clods the corn is seen
Sprouting its spirey points of tender green
Where squats the hare to terrors wide awake
Like some brown clod the harrows failed to break
While 'neath the warm hedge boys stray far from home
To crop the early blossoms as they come
Where buttercups will make them eager run
10 Opening their golden caskets to the sun
To see who shall be first to pluck the prize
And from their hurry up the skylark flies
And o'er her half-formed nest with happy wings
Winnows the air – till in the clouds she sings
Then hangs a dust spot in the sunny skies
And drops and drops till in her nest she lies
Where boys unheeding passed, ne'er dreaming then
That birds which flew so high would drop again
To nests upon the ground where any thing
20 May come at to destroy. Had they the wing
Like such a bird, themselves would be too proud
And build on nothing but a passing cloud
As free from danger as the heavens are free
From pain and toil – there would they build and be
And sail about the world to scenes unheard
Of and unseen – O were they but a bird –
So think they while they listen to its song
And smile and fancy and so pass along
While its low nest moist with the dews of morn
30 Lye safely with the leveret in the corn

The Badger

The badger grunting on his woodland track
With shaggy hide and sharp nose scrowed[1] with black
Roots in the bushes and the woods and makes
A great hugh[2] burrow in the ferns and brakes
With nose on ground he runs an awkard pace
And anything will beat him in the race
The shepherd's dog will run him to his den
Followed and hooted by the dogs and men
The woodman when the hunting comes about
10 Go round at night to stop the foxes out
And hurrying through the bushes ferns and brakes
Nor sees the many holes the badger makes
And often through the bushes to the chin
Breaks the old holes and tumbles headlong in

Some keep a baited badger tame as hog
And tame him till he follows like the dog
They urge him on like dogs and show fair play
He beats and scarcely wounded goes away
Lapt[3] up as if asleep he scorns to fly
20 And siezes any dog that ventures nigh
Clapt[4] like a dog he never bites the men
But worrys dogs and hurrys to his den
They let him out and turn a harrow down
And there he fights the host of all the town
He licks the patting hand and trys to play
And never trys to bite or run away
And runs away from noise in hollow trees
Burnt by the boys to get a swarm of bees

1. Marked with lines.
2. Huge.
3. Curled up in a bundle.
4. Set on.

When midnight comes a host of dogs and men
30   Go out and track the badger to his den
And put a sack within the hole and lye
Till the old grunting badger passes bye
He comes and hears they let the strongest loose
The old fox hears the noise and drops the goose
The poacher shoots and hurrys from the cry
And the old hare half-wounded buzzes bye
They get a forked stick to bear him down
And clap the dogs and bear him to the town
And bait him all the day with many dogs
40   And laugh and shout and fright the scampering hogs
He runs along and bites at all he meets
They shout and hollo down the noisey streets

He turns about to face the loud uproar
And drives the rebels to their very doors
The frequent stone is hurled where e'er they go
When badgers fight and every one's a foe
The dogs are clapt and urged to join the fray
The badger turns and drives them all away
Though scarcly half as big, dimute[1] and small,
50   He fights with dogs for hours and beats them all
The heavy mastiff savage in the fray
Lies down and licks his feet and turns away
The bull-dog knows his match and waxes cold
The badger grins and never leaves his hold
He drives the crowd and follows at their heels
And bites them through. The drunkard swears and reels,

The frighted women takes the boys away
The blackguard laughs and hurrys on the fray:
He tries to reach the woods, an awkard race,
60   But sticks and cudgels quickly stop the chace
He turns agen and drives the noisey crowd
And beats the many dogs in noises loud

1. Diminutive (small).

He drives away and beats them every one
And then they loose them all and set them on
He falls as dead and kicked by boys and men
Then starts and grins and drives the crowd agen
Till kicked and torn and beaten out he lies
And leaves his hold and cackles groans and dies

John Keats
(1795–1821)

Keats was born in London. His father kept a riding stable, and although he had little education himself, sent John and his younger brothers George and Tom to the Reverend John Clarke's school at Enfield, where he was a popular boy, though known more for fighting than for studying. Keats was only nine years old, and his brothers and sister seven, five and one, when their father died. Their mother remarried, and the children went to live with her parents in Enfield, although they later moved to Edmonton. Enfield and Edmonton were both country areas at that time, and Keats's love of nature is evident in many of his poems. Five years later their mother also died.

At the age of fifteen, Keats was apprenticed to a surgeon and later studied medicine at Guy's Hospital in London. When he passed his medical examinations in 1816, he was licensed to practise as an apothecary (pharmacist), physician or surgeon. However, he never practised his profession. He had already begun to write poetry, and decided that he wanted to devote his life to being a poet.

One of Keats's first published poems was the sonnet, 'On First Looking into Chapman's *Homer*'. His friend, Cowden Clarke, had given him a copy of Chapman's translation of Homer's *Odyssey*, and described Keats's delight and amazement at the new world it opened to him. Keats rushed home at dawn from Clarke's house, and by ten o'clock that morning had sent him the sonnet. In it, he likens his reactions to those of the Spanish explorers who stood silent in wonder when they saw for the first time the vast new world of the Pacific Ocean.

Keats's second volume of poetry, *Endymion*, was based on the

Greek myth of a shepherd-prince's search for the moon-goddess who had fallen in love with him. Its opening lines sum up a philosophy Keats expresses in several other poems:

> A thing of beauty is a joy for ever:
> Its loveliness increases; it will never
> Pass into nothingness . . .

In 1818 Keats nursed his brother Tom, who was dying of tuberculosis (called consumption in those days), the disease that had killed their mother. After Tom's death, Keats himself became ill with consumption in 1820. Many of his poems are concerned with the problems of evil, suffering, death and immortality. The poet Robert Graves wrote of Keats's poem 'La Belle Dame sans Merci' that the beautiful lady 'represented Love, Death by Consumption and Poetry all at once'. Other critics have seen in the poem an expression of Keats's unhappy emotional relationship with Fanny Brawne, a young woman with whom he had fallen violently in love. In the poem, the beautiful lady seems to be leading the knight to destruction.

The title of 'La Belle Dame sans Merci' came from a medieval French ballad. He also refers to it in his long narrative poem 'The Eve of St Agnes'. In this and other poems, Keats often takes his subject and style from traditional ballads and stories as well as classical myths and legends. He was also influenced by medieval and Renaissance writers, especially Chaucer and Spenser. These and other works, including his odes 'To Autumn' and 'Ode to a Nightingale', appear in his third volume of poems, published in 1820 despite his increasing ill health.

In the summer of 1820 Keats's doctor ordered him to go to Italy, in the hope that the warmer climate would help him. However, within a few months of arriving he died and was buried in the Protestant cemetery in Rome.

Although Keats's life was short and his output of poetry relatively small, he is agreed to be one of the greatest English poets and a key figure in the Romantic movement. His poems are rich in imagery and he captures the natural and physical world with sensuous detail. 'To Autumn' captures the ripeness and beauty of the season like no other poem in the language.

On First Looking into Chapman's Homer

Much have I travelled in the realms of gold,[1]
    And many goodly states and kingdoms seen;
    Round many western islands have I been
Which bards in fealty[2] to Apollo hold.
Oft of one wide expanse had I been told
    That deep-browed Homer ruled as his demesne;[3]
    Yet did I never breathe its pure serene
Till I heard Chapman speak out loud and bold:
Then felt I like some watcher of the skies
10   When a new planet swims into his ken;
Or like stout Cortez[4] when with eagle eyes
    He stared at the Pacific – and all his men
Looked at each other with a wild surmise –
    Silent, upon a peak in Darien.

1. Possibly El Dorado, the mythical country of gold which the Spaniards Balboa and Cortez sought in South America, but possibly also a reference to the gold leaf embossing on book covers.
2. Poets are bound to Apollo by an oath of faithfulness.
3. Territory.
4. Strictly, it was Balboa who first sighted the Pacific from a mountain in a region just south of where the Panama Canal is now, between the town of Darien and Colombia, so Keats is using poetic licence for the sake of his rhythm here. In the days when half the world was unexplored, the sight of a vast, unknown ocean must have been awe-inspiring. Keats compares this to his feelings on first reading Chapman's translation of Homer's *Odyssey*.

On the Grasshopper and Cricket

The poetry of earth is never dead:
  When all the birds are faint with the hot sun,
  And hide in cooling trees, a voice will run
From hedge to hedge about the new-mown mead[1] –
That is the Grasshopper's. He takes the lead
  In summer luxury; he has never done
  With his delights, for when tired out with fun
He rests at ease beneath some pleasant weed.
The poetry of earth is ceasing never:
10   On a lone winter evening, when the frost
        Has wrought a silence, from the stove there shrills
The Cricket's song, in warmth increasing ever,
      And seems to one in drowsiness half lost,
        The Grasshopper's among some grassy hills.

1. Meadow.

Written on a blank space at the end of Chaucer's tale of The Floure and the Leafe

This pleasant tale is like a little copse:
  The honeyed lines do freshly interlace
  To keep the reader in so sweet a place,
So that he here and there full-hearted stops;
And oftentimes he feels the dewy drops
  Come cool and suddenly against his face,
  And by the wandering melody may trace
Which way the tender-leggèd linnet hops.
Oh! what a power has white simplicity!
10   What mighty power has this gentle story!
      I that do ever feel athirst for glory

Could at this moment be content to lie
    Meekly upon the grass, as those whose sobbings
Were heard of none beside the mournful robins.

'Over the hill and over the dale'

Over the hill and over the dale,
And over the bourn[1] to Dawlish –
Where gingerbread wives have a scanty sale
And gingerbread nuts are smallish.

Rantipole Betty she ran down a hill
And kicked up her petticoats fairly.
Says I, 'I'll be Jack if you will be Jill.'
So she sat on the grass debonairly.[2]

'Here's somebody coming, here's somebody coming!'
Says I, ''Tis the wind at a parley.'[3]
So without any fuss, any hawing and humming,
She lay on the grass debonairly.

'Here's somebody here, and here's somebody *there*!'
Says I, 'Hold your tongue, you young gipsy.'
So she held her tongue and lay plump and fair,
And dead as a Venus tipsy.

O who wouldn't hie[4] to Dawlish fair,
O who wouldn't stop in a meadow?
O who would not rumple the daisies there,
And make the wild fern for a bed do?

1. Small stream.
2. Cheerfully.
3. Conference.
4. Hurry.

'Old Meg she was a gipsy'

Old Meg she was a gipsy,
    And lived upon the moors,
Her bed it was the brown heath turf,
    And her house was out of doors.

Her apples were swart blackberries,
    Her currants pods o' broom,
Her wine was dew o' the wild white rose,
    Her book a churchyard tomb.

Her brothers were the craggy hills,
10   Her sisters larchen trees –
Alone with her great family
    She lived as she did please.

No breakfast had she many a morn,
    No dinner many a noon,
And 'stead of supper she would stare
    Full hard against the moon.

But every morn of woodbine fresh
    She made her garlanding,
And every night the dark glen yew
20   She wove, and she would sing.

And with her fingers old and brown
    She plaited mats o' rushes,
And gave them to the cottagers
    She met among the bushes.

Old Meg was brave as Margaret Queen
    And tall as Amazon,
An old red blanket cloak she wore,
    A chip-hat had she on.
God rest her agèd bones somewhere –
30   She died full long agone!

from *A Song about Myself*

IV
There was a naughty boy,
    And a naughty boy was he,
He ran away to Scotland
    The people for to see –
        There he found
        That the ground
        Was as hard,
        That a yard
        Was as long,
10   That a song
        Was as merry,
        That a cherry
        Was as red,
        That lead
        Was as weighty,
        That fourscore
        Was as eighty,
        That a door
        Was as wooden
20   As in England –
    So he stood in his shoes
        And he wondered,
        He wondered,
    He stood in his
        Shoes and he wondered.

Song

I had a dove and the sweet dove died;
    And I have thought it died of grieving.
O, what could it grieve for? Its feet were tied,
    With a silken thread of my own hand's weaving.
Sweet little red feet! why would you die –
Why should you leave me, sweet bird! why?
You lived alone on the forest-tree,
Why, pretty thing, could you not live with me?
I kissed you oft and gave you white peas;
10   Why not live sweetly, as in the green trees?

To Autumn

I

Season of mists and mellow fruitfulness,
    Close bosom-friend of the maturing sun,
Conspiring with him how to load and bless
    With fruit the vines that round the thatch-eves run;
To bend with apples the mossed cottage-trees,
    And fill all fruit with ripeness to the core;
        To swell the gourd, and plump the hazel shells
    With a sweet kernel; to set budding more,
And still more, later flowers for the bees,
10   Until they think warm days will never cease,
        For Summer has o'er-brimmed their clammy cells.

II

Who hath not seen thee oft amid thy store?
    Sometimes whoever seeks abroad may find
Thee sitting careless on a granary floor,
    Thy hair soft-lifted by the winnowing wind;

Or on a half-reaped furrow sound asleep,
   Drowsed with the fume of poppies, while thy hook
      Spares the next swath and all its twinèd flowers;
And sometimes like a gleaner thou dost keep
20   Steady thy laden head across a brook;
      Or by a cider-press, with patient look,
         Thou watchest the last oozings hours by hours.

III

Where are the songs of Spring? Ay, where are they?
   Think not of them, thou hast thy music too —
While barrèd clouds bloom the soft-dying day,
   And touch the stubble-plains with rosy hue:
Then in a wailful choir the small gnats mourn
   Among the river sallows, borne aloft
      Or sinking as the light wind lives or dies;
30 And full-grown lambs loud bleat from hilly bourn;
   Hedge-crickets sing; and now with treble soft
   The red-breast whistles from a garden-croft;
      And gathering swallows twitter in the skies.

Ode to a Nightingale

I

My heart aches, and a drowsy numbness pains
   My sense, as though of hemlock[1] I had drunk,
Or emptied some dull opiate to the drains
   One minute past, and Lethe-wards[2] had sunk:

1. A plant which can produce a sedative or a poison.
2. Souls waiting in Hades to be reborn drink the waters of the River
Lethe to forget their previous existence.

'Tis not through envy of thy happy lot,
　　But being too happy in thine happiness –
　　　　That thou, light-wingèd Dryad of the trees,
　　　　　　In some melodious plot
　　Of beechen green, and shadows numberless,
10　　　　Singest of summer in full-throated ease.

II

O, for a draught of vintage! that hath been
　　Cooled a long age in the deep-delvèd earth,
Tasting of Flora[1] and the country green,
Dance, and Provençal song, and sunburnt mirth!
O for a beaker full of the warm South,
　　Full of the true, the blushful Hippocrene,[2]
　　　　With beaded bubbles winking at the brim,
　　　　　　And purple-stainèd mouth,
　　That I might drink, and leave the world unseen,
20　　　　And with thee fade away into the forest dim –

III

Fade far away, dissolve, and quite forget
　　What thou among the leaves hast never known,
The weariness, the fever, and the fret
　　Here, where men sit and hear each other groan;
Where palsy shakes a few, sad, last grey hairs,
　　Where youth grows pale, and spectre-thin, and dies;
　　　　Where but to think is to be full of sorrow
　　　　And leaden-eyed despairs;
Where Beauty cannot keep her lustrous eyes,
30　　Or new Love pine at them beyond to-morrow.

1. Goddess of flowers, not margarine!
2. Hippocrene was a fountain near Mount Helicon, sacred to the muses, and thus the fountain of inspiration. Keats is saying here that red wine is the true source of his inspiration.

IV

Away! away! for I will fly to thee,
   Not charioted by Bacchus and his pards,[1]
But on the viewless wings of Poesy,
   Though the dull brain perplexes and retards.
Already with thee! tender is the night,
    And haply the Queen-Moon is on her throne,
      Clustered around by all her starry Fays;[2]
        But here there is no light,
    Save what from heaven is with the breezes blown
40   Through verdurous[3] glooms and winding mossy ways.

V

I cannot see what flowers are at my feet,
   Nor what soft incense hangs upon the boughs,
But, in embalmèd darkness, guess each sweet
   Wherewith the seasonable month endows
The grass, the thicket, and the fruit-tree wild –
    White hawthorn, and the pastoral eglantine;
      Fast fading violets covered up in leaves;
        And mid-May's eldest child,
The coming musk-rose, full of dewy wine,
50   The murmurous haunt of flies on summer eves.

VI

Darkling I listen; and, for many a time
   I have been half in love with easeful Death,
Called him soft names in many a musèd rhyme,
   To take into the air my quiet breath;
Now more than ever seems it rich to die,
   To cease upon the midnight with no pain,
      While thou art pouring forth thy soul abroad

1. Bacchus, the god of wine, had a chariot drawn by leopards.
2. Fairies.
3. Green with vegetation.

In such an ecstasy!
Still wouldst thou sing, and I have ears in vain –
60   To thy high requiem become a sod.[1]

VII

Thou wast not born for death, immortal Bird!
    No hungry generations tread thee down;
The voice I hear this passing night was heard
    In ancient days by emperor and clown:[2]
Perhaps the self-same song that found a path
    Through the sad heart of Ruth, when, sick for home,
        She stood in tears amid the alien corn;[3]
            The same that oft-times hath
    Charmed magic casements[4] opening on the foam
70   Of perilous seas, in faery lands forlorn.

VIII

Forlorn! the very word is like a bell
    To toll me back from thee to my sole self!
Adieu! the fancy cannot cheat so well
    As she is famed to do, deceiving elf.
Adieu! adieu! thy plaintive anthem fades
    Past the near meadows, over the still stream,
        Up the hill-side; and now 'tis buried deep
            In the next valley-glades:
    Was it a vision, or a waking dream?
80   Fled is that music – Do I wake or sleep?

1. The poet will be changed into earth by death, but the nightingale's song will continue and be a requiem.
2. Peasant.
3. See the Old Testament book of Ruth, chapter 2: v. 1–3. Ruth left her own land of Moab to accompany her mother-in-law Naomi to Bethlehem in Judaea. There, she became a gleaner in the fields of Boaz.
4. Windows.

La Belle Dame sans Merci. A Ballad

I

O what can ail thee, knight-at-arms,
    Alone and palely loitering?
The sedge has withered from the lake,
    And no birds sing.

II

O what can ail thee, knight-at-arms,
    So haggard and so woe-begone?
The squirrel's granary is full,
    And the harvest's done.

III

I see a lily on thy brow,
10   With anguish moist and fever-dew,
And on thy cheeks a fading rose
    Fast withereth too.

IV

I met a lady in the meads,
    Full beautiful – a faery's child,
Her hair was long, her foot was light,
    And her eyes were wild.

V

I made a garland for her head,
    And bracelets too, and fragrant zone;
She looked at me as she did love,
20   And made sweet moan.

VI

I set her on my pacing steed,
    And nothing else saw all day long,
For sidelong would she bend, and sing
    A faery's song.

VII

She found me roots of relish sweet,
  And honey wild, and manna-dew,
And sure in language strange she said –
  'I love thee true'.

VIII

She took me to her elfin grot,
30 And there she wept and sighed full sore,
And there I shut her wild wild eyes
  With kisses four.

IX

And there she lullèd me asleep
  And there I dreamed – Ah! woe betide! –
The latest dream I ever dreamt
  On the cold hill side.

X

I saw pale kings and princes too,
  Pale warriors, death-pale were they all;
They cried – 'La Belle Dame sans Merci
40 Thee hath in thrall!'

XI

I saw their starved lips in the gloam,
  With horrid warning gapèd wide,
And I awoke and found me here,
  On the cold hill's side.

XII

And this is why I sojourn here
  Alone and palely loitering,
Though the sedge is withered from the lake,
  And no birds sing.

Elizabeth Barrett Browning
(1806–1861)

Elizabeth Barrett was born at Coxhoe Hall, Durham. She was the
eldest of twelve children, and her father's favourite. She was
educated at home, and learned Greek, Latin and Hebrew when
she was very young. Her first poems, written in the style of Pope,
were published when she was only fourteen. After a back injury
when she was fifteen, she was treated as an invalid by her father.

The family moved to Wimpole Street in London, after which
Elizabeth stayed mainly in her room. She continued to write and
publish her work, which was highly praised. Some of her poems
are intensely intellectual, and others more simple and direct.
Among these are an affectionate tribute 'To Flush, My Dog', and
'The Romance of the Swan's Nest', in which a young girl builds a
romantic daydream about an ideal lover to whom she will reveal a
wild swan's nest she has kept secret, only to find that when she
looks for it again, it has gone.

Although Elizabeth rarely received visitors, she often exchanged
letters with literary admirers. One of those was the poet Robert
Browning, six years younger and at that time much less well
known. After a volume of her poems was published in 1844, to
great critical acclaim, he wrote to her, 'I love your verse with all
my heart, dear Miss Barrett.' Although one of his recent poems
had been very unsuccessful, she recognized his quality as a poet
and wrote encouragingly to him, eventually inviting him to come
and see her.

A woman's life in the 1840s was very confined. Few middle-
class women were truly independent; a woman lived with her
family until she married, and was her husband's property afterwards. Elizabeth Barrett's father's attitude to his children's relation-

ships was oppressive and disapproving, and so when she and Robert Browning fell in love she crept out of the house secretly one morning in 1846, with her maid and her dog Flush, and eloped with him to Italy. In the warm climate her health improved dramatically, she had a baby son, and the Brownings lived very happily together until her death.

Elizabeth Barrett Browning had always had a social conscience. Before she was married, she wrote 'The Cry of the Children' as a protest against the dreadful conditions in which working-class children lived and worked in mines and factories. Later, she wrote political poems about the Italian struggle for freedom and unification.

Although not a feminist in the modern sense of the word, she had strong views about the general attitude to women at that time. She wrote to a friend in 1845 about a man whom she felt patronized her: 'For a woman to hang down her head like a lily through life ... [or] to lounge as in a Book of Beauty, and be "defended" by the strong and mighty thinkers on all sides of her – this he thinks, is her destiny and glory. It is not the pudding-making and stocking-darning theory – it is more graceful and picturesque. But the significance is precisely the same – and the absurdity a hundred times over, greater. Who makes my pudding is useful to me, but who looks languishing in a Book of Beauty, is good for nothing so far.'

Among her best loved works is a series of 44 sonnets which she published in 1850 under the title of *Sonnets from the Portuguese*. The title is deceptive; no Portuguese works were involved, and the title was adopted to conceal the intensely personal nature of the poems. They were written during the secret period of courtship between her and Robert Browning. The sonnets express her intense love and longing for him, her admiration of his qualities, and her doubts and fears that he is marrying her out of pity or that she is not worthy of him. Her poem 'Amy's Cruelty' shows the uncompromising demands she felt were involved in an equal love between two people. She chose wisely in marrying a man who valued her work as highly as his own.

The Romance of the Swan's Nest

'So the dreams depart,
So the fading phantoms flee,
And the sharp reality
Now must act its part.'

WESTWOOD'S
Beads from a Rosary.

I

Little Ellie sits alone
   'Mid the beeches of a meadow,
      By a stream-side on the grass,
And the trees are showering down
   Doubles of their leaves in shadow
      On her shining hair and face.

II

She has thrown her bonnet by,
   And her feet she has been dipping
      In the shallow water's flow:
10   Now she holds them nakedly
   In her hands, all sleek and dripping,
      While she rocketh to and fro.

III

Little Ellie sits alone,
   And the smile she softly uses
      Fills the silence like a speech,
While she thinks what shall be done,
   And the sweetest pleasure chooses
      For her future within reach.

IV

Litle Ellie in her smile

20   Chooses – 'I will have a lover
         Riding on a steed of steeds:
He shall love me without guile,
      And to *him* I will discover[1]
         The swan's nest among the reeds.

V

'And the steed shall be red-roan,[2]
      And the lover shall be noble,
         With an eye that takes the breath:
And the lute he plays upon
      Shall strike ladies into trouble,
30   As his sword strikes men to death.

VI

'And the steed it shall be shod
      All in silver, housed in azure.
         And the mane shall swim the wind;
And the hoofs along the sod[3]
      Shall flash onward and keep measure,
         Till the shepherds look behind.

VII

'But my lover will not prize
      All the glory that he rides in,
         When he gazes in my face:
40   He will say, 'O Love, thine eyes
      Build the shrine my soul abides in,
         And I kneel here for thy grace!'

1. Reveal.
2. Reddish-brown.
3. Turf.

VIII

'Then, ay, then he shall kneel low,
    With the red-roan steed anear him
        Which shall seem to understand,
Till I answer, "Rise and go!
    For the world must love and fear him
        Whom I gift with heart and hand."

IX

'Then he will arise so pale,
50   I shall feel my own lips tremble
            With a *yes* I must not say,
Nathless¹ maiden-brave, "Farewell,"
        I will utter, and dissemble –
            "Light to-morrow with to-day!"

X

'Then he'll ride among the hills
    To the wide world past the river,
        There to put away all wrong;
To make straight distorted wills,
    And to empty the broad quiver
60   Which the wicked bear along.

XI

'Three times shall a young foot-page
    Swim the stream and climb the mountain
        And kneel down beside my feet –
"Lo, my master sends this gage,²
    Lady, for thy pity's counting!
        What wilt thou exchange for it?"

1. Nevertheless.
2. Pledge of his love.

XII

'And the first time I will send
  A white rosebud for a guerdon,[1]
    And the second time, a glove;
70 But the third time – I may bend
    From my pride, and answer – "Pardon
      If he comes to take my love."

XIII

'Then the young foot-page will run,
  Then my lover will ride faster,
    Till he kneeleth at my knee:
"I am a duke's eldest son,
  Thousand serfs do call me master,
    But, O Love, I love but *thee!*"

XIV

'He will kiss me on the mouth
80   Then, and lead me as a lover
      Through the crowds that praise his deeds;
And, when soul-tied by one troth,
    Unto *him* I will discover
      That swan's nest among the reeds.'

XV

Little Ellie with her smile
  Not yet ended, rose up gaily,
    Tied the bonnet, donned the shoe,
And went homeward, round a mile,
    Just to see, as she did daily,
90   What more eggs were with the two.

1. Reward.

XVI

Pushing through the elm-tree copse,
   Winding up the stream, light-hearted,
      Where the osier[1] pathway leads,
Past the boughs she stoops – and stops.
   Lo, the wild swan had deserted,
      And a rat had gnawed the reeds!

XVII

Ellie went home sad and slow.
   If she found the lover ever,
      With his red-roan steed of steeds,
100 Sooth I know not; but I know
   She could never show him – never,
      That swan's nest among the reeds!

1. Willow.

To Flush, My Dog

I

Loving friend, the gift of one
Who her own true faith has run
   Through thy lower nature,
Be my benediction[1] said
With my hand upon thy head,
   Gentle fellow-creature!

II

Like a lady's ringlets brown,
Flow thy silken ears adown
   Either side demurely
10 Of thy silver-suited breast
Shining out from all the rest
   Of thy body purely.

1. Blessing.

III

Darkly brown thy body is,
Till the sunshine striking this
    Alchemize¹ its dulness,
When the sleek curls manifold²
Flash all over into gold
    With a burnished fulness.

IV

Underneath my stroking hand,
20   Startled eyes of hazel bland
    Kindling, growing larger,
Up thou leapest with a spring,
Full of prank and curveting,³
    Leaping like a charger.

V

Leap! thy broad tail waves a light,
Leap! thy slender feet are bright,
    Canopied in fringes;
Leap! those tasselled ears of thine
Flicker strangely, fair and fine
30   Down their golden inches.

VI

Yet, my pretty, sportive friend,
Little is't to such an end
    That I praise thy rareness;
Other dogs may be thy peers
Haply in these drooping ears
    And this glossy fairness.

1. Turn it into gold.
2. Many.
3. Frisking.

VII

But of *thee* it shall be said,
This dog watched beside a bed
   Day and night unweary,
40 Watched within a curtained room
Where no sunbeam brake the gloom
   Round the sick and dreary.

VIII

Roses, gathered for a vase,
In that chamber died apace,
   Beam and breeze resigning;
This dog only, waited on,
Knowing that when light is gone
   Love remains for shining.

IX

Other dogs in thymy dew
50 Tracked the hares and followed through
   Sunny moor or meadow;
This dog only, crept and crept
Next a languid cheek that slept,
   Sharing in the shadow.

X

Other dogs of loyal cheer
Bounded at the whistle clear,
   Up the woodside hieing;[1]
This dog only, watched in reach
Of a faintly uttered speech
60   Or a louder sighing.

1. Hurrying.

XI

And if one or two quick tears
Dropped upon his glossy ears
   Or a sigh came double,
Up he sprang in eager haste,
Fawning, fondling, breathing fast,
   In a tender trouble.

XII

And this dog was satisfied
If a pale thin hand would glide
   Down his dewlaps sloping, –
70 Which he pushed his nose within,
After, – platforming his chin
   On the palm left open.

XIII

This dog, if a friendly voice
Call him now to blither choice
   Than such chamber-keeping,
'Come out!' praying from the door, –
Presseth backward as before,
   Up against me leaping.

XIV

Therefore to this dog will I,
80 Tenderly not scornfully,
   Render praise and favour:
With my hand upon his head,
Is my benediction said
   Therefore and for ever.

XV

And because he loves me so,
Better than his kind will do
   Often man or woman,
Give I back more love again
Than dogs often take of men,
90   Leaning from my Human.

XVI

Blessings on thee, dog of mine,
Pretty collars make thee fine,
    Sugared milk make fat thee!
Pleasures wag on in thy tail,
Hands of gentle motion fail
    Nevermore, to pat thee!

XVII

Downy pillow take thy head,
Silken coverlid bestead,
    Sunshine help thy sleeping!
100 No fly's buzzing wake thee up,
No man break thy purple cup
    Set for drinking deep in.

XVIII

Whiskered cats arointed¹ flee,
Sturdy stoppers keep from thee
    Cologne distillations;
Nuts lie in thy path for stones,
And thy feast-day macaroons
    Turn to daily rations!

110 XIX

Mock I thee, in wishing weal?²
Tears are in my eyes to feel
    Thou art made so straitly,³
Blessing needs must straiten too, –
Little canst thou joy or do,
    Thou who lovest *greatly*.

1. Banished.
2. Well, good.
3. Confined so much.

XX

Yet be blessèd to the height
Of all good and all delight
   Pervious to thy nature;
Only *loved* beyond that line,
With a love that answers thine,

120   Loving fellow-creature!

from SONNETS FROM THE PORTUGUESE

XIV

If thou must love me, let it be for nought
Except for love's sake only. Do not say
'I love her for her smile – her look – her way
Of speaking gently, – for a trick of thought
That falls in well with mine, and certes[1] brought
A sense of pleasant ease on such a day' –
For these things in themselves, Belovèd, may
Be changed, or change for thee, – and love, so wrought,
May be unwrought so. Neither love me for

10   Thine own dear pity's wiping my cheeks dry, –
A creature might forget to weep, who bore
Thy comfort long, and lose thy love thereby!
But love me for love's sake, that evermore
Thou mayst love on, through love's eternity.

1. Certainly.

XX

Belovèd, my Belovèd, when I think
That thou wast in the world a year ago,
What time I sat alone here in the snow
And saw no footprint, heard the silence sink
No moment at thy voice, but, link by link,
Went counting all my chains as if that so
They never could fall off at any blow
Struck by thy possible hand, – why, thus I drink
Of life's great cup of wonder! Wonderful,
10 Never to feel thee thrill the day or night
With personal act or speech, – nor ever cull[1]
Some prescience[2] of thee with the blossoms white
Thou sawest growing! Atheists are as dull,
Who cannot guess God's presence out of sight.

1. Gather.
2. Awareness, foreknowledge.

XXI

Say over again, and yet once over again,
That thou dost love me. Though the word repeated
Should seem 'a cuckoo-song', as thou dost treat it,
Remember, never to the hill or plain,
Valley and wood, without her cuckoo-strain
Comes the fresh Spring in all her green completed.
Belovèd, I, amid the darkness greeted
By a doubtful spirit-voice, in that doubt's pain
Cry, 'Speak once more – thou lovest!' Who can fear
10 Too many stars, though each in heaven shall roll,
Too many flowers, though each shall crown the year?
Say thou dost love me, love me, love me – toll
The silver iterance![1] – only minding, Dear,
To love me also in silence with thy soul.

1. Repetition.

XXIX

I think of thee! – my thoughts do twine and bud
About thee, as wild vines, about a tree,
Put out broad leaves, and soon there's nought to see
Except the straggling green which hides the wood.
Yet, O my palm-tree, be it understood
I will not have my thoughts instead of thee
Who art dearer, better! Rather, instantly
Renew thy presence; as a strong tree should,
Rustle thy boughs and set thy trunk all bare,
10   And let these bands of greenery which insphere thee
Drop heavily down, – burst, shattered, everywhere!
Because, in this deep joy to see and hear thee
And breathe within thy shadow a new air,
I do not think of thee – I am too near thee.

XXXIX

Because thou hast the power and own'st the grace
To look through and behind this mask of me
(Against which years have beat thus blanchingly
With their rains), and behold my soul's true face,
The dim and weary witness of life's race, –
Because thou hast the faith and love to see,
Through that same soul's distracting lethargy,
The patient angel waiting for a place
In the new Heavens, – because nor sin nor woe,
10   Nor God's infliction, nor death's neighbourhood,
Nor all which others viewing, turn to go,
Nor all which makes me tired of all, self-viewed, –
Nothing repels thee, . . . Dearest, teach me so
To pour out gratitude, as thou dost, good!

XLIII

How do I love thee? Let me count the ways.
I love thee to the depth and breadth and height
My soul can reach, when feeling out of sight
For the ends of Being and ideal Grace.
I love thee to the level of everyday's
Most quiet need, by sun and candle-light.
I love thee freely, as men strive for Right;
I love thee purely, as they turn from Praise.
I love thee with the passion put to use
10   In my old griefs, and with my childhood's faith.
I love thee with a love I seemed to lose
With my lost saints, – I love thee with the breath,
Smiles, tears, of all my life! – and, if God choose,
I shall but love thee better after death.

Amy's Cruelty

Fair Amy of the terraced house,
    Assist me to discover
Why you who would not hurt a mouse
    Can torture so your lover.

You give your coffee to the cat,
    You stroke the dog for coming,
And all your face grows kinder at
    The little brown bee's humming.

But when *he* haunts your door . . . the town
10   Marks coming and marks going . . .
You seem to have stitched your eyelids down
    To that long piece of sewing!

You never give a look, not you,
　　Nor drop him a 'Good morning,'
To keep his long day warm and blue,
　　So fretted by your scorning.

She shook her head – 'The mouse and bee
　　For crumb or flower will linger:
The dog is happy at my knee,
20　　The cat purrs at my finger.

'But *he* . . . to *him*, the least thing given
　　Means great things at a distance;
He wants my world, my sun, my heaven,
　　Soul, body, whole existence.

'They say love gives as well as takes;
　　But I'm a simple maiden, –
My mother's first smile when she wakes
　　I still have smiled and prayed in.

'I only know my mother's love
30　　Which gives all and asks nothing;
And this new loving sets the groove
　　Too much the way of loathing.

'Unless he gives me all in change,
　　I forfeit all things by him:
The risk is terrible and strange –
　　I tremble, doubt, . . . deny him.

'He's sweetest friend or hardest foe,
　　Best angel or worst devil;
I either hate or . . . love him so,
40　　I can't be merely civil!

'You trust a woman who puts forth
　　Her blossoms thick as summer's?
You think she dreams what love is worth,
　　Who casts it to new-comers?

'Such love's a cowslip-ball to fling,
    A moment's pretty pastime;
I give . . . all me, if anything,
    The first time and the last time.

'Dear neighbour of the trellised house,
50   A man should murmur never,
Though treated worse than dog and mouse,
    Till doated on for ever!'

The Forced Recruit

SOLFERINO[1] 1859

In the ranks of the Austrian you found him,
    He died with his face to you all;
Yet bury him here where around him
    You honour your bravest that fall.

Venetian, fair-featured and slender,
    He lies shot to death in his youth,
With a smile on his lips over-tender
    For any mere soldier's dead mouth.

No stranger, and yet not a traitor,
10   Though alien the cloth on his breast,
Underneath it how seldom a greater
    Young heart has a shot sent to rest!

1. The battle of Solferino was fought in Lombardy, between Franco-Italian forces commanded by Napoleon III and the Austrians under Emperor Franz-Joseph I. The Austrians lost, and the suffering of the wounded inspired Jean Dunant, a Swiss philanthropist, to establish the Red Cross.

By your enemy tortured and goaded
   To march with them, stand in their file,
His musket (see) never was loaded,
   He facing your guns with that smile!

As orphans yearn on to their mothers,
   He yearned to your patriot bands; –
'Let me die for our Italy, brothers,
20   If not in your ranks, by your hands!

'Aim straightly, fire steadily! spare me
   A ball in the body which may
Deliver my heart here, and tear me
   This badge of the Austrian away!'

So thought he, so died he this morning.
   What then? many others have died.
Ay, but easy for men to die scorning
   The death-stroke, who fought side by side –

One tricolor floating above them;
30   Struck down 'mid triumphant acclaims
   Of an Italy rescued to love them
And blazon the brass with their names.

But he, – without witness or honour,
   Mixed, shamed in his country's regard,
With the tyrants who march in upon her,
   Died faithful and passive: 't was hard.

'T was sublime. In a cruel restriction
   Cut off from the guerdon[1] of sons,
With most filial obedience, conviction,
40   His soul kissed the lips of her guns.

1. Reward.

That moves you? Nay, grudge not to show it,
   While digging a grave for him here:
The others who died, says your poet,
   Have glory, – let *him* have a tear.

Alfred, Lord Tennyson
(1809–1892)

Tennyson was born in Somersby, Lincolnshire. He was the fourth of eleven children of a country clergyman. His father had a large collection of books by great authors, and all the children were encouraged to read widely. Tennyson and his brothers all wrote poetry as young children, and they experimented with many different verse forms. In 1827, the year he went up to Trinity College, Cambridge, Tennyson and his brother Charles published some of their boyhood works in *Poems by Two Brothers*.

Once at university, Tennyson continued to work on his poetry. He published *Poems, Chiefly Lyrical* in 1830, and a further volume of poems in 1832. This second volume contains 'The Lady of Shalott', one of his most popular works. It was enthusiastically received by his admirers, but severely criticized by reviewers.

In 1830 Tennyson briefly joined a Spanish revolutionary army with his friend Arthur Hallam, although they did no fighting. After his father died in 1831, he left Cambridge without taking a degree. In 1833 Arthur Hallam died suddenly. This affected Tennyson deeply, and in his depression he vowed not to publish any more verse for ten years. During this time, however, he continued to write, and as well as other poetry he began work on *In Memoriam*, an elegy for Hallam that combines grief for his friend with meditation on spiritual conflicts and religious faith.

At the end of his period of silence, Tennyson published two volumes of poetry. These included 'Morte d'Arthur', a poem based on the Arthurian legends to which he later returned in his longer work *Idylls of the King*, and the short lyric 'Break, Break, Break'. His work was hugely successful, and he was acclaimed as the leading poet of his day. In 1850 his literary reputation was confirmed by the publication of *In Memoriam*, and he was made Poet Laureate after Wordsworth died. At last he felt financially secure enough to marry Emily Sellwood, to whom he had been engaged for seven years.

Tennyson took his duties as Poet Laureate seriously, and produced several memorable poems in that role. Among these was 'The Charge of the Light Brigade' in 1854, which commemorated a courageous, if disastrous, charge by a British cavalry unit in the Crimean War. He continued to write and publish poems and plays until he was over 80. Of all English poets, he was the most famous and honoured during his lifetime. Sightseers used to wait near his house for a glimpse of him, but he had a shy nature and tried hard to avoid them. In 1884 he was created a peer and took the title Baron Tennyson of Freshwater and Aldworth, after his estate on the Isle of Wight.

A wide range of subject matter provided sources for Tennyson's poetry. He ranged from medieval legends to classical myths, and from domestic situations to close observation of nature. The richness of his imagery and descriptive writing shows the influence of Keats and other Romantic poets, for example in 'Now sleeps the crimson petal, now the white' from *The Princess*. However, he was also a master at handling rhythm. The sadness of 'Break, break, break' owes as much to the insistent beat as to the subject. He used the musical qualities of words to emphasize his rhythms and meanings. The language of 'I come from haunts of coot and hern' ripples and lilts like the brook it portrays, and the last two lines of 'Come down O maid from yonder mountain height' provide one of the most beautiful examples of alliteration, assonance and onomatopoeia in English poetry:

> The moan of doves in immemorial elms
> And murmuring of innumerable bees.

Tennyson was a craftsman in his poetry. His manuscripts were carefully polished and revised until they were perfect. His understanding of metre was exact, and few poets have used such a wide variety of styles. He is very Victorian in his feeling for order and in his occasional tendency to moralize and indulge himself in melancholy, but the energy and beauty of so much of his poetry have maintained its popularity since his death.

The Owl

I

When cats run home and light is come,
    And dew is cold upon the ground,
And the far-off stream is dumb,
    And the whirring sail goes round,[1]
    And the whirring sail goes round;
        Alone and warming his five wits,
        The white owl in the belfry sits.

II

When merry milkmaids click the latch,
    And rarely smells the new-mown hay,
10   And the cock hath sung beneath the thatch
        Twice or thrice his roundelay,[2]
        Twice or thrice his roundelay;
            Alone and warming his five wits,
            The white owl in the belfry sits.

1. The sail is on a windmill.
2. A simple song, also a bird's song.

The Eagle

He clasps the crag with crooked hands;
Close to the sun in lonely lands,
Ring'd with the azure world, he stands.

The wrinkled sea beneath him crawls;
He watches from his mountain walls,
And like a thunderbolt he falls.

The Kraken[1]

Below the thunders of the upper deep;
Far far beneath in the abysmal sea,
His ancient, dreamless, uninvaded sleep
The Kraken sleepeth: faintest sunlights flee
About his shadowy sides: above him swell
Huge sponges of millennial growth and height;
And far away into the sickly light,
From many a wondrous grot and secret cell
Unnumber'd and enormous polypi
10 Winnow with giant fins the slumbering green.
There hath he lain for ages and will lie
Battening upon huge seaworms in his sleep,
Until the latter fire shall heat the deep;
Then once by men and angels to be seen,
In roaring he shall rise and on the surface die.

1. A fabulous sea-monster, supposed to have been seen off the coast of
Norway.

The Lady of Shalott

PART I

On either side the river lie
Long fields of barley and of rye,
That clothe the wold[1] and meet the sky;
And thro' the field the road runs by
          To many-tower'd Camelot;
And up and down the people go,
Gazing where the lilies blow
Round an island there below,
          The island of Shalott.

1. Hilly land.

10   Willows whiten, aspens quiver,
     Little breezes dusk and shiver
     Thro' the wave that runs for ever
     By the island in the river
          Flowing down to Camelot.
     Four grey walls, and four grey towers,
     Overlook a space of flowers,
     And the silent isle imbowers
          The Lady of Shalott.

     By the margin, willow-veil'd,
20   Slide the heavy barges trail'd
     By slow horses; and unhail'd
     The shallop flitteth silken-sail'd
          Skimming down to Camelot:
     But who hath seen her wave her hand?
     Or at the casement seen her stand?
     Or is she known in all the land,
          The Lady of Shalott?

     Only reapers, reaping early
     In among the bearded barley,
30   Hear a song that echoes cheerly
     From the river winding clearly,
          Down to tower'd Camelot:
     And by the moon the reaper weary,
     Piling sheaves in uplands airy,
     Listening, whispers ''Tis the fairy
          Lady of Shalott.'

PART II
     There she weaves by night and day
     A magic web with colours gay.
     She has heard a whisper say,
40   A curse is on her if she stay

To look down to Camelot.
She knows not what the curse may be,
And so she weaveth steadily,
And little other care hath she,
     The Lady of Shalott.

And moving thro' a mirror clear
That hangs before her all the year,
Shadows of the world appear.
There she sees the highway near
50   Winding down to Camelot:
There the river eddy whirls,
And there the surly village-churls,
And the red cloaks of market girls,
     Pass onward from Shalott.

Sometimes a troop of damsels glad,
An abbot on an ambling pad,
Sometimes a curly shepherd-lad,
Or long-hair'd page in crimson clad,
     Goes by to tower'd Camelot;
60   And sometimes thro' the mirror blue
The knights come riding two and two:
She hath no loyal knight and true,
     The Lady of Shalott.

But in her web she still delights
To weave the mirror's magic sights,
For often thro' the silent nights
A funeral, with plumes and lights,
     And music, went to Camelot:
Or when the moon was overhead,
70   Came two young lovers lately wed;
'I am half sick of shadows,' said
     The Lady of Shalott.

PART III

A bow-shot from her bower-eaves,
He rode between the barley-sheaves,
The sun came dazzling thro' the leaves,
And flamed upon the brazen greaves
        Of bold Sir Lancelot.
A red-cross knight for ever kneel'd
To a lady in his shield,
80 That sparkled on the yellow field,
        Beside remote Shalott.

The gemmy[1] bridle glitter'd free,
Like to some branch of stars we see
Hung in the golden Galaxy.
The bridle bells rang merrily
        As he rode down to Camelot:
And from his blazon'd baldric[2] slung
A mighty silver bugle hung,
And as he rode his armour rung,
90   Beside remote Shalott.

All in the blue unclouded weather
Thick-jewell'd shone the saddle-leather,
The helmet and the helmet-feather
Burn'd like one burning flame together,
        As he rode down to Camelot.
As often thro' the purple night,
Below the starry clusters bright,
Some bearded meteor, trailing light,
        Moves over still Shalott.

100 His broad clear brow in sunlight glow'd;
On burnish'd hooves his war-horse trode;
From underneath his helmet flow'd
His coal-black curls as on he rode,
        As he rode down to Camelot.

1. Covered in gems.
2. A richly ornamented belt, passing over one shoulder and under the
opposite arm, used to support a weapon or an instrument.

From the bank and from the river
He flash'd into the crystal mirror,
'Tirra lirra,' by the river
    Sang Sir Lancelot.

She left the web, she left the loom,
110 She made three paces thro' the room,
She saw the water-lily bloom,
She saw the helmet and the plume,
    She look'd down to Camelot.
Out flew the web and floated wide;
The mirror crack'd from side to side;
'The curse is come upon me,' cried
    The Lady of Shalott.

PART IV
In the stormy east-wind straining,
The pale yellow woods were waning,
120 The broad stream in his banks complaining,
Heavily the low sky raining
    Over tower'd Camelot;
Down she came and found a boat
Beneath a willow left afloat,
And round about the prow she wrote
    The Lady of Shalott.

And down the river's dim expanse –
Like some bold seër in a trance,
Seeing all his own mischance –
130 With a glassy countenance
    Did she look to Camelot.
And at the closing of the day
She loosed the chain, and down she lay;
The broad stream bore her far away,
    The Lady of Shalott.

Lying, robed in snowy white
That loosely flew to left and right –
The leaves upon her falling light –
Thro' the noises of the night
140   She floated down to Camelot:
And as the boat-head wound along
The willowy hills and fields among,
They heard her singing her last song,
        The Lady of Shalott.

Heard a carol, mournful, holy,
Chanted loudly, chanted lowly,
Till her blood was frozen slowly,
And her eyes were darken'd wholly,
        Turn'd to tower'd Camelot.
150 For ere she reach'd upon the tide
The first house by the water-side,
Singing in her song she died,
        The Lady of Shalott.

Under tower and balcony,
By garden-wall and gallery,
A gleaming shape she floated by,
Dead-pale between the houses high,
        Silent into Camelot.
Out upon the wharfs they came,
160 Knight and burgher, lord and dame,
And round the prow they read her name,
        The Lady of Shalott.

Who is this? and what is here?
And in the lighted palace near
Died the sound of royal cheer;
And they cross'd themselves for fear,
        All the knights at Camelot:
But Lancelot mused a little space;
He said, 'She has a lovely face;
170 God in his mercy lend her grace,
        The Lady of Shalott.'

Break, break, break

Break, break, break
    On thy cold grey stones, O Sea!
And I would that my tongue could utter
    The thoughts that arise in me.

O well for the fisherman's boy,
    That he shouts with his sister at play!
O well for the sailor lad,
    That he sings in his boat on the bay!

And the stately ships go on
    To their haven under the hill;
10 But O for the touch of a vanish'd hand,
    And the sound of a voice that is still!

Break, break, break
    At the foot of thy crags, O Sea!
But the tender grace of a day that is dead
    Will never come back to me.

from IN MEMORIAM

CVI

Ring out, wild bells, to the wild sky,
        The flying cloud, the frosty light:
        The year is dying in the night;
Ring out, wild bells, and let him die.

Ring out the old, ring in the new,
        Ring, happy bells, across the snow:
        The year is going, let him go;
Ring out the false, ring in the true.

Ring out the grief that saps the mind,
10   For those that here we see no more;
        Ring out the feud of rich and poor,
Ring in redress to all mankind.

Ring out a slowly dying cause,
        And ancient forms of party strife;
        Ring in the nobler modes of life,
With sweeter manners, purer laws.

Ring out the want, the care, the sin,
        The faithless coldness of the times;
        Ring out, ring out my mournful rhymes,
20 But ring the fuller minstrel in.

Ring out false pride in place and blood,
        The civic slander and the spite;
        Ring in the love of truth and right,
Ring in the common love of good.

Ring out old shapes of foul disease;
        Ring out the narrowing lust of gold;
        Ring out the thousand wars of old,
Ring in the thousand years of peace.

Ring in the valiant man and free,
30   The larger heart, the kindlier hand;
        Ring out the darkness of the land,
Ring in the Christ that is to be.

Songs from 'The Brook'

I come from haunts of coot and hern,[1]
    I make a sudden sally
And sparkle out among the fern,
    To bicker down a valley.

1. Water-birds.

By thirty hills I hurry down,
    Or slip between the ridges,
By twenty thorps,[1] a little town,
    And half a hundred bridges.

Till last by Philip's farm I flow
10   To join the brimming river,
For men may come and men may go,
    But I go on for ever.

I chatter over stony ways,
    In little sharps and trebles,
I bubble into eddying bays,
    I babble on the pebbles.

With many a curve my banks I fret
    By many a field and fallow,
And many a fairy foreland set
20   With willow-weed and mallow.

I chatter, chatter, as I flow
    To join the brimming river,
For men may come and men may go,
    But I go on for ever.

I wind about, and in and out,
    With here a blossom sailing,
And here and there a lusty trout,
    And here and there a grayling,

And here and there a foamy flake
30   Upon me, as I travel
With many a silvery waterbreak
    Above the golden gravel,

And draw them all along, and flow
    To join the brimming river,
For men may come and men may go,
    But I go on for ever.

1. Small villages.

I steal by lawns and grassy plots,
   I slide by hazel covers;
I move the sweet forget-me-nots
40   That grow for happy lovers.

I slip, I slide, I gloom, I glance
   Among my skimming swallows;
I make the netted sunbeam dance
   Against my sandy shallows.

I murmur under moon and stars
   In brambly wildernesses;
I linger by my shingly bars;
   I loiter round my cresses;

And out again I curve and flow
50   To join the brimming river,
For men may come and men may go,
   But I go on for ever.

Crossing the Bar[1]

Sunset and evening star,
   And one clear call for me.
And may there be no moaning of the bar,
   When I put out to sea,

But such a tide as moving seems asleep,
   Too full for sound and foam,
When that which drew from out the boundless deep
   Turns again home.

1. A bank of silt, sand or gravel deposited across the mouth of a river or harbour.

Twilight and evening bell,
10   And after that the dark:
And may there be no sadness of farewell,
     When I embark;

For tho' from out our bourne[1] of Time and Place
     The flood may bear me far,
I hope to see my Pilot face to face,
     When I have crost[2] the bar.

1. Boundary.
2. Crossed.

Songs from 'The Princess'

II

Sweet and low, sweet and low,
     Wind of the western sea,
Low, low, breathe and blow,
     Wind of the western sea!
Over the rolling waters go,
Come from the dying moon, and blow,
     Blow him again to me;
While my little one, while my pretty one, sleeps.

Sleep and rest, sleep and rest,
10   Father will come to thee soon;
Rest, rest, on mother's breast,
     Father will come to thee soon;

Father will come to his babe in the nest,
Silver sails all out of the west
     Under the silver moon:
Sleep, my little one, sleep, my pretty one, sleep.

III

The splendour falls on castle walls
    And snowy summits old in story:
The long light shakes across the lakes,
    And the wild cataract leaps in glory.
Blow, bugle, blow, set the wild echoes flying,
Blow, bugle; answer, echoes, dying, dying, dying.

O hark, O hear! how thin and clear,
    And thinner, clearer, farther going!
O sweet and far from cliff and scar
    The horns of Elfland faintly blowing!
Blow, let us hear the purple glens replying:
Blow, bugle; answer, echoes, dying, dying, dying.

O love, they die in yon rich sky,
    They faint on hill or field or river:
Our echoes roll from soul to soul,
    And grow for ever and for ever.
Blow, bugle, blow, set the wild echoes flying,
And answer, echoes, answer, dying, dying, dying.

IX

Now sleeps the crimson petal, now the white;
Nor waves the cypress in the palace walk;
Nor winks the gold fin in the porphyry[1] font:
The fire-fly wakens: waken thou with me.

Now droops the milkwhite peacock like a ghost,
And like a ghost she glimmers on to me.

Now lies the Earth all Danaë[2] to the stars,
And all thy heart lies open unto me.

1. Made of a purple stone with feldspar crystals in it.
2. Danaë was the daughter of the King of Argos. He was told that her
son would kill him, so resolved she should never marry and locked her
in a tower. However, Zeus changed himself into a shower of gold and
fell on her from the sky, and she thus became the mother of Perseus.

Now slides the silent meteor on, and leaves
10   A shining furrow, as thy thoughts in me.

Now folds the lily all her sweetness up,
And slips into the bosom of the lake:
So fold thyself, my dearest, thou, and slip
Into my bosom and be lost in me.

The Charge of the Light Brigade

I

Half a league, half a league,
   Half a league onward,
All in the valley of Death
   Rode the six hundred.
'Forward, the Light Brigade!
Charge for the guns!' he said;
Into the valley of Death
   Rode the six hundred.

II

'Forward, the Light Brigade!'
10   Was there a man dismay'd?
Not tho' the soldier knew
   Some one had blunder'd:
Theirs not to make reply,
Theirs not to reason why,
Theirs but to do and die:
Into the valley of Death
   Rode the six hundred.

III

Cannon to right of them,
Cannon to left of them,
20 Cannon in front of them
    Volley'd and thunder'd;
Storm'd at with shot and shell,
Boldly they rode and well,
    Into the jaws of Death,
    Into the mouth of Hell
        Rode the six hundred.

IV

Flash'd all their sabres bare,
Flash'd as they turn'd in air,
Sabring the gunners there,
30 Charging an army, while
    All the world wonder'd:
Plunged in the battery-smoke
Right thro' the line they broke;
    Cossack and Russian
Reel'd from the sabre-stroke
    Shatter'd and sunder'd.
Then they rode back, but not,
    Not the six hundred.

V

Cannon to right of them,
40 Cannon to left of them,
Cannon behind them
    Volley'd and thunder'd;
Storm'd at with shot and shell,
While horse and hero fell,
They that had fought so well
Came thro' the jaws of Death
Back from the mouth of Hell,
All that was left of them,
    Left of six hundred.

VI

50   When can their glory fade?
O the wild charge they made!
    All the world wonder'd.
Honour the charge they made!
Honour the Light Brigade,
    Noble six hundred!

Morte d'Arthur[1]

So all day long the noise of battle roll'd
Among the mountains by the winter sea;
Until King Arthur's table, man by man,
Had fall'n in Lyonnesse about their Lord,
King Arthur: then, because his wound was deep,
The bold Sir Bedivere uplifted him,
Sir Bedivere, the last of all his knights,
And bore him to a chapel nigh the field,
A broken chancel with a broken cross,
10   That stood on a dark strait of barren land.
On one side lay the Ocean, and on one
Lay a great water, and the moon was full.
    Then spake King Arthur to Sir Bedivere:
'The sequel of to-day unsolders[2] all
The goodliest fellowship of famous knights
Whereof this world holds record. Such a sleep
They sleep – the men I loved. I think that we
Shall never more, at any future time,
Delight our souls with talk of knightly deeds,
20   Walking about the gardens and the halls
Of Camelot, as in the days that were.
I perish by this people which I made, –

1. The death of Arthur.
2. Separates.

Tho' Merlin sware that I should come again
To rule once more – but let what will be, be.
I am so deeply smitten thro' the helm
That without help I cannot last till morn.
Thou therefore take my brand[1] Excalibur,
Which was my pride: for thou rememberest how
In those old days, one summer noon, an arm
30   Rose up from out the bosom of the lake,
Clothed in white samite,[2] mystic, wonderful,
Holding the sword – and how I row'd across
And took it, and have worn it, like a king:
And, wheresoever I am sung or told
In aftertime, this also shall be known:
But now delay not: take Excalibur,
And fling him far into the middle mere:[3]
Watch what thou seëst, and lightly bring me word.'
     To him replied the bold Sir Bedivere:
40   'It is not meet, Sir King, to leave thee thus,
Aidless, alone, and smitten thro' the helm.
A little thing may harm a wounded man.
Yet I thy hest will all perform at full,
Watch what I see, and lightly bring thee word.'
     So saying, from the ruin'd shrine he stept
And in the moon athwart the place of tombs,
Where lay the mighty bones of ancient men,
Old knights, and over them the sea-wind sang
Shrill, chill, with flakes of foam. He, stepping down
50   By zig-zag paths, and juts of pointed rock,
Came on the shining levels of the lake.
     There drew he forth the brand Excalibur,
And o'er him, drawing it, the winter moon,
Brightening the skirts of a long cloud, ran forth
And sparkled keen with frost against the hilt:
For all the haft twinkled with diamond sparks,

1. Sword.
2. A rich medieval silk fabric.
3. Lake.

Myriads of topaz-lights, and jacinth[1]-work
Of subtlest jewellery. He gazed so long
That both his eyes were dazzled, as he stood,
60   This way and that dividing the swift mind,
In act to throw: but at the last it seem'd
Better to leave Excalibur conceal'd
There in the many-knotted waterflags,[2]
That whistled stiff and dry about the marge.
So strode he back slow to the wounded King.
    Then spake King Arthur to Sir Bedivere:
'Hast thou perform'd my mission which I gave?
What is it thou hast seen? or what hast heard?'
    And answer made the bold Sir Bedivere:
70   'I heard the ripple washing in the reeds,
And the wild water lapping on the crag.'
    To whom replied King Arthur, faint and pale:
'Thou hast betray'd thy nature and thy name,
Not rendering true answer, as beseem'd
Thy fëalty,[3] nor like a noble knight:
For surer sign had follow'd, either hand,
Or voice, or else a motion of the mere.
This is a shameful thing for men to lie.
Yet now, I charge thee, quickly go again
80   As thou art lief[4] and dear, and do the thing
I bad thee, watch, and lightly bring me word.'
    Then went Sir Bedivere the second time
Across the ridge, and paced beside the mere,
Counting the dewy pebbles, fix'd in thought;
But when he saw the wonder of the hilt,
How curiously and strangely chased, he smote
His palms together, and he cried aloud,
    'And if indeed I cast the brand away,
Surely a precious thing, one worthy note,

1. A semi-precious stone.
2. Yellow iris.
3. Loyal oath.
4. Willing.

90   Should thus be lost for ever from the earth,
    Which might have pleased the eyes of many men.
    What good should follow this, if this were done?
    What harm, undone? deep harm to disobey,
    Seeing obedience is the bond of rule.
    Were it well to obey then, if a king demand
    An act unprofitable, against himself?
    The King is sick, and knows not what he does.
    What record, or what relic of my lord
    Should be to aftertime, but empty breath
100   And rumours of a doubt? but were this kept,
    Stored in some treasure-house of mighty kings,
    Some one might show it at a joust of arms,
    Saying, "King Arthur's sword, Excalibur,
    Wrought by the lonely maiden of the Lake,
    Nine years she wrought it, sitting in the deeps
    Upon the hidden bases of the hills."
    So might some old man speak in the aftertime
    To all the people, winning reverence.
    But how much honour and much fame were lost.'
110   So spake he, clouded with his own conceit,
    And hid Excalibur the second time,
    And so strode back slow to the wounded King.

     Then spoke King Arthur, breathing heavily:
    'What is it thou hast seen? or what hast heard?'

     And answer made the bold Sir Bedivere:
    'I heard the water lapping on the crag,
    And the long ripple washing in the reeds.'

     To whom replied King Arthur, much in wrath:
    'Ah, miserable and unkind, untrue,
120   Unknightly, traitor-hearted! Woe is me!
    Authority forgets a dying king,
    Laid widow'd of the power in his eye
    That bow'd the will. I see thee what thou art,
    For thou, the latest-left of all my knights,
    In whom should meet the offices of all,
    Thou wouldst betray me for the precious hilt;

Either from lust of gold, or like a girl
Valuing the giddy pleasure of the eyes.
Yet, for a man may fail in duty twice,
130　And the third time may prosper, get thee hence:
But, if thou spare to fling Excalibur,
I will arise and slay thee with my hands.'
　　Then quickly rose Sir Bedivere, and ran,
And, leaping down the ridges lightly, plunged
Among the bulrush-beds, and clutch'd the sword,
And strongly wheel'd and threw it. The great brand
Made lightnings in the splendour of the moon,
And flashing round and round, and whirl'd in an arch,
Shot like a streamer of the northern morn,
140　Seen where the moving isles of winter shock
By night, with noises of the northern sea.
So flash'd and fell the brand Excalibur:
But ere he dipt the surface, rose an arm
Clothed in white samite, mystic, wonderful,
And caught him by the hilt, and brandish'd him
Three times, and drew him under in the mere.
And lightly went the other to the King.
　　Then spoke King Arthur, drawing thicker breath:
'Now see I by thine eyes that this is done.
150　Speak out: what is it thou hast heard, or seen?'
　　And answer made the bold Sir Bedivere:
'Sir King, I closed mine eyelids, lest the gems
Should blind my purpose, for I never saw,
Nor shall see, here or elsewhere, till I die,
Not tho' I live three lives of mortal men,
So great a miracle as yonder hilt.
Then with both hands I flung him, wheeling him;
But when I look'd again, behold an arm,
Clothed in white samite, mystic, wonderful,
160　That caught him by the hilt, and brandish'd him
Three times, and drew him under in the mere.'
　　And answer made King Arthur, breathing hard:
'My end draws nigh: 'tis time that I were gone.

Make broad thy shoulders to receive my weight,
And bear me to the margin; yet I fear
My wound hath taken cold, and I shall die.'
    So saying, from the pavement he half rose,
Slowly, with pain, reclining on his arm,
And looking wistfully with wide blue eyes
170 As in a picture. Him Sir Bedivere
Remorsefully regarded thro' his tears,
And would have spoken, but he found not words,
Then took with care, and kneeling on one knee,
O'er both his shoulders drew the languid hands,
And rising bore him thro' the place of tombs.
    But, as he walk'd, King Arthur panted hard,
Like one that feels a nightmare on his bed
When all the house is mute. So sigh'd the King,
Muttering and murmuring at his ear, 'Quick, quick!
180 I fear it is too late, and I shall die.'
But the other swiftly strode from ridge to ridge,
Clothed with his breath, and looking, as he walk'd,
Larger than human on the frozen hills.
He heard the deep behind him, and a cry
Before. His own thought drove him like a goad.
Dry clash'd his harness in the icy caves
And barren chasms, and all to left and right
The bare black cliff clang'd round him, as he based
His feet on juts of slippery crag that rang
190 Sharp-smitten with the dint of armed heels —
And on a sudden, lo! the level lake,
And the long glories of the winter moon.
    Then saw they how there hove a dusky barge,
Dark as a funeral scarf from stem to stern,
Beneath them; and descending they were ware
That all the decks were dense with stately forms
Black-stoled, black-hooded, like a dream — by these
Three Queens with crowns of gold — and from them rose
A cry that shiver'd to the tingling stars,
200 And, as it were one voice, an agony

Of lamentation, like a wind, that shrills
All night in a waste land, where no one comes,
Or hath come, since the making of the world.

Then murmur'd Arthur, 'Place me in the barge,'
And to the barge they came. There those three Queens
Put forth their hands, and took the King, and wept.
But she, that rose the tallest of them all
And fairest, laid his head upon her lap,
And loosed the shatter'd casque,[1] and chafed his hands,
210   And call'd him by his name, complaining loud,
And dropping bitter tears against his brow
Striped with dark blood: for all his face was white
And colourless, and like the wither'd moon
Smote by the fresh beam of the springing east;
And all his greaves and cuisses dash'd with drops
Of onset; and the light and lustrous curls –
That made his forehead like a rising sun
High from the daïs-throne – were parch'd with dust;
Or, clotted into points and hanging loose,
220   Mix'd with the knightly growth that fringed his lips.
So like a shatter'd column lay the King;
Not like that Arthur who, with lance in rest,
From spur to plume a star of tournament,
Shot thro' the lists at Camelot, and charged
Before the eyes of ladies and of kings.

Then loudly cried the bold Sir Bedivere,
'Ah! my Lord Arthur, whither shall I go?
Where shall I hide my forehead and my eyes?
For now I see the true old times are dead,
230   When every morning brought a noble chance,
And every chance brought out a noble knight.
Such times have been not since the light that led
The holy Elders with the gift of myrrh.
But now the whole ROUND TABLE is dissolved
Which was an image of the mighty world;

1. Helmet.

And I, the last, go forth companionless,
And the days darken round me, and the years,
Among new men, strange faces, other minds.'
    And slowly answered Arthur from the barge:
240 'The old order changeth, yielding place to new,
And God fulfils Himself in many ways,
Lest one good custom should corrupt the world.
Comfort thyself: what comfort is in me?
I have lived my life, and that which I have done
May He within Himself make pure! but thou,
If thou shouldst never see my face again,
Pray for my soul. More things are wrought by prayer
Than this world dreams of. Wherefore, let thy voice
Rise like a fountain for me night and day.
250 For what are men better than sheep or goats
That nourish a blind life within the brain,
If, knowing God, they lift not hands of prayer
Both for themselves and those who call them friend?
For so the whole round earth is every way
Bound by gold chains about the feet of God.
But now farewell. I am going a long way
With these thou seëst – if indeed I go –
(For all my mind is clouded with a doubt)
To the island-valley of Avilion;
260 Where falls not hail, or rain, or any snow,
Nor ever wind blows loudly; but it lies
Deep-meadow'd, happy, fair with orchard-lawns
And bowery hollows crown'd with summer sea,
Where I will heal me of my grievous wound.'
    So said he, and the barge with oar and sail
Moved from the brink, like some full-breasted swan
That, fluting a wild carol ere her death,
Ruffles her pure cold plume, and takes the flood
With swarthy webs. Long stood Sir Bedivere
Revolving many memories, till the hull
270 Look'd one black dot against the verge of dawn,
And on the mere the wailing died away.

Robert Browning
(1812–1889)

Until he was thirty-four years old, Browning lived in Camberwell, which was then a suburb of London. His mild-tempered and loving father, a bank clerk, was a passionate collector of books and prints, and Browning was educated mainly at home in his father's library. His mother's strong character and Nonconformist faith also influenced him and prevented him from attending Oxford or Cambridge Universities, which were then still closed to members of dissenting faiths. He did attend the new University College in London for a year, but dropped out.

Browning's family was unusually tolerant for that period. He and his sister Sarianna were disciplined mainly by persuasion, and Browning is said to have once appeared naked before guests, with a devil's tail attached to his backside. At fourteen, after reading the works of Shelley, he decided to become an atheist and a vegetarian, a development which his parents apparently took calmly, having themselves given him the poems to read.

As Browning grew up, he remained financially dependent on his father and declared his intention of being a poet. Despite their disapproval of this idea, his parents and his aunt paid for the publication of his early volumes of poetry.

At first, Browning's work was far from successful. He had a slight critical success with some poems and plays, but made little money from them. His long and daringly experimental poem *Sordello* (1840) was universally ridiculed. Thomas Carlyle said his wife read it without ever discovering whether Sordello was a man, a city or a book. Because of this disaster, his next two books, *Dramatic Lyrics* (1842) and *Dramatic Romances and Lyrics* (1845), were generally ignored, even though they contain works such as

'The Pied Piper of Hamelin', 'My Last Duchess' and the paired poems 'Meeting at Night' and 'Parting at Morning', which were later among his most popular.

In January 1845 Browning began corresponding with Elizabeth Barrett, a well-known poet whose ill health kept her a recluse. Their courtship was secret because of her father's opposition, but eventually they eloped and married in 1846. Because of her poor health, and because her small income would stretch further abroad, they went to Italy, where their son was born in 1849. They lived in apartments in a palace known as the Casa Guidi in Florence, although they made some trips to England and France.

Men and Women was published in 1855, and although it was better received than his earlier work, Browning was disappointed at its lack of success and for several years wrote little. When Elizabeth died in 1861, Browning moved back to London with his son. Within four years, two selected editions of his earlier work and the eighteen new poems in *Dramatis Personae* brought him fame and critical recognition. For the first time in his life, he could live on his earnings from writing and enjoyed celebrity status in London society.

Using a series of dramatic monologues, Browning next produced a work many people consider to be his masterpiece, *The Ring and the Book*. Published in four volumes, it tells the story of a seventeenth-century murder and attempts to combine the forms of the novel and the epic poem. This and his later works were so well received that a Browning Society was formed for the appreciation of his works in 1881. His last volume, *Asolando*, was published on 12 December 1889, the day he died in Venice.

Browning's fame today rests mainly on his dramatic monologues and their psychological insights. The words not only convey setting and action, but also reveal the speaker's character. Perhaps the most sensational of these monologues is 'Porphyria's Lover'. The opening lines provide a sinister setting for the macabre events that follow. It is plain that the speaker is insane, as he strangles his lover with her own hair to try and preserve for ever the moment of perfect love she has shown him. These monologues greatly influenced many later poets, including Ezra Pound and T. S.

Eliot. Ironically, Browning's style, which seemed modern and experimental to Victorian readers, owes much to his love of the seventeenth-century poems of John Donne, with their abrupt openings, colloquial phrasing and irregular rhythms.

Spring Song

Dance, yellows and whites and reds, –
Lead your gay orgy, leaves, stalks, heads
Astir with the wind in the tulip-beds!

There's sunshine; scarcely a wind at all
Disturbs starved grass and daisies small
On a certain mound by a churchyard wall.

Daisies and grass be my heart's bedfellows
On the mound wind spares and sunshine mellows:
Dance you, reds and whites and yellows!

Song from Pippa Passes

The year's at the spring
And day's at the morn;
Morning's at seven;
The hill-side's dew-pearled;
The lark's on the wing;
The snail's on the thorn:
God's in his heaven –
All's right with the world!

Porphyria's Lover

The rain set early in tonight,
    The sullen wind was soon awake,
It tore the elm-tops down for spite,
    And did its worst to vex the lake:
    I listened with heart fit to break.
When glided in Porphyria; straight

She shut the cold out and the storm,
And kneeled and made the cheerless grate
   Blaze up, and all the cottage warm;
10   Which done, she rose, and from her form
Withdrew the dripping cloak and shawl,
   And laid her soiled gloves by, untied
Her hat and let the damp hair fall,
   And, last, she sat down by my side
   And called me. When no voice replied,
She put my arm about her waist,
   And made her smooth white shoulder bare,
And all her yellow hair displaced,
   And, stooping, made my cheek lie there,
20   And spread, o'er all, her yellow hair,
Murmuring how she loved me – she
   Too weak, for all her heart's endeavour,
To set its struggling passion free
   From pride, and vainer ties dissever,
   And give herself to me for ever.
But passion sometimes would prevail,
   Nor could tonight's gay feast restrain
A sudden thought of one so pale
   For love of her, and all in vain:
30   So, she was come through wind and rain.
Be sure I looked up at her eyes
   Happy and proud; at last I knew
Porphyria worshipped me; surprise
   Made my heart swell, and still it grew
   While I debated what to do.
That moment she was mine, mine, fair,
   Perfectly pure and good: I found
A thing to do, and all her hair
   In one long yellow string I wound
40   Three times her little throat around,
And strangled her. No pain felt she;
   I am quite sure she felt no pain.
As a shut bud that holds a bee,

I warily oped her lids: again
  Laughed the blue eyes without a stain.
And I untightened next the tress
  About her neck; her cheek once more
Blushed bright beneath my burning kiss:
  I propped her head up as before,
50   Only, this time my shoulder bore
Her head, which droops upon it still:
  The smiling rosy little head,
So glad it has its utmost will,
  That all it scorned at once is fled,
  And I, its love, am gained instead!
Porphyria's love: she guessed not how
  Her darling one wish would be heard.
And thus we sit together now,
  And all night long we have not stirred,
60   And yet God has not said a word!

My Last Duchess

Ferrara

That's my last Duchess painted on the wall,
Looking as if she were alive. I call
That piece a wonder, now: Frà Pandolf's hands
Worked busily a day, and there she stands.
Will't please you sit and look at her? I said
'Frà Pandolf' by design, for never read
Strangers like you that pictured countenance,
The depth and passion of its earnest glance,
But to myself they turned (since none puts by
10   The curtain I have drawn for you, but I)
And seemed as they would ask me, if they durst,
How such a glance came there; so, not the first
Are you to turn and ask thus. Sir, 'twas not
Her husband's presence only, called that spot

Of joy into the Duchess' cheek: perhaps
Frà Pandolf chanced to say 'Her mantle laps
Over my lady's wrist too much,' or 'Paint
Must never hope to reproduce the faint
Half-flush that dies along her throat': such stuff
20 Was courtesy, she thought, and cause enough
For calling up that spot of joy. She had
A heart – how shall I say? – too soon made glad,
Too easily impressed; she liked whate'er
She looked on, and her looks went everywhere.
Sir, 'twas all one! My favour at her breast,
The dropping of the daylight in the West,
The bough of cherries some officious fool
Broke in the orchard for her, the white mule
She rode with round the terrace – all and each
30 Would draw from her alike the approving speech,
Or blush, at least. She thanked men, – good! but thanked
Somehow – I know not how – as if she ranked
My gift of a nine-hundred-years-old name
With anybody's gift. Who'd stoop to blame
This sort of trifling? Even had you skill
In speech – (which I have not) – to make your will
Quite clear to such an one, and say, 'Just this
Or that in you disgusts me; here you miss,
Or there exceed the mark' – and if she let
40 Herself be lessoned so, nor plainly set
Her wits to yours, forsooth, and made excuse,
– E'en then would be some stooping, and I choose
Never to stoop. Oh sir, she smiled, no doubt,
Whene'er I passed her; but who passed without
Much the same smile? This grew; I gave commands;
Then all smiles stopped together. There she stands
As if alive. Will 't please you rise? We'll meet
The company below, then. I repeat,
The Count your master's known munificence
50 Is ample warrant that no just pretence
Of mine for dowry will be disallowed;

Though his fair daughter's self, as I avowed
At starting, is my object. Nay, we'll go
Together down, sir. Notice Neptune, though,
Taming a sea-horse, thought a rarity,
Which Claus of Innsbruck cast in bronze for me!

The Pied Piper of Hamelin

A Child's Story

[*Written for, and inscribed to, W.M. the Younger*][1]

I

Hamelin Town's in Brunswick,[2]
  By famous Hanover city;
The river Weser, deep and wide,
Washes its wall on the southern side;
A pleasanter spot you never spied;
  But, when begins my ditty,
Almost five hundred years ago,
To see the townsfolk suffer so
  From vermin, was a pity.

II

10   Rats!
They fought the dogs and killed the cats,
  And bit the babies in the cradles,
And ate the cheeses out of the vats,
  And licked the soup from the cooks' own ladles,
Split open the kegs of salted sprats,
Made nests inside men's Sunday hats,
And even spoiled the women's chats

1. The poem was written for the young son of William Macready, the actor-manager, to illustrate while he was ill in bed.
2. In Germany.

By drowning their speaking
With shrieking and squeaking
20   In fifty different sharps and flats.

III

At last the people in a body
   To the Town Hall came flocking:
''Tis clear,' cried they, 'our Mayor's a noddy;
   And as for our Corporation – shocking
To think we buy gowns lined with ermine
For dolts that can't or won't determine
What's best to rid us of our vermin!
You hope, because you're old and obese,
To find in the furry civic robe ease?
30   Rouse up, Sirs! Give your brains a racking
To find the remedy we're lacking,
Or, sure as fate, we'll send you packing!'
At this the Mayor and Corporation
Quaked with a mighty consternation.

IV

An hour they sat in council,
   At length the Mayor broke silence:
'For a guilder I'd my ermine gown sell,
   I wish I were a mile hence!
It's easy to bid one rack one's brain –
40   I'm sure my poor head aches again,
I've scratched it so, and all in vain.
Oh for a trap, a trap, a trap!'
Just as he said this, what should hap
At the chamber door but a gentle tap?
'Bless us,' cried the Mayor, 'what's that?'
(With the Corporation as he sat,
Looking little though wondrous fat;
Nor brighter was his eye, nor moister
Than a too-long-opened oyster,
50   Save when at noon his paunch grew mutinous
For a plate of turtle green and glutinous)

'Only a scraping of shoes on the mat?
Anything like the sound of a rat
Makes my heart go pit-a-pat!'

V

'Come in!' – the Mayor cried, looking bigger:
And in did come the strangest figure!
His queer long coat from heel to head
Was half of yellow and half of red,
And he himself was tall and thin,
60   With sharp blue eyes, each like a pin,
And light loose hair, yet swarthy skin,
No tuft on cheek nor beard on chin,
But lips where smiles went out and in;
There was no guessing his kith and kin:
And nobody could enough admire
The tall man and his quaint attire.
Quoth one: 'It's as my great-grandsire,
Starting up at the Trump of Doom's tone,
Had walked this way from his painted tombstone!'

VI

70   He advanced to the council-table:
And, 'Please your honours,' said he, 'I'm able,
By means of a secret charm, to draw
      All creatures living beneath the sun,
      That creep or swim or fly or run,
After me so as you never saw!
And I chiefly use my charm
On creatures that do people harm,
The mole and toad and newt and viper;
And people call me the Pied Piper.'
80   (And here they noticed round his neck,
      A scarf of red and yellow stripe,
To match with his coat of the self-same check;
      And at the scarf's end hung a pipe;
And his fingers, they noticed, were ever straying
As if impatient to be playing

Upon this pipe, as low it dangled
Over his vesture so old-fangled.)
'Yet,' said he, 'poor piper as I am,
In Tartary I freed the Cham,
90   Last June, from his huge swarms of gnats;
I eased in Asia the Nizam
    Of a monstrous brood of vampire-bats:
And as for what your brain bewilders,
    If I can rid your town of rats
Will you give me a thousand guilders?'
'One? fifty thousand!' – was the exclamation
Of the astonished Mayor and Corporation.

VII

Into the street the Piper stept,
    Smiling first a little smile,
100 As if he knew what magic slept
    In his quiet pipe the while;
Then, like a musical adept,
To blow the pipe his lips he wrinkled,
And green and blue his sharp eyes twinkled,
Like a candle-flame where salt is sprinkled;
And ere three shrill notes the pipe uttered,
You heard as if an army muttered;
And the muttering grew to a grumbling;
And the grumbling grew to a mighty rumbling;
110 And out of the houses the rats came tumbling.
Great rats, small rats, lean rats, brawny rats,
Brown rats, black rats, grey rats, tawny rats,
Grave old plodders, gay young friskers,
    Fathers, mothers, uncles, cousins,
Cocking tails and pricking whiskers,
    Families by tens and dozens,
Brothers, sisters, husbands, wives –
Followed the Piper for their lives.
From street to street he piped advancing,
120 And step for step they followed dancing,

Until they came to the river Weser,
   Wherein all plunged and perished!
– Save one who, stout as Julius Caesar,[1]
Swam across and lived to carry
   (As he, the manuscript he cherished)
To Rat-land home his commentary:
Which was, 'At the first shrill notes of the pipe,
I heard a sound as of scraping tripe,
And putting apples, wondrous ripe,
130   Into a cider-press's gripe:
And a moving away of pickle-tub-boards,
And a leaving ajar of conserve-cupboards,
And a drawing the corks of train-oil-flasks,
And a breaking the hoops of butter-casks:
And it seemed as if a voice
   (Sweeter far than bý harp or bý psaltery[2]
Is breathed) called out, "Oh rats, rejoice!
   The world is grown to one vast drysaltery![3]
So munch on, crunch on, take your nuncheon,[4]
140   Breakfast, supper, dinner, luncheon!"
And just as a bulky sugar-puncheon,[5]
All ready staved, like a great sun shone
Glorious scarce an inch before me,
Just as methought it said, "Come, bore me!"
– I found the Weser rolling o'er me.'

VIII
You should have heard the Hamelin people
Ringing the bells till they rocked the steeple.
'Go,' cried the Mayor, 'and get long poles,
Poke out the nests and block up the holes!

---

1. Julius Caesar was supposed to have swum ashore carrying his commentary on the Gallic Wars after his ship was wrecked off Alexandria.
2. Musical instruments.
3. Place where dried and salted meats and pickles are made.
4. Snack.
5. Small barrel.

150 And leave in our town not even a trace
Of the rats!' – when suddenly, up the face
Of the Piper perked in the market-place,
With a, 'First, if you please, my thousand guilders!'

IX

A thousand guilders! The Mayor looked blue;
So did the Corporation too.
For council dinners made rare havoc
With Claret, Moselle, Vin-de-Grave, Hock;
And half the money would replenish
Their cellar's biggest butt with Rhenish.[1]
To pay this sum to a wandering fellow
With a gypsy coat of red and yellow!
'Beside,' quoth the Mayor with a knowing wink,
'Our business was done at the river's brink;
We saw with our eyes the vermin sink,
And what's dead can't come to life, I think.
So, friend, we're not the folks to shrink
From the duty of giving you something for drink,
And a matter of money to put in your poke;[2]
170 But as for the guilders, what we spoke
Of them, as you very well know, was in joke.
Beside, our losses have made us thrifty.
A thousand guilders! Come, take fifty!'

X

The Piper's face fell, and he cried
'No trifling! I can't wait, beside!
I've promised to visit by dinner-time
Bagdat, and accept the prime
Of the Head-Cook's pottage, all he's rich in,
For having left, in the Caliph's kitchen,

1. Wine from the Rhine valley.
2. Purse.

180   Of a nest of scorpions no survivor:
     With him I proved no bargain-driver,
     With you, don't think I'll bate a stiver![1]
     And folks who put me in a passion
     May find me pipe after another fashion.'

     XI
     'How?' cried the Mayor, 'd'ye think I brook
     Being worse treated than a Cook?
     Insulted by a lazy ribald[2]
     With idle pipe and vesture piebald?[3]
     You threaten us, fellow? Do your worst,
190   Blow your pipe there till you burst!'

     XII
     Once more he stept into the street
       And to his lips again
       Laid his long pipe of smooth straight cane;
     And ere he blew three notes (such sweet
     Soft notes as yet musician's cunning
       Never gave the enraptured air)
     There was a rustling that seemed like a bustling
     Of merry crowds justling at pitching and hustling,[4]
     Small feet were pattering, wooden shoes clattering,
200   Little hands clapping and little tongues chattering,
     And, like fowls in a farm-yard when barley is scattering,
     Out came the children running.
     All the little boys and girls,
     With rosy cheeks and flaxen curls,
     And sparkling eyes and teeth like pearls,
     Tripping and skipping, ran merrily after
     The wonderful music with shouting and laughter.

1. Deduct small coin.
2. Ruffian.
3. Clothes in two colours.
4. A gambling game with coins.

XIII

The Mayor was dumb, and the Council stood
As if they were changed into blocks of wood.
210 Unable to move a step, or cry
To the children merrily skipping by,
– Could only follow with the eye
That joyous crowd at the Piper's back.
But how the Mayor was on the rack,
And the wretched Council's bosoms beat,
As the Piper turned from the High Street
To where the Weser rolled its waters
Right in the way of their sons and daughters!
However he turned from South to West,
220 And to Koppelberg Hill his steps addressed,
And after him the children pressed;
Great was the joy in every breast.
'He never can cross that mighty top!
He's forced to let the piping drop,
And we shall see our children stop!'
When, lo, as they reached the mountain-side,
A wondrous portal[1] opened wide,
As if a cavern was suddenly hollowed;
And the Piper advanced and the children followed,
230 And when all were in to the very last,
The door in the mountain-side shut fast.
Did I say, all? No! One was lame,
And could not dance the whole of the way;
And in after years, if you would blame
His sadness, he was used to say, –
'It's dull in our town since my playmates left!
I can't forget that I'm bereft
Of all the pleasant sights they see,
Which the Piper also promised me.
240 For he led us, he said, to a joyous land,
Joining the town and just at hand,

1. Doorway.

Where waters gushed and fruit-trees grew
And flowers put forth a fairer hue,
And everything was strange and new;
The sparrows were brighter than peacocks here,
And their dogs outran our fallow deer,
And honey-bees had lost their stings,
And horses were born with eagles' wings:
And just as I became assured
250 My lame foot would be speedily cured,
The music stopped and I stood still,
And found myself outside the hill,
Left alone against my will,
To go now limping as before,
And never hear of the country more!'

XIV

Alas, alas for Hamelin!
    There came into many a burgher's pate
    A text which says that heaven's gate
    Opes¹ to the rich at as easy rate
260 As the needle's eye takes a camel in!
The Mayor sent East, West, North and South,
To offer the Piper, by word of mouth,
    Wherever it was men's lot to find him,
Silver and gold to his heart's content,
If he'd only return the way he went,
    And bring the children behind him.
But when they saw 'twas a lost endeavour,
And Piper and dancers were gone for ever,
They made a decree that lawyers never
270   Should think their records dated duly
If, after the day of the month and year,
These words did not as well appear,
'And so long after what happened here
    On the Twenty-second of July,

1. Opens.

Thirteen hundred and seventy-six':
And the better in memory to fix
The place of the children's last retreat,
They called it, the Pied Piper's Street –
Where any one playing on pipe or tabor[1]
280 Was sure for the future to lose his labour.
Nor suffered they hostelry or tavern
   To shock with mirth a street so solemn;
But opposite the place of the cavern
   They wrote the story on a column,
And on the great church-window painted
The same, to make the world acquainted
How their children were stolen away,
And there it stands to this very day.
And I must not omit to say
290 That in Transylvania there's a tribe
Of alien people who ascribe
The outlandish ways and dress
On which their neighbours lay such stress,
To their fathers and mothers having risen
Out of some subterraneous prison
Into which they were trepanned[2]
Long time ago in a mighty band
Out of Hamelin town in Brunswick land,
But how or why, they don't understand.

XV
300 So, Willy, let me and you be wipers
Of scores out with all men – especially pipers!
And, whether they pipe us free fróm rats or fróm mice,
If we've promised them aught, let us keep our promise!

1. Small hand drum.
2. Entrapped.

'How They Brought the Good News from Ghent to Aix'[1]

[16—]

I

I sprang to the stirrup, and Joris, and he;
I galloped, Dirck galloped, we galloped all three;
'Good speed!' cried the watch, as the gate-bolts undrew;
'Speed!' echoed the wall to us galloping through;
Behind shut the postern, the lights sank to rest,
And into the midnight we galloped abreast.

II

Not a word to each other; we kept the great pace
Neck by neck, stride by stride, never changing our place;
I turned in my saddle and made its girths tight,
10 Then shortened each stirrup, and set the pique[2] right,
Rebuckled the cheek-strap, chained slacker the bit,
Nor galloped less steadily Roland a whit.

III

'Twas moonset at starting; but while we drew near
Lokeren, the cocks crew and twilight dawned clear;
At Boom, a great yellow star came out to see;
At Düffeld, 'twas morning as plain as could be;
And from Mecheln church-steeple we heard the half-chime,
So, Joris broke silence with, 'Yet there is time!'

1. An imaginary story, in which Aix-la-Chapelle is besieged and the good news is that help is on the way. All the towns named are in Belgium, except Aix which is now called Aachen and is in Germany.
2. Browning defined this as 'the old-fashioned projection in front of the military saddle on the Continent'.

IV

At Aershot, up leaped of a sudden the sun,
20   And against him the cattle stood black every one,
To stare through the mist at us galloping past,
And I saw my stout¹ galloper Roland at last,
With resolute shoulders, each butting away
The haze, as some bluff river headland its spray:

V

And his low head and crest, just one sharp ear bent back
For my voice, and the other pricked out on his track;
And one eye's black intelligence, – ever that glance
O'er its white edge at me, his own master, askance!
And the thick heavy spume-flakes which aye and anon
30   His fierce lips shook upwards in galloping on.

VI

By Hasselt, Dirck groaned; and cried Joris, 'Stay spur!
Your Roos galloped bravely, the fault's not in her,
We'll remember at Aix' – for one heard the quick wheeze
Of her chest, saw the stretched neck and staggering knees,
And sunk tail, and horrible heave of the flank,
As down on her haunches she shuddered and sank.

VII

So, we were left galloping, Joris and I,
Past Looz and past Tongres, no cloud in the sky;
The broad sun above laughed a pitiless laugh,
40   'Neath our feet broke the brittle bright stubble like chaff;
Till over by Dalhem a dome-spire sprang white,
And 'Gallop,' gasped Joris, 'for Aix is in sight!'

1. Strong and steady.

VIII

'How they'll greet us!' – and all in a moment his roan
Rolled neck and croup over, lay dead as a stone;
And there was my Roland to bear the whole weight
Of the news which alone could save Aix from her fate,
With his nostrils like pits full of blood to the brim,
And with circles of red for his eye-sockets' rim.

IX

Then I cast loose my buffcoat, each holster let fall,
50   Shook off both my jack-boots, let go belt and all,
Stood up in the stirrup, leaned, patted his ear,
Called my Roland his pet-name, my horse without peer;
Clapped my hands, laughed and sang, any noise, bad or
   good,
Till at length into Aix Roland galloped and stood.

X

And all I remember is – friends flocking round
As I sat with his head 'twixt my knees on the ground;
And no voice but was praising this Roland of mine,
As I poured down his throat our last measure of wine,
Which (the burgesses voted by common consent)
60   Was no more than his due who brought good news from
   Ghent.

Meeting at Night

I

The grey sea and the long black land;
And the yellow half-moon large and low;
And the startled little waves that leap
In fiery ringlets from their sleep,
As I gain the cove with pushing prow,
And quench its speed i' the slushy sand.

II
Then a mile of warm sea-scented beach;
Three fields to cross till a farm appears;
A tap at the pane, the quick sharp scratch
10 And blue spurt of a lighted match,
And a voice less loud, through its joys and fears,
Than the two hearts beating each to each!

Parting at Morning

Round the cape of a sudden came the sea,
And the sun looked over the mountain's rim:
And straight was a path of gold for him,[1]
And the need of a world of men for me.

1. The 'him' here is the sun; the speaker is a man. When Browning was
asked what the last line meant, he said: '. . . it is his confession of how
fleeting is the belief that [the raptures of love] are self-sufficient and
enduring – as for the time they appear'.

The Patriot

An Old Story[1]

I
It was roses, roses, all the way,
    With myrtle mixed in my path like mad:
The house-roofs seemed to heave and sway,
    The church-spires flamed, such flags they had,
A year ago on this very day.

1. The poem is associated with the Italian struggle for liberation from
Austrian rule, but Browning revised it so that it could be any leader
once hailed by the fickle mob as a hero and later executed as a traitor.

II

The air broke into a mist with bells,
    The old walls rocked with the crowd and cries.
Had I said, 'Good folk, mere noise repels –
    But give me your sun from yonder skies!'
10   They had answered, 'And afterward, what else?'

III

Alack, it was I who leaped at the sun
    To give it my loving friends to keep!
Naught man could do, have I left undone:
    And you see my harvest, what I reap
This very day, now a year is run.

IV

There's nobody on the house-tops now –
    Just a palsied few at the windows set;
For the best of the sight is, all allow,
    At the Shambles' Gate[1] – or, better yet,
20   By the very scaffold's foot, I trow.

V

I go in the rain, and, more than needs,
    A rope cuts both my wrists behind;
And I think, by the feel, my forehead bleeds,
    For they fling, whoever has a mind,
Stones at me for my year's misdeeds.

VI

Thus I entered, and thus I go!
    In triumphs, people have dropped down dead.
'Paid by the world, what dost thou owe
    Me?' – God might question; now instead,
30   'Tis God shall repay: I am safer so.

1. A shambles was a place where animals were slaughtered. Here it is
the place of execution.

Home-Thoughts, from Abroad

I

Oh, to be in England
Now that April's there,
And whoever wakes in England
Sees, some morning, unaware,
That the lowest boughs and the brushwood sheaf
Round the elm-tree bole are in tiny leaf,
While the chaffinch sings on the orchard bough
In England – now!

II

And after April, when May follows,
10   And the whitethroat builds, and all the swallows!
Hark, where my blossomed pear-tree in the hedge
Leans to the field and scatters on the clover
Blossoms and dewdrops – at the bent spray's edge –
That's the wise thrush; he sings each song twice over,
Lest you should think he never could recapture
The first fine careless rapture!
And though the fields look rough with hoary dew,
All will be gay when noontide wakes anew
The buttercups, the little children's dower
20   – Far brighter than this gaudy melon-flower!

Emily Jane Brontë

(1818–1848)

Emily Brontë was born in Thornton, Yorkshire, although she is usually associated with Haworth, a village on the Yorkshire moors where her father became rector in 1820. Her sisters Maria, Elizabeth, Charlotte and her brother Branwell were older than Emily; her sister Anne was younger. Their mother died in 1824, and their aunt then lived in the household and looked after the children.

Maria and Elizabeth were sent to Cowan Bridge School during their mother's illness, and after her death Charlotte and Emily joined them. The school was a charitable institution for the daughters of clergymen, and at that time conditions there were very harsh. Charlotte Brontë later used it as a model for Lowood School in her novel *Jane Eyre*. Both Maria and Elizabeth returned in ill health and died the following year, after which Charlotte and Emily were taken away and mainly educated at home.

In 1826 their father went to Leeds and brought home some presents for the children which included a box of toy soldiers. For the next six years, the children wrote stories in tiny, home-made books about the imaginary adventures of the soldiers in two kingdoms they called Gondal and Angria. Many of Charlotte's Angria stories survive, but some of Emily's poems are the only trace of the Gondal saga.

Emily tried several times to leave Haworth, first to go to another school and later to work as a teacher, but each time her health suffered. It seemed that she could only be happy at Haworth, near the moors where she spent hours walking alone. For a short time she stayed at a school in Brussels with Charlotte, but when her aunt died in 1842, she returned home and never left again except for short trips.

In 1844 Emily began to transcribe the rough copies of her poems into two notebooks. Charlotte found them, and persuaded Emily to let her send them to a publisher, along with her own poems and others by Anne. Women were not always taken seriously as writers at that time, so the sisters sent their work as *Poems by Currer, Ellis and Acton Bell*, each keeping her own initials.

The poems did not sell, and the sisters began to write novels. *Jane Eyre* was published first, followed quickly by Emily's novel *Wuthering Heights* and Anne's *Agnes Grey*. The sisters had again used the names of Currer, Ellis and Acton Bell, and the publishers began to wonder if the three names were in fact one person. Anne and Charlotte travelled to London to reveal the truth about themselves, much against Emily's will. Emily was very shy and hated the thought of publicity.

Emily's beloved moors provided the setting and the atmosphere for *Wuthering Heights*, a passionate love story with strong, dramatic characters. It was criticized at first for being too harsh, but was later recognized as a major work of literature. Emily's mystical love of nature and her sense of harmony with it is a fundamental part of the novel and also very important to her poems. Such poems as 'A little while, a little while' and 'Loud without the wind was roaring' draw attention to the starkly beautiful landscape of the moors and make clear her unhappiness away from them.

Emily's personal life was not particularly happy. The early deaths of her mother and sisters greatly affected her. Her retiring nature made it impossible for her to be happy at school or at work, and made it hard for her to cope with the duties expected of the rector's daughter. Her only brother, Branwell, had tormented the family by his decline into drink and drug addiction. This unhappiness comes over in many of her poems, as does the strength of spirit that enabled her to battle against years of ill health. 'No coward soul is mine' expresses these feelings clearly.

When Branwell died in September 1848, after a long and harrowing illness at home, during which all three sisters shared in nursing him, Emily caught a cold at his funeral. This sent her already delicate health into a decline, and she died three months later.

She dried her tears and they did smile

She dried her tears and they did smile
To see her cheeks' returning glow
How little dreaming all the while
That full heart throbbed to overflow

With that sweet look and lively tone
And bright eye shining all the day
They could not guess at midnight lone
How she would weep the time away

Love and friendship

Love is like the wild rose briar,
Friendship, like the holly tree
The holly is dark when the rose briar blooms,
But which will bloom most constantly?

The wild rose briar is sweet in spring,
Its summer blossoms scent the air
Yet wait till winter comes again
And who will call the wild-briar fair

Then scorn the silly rose-wreath now
And deck thee with the holly's sheen
That when December blights thy brow
He still may leave thy garland green –

The Bluebell

The Bluebell is the sweetest flower
    That waves in summer air:
Its blossoms have the mightiest power
    To soothe my spirit's care.

There is a spell in purple heath
    Too wildly, sadly dear;
The violet has a fragrant breath,
    But fragrance will not cheer.

The trees are bare, the sun is cold,
10   And seldom, seldom seen;
The heavens have lost their zone of gold,
    And earth her robe of green.

And ice upon the glancing stream
    Has cast its sombre shade;
And distant hills and valleys seem
    In frozen mist arrayed.

The Bluebell cannot charm me now,
    The heath has lost its bloom;
The violets in the glen below,
20   They yield no sweet perfume.

But, though I mourn the sweet Bluebell,
    'Tis better far away;
I know how fast my tears would swell
    To see it smile to-day.

For, oh! when chill the sunbeams fall
    Adown that dreary sky,
And gild yon dank and darkened wall
    With transient brilliancy;

How do I weep, how do I pine
30   For the time of flowers to come,
And turn me from that fading shine,
    To mourn the fields of home!

No coward soul is mine

No coward soul is mine
No trembler in the world's storm-troubled sphere
I see Heaven's glories shine
And Faith shines equal arming me from Fear

O God within my breast
Almighty ever-present Deity
Life, that in me hast rest
As I Undying Life, have power in thee

Vain are the thousand creeds
10   That move men's hearts, unutterably vain,
Worthless as withered weeds
Or idlest froth amid the boundless main

To waken doubt in one
Holding so fast by thy infinity
So surely anchored on
The steadfast rock of Immortality

With wide-embracing love
Thy spirit animates eternal years
Pervades and broods above,
20   Changes, sustains, dissolves, creates and rears

Though Earth and moon were gone
And suns and universes ceased to be
And thou wert left alone
Every Existence would exist in thee

There is not room for Death
Nor atom that his might could render void
Since thou art Being and Breath
And what thou art may never be destroyed

Hope

Hope was but a timid friend;
    She sat without the grated den,
Watching how my fate would tend,
    Even as selfish-hearted men.

She was cruel in her fear;
    Through the bars, one dreary day,
I looked out to see her there,
    And she turned her face away!

Like a false guard, false watch keeping,
10   Still in strife, she whispered peace;
She would sing while I was weeping;
    If I listened, she would cease.

False she was, and unrelenting;
    When my last joys strewed the ground,
Even Sorrow saw, repenting,
    Those sad relics scattered round;

Hope, whose whisper would have given
    Balm to all my frenzied pain,
Stretched her wings, and soared to heaven,
20   Went, and ne'er returned again!

Honour's Martyr

The moon is full this winter night;
    The stars are clear, though few;
And every window glistens bright,
    With leaves of frozen dew.

The sweet moon through your lattice gleams
    And lights your room like day;
And there you pass, in happy dreams,
    The peaceful hours away!

While I, with effort hardly quelling
10   The anguish in my breast,
Wander about the silent dwelling,
    And cannot think of rest.

The old clock in the gloomy hall
    Ticks on, from hour to hour;
And every time its measured call
    Seems lingering slow and slower:

And oh, how slow that keen-eyed star
    Has tracked the chilly grey!
What, watching yet! how very far
20   The morning lies away!

Without your chamber door I stand;
    Love, are you slumbering still?
My cold heart, underneath my hand,
    Has almost ceased to thrill.

Bleak, bleak the east wind sobs and sighs,
    And drowns the turret bell,
Whose sad note, undistinguished, dies
    Unheard, like my farewell!

Tomorrow, Scorn will blight my name,
30   And Hate will trample me,
Will load me with a coward's shame –
    A traitor's perjury.

False friends will launch their covert sneers;
    True friends will wish me dead;
And I shall cause the bitterest tears
    That you have ever shed.

It was night and on the mountains

It was night and on the mountains
Fathoms deep the snow drifts lay
Streams and waterfalls and fountains
Down in darkness stole away

Long ago the hopeless peasant
Left his sheep all buried there
Sheep that through the summer pleasant
He had watched with fondest care

Now no more a cheerful ranger
10   Following pathways known of yore
Sad he stood a wildered stranger
On his own unbounded moor

It is not pride it is not shame

It is not pride it is not shame
That makes her leave the gorgeous hall
And though neglect her heart might tame
She mourns not for her sudden fall

'Tis true she stands among the crowd
An unmarked and an unloved child
While each young comrade blithe and proud
Glides through the maze of pleasure wild

And all do homage to their will
10   And all seem glad their voice to hear
She heeds not that but hardly still
Her eye can hold the quivering tear

What made her weep what made her glide
Out to the park this dreary day
And cast her jewelled chains aside
And seek a rough and lonely way

And down beneath a cedar's shade
On the wet grass regardless lie
With nothing but its gloomy head
20   Between her and the showery sky

I saw her stand in the gallery long
Watching the little children there
As they were playing the pillars among
And bounding down the marble stair

All day I've toiled but not with pain

All day I've toiled but not with pain
In learning's golden mine
And now at eventide again
The moonbeams softly shine

There is no snow upon the ground
No frost on wind or wave
The south wind blew with gentlest sound
And broke their icy grave

'Tis sweet to wander here at night
10   To watch the winter die
With heart as summer sunshine light
And warm as summer's sky.

O may I never lose the peace
That lulls me gently now
Though time should change my youthful face
And years should shade my brow

True to myself and true to all
May I be healthful still
And turn away from passion's call
20   And curb my own wild will

A little while, a little while

A little while, a little while
The noisy crowd are barred away;
And I can sing and I can smile
A little while I've holiday!

Where wilt thou go my harassed heart?
Full many a land invites thee now;
And places near, and far apart
Have rest for thee, my weary brow –

There is a spot 'mid barren hills
10 Where winter howls and driving rain
But if the dreary tempest chills
There is a light that warms again

The house is old, the trees are bare
And moonless bends the misty dome
But what on earth is half so dear –
So longed for as the hearth of home?

The mute bird sitting on the stone,
The dank moss dripping from the wall,
The garden-walk with weeds o'ergrown
20 I love them – how I love them all!

Shall I go there? or shall I seek
Another clime, another sky.
Where tongues familiar music speak
In accents dear to memory?

Yes, as I mused, the naked room,
The flickering firelight died away
And from the midst of cheerless gloom
I passed to bright, unclouded day –

A little and a lone green lane
30   That opened on a common wide
A distant, dreamy, dim blue chain
Of mountains circling every side –

A heaven so clear, an earth so calm,
So sweet, so soft, so hushed an air
And, deepening still the dreamlike charm,
Wild moor-sheep feeding everywhere –

That was the scene – I knew it well
I knew the pathways far and near
That winding o'er each billowy swell
40   Marked out the tracks of wandering deer

Could I have lingered but an hour
It well had paid a week of toil
But truth has banished fancy's power
I hear my dungeon bars recoil –

Even as I stood with raptured eye
Absorbed in bliss so deep and dear
My hour of rest had fleeted by
And given me back to weary care –

Loud without the wind was roaring

Loud without the wind was roaring
    Through the waned Autumnal sky,
Drenching wet, the cold rain pouring
    Spoke of stormy winters nigh.

All too like that dreary eve
Sighed within repining grief –
Sighed at first – but sighed not long
Sweet – How softly sweet it came!
Wild words of an ancient song –
10   Undefined, without a name –

'It was spring, for the skylark was singing.'
Those words they awakened a spell –
They unlocked a deep fountain whose springing
Nor Absence nor Distance can quell.

In the gloom of a cloudy November
They uttered the music of May –
They kindled the perishing ember
Into fervour that could not decay.

Awaken on all my dear moorlands
20 The wind in its glory and pride!
O call me from valleys and highlands
To walk by the hill-river's side!

It is swelled with the first snowy weather;
The rocks they are icy and hoar
And darker waves round the long heather
And the fern-leaves are sunny no more.

There are no yellow-stars on the mountain,
The blue bells have long died away
From the brink of the moss-bedded fountain,
30 From the side of the wintery brae –

But lovelier than corn-fields all waving
In emerald and scarlet and gold
Are the slopes where the north wind is raving
And the glens where I wandered of old –

'It was morning; the bright sun was beaming.'
How sweetly that brought back to me
The time when nor labour nor dreaming
Broke the sleep of the happy and free

But blithely we rose as the dusk heaven
40 Was melting to amber and blue –
And swift were the wings to our feet given
While we traversed the meadows of dew.

For the moors, for the moors where the short grass
Like velvet beneath us should lie!
For the moors, for the moors where each high pass
Rose sunny against the clear sky!

For the moors, where the linnet was trilling
Its song on the old granite stone –
Where the lark – the wild skylark was filling
50 Every breast with delight like its own.

What language can utter the feeling
That rose when, in exile afar,
On the brow of a lonely hill kneeling
I saw the brown heath growing there.

It was scattered and stunted, and told me
That soon even that would be gone.
It whispered, 'The grim walls enfold me
I have bloomed in my last summer's sun.'

But not the loved music whose waking
60 Makes the soul of the Swiss die away
Has a spell more adored and heart-breaking
Than in its half-blighted bells lay –

The spirit that bent 'neath its power
How it longed, how it burned to be free!
If I could have wept in that hour
Those tears had been heaven to me –

Well, well the sad minutes are moving
Though loaded with trouble and pain –
And sometimes the loved and the loving
70 Shall meet on the mountains again.

Christina Rossetti
(1830–1894)

Christina Rossetti was the youngest of four children of Gabriele
Rossetti, an Italian patriot who came to London in 1824. She had
one sister, Maria, and two brothers, Dante Gabriel and William.
Christina and her sister were mainly educated at home by their
mother, and brought up as devout Anglo-Catholics. Her brothers
went to King's College School in London, and were founder
members of the Pre-Raphaelite Brotherhood, a group of artists,
poets and critics who tried to infuse art with moral qualities by a
closely detailed study of nature and by choosing morally uplifting
subjects. They chose the name of their group to indicate that they
thought all art since Raphael (an Italian painter who lived from
1483 to 1520) was degenerate.

Although some of Christina Rossetti's earliest verse was published in *The Germ*, a magazine produced for a short time by the
Pre-Raphaelites, and she sat as a model for several of Dante
Gabriel Rossetti's paintings, she was not a member of the movement. By modern standards, their work seems too rich and
cloying; hers, by comparison, is far more sensitive.

Christina Rossetti's family was very important to her. Although
she is known to have had a relationship with two different men, and
it is clear from her poetry that both love and its loss were known to
her, she never married or broke away from home, and her brothers
and sister were central to her emotions. She spent the last fifteen
years of her life as a recluse, concentrating on her religious
life.

Much of Rossetti's work was religious in nature. Poems such as
'When I am dead, my dearest', 'Remember' and 'Up-Hill' concern
themselves with the nearness of death and the renunciation of
earthly love. Her love of God is passionately expressed in 'Long

Barren', and her poem 'In the Bleak Mid-Winter' is well known as a Christmas carol. However, she is also a poet who demonstrates in her work a love of nature. 'Another Spring' and 'Spring Quiet' show an exactness of observation which her Pre-Raphaelite brothers would have undoubtedly appreciated.

Although she is thought of as a somewhat melancholy poet, and indeed much of her writing inclines to be sad, she can also express the lighter side of life. Her poem 'A Birthday' is a rapturous expression of delight in love. She also shows a malicious appreciation of sisterly jealousies in her poem 'Noble Sisters'. Among her works is *Sing-Song, A Nursery Rhyme Book*, published in 1872, containing lyrics for young children.

Many people consider that her best work is 'Goblin Market' (1862), the longest of her poems. Because goblins sound as if they belong in a fairy story, it is often put in collections for young children. However, it is really a short epic poem for adults. The most notable quality of the writing is the exactness and sensuousness of her descriptions of the fruit sold by the goblins. The nearest comparison in English poetry to this must be the description of the feast in Keats's 'The Eve of St Agnes'. The most striking thing about the subject matter is its eeriness. Two sisters, Lizzie and Laura, see goblin merchants going to market with mouth-wateringly tempting fruit to sell. Laura buys the fruit with one of her golden curls, and when it is gone pines for more, which the goblins refuse to sell her. She sickens and nearly dies, but her sister braves the temptations of the fruit to bring back juices which the goblins have squeezed onto her in their efforts to force her to eat. By offering herself in this way, she redeems her sister.

Some people have seen this poem as an allegory, in which the fruits offered by the goblins stand for the pleasures of the world. However, many modern readers may make a connection with the temptations and effects of narcotic drugs. This may not be a connection that Rossetti intended, but the description of Laura yielding to temptation and her subsequent illness would have been familiar to such families as the Brontës, whose brother Branwell died of an addiction to drink and drugs, and to Coleridge, who suffered from a life-long addiction to opium.

Summer

Winter is cold-hearted,
  Spring is yea and nay,
Autumn is a weathercock
  Blown every way:
Summer days for me
When every leaf is on the tree;

When Robin's not a beggar,
  And Jenny Wren's a bride,
10 And larks hang singing, singing, singing,
    Over the wheatfields wide,
    And anchored lilies ride,
And the pendulum spider
    Swings from side to side,

And blue-black beetles transact business,
  And gnats fly in a host,
And furry caterpillars hasten
  That no time be lost,
And moths grow fat and thrive,
20 And ladybirds arrive.

Before green apples blush,
  Before green nuts embrown,
Why, one day in the country
  Is worth a month in town;
  Is worth a day and a year
Of the dusty, musty, lag-last fashion
  That days drone elsewhere.

Goblin Market

Morning and evening
Maids heard the goblins cry:
'Come buy our orchard fruits,
Come buy, come buy:
Apples and quinces,
Lemons and oranges,
Plump unpecked cherries,
Melons and raspberries,
Bloom-down-cheeked peaches,
10   Swart-headed mulberries,
Wild free-born cranberries,
Crab-apples, dewberries,
Pine-apples, blackberries,
Apricots, strawberries; –
All ripe together
In summer weather, –
Morns that pass by,
Fair eves that fly;
Come buy, come buy:
20   Our grapes fresh from the vine,
Pomegranates full and fine,
Dates and sharp bullaces,[1]
Rare pears and greengages,
Damsons and bilberries,
Taste them and try:
Currants and gooseberries,
Bright-fire-like barberries,
Figs to fill your mouth,
Citrons from the South,
30   Sweet to tongue and sound to eye;
Come buy, come buy.'

1. A type of wild plum.

Evening by evening
Among the brookside rushes,
Laura bowed her head to hear,
Lizzie veiled her blushes:
Crouching close together
In the cooling weather,
With clasping arms and cautioning lips,
With tingling cheeks and finger tips.
40 'Lie close,' Laura said,
Pricking up her golden head:
'We must not look at goblin men,
We must not buy their fruits:
Who knows upon what soil they fed
Their hungry thirsty roots?'
'Come buy,' call the goblins
Hobbling down the glen.
'Oh,' cried Lizzie, 'Laura, Laura,
You should not peep at goblin men.'
50 Lizzie covered up her eyes,
Covered close lest they should look;
Laura reared her glossy head,
And whispered like the restless brook:
'Look, Lizzie, look, Lizzie,
Down the glen tramp little men.
One hauls a basket,
One bears a plate,
One lugs a golden dish
Of many pounds weight.
60 How fair the vine must grow
Whose grapes are so luscious;
How warm the wind must blow
Through those fruit bushes.'
'No,' said Lizzie: 'No, no, no;
Their offers should not charm us,
Their evil gifts would harm us.'
She thrust a dimpled finger
In each ear, shut eyes and ran:

Curious Laura chose to linger
70 Wondering at each merchant man.
One had a cat's face,
One whisked a tail,
One tramped at a rat's pace,
One crawled like a snail,
One like a wombat prowled obtuse and furry,
One like a ratel[1] tumbled hurry skurry.
She heard a voice like voice of doves
Cooing all together:
They sounded kind and full of loves
80 In the pleasant weather.

Laura stretched her gleaming neck
Like a rush-imbedded swan,
Like a lily from the beck,
Like a moonlit poplar branch,
Like a vessel at the launch
When its last restraint is gone.

Backwards up the mossy glen
Turned and trooped the goblin men,
With their shrill repeated cry,
90 'Come buy, come buy.'
When they reached where Laura was
They stood stock still upon the moss,
Leering at each other,
Brother with queer brother;
Signalling each other,
Brother with sly brother.
One set his basket down,
One reared his plate;
One began to weave a crown
100 Of tendrils, leaves, and rough nuts brown
(Men sell not such in any town);
One heaved the golden weight

1. A type of badger.

Of dish and fruit to offer her:
'Come buy, come buy,' was still their cry.
Laura stared but did not stir,
Longed but had no money:
The whisk-tailed merchant bade her taste
In tones as smooth as honey,
The cat-faced purr'd,
110 The rat-paced spoke a word
Of welcome, and the snail-paced even was heard;
One parrot-voiced and jolly
Cried 'Pretty Goblin' still for 'Pretty Polly'; –
One whistled like a bird.

But sweet-tooth Laura spoke in haste:
'Good folk, I have no coin;
To take were to purloin:[1]
I have no copper in my purse,
I have no silver either,
120 And all my gold is on the furze
That shakes in windy weather
Above the rusty heather.'
'You have much gold upon your head,'
They answered all together:
'Buy from us with a golden curl.'
She clipped a precious golden lock,
She dropped a tear more rare than pearl,
Then sucked their fruit globes fair or red:
Sweeter than honey from the rock,
130 Stronger than man-rejoicing wine,
Clearer than water flowed that juice;
She never tasted such before,
How should it cloy with length of use?
She sucked and sucked and sucked the more
Fruits which that unknown orchard bore;
She sucked until her lips were sore;

1. Steal.

Then flung the emptied rinds away
But gathered up one kernel stone,
And knew not was it night or day
140 As she turned home alone.

  Lizzie met her at the gate
Full of wise upbraidings:
'Dear, you should not stay so late,
Twilight is not good for maidens;
Should not loiter in the glen
In the haunts of goblin men.
Do you not remember Jeanie,
How she met them in the moonlight,
Took their gifts both choice and many,
150 Ate their fruits and wore their flowers
Plucked from bowers
Where summer ripens at all hours?
But ever in the noonlight
She pined and pined away;
Sought them by night and day,
Found them no more but dwindled and grew grey;
Then fell with the first snow,
While to this day no grass will grow
Where she lies low:
160 I planted daisies there a year ago
That never blow.
You should not loiter so.'
  'Nay, hush,' said Laura:
'Nay, hush, my sister:
I ate and ate my fill,
Yet my mouth waters still;
To-morrow night I will
Buy more': and kissed her:
'Have done with sorrow;
170 I'll bring you plums to-morrow
Fresh on their mother twigs,
Cherries worth getting;

You cannot think what figs
My teeth have met in,
What melons icy-cold
Piled on a dish of gold
Too huge for me to hold,
What peaches with a velvet nap,
Pellucid grapes without one seed:
180 Odorous indeed must be the mead
Whereon they grow, and pure the wave they drink
With lilies at the brink,
And sugar-sweet their sap.'

Golden head by golden head,
Like two pigeons in one nest
Folded in each other's wings,
They lay down in their curtained bed:
Like two blossoms on one stem,
Like two flakes of new-fall'n snow,
190 Like two wands of ivory
Tipped with gold for awful kings.
Moon and stars gazed in at them,
Wind sang to them lullaby,
Lumbering owls forbore to fly,
Not a bat flapped to and fro
Round their nest:
Cheek to cheek and breast to breast
Locked together in one nest.

Early in the morning
200 When the first cock crowed his warning,
Neat like bees, as sweet and busy,
Laura rose with Lizzie:
Fetched in honey, milked the cows,
Aired and set to rights the house,
Kneaded cakes of whitest wheat,
Cake for dainty mouths to eat,
Next churned butter, whipped up cream,
Fed their poultry, sat and sewed;

Talked as modest maidens should:
210 Lizzie with an open heart,
Laura in an absent dream,
One content, one sick in part;
One warbling for the mere bright day's delight,
One longing for the night.

At length slow evening came:
They went with pitchers to the reedy brook;
Lizzie most placid in her look,
Laura most like a leaping flame.
They drew the gurgling water from its deep;
220 Lizzie plucked purple and rich golden flags,
Then turning homewards said: 'The sunset flushes
Those furthest loftiest crags;
Come, Laura, not another maiden lags,
No wilful squirrel wags,
The beasts and birds are fast asleep.'
But Laura loitered still among the rushes
And said the bank was steep.

And said the hour was early still,
The dew not fall'n, the wind not chill:
230 Listening ever, but not catching
The customary cry,
'Come buy, come buy,'
With its iterated[1] jingle
Of sugar-baited words:
Not for all her watching
Once discerning even one goblin
Racing, whisking, tumbling, hobbling;
Let alone the herds
That used to tramp along the glen,
240 In groups or single,
Of brisk fruit-merchant men.

1. Repeated.

Till Lizzie urged, 'O Laura, come;
I hear the fruit-call but I dare not look:
You should not loiter longer at this brook:
Come with me home.
The stars rise, the moon bends her arc,
Each glowworm winks her spark,
Let us get home before the night grows dark:
For clouds may gather
250 Though this is summer weather,
Put out the lights and drench us through;
Then if we lost our way what should we do?'

Laura turned cold as stone
To find her sister heard that cry alone,
That goblin cry,
'Come buy our fruits, come buy.'
Must she then buy no more such dainty fruit?
Must she no more such succous[1] pasture find,
Gone deaf and blind?
260 Her tree of life drooped from the root:
She said not one word in her heart's sore ache;
But peering thro' the dimness, nought discerning,
Trudged home, her pitcher dripping all the way;
So crept to bed, and lay
Silent till Lizzie slept;
Then sat up in a passionate yearning,
And gnashed her teeth for baulked desire, and wept
As if her heart would break.

Day after day, night after night,
270 Laura kept watch in vain
In sullen silence of exceeding pain.
She never caught again the goblin cry:
'Come buy, come buy'; –
She never spied the goblin men
Hawking their fruits along the glen:

1. Juicy.

But when the noon waxed bright
Her hair grew thin and grey;
She dwindled, as the fair full moon doth turn
To swift decay and burn
280   Her fire away.

One day remembering her kernel-stone
She set it by a wall that faced the south;
Dewed it with tears, hoped for a root,
Watched for a waxing shoot,
But there came none;
It never saw the sun,
It never felt the trickling moisture run:
While with sunk eyes and faded mouth
She dreamed of melons, as a traveller sees
290   False waves in desert drouth[1]
With shade of leaf-crowned trees,
And burns the thirstier in the sandful breeze.

She no more swept the house,
Tended the fowls or cows,
Fetched honey, kneaded cakes of wheat,
Brought water from the brook:
But sat down listless in the chimney-nook
And would not eat.

Tender Lizzie could not bear
300   To watch her sister's cankerous[2] care
Yet not to share.
She night and morning
Caught the goblins' cry:
'Come buy our orchard fruits,
Come buy, come buy'; –
Beside the brook, along the glen,
She heard the tramp of goblin men,

1. Thirst or drought.
2. Corroding, destroying.

The voice and stir
Poor Laura could not hear;
310 Longed to buy fruit to comfort her,
But feared to pay too dear.
She thought of Jeanie in her grave,
Who should have been a bride;
But who for joys brides hope to have
Fell sick and died
In her gay prime,
In earliest Winter time,
With the first glazing rime,
With the first snow-fall of crisp Winter time.

320   Till Laura dwindling
Seemed knocking at Death's door:
Then Lizzie weighed no more
Better and worse;
But put a silver penny in her purse,
Kissed Laura, crossed the heath with clumps of furze
At twilight, halted by the brook:
And for the first time in her life
Began to listen and look.

    Laughed every goblin
330 When they spied her peeping:
Came towards her hobbling,
Flying, running, leaping,
Puffing and blowing,
Chuckling, clapping, crowing,
Clucking and gobbling,
Mopping and mowing,
Full of airs and graces,
Pulling wry faces,
Demure grimaces,
340 Cat-like and rat-like,
Ratel- and wombat-like,
Snail-paced in a hurry,
Parrot-voiced and whistler,

Helter skelter, hurry skurry,
Chattering like magpies,
Fluttering like pigeons,
Gliding like fishes, –
Hugged her and kissed her:
Squeezed and caressed her:
350　Stretched up their dishes,
Panniers, and plates:
'Look at our apples
Russet and dun,
Bob at our cherries,
Bite at our peaches,
Citrons and dates,
Grapes for the asking,
Pears red with basking
Out in the sun,
360　Plums on their twigs;
Pluck them and suck them,
Pomegranates, figs.' –

　　'Good folk,' said Lizzie,
Mindful of Jeanie:
'Give me much and many'; –
Held out her apron,
Tossed them her penny.
'Nay, take a seat with us,
Honour and eat with us,'
370　They answered grinning:
'Our feast is but beginning.
Night yet is early,
Warm and dew-pearly,
Wakeful and starry:
Such fruits as these
No man can carry;
Half their bloom would fly,
Half their dew would dry,
Half their flavour would pass by.

380 Sit down and feast with us,
    Be welcome guest with us,
    Cheer you and rest with us.' –
    'Thank you,' said Lizzie: 'But one waits
    At home alone for me:
    So without further parleying,
    If you will not sell me any
    Of your fruits though much and many,
    Give me back my silver penny
    I tossed you for a fee.' –

390 They began to scratch their pates,
    No longer wagging, purring,
    But visibly demurring,[1]
    Grunting and snarling.
    One called her proud,
    Cross-grained, uncivil;
    Their tones waxed loud,
    Their looks were evil.
    Lashing their tails
    They trod and hustled her,

400 Elbowed and jostled her,
    Clawed with their nails,
    Barking, mewing, hissing, mocking,
    Tore her gown and soiled her stocking,
    Twitched her hair out by the roots,
    Stamped upon her tender feet,
    Held her hands and squeezed their fruits
    Against her mouth to make her eat.

    White and golden Lizzie stood,
    Like a lily in a flood, –

410 Like a rock of blue-veined stone
    Lashed by tides obstreperously,[2] –
    Like a beacon left alone

    1. Hesitating.
    2. Boisterously.

In a hoary roaring sea,
Sending up a golden fire, –
Like a fruit-crowned orange-tree
White with blossoms honey-sweet
Sore beset by wasp and bee, –
Like a royal virgin town
Topped with gilded dome and spire
420 Close beleaguered by a fleet
Mad to tug her standard down.

One may lead a horse to water,
Twenty cannot make him drink.
Though the goblins cuffed and caught her,
Coaxed and fought her,
Bullied and besought her,
Scratched her, pinched her black as ink,
Kicked and knocked her,
Mauled and mocked her,
430 Lizzie uttered not a word;
Would not open lip from lip
Lest they should cram a mouthful in:
But laughed in heart to feel the drip
Of juice that syrupped all her face,
And lodged in dimples of her chin,
And streaked her neck which quaked like curd.
At last the evil people
Worn out by her resistance
Flung back her penny, kicked their fruit
440 Along whichever road they took,
Not leaving root or stone or shoot;
Some writhed into the ground,
Some dived into the brook
With ring and ripple,
Some scudded on the gale without a sound,
Some vanished in the distance.

In a smart, ache, tingle,
Lizzie went her way;

Knew not was it night or day;
450 Sprang up the bank, tore thro' the furze,
Threaded copse and dingle,
And heard her penny jingle
Bouncing in her purse, –
Its bounce was music to her ear.
She ran and ran
As if she feared some goblin man
Dogged her with gibe or curse
Or something worse:
But not one goblin skurried after,
460 Nor was she pricked by fear;
The kind heart made her windy-paced
That urged her home quite out of breath with haste
And inward laughter.

She cried 'Laura,' up the garden,
'Did you miss me?
Come and kiss me.
Never mind my bruises,
Hug me, kiss me, suck my juices
Squeezed from goblin fruits for you,
470 Goblin pulp and goblin dew.
Eat me, drink me, love me;
Laura, make much of me:
For your sake I have braved the glen
And had to do with goblin merchant men.'

Laura started from her chair,
Flung her arms up in the air,
Clutched her hair:
'Lizzie, Lizzie, have you tasted
For my sake the fruit forbidden?
480 Must your light like mine be hidden,
Your young life like mine be wasted,
Undone in mine undoing
And ruined in my ruin,
Thirsty, cankered, goblin-ridden?' –

She clung about her sister,
Kissed and kissed and kissed her:
Tears once again
Refreshed her shrunken eyes,
Dropping like rain
490   After long sultry drouth;
Shaking with anguish fear, and pain,
She kissed and kissed her with a hungry mouth.

      Her lips began to scorch,
That juice was wormwood[1] to her tongue,
She loathed the feast:
Writhing as one possessed she leaped and sung,
Rent all her robe, and wrung
Her hands in lamentable haste,
And beat her breast.
500   Her locks streamed like the torch
Borne by a racer at full speed,
Or like the mane of horses in their flight,
Or like an eagle when she stems the light
Straight toward the sun,
Or like a caged thing freed,
Or like a flying flag when armies run.

      Swift fire spread through her veins, knocked at her heart,
Met the fire smouldering there
And overbore its lesser flame;
510   She gorged on bitterness without a name:
Ah! fool, to choose such part
Of soul-consuming care!
Sense failed in the mortal strife:
Like the watch-tower of a town
Which an earthquake shatters down,
Like a lightning-stricken mast,
Like a wind-uprooted tree
Spun about,

1. A very bitter herb.

Like a foam-topped waterspout
520 Cast down headlong in the sea,
She fell at last;
Pleasure past and anguish past,
Is it death or is it life?

    Life out of death.
That night long Lizzie watched by her,
Counted her pulse's flagging stir,
Felt for her breath,
Held water to her lips, and cooled her face
With tears and fanning leaves:
530 But when the first birds chirped about their eaves,
And early reapers plodded to the place
Of golden sheaves,
And dew-wet grass
Bowed in the morning winds so brisk to pass,
And new buds with new day
Opened of cup-like lilies on the stream,
Laura awoke as from a dream,
Laughed in the innocent old way,
Hugged Lizzie but not twice or thrice;
540 Her gleaming locks showed not one thread of grey,
Her breath was sweet as May
And light danced in her eyes.

    Days, weeks, months, years
Afterwards, when both were wives
With children of their own;
Their mother-hearts beset with fears,
Their lives bound up in tender lives;
Laura would call the little ones
And tell them of her early prime,
550 Those pleasant days long gone
Of not-returning time:
Would talk about the haunted glen,
The wicked, quaint fruit-merchant men,
Their fruits like honey to the throat

But poison in the blood;
(Men sell not such in any town:)
Would tell them how her sister stood
In deadly peril to do her good,
And win the fiery antidote:
560   Then joining hands to little hands
Would bid them cling together,
'For there is no friend like a sister
In calm or stormy weather;
To cheer one on the tedious way,
To fetch one if one goes astray,
To lift one if one totters down,
To strengthen whilst one stands.'

Noble Sisters

'Now did you mark a falcon,
   Sister dear, sister dear,
Flying toward my window
   In the morning cool and clear?
With jingling bells about her neck,
   But what beneath her wing?
It may have been a ribbon,
   Or it may have been a ring.' –
      'I marked a falcon swooping
10   At the break of day:
      And for your love, my sister dove,
         I 'frayed the thief away.' –

'Or did you spy a ruddy hound,
   Sister fair and tall,
Went snuffing round my garden bound,
   Or crouched by my bower wall?
With a silken leash about his neck;
   But in his mouth may be
A chain of gold and silver links,

Or a letter writ to me.' –

20   'I heard a hound, highborn sister,
            Stood baying at the moon:
        I rose and drove him from your wall
            Lest you should wake too soon.' –

'Or did you meet a pretty page
    Sat swinging on the gate;
Sat whistling whistling like a bird,
    Or may be slept too late:
With eaglets broidered on his cap,
    And eaglets on his glove?
30 If you had turned his pockets out,
        You had found some pledge of love.' –
            'I met him at this daybreak,
                Scarce the east was red:
            Lest the creaking gate should anger you,
                I packed him home to bed.' –

'Oh patience sister. Did you see
    A young man tall and strong,
Swift-footed to uphold the right
    And to uproot the wrong,
40 Come home across the desolate sea
    To woo me for his wife?
And in his heart my heart is locked,
    And in his life my life.' –
        'I met a nameless man, sister,
            Hard by your chamber door:
        I said: Her husband loves her much.
            And yet she loves him more.' –

'Fie, sister, fie, a wicked lie,
    A lie, a wicked lie,
50 I have none other love but him,
    Nor will have till I die.
And you have turned him from our door,
    And stabbed him with a lie:

I will go seek him thro' the world
　　In sorrow till I die.' –
　　　　'Go seek in sorrow, sister,
　　　　　And find in sorrow too:
　　　If thus you shame our father's name
　　　　My curse go forth with you.'

Spring

　　Frost-locked all the winter,
　　Seeds, and roots, and stones of fruits,
　　What shall make their sap ascend
　　That they may put forth shoots?
　　Tips of tender green,
　　Leaf, or blade, or sheath;
　　Telling of the hidden life
　　That breaks forth underneath,
　　Life nursed in its grave by Death.

10　Blows the thaw-wind pleasantly,
　　Drips the soaking rain,
　　By fits looks down the waking sun:
　　Young grass springs on the plain;
　　Young leaves clothe early hedgerow trees;
　　Seeds, and roots, and stones of fruits,
　　Swollen with sap put forth their shoots;
　　Curled-headed ferns sprout in the lane;
　　Birds sing and pair again.

　　There is no time like Spring,
20　When life's alive in everything,
　　Before new nestlings sing,
　　Before cleft swallows speed their journey back
　　Along the trackless track –
　　God guides their wing,
　　He spreads their table that they nothing lack, –

Before the daisy grows a common flower,
Before the sun has power
To scorch the world up in his noontide hour.

There is no time like Spring,
30   Like Spring that passes by:
There is no life like Spring-life born to die, –
Piercing the sod,
Clothing the uncouth clod,
Hatched in the nest,
Fledged on the windy bough,
Strong on the wing;
There is no time like Spring that passes by,
Now newly born, and now
Hastening to die.

Remember

SONNET

Remember me when I am gone away,
    Gone far away into the silent land;
    When you can no more hold me by the hand,
Nor I half turn to go yet turning stay.
Remember me when no more day by day
    You tell me of our future that you planned:
    Only remember me; you understand
It will be late to counsel then or pray.
Yet if you should forget me for a while
10   And afterwards remember, do not grieve:
    For if the darkness and corruption leave
    A vestige of the thoughts that once I had,
Better by far you should forget and smile
    Than that you should remember and be sad.

Song

When I am dead, my dearest,
　　Sing no sad songs for me;
Plant thou no roses at my head,
　　Nor shady cypress tree:
Be the green grass above me
　　With showers and dewdrops wet;
And if thou wilt, remember,
　　And if thou wilt, forget.
I shall not see the shadows,
10　　I shall not feel the rain;
I shall not hear the nightingale
　　Sing on, as if in pain:
And dreaming through the twilight
　　That doth not rise nor set,
Haply I may remember,
　　And haply may forget.

Spring Quiet

Gone were but the Winter,
　　Come were but the Spring,
I would go to a covert[1]
　　Where the birds sing;

Where in the whitethorn
　　Singeth a thrush,
And a robin sings
　　In the holly-bush.

1. Small area of woodland, a cover for game birds.

Full of fresh scents
10 Are the budding boughs
Arching high over
    A cool green house:

Full of sweet scents,
    And whispering air
Which sayeth softly:
    'We spread no snare;

'Here dwell in safety,
    Here dwell alone,
With a clear stream
20   And a mossy stone.

'Here the sun shineth
    Most shadily;
Here is heard an echo
    Of the far sea,
        Though far off it be.'

Up-Hill

Does the road wind up-hill all the way?
    Yes, to the very end.
Will the day's journey take the whole long day?
    From morn to night, my friend.

But is there for the night a resting-place?
    A roof for when the slow dark hours begin.
May not the darkness hide it from my face?
    You cannot miss that inn.

Shall I meet other wayfarers at night?
10   Those who have gone before.
Then must I knock, or call when just in sight?
    They will not keep you standing at that door.

Shall I find comfort, travel-sore and weak?
　　Of labour you shall find the sum.
Will there be beds for me and all who seek?
　　Yea, beds for all who come.

Song

Two doves upon the selfsame branch,
　　Two lilies on a single stem,
Two butterflies upon one flower: –
　　Oh happy they who look on them.

Who look upon them hand in hand
　　Flushed in the rosy summer light;
Who look upon them hand in hand
　　And never give a thought to night.

Bitter for Sweet

Summer is gone with all its roses,
　　Its sun and perfumes and sweet flowers,
　　Its warm air and refreshing showers:
　　　　And even Autumn closes.

Yea, Autumn's chilly self is going,
　　And winter comes which is yet colder;
　　Each day the hoar-frost waxes bolder
　　　　And the last buds cease blowing.

A Birthday

My heart is like a singing bird
    Whose nest is in a watered shoot;
My heart is like an apple-tree
    Whose boughs are bent with thick-set fruit;
My heart is like a rainbow shell
    That paddles in a halcyon[1] sea;
My heart is gladder than all these
    Because my love is come to me.

Raise me a dais of silk and down;
10   Hang it with vair[2] and purple dyes;
Carve it in doves, and pomegranates,
    And peacocks with a hundred eyes;
Work it in gold and silver grapes,
    In leaves, and silver fleurs-de-lys;
Because the birthday of my life
    Is come, my love is come to me.

1. Calm, peaceful.
2. Fur.

Matthew Arnold
(1822–1888)

Matthew Arnold was born at Laleham, near Staines in Middlesex. His father, Thomas Arnold, became headmaster of Rugby School in 1828 and in that role was immortalized in Thomas Hughes's novel *Tom Brown's Schooldays*. Arnold was educated first at Winchester, and then from 1837 to 1841 at Rugby, where he made friends with both Thomas Hughes and the poet Arthur Hugh Clough. He won a scholarship to Balliol College, Oxford, a prize for English verse with a poem on Cromwell, and was eventually elected a Fellow of Oriel College in 1845. A vacation in Switzerland in 1847 inspired among others his poem 'The Dream', which vividly captures the crispness and clarity of the Alps.

Arnold married Frances Wightman in 1851, and from then until 1886 he was an inspector of schools. This job required him to travel throughout England and Wales, visiting and reporting on elementary and secondary schools. He also made several trips to Europe as a Commissioner to enquire into the state of education in France, Germany and Holland. Arnold believed that access to education was needed above everything else in England, and there is no doubt that by his work he did great service to the cause of education.

Arnold's first two volumes of poetry, *The Strayed Reveller and other Poems by A*, and *Empedocles on Etna and other Poems by A* were published anonymously in 1849 and 1852. Both these volumes were withdrawn from sale quite soon, because Arnold was dissatisfied with one of the poems, but in 1853 and 1855 he published two volumes of *Poems by Matthew Arnold*, which included many of the poems that had already appeared and a few more, especially 'Sohrab and Rustum' and 'The Scholar-Gipsy'.

In 1857 Arnold was elected as the first Professor of Poetry at Oxford, and was re-elected for a second five-year term in 1862. This post was not a full-time job, but required the holder to give three lectures a year during his term in office. Arnold's first lecture was entitled 'On the Modern Element in Literature'. Eventually, his critical writings were published in 1865 as *Essays in Criticism* and greatly influenced the next generation of literary scholars.

His last volume of new works, *New Poems by Matthew Arnold*, appeared in 1867, although collected editions appeared over the next twenty years. After this, he only occasionally wrote poetry, though he published several volumes of literary, social and religious criticism. In 1883 he was awarded a pension of £250 a year 'in public recognition of service to the poetry and literature of England'.

After his retirement in 1886 Arnold made a lecture tour of America, where he visited his daughter Lucy, who had married a New Yorker. In 1888 he died quite suddenly of heart failure in Liverpool, where he had gone to meet Lucy, who was making a visit to England.

The mood of Arnold's poetry tends to be of plaintive reflection, and he is restrained in expressing emotion. He felt that poetry should be the 'criticism of life' and express a philosophy. Arnold's philosophy is that true happiness comes from within, and that people should seek within themselves for good, while being resigned in acceptance of outward things and avoiding the pointless turmoil of the world. However, he argues that we should not live in the belief that we shall one day inherit eternal bliss. If we are not happy on earth, we should moderate our desires rather than live in dreams of something that may never be attained. This philosophy is clearly expressed in such poems as 'Dover Beach' and in these lines from 'Stanzas from the Grande Chartreuse':

Wandering between two worlds, one dead
The other powerless to be born,
With nowhere yet to rest my head
Like these, on earth I wait forlorn.

Arnold valued natural scenery for its peace and permanence in contrast with the ceaseless change of human things. He liked subdued colours, mist and moonlight. He seems to prefer the 'spent lights' of the sea-depths in 'The Forsaken Merman' to the village life preferred by the merman's lost wife. At the same time, his descriptions are often picturesque, and marked by striking similes.

The Hayswater Boat

A region desolate and wild.
Black, chafing water: and afloat,
And lonely as a truant child
In a waste wood, a single boat:
No mast, no sails are set thereon;
It moves, but never moveth on:
And welters[1] like a human thing
Amid the wild waves weltering.

Behind, a buried vale doth sleep,
10   Far down the torrent cleaves its way:
In front the dumb rock rises steep,
A fretted wall of blue and grey;
Of shooting cliff and crumbled stone
With many a wild weed overgrown:
All else, black water: and afloat,
One rood[2] from shore, that single boat.

Last night the wind was up and strong;
The grey-streak'd waters labour still:
The strong blast brought a pigmy throng
20   From that mild hollow in the hill;
From those twin brooks, that beached strand
So featly[3] strewn with drifted sand;
From those weird domes of mounded green
That spot the solitary scene.

This boat they found against the shore:
The glossy rushes nodded by.
One rood from land they push'd, no more;

1. Rolls and tumbles.
2. A quarter of an acre.
3. Skilfully.

Then rested, listening silently.
The loud rains lash'd the mountain's crown,
30 The grating shingle straggled down:
All night they sat; then stole away,
And left it rocking in the bay.

Last night? – I look'd, the sky was clear.
The boat was old, a batter'd boat.
In sooth, it seems a hundred year
Since that strange crew did ride afloat.
The boat hath drifted in the bay –
The oars have moulder'd as they lay –
The rudder swings – yet none doth steer.
40 What living hand hath brought it here?

The Forsaken Merman[1]

Come, dear children, let us away;
Down and away below!
Now my brothers call from the bay,
Now the great winds shoreward blow,
Now the salt tides seaward flow;
Now the wild white horses play,
Champ and chafe and toss in the spray.
Children dear, let us away!
This way, this way!

10 Call her once before you go –
Call once yet!
In a voice that she will know:
'Margaret! Margaret!'

1. The original mermen and mermaids of mythology did not have the fish-shaped lower halves of modern myth, and so were able to come on shore and associate with humans. However, unlike humans, they had no souls and would vanish into the sea-foam when they died.

Children's voices should be dear
(Call once more) to a mother's ear;
Children's voices, wild with pain –
Surely she will come again!
Call her once and come away;
This way, this way!
20 'Mother dear, we cannot stay!
The wild white horses foam and fret.'
Margaret! Margaret!

Come, dear children, come away down;
Call no more!
One last look at the white-wall'd town,
And the little grey church on the windy shore,
Then come down!
She will not come though you call all day;
Come away, come away!

30 Children dear, was it yesterday
We heard the sweet bells over the bay?
In the caverns where we lay,
Through the surf and through the swell,
The far-off sound of a silver bell?
Sand-strewn caverns, cool and deep,
Where the winds are all asleep;
Where the spent lights quiver and gleam,
Where the salt weed sways in the stream,
Where the sea-beasts, ranged all round,
40 Feed in the ooze of their pasture-ground;
Where the sea-snakes coil and twine,
Dry their mail and bask in the brine;
Where great whales come sailing by,
Sail and sail, with unshut eye,
Round the world for ever and aye?
When did music come this way?
Children dear, was it yesterday?

Children dear, was it yesterday
(Call yet once) that she went away?
50 Once she sate with you and me,
On a red gold throne in the heart of the sea,
And the youngest sate on her knee.
She comb'd its bright hair, and she tended it well,
When down swung the sound of a far-off bell.
She sigh'd, she look'd up through the clear green sea;
She said: 'I must go, for my kinsfolk pray
In the little grey church on the shore to-day.
'Twill be Easter-time in the world – ah me!
And I lose my poor soul, Merman! here with thee.'
60 I said: 'Go up, dear heart, through the waves;
Say thy prayer, and come back to the kind sea-caves!'
She smiled, she went up through the surf in the bay.
Children dear, was it yesterday?

Children dear, were we long alone?
'The sea grows stormy, the little ones moan;
Long prayers,' I said, 'in the world they say;
Come!' I said; and we rose through the surf in the bay.
We went up the beach, by the sandy down
Where the sea-stocks bloom, to the white-wall'd town;
70 Through the narrow paved streets, where all was still,
To the little grey church on the windy hill.
From the church came a murmur of folk at their prayers,
But we stood without in the cold blowing airs.
We climb'd on the graves, on the stones worn with rains,
And we gazed up the aisle through the small leaded panes.
She sate by the pillar; we saw her clear:
'Margaret, hist! come quick, we are here!
Dear heart,' I said, 'we are long alone;
The sea grows stormy, the little ones moan.'
80 But, ah, she gave me never a look,
For her eyes were seal'd to the holy book!
Loud prays the priest; shut stands the door.
Come away, children, call no more!
Come away, come down, call no more!

Down, down, down!
Down to the depths of the sea!
She sits at her wheel in the humming town,
Singing most joyfully.
Hark what she sings: 'O joy, O joy,
90   For the humming street, and the child with its toy!
For the priest, and the bell, and the holy well;
For the wheel where I spun,
And the blessed light of the sun!'
And so she sings her fill,
Singing most joyfully,
Till the spindle drops from her hand,
And the whizzing wheel stands still.
She steals to the window, and looks at the sand,
And over the sand at the sea;
100 And her eyes are set in a stare;
And anon[1] there breaks a sigh,
And anon there drops a tear,
From a sorrow-clouded eye,
And a heart sorrow-laden,
A long, long sigh;
For the cold strange eyes of a little Mermaiden
And the gleam of her golden hair.

Come away, away children;
Come children, come down!
110 The hoarse wind blows coldly;
Lights shine in the town.
She will start from her slumber
When gusts shake the door;
She will hear the winds howling,
Will hear the waves roar.
We shall see, while above us
The waves roar and whirl,
A ceiling of amber,
A pavement of pearl.

1. In a little while.

120   Singing: 'Here came a mortal,
      But faithless was she!
      And alone dwell for ever
      The kings of the sea.'

      But, children, at midnight,
      When soft the winds blow,
      When clear falls the moonlight,
      When spring-tides are low;
      When sweet airs come seaward
      From heaths starr'd with broom,
130   And high rocks throw mildly
      On the blanch'd sands a gloom;
      Up the still, glistening beaches,
      Up the creeks we will hie,
      Over banks of bright seaweed
      The ebb-tide leaves dry.
      We will gaze, from the sand-hills,
      At the white, sleeping town;
      At the church on the hill-side –
      And then come back down.
140   Singing: 'There dwells a loved one,
      But cruel is she!
      She left lonely for ever
      The kings of the sea.'

Dover Beach

      The sea is calm to-night.
      The tide is full, the moon lies fair
      Upon the straits; – on the French coast the light
      Gleams and is gone; the cliffs of England stand,
      Glimmering and vast, out in the tranquil bay.
      Come to the window, sweet is the night-air!
      Only, from the long line of spray
      Where the sea meets the moon-blanch'd land,

Listen! you hear the grating roar
10 Of pebbles which the waves draw back, and fling,
At their return, up the high strand,
Begin, and cease, and then again begin,
With tremulous cadence slow, and bring
The eternal note of sadness in.

Sophocles[1] long ago
Heard it on the Aegean,[2] and it brought
Into his mind the turbid ebb and flow
Of human misery; we
Find also in the sound a thought,
20 Hearing it by this distant northern sea.

The Sea of Faith[3]
Was once, too, at the full, and round earth's shore
Lay like the folds of a bright girdle furl'd.
But now I only hear
Its melancholy, long, withdrawing roar,
Retreating, to the breath
Of the night-wind, down the vast edges drear
And naked shingles of the world.

Ah, love, let us be true
30 To one another! for the world, which seems
To lie before us like a land of dreams,
So various, so beautiful, so new,
Hath really neither joy, nor love, nor light,

1. One of the three great ancient Greek writers of tragedy. In his play
Antigone, the evil coming upon a doomed house is compared to the
gathering of a storm on the sea: 'As the swelling wave, when driven by
Thracian sea-blasts it rushes over the gloom which lies beneath the sea,
rolls up the dark shingle from the depth, and the beach on which it
breaks resounds with a stormy moan.'
2. The Aegean is the sea that washes the eastern coast of Greece.
3. The religious faith of the early Christians.

Nor certitude, nor peace, nor help for pain;
And we are here as on a darkling plain
Swept with confused alarms of struggle and flight,
Where ignorant armies clash by night.

A Dream

Was it a dream? We sail'd, I thought we sail'd,
Martin and I, down a green Alpine stream,
Border'd, each bank, with pines; the morning sun,
On the wet umbrage[1] of their glossy tops,
On the red pinings of their forest-floor,
Drew a warm scent abroad; behind the pines
The mountain-skirts, with all their sylvan[2] change
Of bright-leaf'd chestnuts and moss'd walnut-trees
And the frail scarlet-berried ash, began.
10 Swiss chalets glitter'd on the dewy slopes,
And from some swarded[3] shelf, high up, there came
Notes of wild pastoral music – over all
Ranged, diamond-bright, the eternal wall of snow.
Upon the mossy rocks at the stream's edge,
Back'd by the pines, a plank-built cottage stood,
Bright in the sun; the climbing gourd-plant's leaves
Muffled its walls, and on the stone-strewn roof
Lay the warm golden gourds; golden, within,
Under the eaves, peer'd rows of Indian corn.
20 We shot beneath the cottage with the stream.
On the brown rude-carved[4] balcony, two forms
Came forth – Olivia's, Marguerite! and thine.
Clad were they both in white, flowers in their breast;
Straw hats bedeck'd their heads, with ribbons blue,

1. Shade-giving.
2. Belonging to woods or forests.
3. Grassy.
4. Roughly carved.

Which danced, and on their shoulders, fluttering, play'd.
They saw us, they conferr'd; their bosoms heaved,
And more than mortal impulse fill'd their eyes.
Their lips moved; their white arms, waved eagerly,
Flash'd once, like falling streams; we rose, we gazed.
30 One moment on the rapid's top, our boat
Hung poised – and then the darting river of Life
(Such now, methought, it was), the river of Life
Loud thundering, bore us by; swift, swift it foam'd,
Black under cliffs it raced, round headlands shone.
Soon the plank'd cottage by the sun-warm'd plains,
Bristled with cities, us the sea received.

'Below the surface-stream, shallow and light'

Below the surface-stream, shallow and light,
Of what we *say* we feel – below the stream,
As light, of what we *think* we feel – there flows
With noiseless current strong, obscure and deep,
The central stream of what we feel indeed.

A Picture at Newstead[1]

What made my heart, at Newstead, fullest swell? –
'Twas not the thought of Byron, of his cry
Stormily sweet, his Titan-agony,[2]
It was the sight of that Lord Arundel

1. Newstead Abbey, in Nottinghamshire, originally belonged to the
Arundel family. Later it was the home of Lord Byron, who sold it
when he left England for Italy.
2. Byron's struggle with the forces by which he felt oppressed is
compared to the war of the ancient Greek Titans with the newer race
of gods.

Who struck, in heat, his child he loved so well.
And his child's reason flicker'd and did die.
Painted (he will'd it) in the gallery
They hang; the picture doth the story tell.

Behold the stern, mail'd father, staff in hand!
10   The little fair-hair'd son, with vacant gaze,
Where no more lights of sense or knowledge are!

Methinks the woe, which made that father stand
Baring his dumb remorse to future days,
Was woe than Byron's woe more tragic far.

from Sohrab and Rustum[1]

   Rustum strode to his tent-door, and call'd
His followers in, and bade them bring his arms,
And clad himself in steel; the arms he chose
Were plain, and on his shield was no device,
Only his helm was rich, inlaid with gold,
And, from the fluted spine atop, a plume

1. Arnold took the story of this poem from Sir John Malcolm's *History of Persia*. The young Sohrab was the son of the world-renowned Persian champion Rustum, born of a love affair in Rustum's youth. His mother, fearing that Rustum would remove the child from her care and rear it as a warrior if he knew it was a boy, had written to Rustum that their baby was a girl. When he grew up, Sohrab left his mother and sought fame under the banners of the Tartar king Afrasiab. He gained command of the army and was more famous than any other hero except his father. He had always sought his father, but never met him.

   When the Tartar armies faced the Persians on a plain by the River Oxus, Sohrab challenged the Persians to produce a champion and settle the issue by single combat. He did not know that Rustum had secretly arrived during the night. The Persian chiefs asked Rustum to be their champion. At first, Rustum was reluctant to fight, but when taunted that he appeared to be frightened to risk his reputation by fighting a younger man, he angrily agreed, saying only that he would fight without revealing his identity so as not to heap too much honour on his opponent.

Of horsehair waved, a scarlet horsehair plume.
So arm'd, he issued forth; and Ruksh, his horse,
Follow'd him like a faithful hound at heel –

10 Ruksh, whose renown was noised through all the earth,
The horse, whom Rustum on a foray once
Did in Bokhara by the river find
A colt beneath its dam, and drove him home,
And rear'd him; a bright bay, with lofty crest,
Dight[1] with a saddle-cloth of broider'd green
Crusted with gold, and on the ground were work'd
All beasts of chase, all beasts which hunters know.
So follow'd, Rustum left his tents, and cross'd
The camp, and to the Persian host appear'd.

20 And all the Persians knew him, and with shouts
Hail'd; but the Tartars knew not who he was.
And dear as the wet diver to the eyes
Of his pale wife who waits and weeps on shore,
By sandy Bahrein, in the Persian Gulf,
Plunging all day in the blue waves, at night,
Having made up his tale of precious pearls,
Rejoins her in their hut upon the sands –
So dear to the pale Persians Rustum came.

  And Rustum to the Persian front advanced,
30 And Sohrab arm'd in Haman's tent, and came.
And as afield the reapers cut a swath
Down through the middle of a rich man's corn,
And on each side are squares of standing corn,
And in the midst a stubble, short and bare –
So on each side were squares of men, with spears
Bristling, and in the midst, the open sand.
And Rustum came upon the sand, and cast
His eyes toward the Tartar tents, and saw
Sohrab come forth, and eyed him as he came.

40   As some rich woman, on a winter's morn,
Eyes through her silken curtains the poor drudge

1. Dressed or adorned.

Who with numb blacken'd fingers makes her fire –
At cock-crow, on a starlit winter's morn,
When the frost flowers the whiten'd window-panes –
And wonders how she lives, and what the thoughts
Of that poor drudge may be; so Rustum eyed
The unknown adventurous youth, who from afar
Came seeking Rustum, and defying forth
All the most valiant chiefs; long he perused
50 His spirited air, and wonder'd who he was.
For very young he seem'd, tenderly rear'd;
Like some young cypress, tall, and dark, and straight,
Which in a queen's secluded garden throws
Its slight dark shadow on the moonlit turf,
By midnight, to a bubbling fountain's sound –
So slender Sohrab seem'd, so softly rear'd.
And a deep pity enter'd Rustum's soul
As he beheld him coming; and he stood,
And beckon'd to him with his hand, and said: –
60 'O thou young man, the air of Heaven is soft,
And warm, and pleasant; but the grave is cold!
Heaven's air is better than the cold dead grave.
Behold me! I am vast, and clad in iron,
And tried; and I have stood on many a field
Of blood, and I have fought with many a foe –
Never was that field lost, or that foe saved.
O Sohrab, wherefore wilt thou rush on death?
Be govern'd! quit the Tartar host, and come
To Iran,[1] and be as my son to me,
70 And fight beneath my banner till I die!
There are no youths in Iran brave as thou.'
    So he spake, mildly: Sohrab heard his voice,
The mighty voice of Rustum, and he saw
His giant figure planted on the sand,
Sole, like some single tower, which a chief

1. The country known as Persia in Matthew Arnold's time was originally called Iran, and has now resumed that name.

Hath builded on the waste in former years
Against the robbers: and he saw that head,
Streak'd with its first grey hairs; – hope filled his soul,
And he ran forward and embraced his knees,
80   And clasp'd his hand within his own, and said: –
      'O, by thy father's head! by thine own soul!
Art thou not Rustum? speak! art thou not he?'
      But Rustum eyed askance the kneeling youth,
And turn'd away, and spake to his own soul: –
      'Ah me, I muse what this young fox may mean!
False, wily, boastful, are these Tartar boys.
For if I now confess this thing he asks,
And hide it not, but say: *Rustum is here!*
He will not yield indeed, nor quit our foes,
90   But he will find some pretext not to fight,
And praise my fame, and proffer courteous gifts.
A belt or sword perhaps, and go his way.
And on a feast-tide, in Afrasiab's hall,
In Samarcand, he will arise and cry:
'I challenged once, when the two armies camp'd
Beside the Oxus, all the Persian lords
To cope with me in single fight; but they
Shrank, only Rustum dared; then he and I
Changed gifts, and went on equal terms away.'
100 So will he speak, perhaps, while men applaud;
Then were the chiefs of Iran shamed through me.'
      And then he turn'd, and sternly spake aloud: –
   'Rise! wherefore dost thou vainly question thus
Of Rustum? I am here, whom thou hast call'd
By challenge forth; make good thy vaunt,[1] or yield!
Is it with Rustum only thou wouldst fight?
Rash boy, men look on Rustum's face and flee!
For well I know, that did great Rustum stand
Before thy face this day, and were reveal'd,
110 There would be then no talk of fighting more.

1. Boast.

But being what I am, I tell thee this –
Do thou record it in thine inmost soul:
Either thou shalt renounce thy vaunt and yield,
Or else thy bones shall strew this sand, till winds
Bleach them, or Oxus with his summer-floods,
Oxus in summer wash them all away.'
    He spoke; and Sohrab answer'd, on his feet: –
'Art thou so fierce? Thou wilt not fright me so!
120 I am no girl, to be made pale by words.
Yet this thou hast said well, did Rustum stand
Here on this field, there were no fighting then.
But Rustum is far hence, and we stand here.
Begin! thou art more vast, more dread than I,
And thou art proved, I know, and I am young –
But yet success sways with the breath of Heaven.
And though thou thinkest that thou knowest sure
Thy victory, yet thou canst not surely know.
For we are all, like swimmers in the sea,
130 Poised on the top of a huge wave of fate,
Which hangs uncertain to which side to fall.
And whether it will heave us up to land,
Or whether it will roll us out to sea,
Back out to sea, to the deep waves of death,
We know not, and no search will make us know;
Only the event will teach us in its hour.'
    He spoke, and Rustum answer'd not, but hurl'd
His spear; down from the shoulder, down it came,
As on some partridge in the corn a hawk,
140 That long has tower'd in the airy clouds,
Drops like a plummet; Sohrab saw it come,
And sprang aside, quick as a flash; the spear
Hiss'd, and went quivering down into the sand,
Which it sent flying wide; – then Sohrab threw
In turn, and full struck Rustum's shield; sharp rang,
The iron plates rang sharp, but turn'd the spear.
And Rustum seized his club, which none but he
Could wield; an unlopp'd trunk it was, and huge,

Still rough – like those which men in treeless plains
150 To build them boats fish from the flooded rivers,
Hyphasis or Hydaspes, when, high up
By their dark springs, the wind in winter-time
Hath made in Himalayan forests wrack,
And strewn the channels with torn boughs – so huge
The club which Rustum lifted now, and struck
One stroke; but again Sohrab sprang aside,
Lithe as the glancing snake, and the club came
Thundering to earth, and leapt from Rustum's hand.
And Rustum follow'd his own blow, and fell
160 To his knees, and with his fingers clutch'd the sand;
And now might Sohrab have unsheathed his sword,
And pierced the mighty Rustum while he lay
Dizzy, and on his knees, and choked with sand;
But he look'd on, and smiled, nor bared his sword,
But courteously drew back, and spoke, and said: –

  'Thou strik'st too hard! that club of thine will float
Upon the summer-floods, and not my bones.
But rise, and be not wroth! not wroth am I;
No, when I see thee, wrath forsakes my soul.
170 Thou say'st, thou art not Rustum; be it so!
Who art thou then, that canst so touch my soul?
Boy as I am, I have seen battles too –
Have waded foremost in their bloody waves,
And heard their hollow roar of dying men;
But never was my heart thus touch'd before.
Are they from Heaven, these softenings of the heart?
O thou old warrior, let us yield to Heaven!
Come, plant we here in earth our angry spears,
And make a truce, and sit upon this sand,
180   And pledge each other in red wine, like friends,
And thou shalt talk to me of Rustum's deeds.
There are enough foes in the Persian host,
Whom I may meet, and strike, and feel no pang;
Champions enough Afrasiab has, whom thou
Mayst fight; fight *them*, when they confront thy spear!

But oh, let there be peace 'twixt thee and me!'
   He ceased, but while he spake, Rustum had risen,
And stood erect, trembling with rage; his club
He left to lie, but had regain'd his spear,
190 Whose fiery point now in his mail'd right-hand
Blazed bright and baleful, like that autumn-star,
The baleful sign of fevers; dust had soil'd
His stately crest, and dimm'd his glittering arms.
His breast heaved, his lips foam'd, and twice his voice
Was choked with rage; at last these words broke way: –
   'Girl! nimble with thy feet, not with thy hands!
Curl'd minion,[1] dancer, coiner of sweet words!
Fight, let me hear thy hateful voice no more!
Thou art not in Afrasiab's gardens now
200 With Tartar girls, with whom thou art wont to dance;
But on the Oxus-sands, and in the dance
Of battle, and with me, who make no play
Of war; I fight it out, and hand to hand.
Speak not to me of truce, and pledge, and wine!
Remember all thy valour; try thy feints
And cunning! all the pity I had is gone;
Because thou hast shamed me before both the hosts
With thy light skipping tricks, and thy girl's wiles.'
   He spoke, and Sohrab kindled at his taunts,
210 And he too drew his sword; at once they rush'd
Together, as two eagles on one prey
Come rushing down together from the clouds,
One from the east, one from the west; their shields
Dash'd with a clang together, and a din
Rose, such as that the sinewy woodcutters
Make often in the forest's heart at morn,
Of hewing axes, crashing trees – such blows
Rustum and Sohrab on each other hail'd.
And you would say that sun and stars took part
220 In that unnatural conflict; for a cloud

1. Darling, favourite.

Grew suddenly in Heaven, and dark'd the sun
Over the fighters' heads; and a wind rose
Under their feet, and moaning swept the plain,
And in a sandy whirlwind wrapp'd the pair.
In gloom they twain were wrapp'd, and they alone;
For both the on-looking hosts on either hand
Stood in broad daylight, and the sky was pure,
And the sun sparkled on the Oxus stream.
But in the gloom they fought, with bloodshot eyes
230   And labouring breath; first Rustum struck the shield
Which Sohrab held stiff out; the steel-spiked spear
Rent the tough plates, but fail'd to reach the skin,
And Rustum pluck'd it back with angry groan.
Then Sohrab with his sword smote Rustum's helm,
Nor clove its steel quite through; but all the crest
He shore away, and that proud horsehair plume,
Never till now defiled, sank to the dust;
And Rustum bow'd his head; but then the gloom
Grew blacker, thunder rumbled in the air,
240   And lightnings rent the cloud; and Ruksh, the horse,
Who stood at hand, utter'd a dreadful cry; –
No horse's cry was that, most like the roar
Of some pain'd desert-lion, who all day
Hath trail'd the hunter's javelin in his side,
And comes at night to die upon the sand.
The two hosts heard that cry, and quaked for fear,
And Oxus curdled as it cross'd his stream.
But Sohrab heard, and quail'd not, but rush'd on,
And struck again; and again Rustum bow'd
250   His head; but this time all the blade, like glass,
Sprang in a thousand shivers on the helm,
And in the hand the hilt remain'd alone.
Then Rustum raised his head; his dreadful eyes
Glared, and he shook on high his menacing spear,
And shouted: *Rustum!* – Sohrab heard that shout,
And shrank amazed; back he recoil'd one step,
And scann'd with blinking eyes the advancing form;

And then he stood bewilder'd; and he dropp'd
His covering shield, and the spear pierced his side.
260 He reel'd, and staggering back, sank to the ground;
And then the gloom dispersed, and the wind fell,
And the bright sun broke forth, and melted all
The cloud; and the two armies saw the pair –
Saw Rustum standing, safe upon his feet,
And Sohrab, wounded, on the bloody sand.

*   *   *

*[Sohrab, writhing in the pangs of death, warns his conqueror to dread
the rage of the mighty Rustum, who will soon learn that his son
Sohrab has been slain. At first incredulous, Rustum asks for proof
of what Sohrab has said. The dying youth tears open his armour and
shows his father a seal which his mother gave him when she revealed
to him the secret of his birth and told him to seek his father. The
sight of his own signet drives Rustum frantic, and only his dying
son's words prevent him from committing suicide.]*

So, on the bloody sand, Sohrab lay dead;
And the great Rustum drew his horseman's cloak
Down o'er his face, and sate by his dead son.
As those black granite pillars, once high-rear'd
270 By Jemshid[1] in Persepolis,[2] to bear
His house, now 'mid their broken flights of steps
Lie prone, enormous, down the mountain side –
So in the sand lay Rustum by his son.
And night came down over the solemn waste,
And the two gazing hosts, and that sole pair,
And darken'd all; and a cold fog, with night,
Crept from the Oxus. Soon a hum arose,
As of a great assembly loosed, and fires
Began to twinkle through the fog; for now

1. An ancient king of Iran.
2. The ancient capital city of Iran.

280 Both armies moved to camp, and took their meal;
The Persians took it on the open sands
Southward, the Tartars by the river marge;[1]
And Rustum and his son were left alone.
　　But the majestic river floated on,
Out of the mist and hum of that low land,
Into the frosty starlight, and there moved,
Rejoicing, through the hush'd Chorasmian[2] waste,
Under the solitary moon; – he flow'd
Right for the polar star, past Orgunjè,
280 Brimming, and bright, and large; then sands begin
To hem his watery march, and dam his streams,
And split his currents; that for many a league
The shorn and parcell'd Oxus strains along
Through beds of sand and matted rushy isles –
Oxus, forgetting the bright speed he had
In his high mountain-cradle in Pamere,
A foil'd circuitous wanderer – till at last
The long'd-for dash of waves is heard, and wide
His luminous home of waters opens, bright
300 And tranquil, from whose floor the new-bathed stars
Emerge, and shine upon the Aral Sea.

1. Edge.
2. All the places named here were on the boundaries between the
Mongol Empire and the land ruled by the Persians. They are now in
Uzbekhistan and Kazakhstan, southern territories of the former
USSR.

Gerard Manley Hopkins

(1844–1889)

Gerard Manley Hopkins was born at Stratford in Essex, the eldest of eight children in a middle-class family. His mother was devout, and his father a man with wide-ranging interests who had published a volume of verse as well as other books. Artistic pursuits were encouraged, and two of Hopkins's brothers became professional artists. Hopkins himself was a good amateur artist, who was influenced by the Pre-Raphaelites – a group of artists and poets who tried to infuse art with moral qualities by observing nature closely.

At Highgate School, where he won a prize for poetry in 1860, Hopkins was popular, partly for championing the rights of the schoolboys against a tyrannical headmaster. He had a reputation for eccentricity and once won a bet by not drinking liquids for a week.

In 1863 Hopkins won a scholarship to Balliol College, Oxford, where he met Robert Bridges, a lifelong friend who later preserved and published his poetry after his death. Oxford was then still greatly influenced by Tractarianism, a movement within the Anglican Church to make the ceremonies of church worship Catholic in everything except submission to the Pope. Hopkins was greatly influenced by the Anglo-Catholics in his religious practices; among his favourite reading was the poetry of George Herbert and Christina Rossetti. Eventually, he converted to Catholicism in 1866.

At Oxford, Hopkins continued to write and develop his theories of poetry. His diaries show that he carefully observed the natural world, searching for the essential quality of any object which, when perceived by the senses, could strike the mind with a feeling of originality. He coined the words 'inscape' for this individually distinctive form, and 'instress' for the force that upholds it and allows the beholder a sudden glimpse of the inner unity which gives meaning to external forms. These qualities suffuse his poems, particularly 'God's Grandeur' and 'Pied Beauty'.

After leaving university, Hopkins taught for two years, and then in 1868 entered the Catholic religious order of the Society of Jesus (Jesuits). Upon entering the order he destroyed all the poetry he had written so far, though some was preserved without his knowledge. During his theological studies, however, he came across the work of the medieval philosopher and theologian Duns Scotus, whose writings seemed to confirm the theory of 'inscape' that he had formulated at Oxford. Flushed with enthusiasm, he began writing again, and the theories of Scotus greatly influenced the writing of poems like 'As kingfishers catch fire' and 'Duns Scotus's Oxford'.

Hopkins was ordained in 1877 and served as a parish priest and teacher in England before being appointed Professor of Greek at the University of Dublin. The poetry he wrote at the time of his ordination was markedly joyous; some, such as 'Felix Randal', was influenced by his personal experience as a priest. However, his time in Ireland was overshadowed by ill health and the personal conflict between his religious vocation and his attraction to the world of the senses, which found expression in his poetry. This depression led to the writing of a series of poems known as the 'terrible sonnets', of which one, 'No worst, there is none', is printed here. He died in 1889, of typhoid fever.

One of Hopkins's skills as a poet lay in his striking use of language. His work is characterized by splendid imagery ranging from simple, as in 'Heaven-Haven', to the metaphysical intricacies of 'God's Grandeur'. He uses many archaic and dialect words, but also coins new words (such as 'twindles') and creates compound adjectives, sometimes with a hyphen (such as *dapple-dawn-drawn* Falcon') but often without, as in *rolling level underneath him steady* air'. This concentrates his images, communicating the 'instress' of the poet's perceptions to his reader. Added richness comes from Hopkins's extensive use of alliteration, assonance and rhyme, both at the end of lines and internally.

Lastly, his work is distinguished by a metrical technique he called 'sprung rhythm'. Unlike 'running rhythm', which uses a fixed number of syllables to a line, arranged in a fairly predictable pattern of stressed and unstressed syllables, sprung rhythm uses a fixed number of stressed syllables but takes no account of the number of unstressed syllables.

Heaven-Haven[1]

A nun takes the veil

I have desired to go
　　Where springs not fail,
To fields where flies no sharp and sided hail
　　And a few lilies blow.

And I have asked to be
　　Where no storms come,
Where the green swell is in the havens dumb,
　　And out of the swing of the sea.

1. A harbour or a refuge. Both ideas connect the imagery of this poem.

God's Grandeur

The world is charged with the grandeur of God.
　It will flame out, like shining from shook foil;
　It gathers to a greatness, like the ooze of oil
Crushed. Why do men then now not reck[1] his rod?
Generations have trod, have trod, have trod;
　And all is seared with trade; bleared, smeared with toil;
　And wears man's smudge and shares man's smell: the soil
Is bare now, nor can foot feel, being shod.

And for all this, nature is never spent;
10　There lives the dearest freshness deep down things;
And though the last lights off the black West went
　Oh, morning, at the brown brink eastward, springs –
Because the Holy Ghost[2] over the bent
　World broods with warm breast and with ah! bright wings.

1. Pay heed to, care about.
2. The Holy Ghost is often pictured in the form of a dove.

Spring

Nothing is so beautiful as Spring –
　　When weeds, in wheels, shoot long and lovely and lush;
　　Thrush's eggs[1] look little low heavens, and thrush
Through the echoing timber does so rinse and wring
The ear, it strikes like lightnings to hear him sing;
　　The glassy peartree leaves and blooms, they brush
　　The descending blue; that blue is all in a rush
With richness; the racing lambs too have fair their fling.

What is all this juice and all this joy?
　　A strain of the earth's sweet being in the beginning
In Eden garden. – Have, get, before it cloy,
　　Before it cloud, Christ, lord, and sour with sinning,
Innocent mind and Mayday in girl and boy,
　　Most, O maid's child, thy choice and worthy the winning.

1. Thrush's eggs are light blue in colour.

The Windhover[1]

To Christ our Lord

I caught this morning morning's minion,[2] king-
　　dom of daylight's dauphin,[3] dapple-dawn-drawn Falcon,
　　　　in his riding
　　Of the rolling level underneath him steady air, and
　　　　striding

1. A kestrel.
2. Favourite.
3. Prince.

High there, how he rung upon the rein of a wimpling[1] wing
In his ecstasy! then off, off forth on swing,
   As a skate's heel sweeps smooth on a bow-bend: the hurl
     and gliding
10   Rebuffed the big wind. My heart in hiding
Stirred for a bird, – the achieve of, the mastery of the thing!

Brute beauty and valour and act, oh, air, pride, plume, here
  Buckle![2] AND the fire that breaks from thee then, a billion
Times told lovelier, more dangerous, O my chevalier![3]

  No wonder of it: shéer plód makes plough down sillion[4]
Shine, and blue-bleak embers,[5] ah my dear,
  Fall, gall themselves, and gash gold-vermilion.

1. 'To ring on a rein' is to circle a horse at the end of a long rein held
by the trainer; 'to ring' in falconry is to rise in spirals. 'Wimpling'
means falling in folds, like the wimple worn on the head of a nun.
2. This word has several meanings: prepare for action, clasp together,
and collapse. All of them are relevant to the poem.
3. Lord. Here, Hopkins means Christ.
4. Sillion is the furrow made by a plough. When clay soil falls in
furrows, it is smooth and shiny when it catches the sun.
5. Embers are the dead-looking surface coals of a fire. When they slip,
the red-gold heat of the coals beneath shines through.

Pied Beauty

Glory be to God for dappled things –
  For skies of couple-colour as a brinded cow;
    For rose-moles in all stipple upon trout that swim;
Fresh-firecoal chestnut-falls; finches' wings;
  Landscape plotted and pieced – fold, fallow, and plough;
    And áll trádes, their gear and tackle and trim.

All things counter, original, spare, strange;
　　Whatever is fickle, freckled (who knows how?)
　　　With swift, slow; sweet, sour; adazzle, dim;
10　He fathers-forth[1] whose beauty is past change:
　　　　　　　Praise him.

　　1. Brings out of himself, like a father.

Hurrahing in Harvest

Summer ends now; now, barbarous in beauty, the stooks
　rise
　　Around; up above, what wind-walks! what lovely
　　　behaviour
　　Of silk-sack clouds! has wilder, wilful-wavier
Meal-drift[1] moulded ever and melted across skies?

I walk, I lift up, I lift up heart, eyes,
　　Down all that glory in the heavens to glean[2] our Saviour;
　　And, éyes, heárt, what looks, what lips yet gave you a
Rapturous love's greeting of realer,[3] of rounder replies?

And the azurous[4] hung hills are his world-wielding shoulder
10　　Majestic – as a stallion stalwart, very-violet-sweet! –
These things, these things were here and but the beholder
　　Wanting; which two when they once meet,
The heart réars wíngs bold and bolder
　　And hurls for him, O half hurls earth for him off under
　　　his feet.

　　1. The image is of heaps of flour (meal), piled in drifts.
　　2. 'To glean' is to gather ears of corn left by reapers, but it is also used
figuratively to mean collecting small scraps of information.
　　3. More real.
　　4. Sky-blue.

Binsey Poplars

felled 1879

My aspens dear, whose airy cages quelled,
Quelled or quenched in leaves the leaping sun,
All felled, felled, are all felled;
    Of a fresh and following folded rank
        Not spared, not one
        That dandled[1] a sandalled
      Shadow that swam or sank
On meadow and river and wind-wandering weed-
    winding bank.

10   O if we but knew what we do
        When we delve[2] or hew[3] —
    Hack and rack the growing green!
        Since country is so tender
    To touch, her being só slender,
    That, like this sleek and seeing ball
    But a prick will make no eye at all,
    Where we, even where we mean

        To mend her we end her,
      When we hew or delve:
20 After-comers cannot guess the beauty been.
    Ten or twelve, only ten or twelve
      Strokes of havoc únselve[4]
        The sweet especial scene,
      Rural scene, a rural scene,
      Sweet especial rural scene.

1. Danced.
2. Dig.
3. Cut.
4. Make unlike itself, deprive of its particular character.

Duns Scotus's[1] Oxford

Towery city and branchy between towers;
Cuckoo-echoing, bell-swarmèd, lark-charmèd, rook-racked,
   river-rounded;
The dapple-eared lily below thee; that country and town did
Once encounter in, here coped and poisèd powers;

Thou hast a base and brickish skirt there, sours
That neighbour-nature thy grey beauty is grounded
Best in; graceless growth, thou hast confounded
Rural rural keeping – folk, flocks, and flowers.

Yet ah! this air I gather and I release
10 He lived on; these weeds and waters, these walls are what
He haunted who of all men most sways my spirits to peace;

Of realty the rarest-veinèd unraveller; a not
Rivalled insight, be rival Italy or Greece;
Who fired France for Mary without spot.[2]

1. Duns Scotus (?1265–1308) was a teacher of theology who lectured in
the ecclesiastical schools at Paris and Cologne, but was also thought to
have taught in Oxford around 1301. He opposed the teachings of St
Thomas Aquinas (?1225–1274) on the Immaculate Conception of Mary,
mother of Christ. Followers of each man argued fiercely for their point
of view. Hopkins was fired with enthusiasm by reading the works of
Scotus.
2. Without sin.

Felix Randal

Felix Randal the farrier,[1] O is he dead then? my duty all
    ended,
Who have watched his mould of man, big-boned and hardy-
    handsome
Pining, pining, till time when reason rambled in it and some
Fatal four disorders, fleshed there, all contended?

Sickness broke him. Impatient, he cursed at first, but mended
Being anointed and all; though a heavenlier heart began some
Months earlier, since I had our sweet reprieve and ransom
Tendered to him. Ah well, God rest him all road ever he
    offended!

This seeing the sick endears them to us, us too it endears.
10 My tongue had taught thee comfort, touch had quenched
    thy tears,
Thy tears that touched my heart, child, Felix, poor Felix
    Randal;

How far from then forethought of, all thy more boisterous
    years,
When thou at the random grim forge, powerful amidst peers,
Didst fettle[2] for the great grey drayhorse his bright and
    battering sandal![3]

1. A smith who shoes horses.
2. To trim or clean.
3. Horseshoe.

Spring and Fall

to a young child

Márgarét, áre you gríeving
Over Goldengrove unleaving?[1]
Leáves líke the things of man, you
With your fresh thoughts care for, can you?
Ah! ás the heart grows older
It will come to such sights colder
By and by, nor spare a sigh
Though worlds of wanwood leafmeal[2] lie;
And yet you will weep and know why.
10   Now no matter, child, the name:
Sórrow's spríngs áre the same.
Nor mouth had, no nor mind, expressed
What heart heard of, ghost guessed:
It ís the blight man was born for,
It is Margaret you mourn for.

1. Losing its leaves.
2. Decayed leaves piled in drifts.

Inversnaid

This darksome burn, horseback brown,
His rollrock highroad roaring down,
In coop[1] and in comb[2] the fleece of his foam
Flutes and low to the lake falls home.

A windpuff-bonnet of fáwn-fróth
Turns and twindles[3] over the broth
Of a pool so pitchblack, féll-fŕowning,
It rounds and rounds Despair to drowning.

Degged[4] with dew, dappled with dew
10 Are the groins of the braes that the brook treads through,
Wiry heathpacks,[5] flitches[6] of fern,
And the beadbonny ash that sits over the burn.

What would the world be, once bereft
Of wet and of wilderness? Let them be left,
O let them be left, wildness and wet;
Long live the weeds and the wilderness yet.

1. Confined places.
2. Hopkins has used this word elsewhere to mean the movement of water over rocks, but it could also be a variant of 'coomb', a valley.
3. A word combining the meanings of 'twists' and 'dwindles'.
4. Sprinkled.
5. Tufts of heather.
6. Ragged, russet-coloured tufts.

'As kingfishers catch fire'

As kingfishers catch fire, dragonflies draw flame;
As tumbled over rim in roundy wells
Stones ring; like each tucked[1] string tells, each hung bell's
Bow swung finds tongue to fling out broad its name;
Each mortal thing does one thing and the same:
Deals out that being indoors each one dwells;
Selves[2] – goes itself; *myself* it speaks and spells,
Crying *Whát I dó is me: for that I came.*

I say móre: the just man justices;
Keeps gráce: thát keeps all his goings graces;
Acts in God's eye what in God's eye he is –
Chríst – for Christ plays in ten thousand places,
Lovely in limbs, and lovely in eyes not his
To the Father through the features of men's faces.[3]

1. Plucked.
2. Asserts its own individual nature.
3. Acts in a godly manner.

'No worst, there is none'

No worst, there is none. Pitched past pitch of grief,
More pangs will, schooled at forepangs, wilder wring.
Comforter, where, where is your comforting?
Mary, mother of us, where is your relief?
My cries heave, herds-long;[1] huddle in a main, a chief
Woe, wórld-sorrow; on an áge-old anvil wince and sing –
Then lull, then leave off. Fury had shrieked 'No ling-
ering! Let me be fell:[2] force I must be brief'.

O the mind, mind has mountains; cliffs of fall
10 Frightful, sheer, no-man-fathomed. Hold them cheap
May who ne'er hung there. Nor does long our small
Durance[3] deal with that steep or deep. Here! creep,
Wretch, under a comfort serves in a whirlwind: all
Life death does end and each day dies with sleep.

1. Like the cries of cattle.
2. Cruel, terrible.
3. Several meanings are implied here: imprisonment, duration and
endurance.

Index of Titles

Index of First Lines

Index of Themes

READ MORE IN PENGUIN

In every corner of the world, on every subject under the sun, Penguin represents quality and variety – the very best in publishing today.

For complete information about books available from Penguin – including Puffins, Penguin Classics and Arkana – and how to order them, write to us at the appropriate address below. Please note that for copyright reasons the selection of books varies from country to country.

In the United Kingdom: Please write to *Dept. EP, Penguin Books Ltd, Bath Road, Harmondsworth, West Drayton, Middlesex UB7 ODA*

In the United States: Please write to *Consumer Sales, Penguin USA, P.O. Box 999, Dept. 17109, Bergenfield, New Jersey 07621-0120*. VISA and MasterCard holders call 1-800-253-6476 to order Penguin titles

In Canada: Please write to *Penguin Books Canada Ltd, 10 Alcorn Avenue, Suite 300, Toronto, Ontario M4V 3B2*

In Australia: Please write to *Penguin Books Australia Ltd, P.O. Box 257, Ringwood, Victoria 3134*

In New Zealand: Please write to *Penguin Books (NZ) Ltd, Private Bag 102902, North Shore Mail Centre, Auckland 10*

In India: Please write to *Penguin Books India Pvt Ltd, 706 Eros Apartments, 56 Nehru Place, New Delhi 110 019*

In the Netherlands: Please write to *Penguin Books Netherlands bv, Postbus 3507, NL-1001 AH Amsterdam*

In Germany: Please write to *Penguin Books Deutschland GmbH, Metzlerstrasse 26, 60594 Frankfurt am Main*

In Spain: Please write to *Penguin Books S. A., Bravo Murillo 19, 1° B, 28015 Madrid*

In Italy: Please write to *Penguin Italia s.r.l., Via Felice Casati 20, I–20124 Milano*

In France: Please write to *Penguin France S. A., 17 rue Lejeune, F–31000 Toulouse*

In Japan: Please write to *Penguin Books Japan, Ishikiribashi Building, 2–5–4, Suido, Bunkyo-ku, Tokyo 112*

In Greece: Please write to *Penguin Hellas Ltd, Dimocritou 3, GR–106 71 Athens*

In South Africa: Please write to *Longman Penguin Southern Africa (Pty) Ltd, Private Bag X08, Bertsham 2013*

READ MORE IN PENGUIN

CRITICAL STUDIES

Described by *The Times Educational Supplement* as 'admirable' and 'superb', Penguin Critical Studies is a specially developed series of critical essays on the major works of literature for use by students in universities, colleges and schools.

Titles published or in preparation include:

The Poetry of William Blake
Dickens' Major Novels
Doctor Faustus
Emma and Persuasion
Great Expectations
The Great Gatsby
Heart of Darkness
The Poetry of Gerard
  Manley Hopkins
Joseph Andrews
Jude the Obscure
The Poetry of Keats
Mansfield Park
The Mayor of Casterbridge
The Metaphysical Poets
Middlemarch
The Mill on the Floss

Milton: The English Poems
The Portrait of a Lady
A Portrait of the Artist as a
  Young Man
The Return of the Native
Rosencrantz and Guildenstern
  are Dead
Sense and Sensibility
The Poetry of Shelley
Sons and Lovers
Tennyson
Tess of the D'Urbervilles
To the Lighthouse
The Waste Land
Wordsworth
Wuthering Heights
The Poetry of W. B. Yeats